Public Administration and Public Policy in Ireland

Theory and Methods

Edited by Maura Adshead and Michelle Millar

 Routledge
Taylor & Francis Group

LONDON AND NEW YORK

First published 2003
by Routledge
11 New Fetter Lane, London EC4P 4EE

Simultaneously published in the USA and Canada
by Routledge
29 West 35th Street, New York, NY 10001

Routledge is an imprint of the Taylor & Francis Group

© 2003 Maura Adshead and Michelle Millar selection and editorial
matter; individual chapters, the contributors

Typeset in Baskerville by Taylor & Francis Ltd
Printed and bound in Great Britain by TJ International Ltd,
Padstow Cornwall

British Library Cataloguing in Publication Data
A catalogue record for this book is available from the British Library
Library of Congress Cataloging in Publication Data
Public administration and public policy in Ireland:theory and
methods/edited by
Maura Adshead and Michelle Millar.
          p.cm
Includes bibliographical references and index.
1. Ireland - - Politics and government - -1949 - 2. Political planning - -
Ireland.
I. Adshead, Maura. II Millar, Michelle, 1973 -
JN1435.P83 2003
320'.6'09417- -dc21
                    200300381

ISBN 0–415–28241–1 (hbk)
ISBN 0–415–28242-X (pbk)

For Sāoirse, Mancur, Seán and Kate,
from their Mammies with love

Contents

Illustrations

Contributors

Maura Adshead is Lecturer in Politics and Public Administration in the Department of Government and Society at the University of Limerick. Her research interests focus on comparative studies of public policy, policy change, and EU involvement in the policy process in West European states. She is author of *Developing European Regions? Comparative governance, policy networks and European integration* (Ashgate, 2002) and has published on aspects of Irish public policy in *Electoral Studies, West European Politics* and *Politics and Policy*. She is currently President of the Political Studies Association of Ireland.

Vani K. Boorah is Professor of Applied Economics in the School of Public Policy and Economics at University of Ulster, Jordanstown. He has published widely in a variety of areas, including social policy in developing countries (with particular reference to the welfare of women and children), unemployment and labour markets, poverty and inequality, and political economy (with particular reference to voting systems).

Liam Coen is a Temporary Teaching Assistant at the Department of Political Science and Sociology, National University of Ireland, Galway. His research focuses on local government reform and the use of strategy in the public sector.

Neil Collins is Professor of Government and Head of the Department of Government at University College Cork. He is the author of the standard text on the local government management system in Ireland. He has written extensively on Irish politics, public participation and the marketing of public-sector services. His publications include *Irish Politics Today* (4th edn, with Terry Cradden, Manchester University Press, 2001) and *Political Issues in Ireland Today* (Manchester University Press, 2003).

Terry Cradden was formerly Head of the School of Commerce and International Business, University of Ulster; he is currently Visiting Lecturer at the Graduate School of Business, University College Dublin. As well as publications on industrial relations and politics, he has also authored two books on labour history.

Mark Evans is Head of the Department of Politics and Provost of Halifax College at the University of York. He is author of *Charter 88: A Successful Challenge to the British Political Tradition?* (Dartmouth, 1996), *Constitution-making and the Labour Party* (Palgrave, 2002) and *Policy Transfer in Global Perspective* (Ashgate, 2002).

His research focuses on three areas: the study of the New Constitutionalism (with a particular emphasis on issues in governance), the study of policy transfer in global perspective and the study of policy development. He has published extensively in these areas in the journals *Public Administration*, *Public Policy and Administration*, *Political Studies* and *British Journal of Politics*.

Lee McGowan is a lecturer at the Institute of European Studies at Queen's University, Belfast. His research interests centre on three strands: the politics of EU policy-making; the role of the European Commission as a quasi-judicial actor in the area of competition policy; the EU dimension of devolution in Northern Ireland and political extremism. He is currently working on an Economic and Social Research Council (ESRC) project examining public knowledge and attitudes towards the EU in Northern Ireland. He has published widely. Among his publications are articles in the *Journal of Common Market Studies*, *Journal of European Public Policy*, *European Journal of Political Research*, *Governance*, *Public Administration* and *Regional and Federal Studies*. He has co-authored a book on *Competition Policy in the European Union* (with Michelle Cini, Macmillan, 1998); has compiled a *Dictionary of the European Union* (with David Phinnemore, Routledge, 2002) and has recently completed a book for Longman on the *The Radical Right in German Politics*.

Michelle Millar is Lecturer in Public and Social Policy in the Department of Political Science and Sociology at the National University of Ireland, Galway. She has carried out consultancy and research work throughout Ireland as well as contributing book chapters to a number of specialist works in public administration. Her research focuses on accountability and performance measurement in the health sector, the implementation of government strategy in healthcare and health inequalities. She has published widely in this area in the *International Review of Administrative Science*, *Administration*, *Public Policy and Administration*, *Irish Medical Journal* and *Journal of Public Money and Management*. She is currently Secretary of the Political Studies Association of Ireland.

Gary Murphy is Senior Lecturer in Government at the School of Law and Government, Dublin City University, where he lectures in public policy. He has published widely on various aspects of the Irish state in a number of journals and texts and is the author of *Economic Realignment and the Politics of EEC Entry* (Maunsel, 2002). He is currently co-editor of *Irish Political Studies*.

Mary Murphy is studying for a doctoral degree within the School of European and International Studies at Queen's University, Belfast. Her thesis explores the relationship between the new devolved institutions in Northern Ireland and the European Union in terms of policy-making and implementation. She has worked on an Economic and Social Research Council (ESRC) project examining the European dimension of the new Northern Ireland devolved institutions.

Pat O'Connor is Professor of Sociology and Social Policy and Dean of the College of Humanities at the University of Limerick. She has been a teacher and researcher for more than thirty years. Before becoming Professor, she was

Course Director of the MA in Women's Studies at the University of Limerick. She has worked at the Economic and Social Research Institute, Dublin, the University of London, the National Institute for Social Work, London, and Waterford Institute of Technology. Since the late 1980s she has published four books and over thirty refereed journal articles. Her last book, *Emerging Voices: Women in Contemporary Irish Society*, was published by the Institute of Public Administration in 1998.

Mary O'Shea is a Lecturer in Politics at the Department of Government, University College Cork. Recent work includes *Understanding Corruption in Irish Politics* (with Neil Collins, Cork University Press, 2000) and chapters in various books on Irish public management and politics.

Eoin O'Sullivan is a Lecturer in Social Policy in the Department of Social Studies, Trinity College, Dublin. His recent publications include *Suffer the Little Children: The Inside Story of Ireland's Industrial Schools* (with Mary Raftery, New Island Books, 1999) and *Crime Control in Ireland: The Politics of Intolerance* (with Ian O'Donnell, Cork University Press, 2001).

William K. Roche is Professor of Industrial Relations and Human Resources at University College Dublin and lectures at the Smurfit School of Business. He has published extensively in the area of industrial relations in Ireland in the *European Journal of Industrial Relations*, *Journal of Management Studies* and *Journal of Industrial Relations*.

Paul Sweeney is a business and economic advisor. A graduate of Trinity College, he has been economic and financial advisor with SIPTU (Services, Industrial, Professional and Technical Union) for many years, where he was regularly involved in company and plant restructurings, as well as analytical work. He is a former inspector of taxes. He has served on several government committees examining issues of company law, mergers and competition law, taxation, tourism and public–private partnerships. He also served on the board of the Electricity Supply Board (ESB) for five years and is the employees' nominee on the board of a telecoms company. He has written extensively on business and economics, including a review of the recent performance of the Irish economy, a second edition of which is *The Celtic Tiger, Ireland's Continuing Economic Miracle*. He is a Member of the Council of the Statistical and Social Enquiry Society of Ireland.

Oliver Wall is currently working with the EU Committee of the American Chamber of Commerce, Brussels. He was formerly a researcher at the Department of Political Science and Sociology at the National University Institute, Galway, where his research focused on the introduction of performance measurement and quality in the Irish universities sector.

Preface
Policy, politics and public administration

This book is designed as a course text for students of Irish Politics and Public Administration. It may also be used to accompany courses in introductory politics, policy analysis and comparative politics or public administration. A range of Irish public policy topics are presented and explained – each by reference to a distinct framework for analysis. The book is intended to highlight (through readily presented Irish examples) the variety of alternative explanations available to students of politics and public administration who are interested in understanding how policy is made.

Aims and objectives

The book is conceived in response to a current gap in the literature for students studying Irish public policy and administration. Generally speaking, most studies in this area tend to be empirically based, with a preference for historical/descriptive modes of explanation. Despite their obvious utility to students of public policy and administration, such studies do not facilitate students in developing an advanced understanding of the policy process and public administration. At the moment, a range of texts already exist that deal exclusively with methodology and political explanation, or that are devoted to detailed descriptions of distinct topics in Irish politics and administration. This book does not seek to supplant either of these literatures. Rather, it is intended to provide students of public administration and public policy in Ireland with concrete illustrations of the operationalisation of alternative methodological approaches in relation to specific issues and topics in Irish politics and public administration. In doing so, it will provide students of Irish politics, public administration and public policy with a unique collection of Irish case studies and source material for further study.

Organisation of the book

Each chapter examines the main concepts and primary advocates of a particular mode of analysis, together with a review of recent developments in the field and the major criticisms of it. All chapters include a select Irish case study, designed to illustrate the particular approach or framework for analysis outlined by that chapter. A review section at the end of the chapter assesses the utility of the approach in the explanation of the case and provides a guide to further reading, plus a range of sources for the policy area under consideration.

Still, however, the book represents the views, ideas and opinions of a range of authors, who are each experts in their field. As a result, although we have tried as much as possible to keep the format uniform, we have left our contributors with a free hand to determine the logic and development of their arguments. Notwithstanding, each chapter is organised around the following themes:

- introduction to the main concepts and concerns of the approach;
- brief review of the evolution of this approach;
- mainstream variants in contemporary usage;
- major criticisms;
- select Irish case study;
- summary review of the theoretical utility.

Study themes

The content of the book is divided thematically. The first part examines where alternative theories situate the location of power in the policy-making world and deals with elitism, pluralism, Marxism and feminism. The second examines alternative approaches to explaining the distribution of policy-making authority, looking at corporatism, clientelism, policy network and institutionalist approaches. The third looks at alternative modes of explaining policy change and discusses the explanatory idioms provided by rational choice theories, policy transfer, Europeanisation and globalisation approaches.

This division of themes is necessarily a loose one, since it is clear that many of the approaches outlined above may fit as easily in one section as another. Moreover, whilst some approaches may be used at one or more levels of analysis, others are best suited to only one. In this respect, the primary concern of this book is not to explain *all* the different approaches to study that exist or to detail *all* of the ways in which the approaches that we do consider might be used. Our more modest ambition is to introduce students of public administration and policy in Ireland to the idea that there are different theoretical, methodological or idiomatic approaches to the explanation of policy outcomes – each of which focuses to a greater or lesser degree on the significance and importance of alternative explanatory variables.

Students should therefore be aware that the explanatory framework they choose to explore any given policy will affect both the terms of their explanation and the conclusions drawn from the study. Key questions such as who holds power?, how does policy change?, and the relative importance of structure versus agency, may receive different answers when different approaches are used to frame the study. Thus, for example, in answer to the question of who holds power: in Chapter 1 the discussion of elite theory points to the importance of individuals, whereas Chapter 2's review of pluralist approaches highlights the significance of groups. By contrast, Marxian approaches, outlined in Chapter 3, focus on the predominance of class, whereas feminist approaches, discussed in Chapter 4, point to the overriding significance of gender.

Chapter 5, dealing with social partnership and corporatism in Ireland, suggests that policy change is brought about primarily by the interplay of sectional interests. The discussion of Clientelism in Chapter 6 by contrast, suggests that in many respects policy output reflects the mass of individual contracts and bargains made. Chapter 7's review of the policy network literature, however, argues that it is the specific configuration of sectional and/or individual interests that is responsible for distinct policy outcomes. Notwithstanding, the analysis of institutionalist approaches contained in Chapter 8 suggests that the attitudes of all interests (sectional, individual, or any combination of the two) are determined primarily by deeply embedded structural and sociological norms and values. This idea is challenged by Chapter 9's examination of rational choice approaches, which focuses on the significance and importance of individual choices made by actors and agents in the policy process.

The significance of both structure and agency is highlighted in Chapter 10's exposition of the policy transfer literature, as well as in Chapters 11 and 12, which deal with Europeanisation and globalisation, respectively. Of all the chapters, these last three highlight the importance of exogenous – as opposed to endogenous – drivers of policy change, that is, those occurring outside the state as a consequence of transnational, supranational and multinational influences. As with all the other chapters in the book, the intention is to show readers that all forms of explanation or analysis carry their own assumptions about the importance of different explanatory variables and may therefore influence the conclusions drawn. If this book helps students to clarify why this is so, our ambition is achieved.

Maura Adshead
Michelle Millar

Acknowledgements

First and foremost we would like to thank all of our contributors, without whom this book would not have been possible. Before embarking on this project, we were warned that edited books can often be more difficult to complete than monographs: we were prepared for delays and now admit to being somewhat 'economical with the truth' in relation to our reporting of deadlines to all contributors. In the end, however, our prudence proved unnecessary. We were blessed with the best bunch of contributors that any editor could wish for, and if there is any merit in this book, then the credit must surely go to them. Notwithstanding, the responsibility for any errors or omissions remains our own. Aside from 'the obvious', there are also many others who contributed to the timely execution of this work. We would both like to thank Craig Fowlie, Mark Kavanagh, Jennifer Lovell and Zoë Botterill at Routledge. In addition, we have each worked up our own debts of gratitude to family and friends.

Maura would like to acknowledge that (in a house that has been in continual need of repair and renovation since she moved in) without the help of a diverse building, painting, cleaning, baby-minding and 'Maura-minding' crew she would be hard pressed to deliver a letter, let alone a baby or book manuscript. Special thanks go – always – to Neil Robinson, who manages 'all of the above' and more besides. Also to: John and Theresa Adshead, Helen and Jim Cahill, Armelle and John Mangan, Noel and Veronica McMahon, Maureen Ryan, Chris Smith, Cecil and Maureen Williamson and Rosemary Wilmot. Last, but by no means least, a very big thank you to Michelle for being an excellent colleague, co-editor and friend.

Michelle would like to acknowledge the many students of public administration and public policy she has had the pleasure of meeting over the years; the inspiration for this book came from them as they toiled with these very methods, I sincerely hope this 'clears things up'. Big thanks to Maura for believing in the idea and being a proficient co-worker. Special thanks go to Seán, Phil, Annette and Janet Millar, Triona and John Woolner, the Halls, Michael Hennessy and Anne O'Connell, my graduate students Oliver Wall and Liam Coen, and to Dave McKevitt, who continues to supervise. Finally, to Padraig Hall, whose love, advice, patience and humour keep me sane.

1 Elitism and agri-environmental policy in Ireland

Mark Evans and Liam Coen

Introduction

Elite theorists argue that the history of politics has been characterized by the history of elite domination. Elite theory therefore challenges the key premises of most western liberal assumptions about politics, the organization of government and the relationship between the state and civil society. As Gaetano Mosca puts it:

> In all societies – from societies that are very meagerly developed and have barely attained the dawning of civilization, down to the most advanced and powerful societies – two classes of people appear – a class that rules and a class that is ruled. The first class, always the less numerous, performs all political functions, monopolizes power and enjoys the advantages that power brings, whereas the second, the more numerous class, is directed and controlled by the first.
>
> (Mosca 1939: 50)

Hence, for elite theorists the nature of any society – whether it is consensual or authoritarian, pacifist or totalitarian, legitimate or illegitimate – is determined by the nature of its elite. This chapter provides a critical review of the content and nature of elite theory and assesses its contribution to our understanding of contemporary political science in general and the study of the Irish policy process in particular. It develops three central arguments. First, it argues that elitism still provides an important focus for the work of political scientists and political sociologists, particularly in the United States, and continues to present a compelling critique of the liberal democratic model. Second, the chapter observes that one of the most striking features of modern and contemporary elitist perspectives lies in their convergence with once-opposite theoretical traditions. Third, it argues that contemporary variants of the elitist approach focus less on providing a grand narrative on who governs and more on highlighting the nature and role of privileged elites in decision-making centres.

Brief review of the evolution of elitist approaches

Although the seeds of elite theory were sown in the ideas of Plato, Machiavelli and others, elitism as a theory of social power is most associated in its earliest form with the work of Pareto, Mosca and Michels. Their common thesis was that the concentration of social power in a small set of controlling elites was inevitable in all societies and they rejected the feasibility of Karl Marx's vision of evolutionary change towards a classless society with power equality. This section provides an overview of the core propositions of classical elitist thought focusing on: Vilfredo Pareto's (1935) reworking of Machiavellian realism and the circulation of elites; Gaetano Mosca's (1896) idea of *The Ruling Class*; and Robert Michels' (1911) main work *Political Parties*, which drew attention to the inevitability of an 'iron law of oligarchy.' Each one of these three texts engages in a critique of Marxism and pluralism which emphasizes the rejection of both class domination and the diffusion of power on pluralist lines. A critical discussion of these texts will enable us to identify a partial, if weak, theory of elite domination.

Pareto and the concept of elite circulation

Pareto argued that historical experience provides testimony to the perpetual circulation of elites and oligarchy. Every field of human enterprise has its own elite. Pareto (1935) borrowed two categories of elites from Machiavelli, 'Foxes' and 'Lions' (1961: 99–110), in order to illustrate the nature of governing elite structures. The two categories stand at opposite ends of a continuum of governance. 'Foxes' govern by attempting to gain consent and are not prepared to use force; they are intelligent and cunning, enterprising, artistic and innovative. However, in times of crisis their misplaced humanitarianism leads them towards compromise and pacifism. Hence, when final attempts to reach a political solution have failed the regime is fatally weakened. 'Lions' represent the opposite pole. They are men of strength, stability and integrity. Cold and unimaginative, they are self-serving and are prepared to use force to achieve or maintain their position. 'Lions' are defenders of the status quo in both the state and civil society. They are likely to be committed to public order, religion and political orthodoxy. For Pareto, the qualities of 'Fox' and 'Lion' are generally mutually exclusive. History is a process of circulation between these two types of elites. Pareto's ideal system of governance would reflect a balance of forces which exhibits characteristics of both 'Fox' and 'Lion.' This ongoing process of elite renewal, circulation and replacement illuminates the thesis that an elite rules in all organized societies.

Pareto's (1935) focus upon the concentration of power in the hands of a political elite represented a rejection of both vulgar Marxist economism and the weak but popular liberal/pluralist view. It undermined the Marxist conception of the state as a mere tool of the capitalist class. It rejects Marx's view that the history of all hitherto existing society is the history of class struggle (for a more detailed discussion of Marxism, see Chapter 3). At the same time, Pareto's (1935) elitist claims are also at odds with the pluralist conception of the state as a co-coordinator of the national interest in a plural society (for a more detailed discussion of pluralism, see Chapter 2).

Mosca and the idea of the ruling class

Mosca (1939) argued that elites were inevitable as all societies are characterized by the dictatorship of the majority by the minority. He posited the existence of a ruling, but not necessarily economically dominant, class from which key office holders were drawn. Within Mosca's (1939) formulation, each ruling class develops a political formula which maintains and legitimates its rule to the rest of the population. Elite circulation will usually occur through inheritance, but, from time to time, power will pass into the hands of another class due to the failure and collapse of the political formula. Mosca's (1939) conceptualization of the political formula has much in common with the concept of hegemony, which springs from the view of Marx and Engels (see Chapter 3) that the ideas of the ruling class are in every historical stage the ruling ideas. Hence, the capitalist class, which is the dominant economic group in society, is simultaneously its ruling intellectual force. In other words, a Marxist would say that those people owning the means of production also control the process of government and can use this source of domination to impose their views on society. This results in a false consciousness among the proletariat, whereby they accept their subordinate position in capitalist society and do not question the existing social and political structure. Mosca (1939), by contrast, failed to develop the concept of political formula in any systematic way, unlike his Marxist contemporary Antonio Gramsci (see Chapter 3, pp. 00–00). The centrality of the ideological dimension to an understanding of the dialectic of power domination and control is an important consideration which Mosca's (1939) research clearly overlooked.

Michels and the 'iron law of oligarchy'

Michels (1911) work needs to be understood in the context of his own personal struggle against the German academic establishment. He wrote from the stand-point of a radical socialist whose ability to secure an academic post at a German university was impaired by his ideological position. However, it was the German Social Democratic Party and its propensity for oligarchy, and not the establishment, which bore the full brunt of his frustrations. Michels' (1962: 364) central explanation of the inevitability of elites represents a further critique of pluralism and Marxism. With regard to the former, Michels (1911) argued that the practical ideal of democracy consisted in the self-government of the masses in conformity with the decision-making of popular assemblies. However, while this system placed limits upon the extension of the principle of delegation, it fails 'to provide any guarantee against the formation of an oligarchic camarilla' (Michels 1962: 364). In short, direct government by the masses was impossible. Michels (1911) applied a similar argument to political parties. In his view, the technical and administrative functions of political parties make first bureaucracy and then oligarchy inevitable. Hence, for Michels, '[w]ho says organization, says oligarchy' (1962: 364). This maxim clearly determined his conception of the nature of elites. The notorious notion of the 'iron law of oligarchy' provides the key to Michels' thoughts on the nature of elite structures, for it ensures the dominance of the leadership over the rank-and-file membership. Elite circulation is maintained by the inability of the masses to mobilize against the leadership view. This ensures their subjugation to the whim of the elite. In essence, it is the very existence of this system of leadership which is incompatible with the tenets of liberal democracy and pluralism.

The work of Robert Michels (1911) is remembered more as a series of 'sound bites' than a seminal contribution to political thought. As a case in point, others than he have given his phrase the 'iron law of oligarchy.' For example, the notion of organization as the basis of oligarchy has been developed much further in the research of organizational theorists such as J.G. March and H.A. Simon (1958), amongst others. The major impact of Michels' work has been on pluralist thinking, insofar as it has compelled pluralists to acknowledge the existence of elites although they continue to reject the argument that elites act cohesively. McConnell, for example, writing from an American perspective, observes:

> The first conclusion that emerges from the present analysis and survey is that a substantial part of the government in the United States has come under the influence of a narrowly based and largely autonomous elites [*sic*]. These elites do not act cohesively with each other on many issues. They do not 'rule' in the sense of commanding the entire nation. Quite the contrary, they tend to pursue a policy of non-involvement in the large issues of statesmanship, save where such issues touch their own particular concerns.
>
> (McConnell 1996: 339)

The classical elitists in perspective

Pareto, Mosca and Michels generally assume the integration of elites without any rigorous empirical investigation. Pareto failed to demonstrate a theory of elite domination in his native Italy. Mosca showed that governments in the past were often characterized by a self-serving elite, but did not establish that this was always the case. Further, while Michels argued that Western European political parties were characterized by elite domination, his fondness for selecting convenient empirical evidence to support his arguments is vulnerable to counter-critique. Perhaps not surprisingly, then, subsequent elite theorists have strongly disagreed about the nature, causes and consequences of elite rule in western industrialized societies. This debate will be considered in the following section, which deals with more modern elitist perspectives.

Mainstream variants of elitism in contemporary usage – from radical elitism to the statists

This section reviews some modern elitist perspectives, from the radical elitists to the statists, by focusing on two key areas of consideration within elitist thought: national elite power network studies and epistemic communities; and state-centered perspectives.

National elite power network studies

The study of national elite power networks (NEPNs) has long been a focus of study in the United States and Britain. The key concern of this literature has been to identify the degree to which national elite structures are unified or diversified. The origins of these studies lie in the pluralist–radical elitist debates of the 1940s and 1950s in the United States. These had two chief protagonists: C. Wright Mills, who in *The Power Elite* (1956) provided an account of the role of power elites within the US Executive; and James Burnham, who argued in *The Managerial Revolution* (1972) that a new managerial elite was in the process of establishing control across all capitalist states. However, it was the work of the radical elitist C. Wright Mills (1956) that had the most impact on future NEPNs. His theory involved a three-level gradation of the distribution of power. At the top level were those in command of the major institutional hierarchies of modern society – the executive branch of the national government, the large business corporations, and the military establishment. The pluralist model of competing interests, Mills (1956) argued, applied only to the 'middle levels,' the semi-organized stalemate of interest group and legislative politics, which pluralists mistook for the entire power structure of the capitalist state. A politically fragmented 'society of the masses' occupied the bottom level. Mills's work suggested a close relationship between economic elites and governmental elites: the 'corporate rich' and the 'political directorate' (1956: 167–9). He maintained that the growing centralization of power in the federal executive branch of government had been accompanied by a declining role for professional politicians and a growing role for 'political outsiders' from the corporate world (Mills 1956: 235). Despite this, Mills contended that it would be a mistake 'to believe that the political apparatus is merely an extension of the corporate world, or that it had been taken over by the representatives of the corporate rich' (1956: 170). Here, Mills wanted to distinguish his position from what he termed the 'simple Marxian view,' which held that economic elites were the real holders of power. For this reason, he used the term 'power elite' rather than 'ruling class' – a term which for him implied too much economic determinism (Mills 1956: 276–7). Crucially, Mills argued that political, military, and economic elites all exercised a considerable degree of autonomy, were often in conflict, and rarely acted in concert.

The Power Elite (Mills 1956) provided the most important critique of pluralism written from an elitist perspective. It emphasized that, far from being an independent arbiter of the national interest, the state was actually dominated by an

NEPN of politicians, military and corporate bosses who melded public policy to suit their own ends. The credibility of Mills's analysis was given a boost by a series of community power studies which compounded the validity of the elitist interpretation of American politics. In the debate which ensued throughout the 1950s and 1960s, pluralists emphasized the non-falsifiability of the claims of the community power theorists.

A United States perspective: from Mills to Domhoff

NEPN theorists in the United States such as Mills and Domhoff have found a considerable amount of elite integration, although with various bases in the national power structure. According to Mills:

> The conception of the power elite and of its unity rests upon the corresponding developments and the coincidence of interests among economic, political, and military organizations. It also rests upon the similarity of origins and outlook, and the social and personal intermingling of the top circles from each of these dominant hierarchies.
>
> (Mills 1956: 292)

The existence of a broad, inclusive network of powerful persons with similar social origins, in different institutions, is an important feature of this view of the power structure. However, the NEPN literature identifies three key dimensions of political elite integration: social homogeneity, which emphasizes shared class and status origins; value consensus, which focuses on agreement among elites on the 'rules of the game'; and personal interaction among elites, both informally through social and personal interaction and formally through membership of common organizations. This third dimension is reflected in the interlocking directorates of major US corporations. These ties are seen as fostering integration, cohesiveness and consensus within the business community. Many social scientists, particularly in the US, have examined these sociometric ties among elites in individual communities (see Kadushin 1974; Laumann and Pappi 1973; Laumann 1976; Laumann *et al.* 1977) but few have turned their attention to the national level.

The pluralist critique of the NEPN studies rests on the view that these elites are not cohesive; that is, that they fail to act together on many issues. Each elite group is distinct and narrowly based, with its influence confined to the issues most relevant to its membership (see Dahl 1961; Polsby 1963). Thus, elites are seen as fragmented rather than integrated since each is involved primarily with its own relatively narrow concerns and constituencies. In a critique of elitism, Dahl (1958) argued that elite theorists frequently make the mistake of equating a capacity for control with facilitative power. The formation of a ruling elite requires not only control over important resources but also the establishment of unity and cohesiveness among its members. Clearly, the Marxist account of ruling-class theory would place less emphasis upon the importance of social origins among members of the political elite in a society with a capitalist economy. The Marxist approach would argue that bias in favour of capitalist interests is built into the policy-making process, guaranteeing that those interests are protected by occupants in key positions within the state apparatus, whatever their origins (see Miliband 1969; Poulantzas 1973).

A United Kingdom perspective: from Sampson to Scott

In the UK NEPNs have rarely reached any degree of sophistication. A number of historians have considered the fate of the English aristocracy (Perrott 1968; Sinclair 1968; Winchester 1981), dwelling on the changing nature of the relationship between landed and mercantile interests. William Guttsman (1963) analysed the decline of the upper class and the rise of the middle class as a principal source of elite renewal. Anthony Sampson (1962, 1965, 1971, 1982), in his exhaustive accounts of the anatomy of Britain, has argued that the aristocracy no longer rules and that there is no longer a real social elite at all. Further, Sampson (1982) contends that the various hierarchies of British society have become gradually more open in their recruitment and that the diversity of these hierarchies is such that there is no single centre of power. However, Sampson's analyses fail to place political power in its broader economic and social context. John Scott (1991) remains one of the most imaginative of contemporary British social scientists working within the NEPN tradition. Scott argues that:

> The view is widely held that in Britain there is a small minority, which holds a ruling position in its economy, society, and political system. This minority has been described in numerous varying ways: 'The establishment', 'the powers that be', 'the ruling few', the 'elite', or more prosaically, 'them'.
>
> (J. Scott 1991: 1)

His work is structured around two key issues which characterize modern elitist thought: is the elite a nominal category of office holders or a real, cohesive, active and self-perpetuating social group?; and do members of the elite use their power for sectional or public purposes? Scott (1991: 119) identified two central forms of power elite, *exclusive* and *inclusive*. The former exists 'where the power bloc is drawn from a restricted and highly uniform social background and so is able to achieve a high level of solidarity'; the latter where 'a solidaristic power bloc is not dominated by any particular class' (J. Scott 1991: 119–20).

Scott's analysis epitomizes the convergence between elitist and Marxist theories of the state, drawing on the work of both Weber and Marx, when he states that '[s]pecifically, I use Weber's analytical distinctions between class, status, and party as ways of clarifying the Marxian concepts of the capitalist state and the ruling class' (1991: 4–5). His work gives much attention to the question of social status:

> The hierarchy of status is seen as an important element in the legitimation of power structures, and the dynamics of status group relations are seen as integral elements in class reproduction and in the formation of power blocs.
>
> (J. Scott 1991: 119)

Thus, for Scott the concepts of 'capitalist class,' 'upper circle,' and 'state elite' are interchangeable terms for describing privileged groups which exercise power deriving from class, status, and politics. His conclusion reflects the balance of these concerns:

> The question 'Who Rules Britain?' can now be answered. Britain is ruled by a capitalist class whose economic dominance is sustained by the operations of the state and whose members are disproportionately represented in the power elite which rules the state apparatus. That is to say, Britain does have a ruling class. Much remains to be done in documenting the anatomy and personnel of this class, but the general picture is, I believe, clear…. Instead of being organized around an upper circle of status superiors, the capitalist class became organized around an inner circle of finance capitalists. This inner circle, espousing the City point of view, predominates in the formulation of state and business policy.
>
> (J. Scott 1991: 151–2)

Epistemic communities

The role and influence of 'special advisers' has demanded greater acknowledgement in public policy studies in recent years. Think-tanks, special committees and subcommittees proliferate around increasingly complex policy areas, allowing decision-makers to progressively rely on external information to assist in the formation and application of public policy. The practice of drafting in a non-political actor with expertise in a specific policy field offers policy-makers an alternative means of formulating policy, one that allows them to use outside experts to introduce new or innovative policy practices that may increase the chance of successful implementation.

With the discovery of new scientific practices, the acquisition of specific knowledge, and the promotion of new techniques, the realm of science has an increasingly important role to play in policy formation. Experts, collectively known as an *epistemic community*, impart specific knowledge to policy-makers in a certain area, which then allows them to make informed choices when formulating policy. Whilst the undoubted proficiency of such groups of experts may offer invaluable advice, concerns have been raised about the undue influence that they might exert over the political process and elected politicians. Once more, we can see that an opportunity arises for distinct and privileged access to the policy process, which may exclude – or at least significantly diminish – the influence of others on the process, such as elected representatives or those with a legitimate or vested interest in the area, who might not be consulted.

In contrast to general or traditional modes of policy formation, the role of epistemic communities in the policy process is usually brought to the fore in times of policy stagnation, where policy-makers encounter unforeseen problems, or if national executives wish to achieve international policy coordination (Verdun 1999: 313). Haas defines an epistemic community as 'a network of professionals with recognized expertise and competence in a particular domain and an authoritative claim to policy relevant knowledge within the domain or issue-area' (P. Haas 1992: 7). Members of the community are brought together through a shared belief system, one that confers authority through peer-related practices and the interpretation of scientific experiment, culminating in the formulation of 'a truth.' Within the community, this truth is unequivocal since it emerges as a result of knowledge acquired through investigation within the issue-area, and because of its specific nature it is knowledge that only a small number possess. This 'truth' is promoted as 'reality,' allowing the group to shape the world within which policy will be formulated. Hence great social and political influence is exerted (Toke 1999: 98). Generally speaking, epistemic communities are associated with a common policy enterprise that concerns 'the enhancement of human welfare,' such that personal gain from policy implementation is not an issue in the offering of policy advice (Toke 1999: 97).

Adler and Haas (1992) outline five ways by which epistemic communities can exert influence: first, through *policy innovation*, which allows members to frame the issue, decide the nature of the issue and outline policy objectives; second, *policy diffusion*, which generates international debate and promotes consensus about the way forward; third, *policy selection*, which despite being a power exerted by decision-makers must be confirmed by the community involved; fourth, *policy persistence*, which confers greater authority upon the community and provides for continual consensus; and, finally, *policy evolution*, which allows for the use of newly acquired knowledge, reproducing the need for the community, hence providing for its own survival (Verdun 1999: 314). Political empowerment can also be conferred in a general way. Technocracy (the use of expertise in technical areas) often 'proliferates under conditions of distrust of politicians. For technocracy to succeed, political decision making must be perceived as slow, corrupt and ultimately irrational' (Radaelli 1999: 760). Thus, while the public might view traditional political actors with suspicion and mistrust, they often show a rejuvenated interest in science and the pursuit of truth, culminating in the public's desire and willingness to believe everything that science champions, thus endorsing the community's undemocratically acquired place within the policy process. As Dunlop notes, 'from this view…all non-epistemic actors are deliberately relegated to the task of amplifying the voices of expert communities, having no truth of their own to purvey' (Dunlop 2000: 138).

Some argue that what results from an epistemic community's role in the policy process is the development of a broadly consensual policy, one based not on ideology but on information. Within this practice class is relegated as a gauge of political activity, and the tendency is for policy measures to focus more on regulation than on redistribution (Radaelli 1999: 759). Epistemic communities become politically empowered through the position they occupy at the policy table and through their ability to translate consensual authoritative knowledge into policy (Dunlop 2000: 140). Others argue that epistemic communities act in an extremely political manner, ensuring that their own view is the only one to be recognized or adopted in the policy process (Dunlop 2000: 141). In our examination of food safety policy in Ireland later in this chapter (pp. 16) we shall see which is the case in the Irish context. Before doing so, however, we shall take a look at the second chief variant in elitist theory, represented by the statist approaches.

The statists

By the mid-1980s virtually every significant current of theoretical work in political science was united in a renewed interest in the state itself as the fundamental unit of analysis. As Peter Evans, Dietrich Rieschemeyer and Theda Skocpol acknowledge, 'the state as an actor or institution has been highlighted' (1985: 3). The two leading exponents of the statist position were Theda Skocpol (1985) and Michael Mann (1988) (for a broader discussion, see Jessop 1990a: 278–88).

Mann and Skocpol on the 'potential' autonomy of the state

Skocpol (1985) advances what she terms an organizational realist approach which rejects the dominant assumption of both liberal and Marxist variants of social theory that political structures and struggles can be reduced (at least 'in the last instance') to socio-economic forces and conflicts. In this view, the state is nothing more than an arena in which social and economic conflict takes place – the crucial difference between these theories rests on whether the arena is legitimate and consensually constructed or a vehicle for coercive domination. For Skocpol (1979), in contrast, the state as a system of organized coercion needs to be treated as an autonomous structure and actor. Skocpol argues that within the terms of these theories 'it is consequently virtually impossible even to raise the possibility that fundamental conflicts of interest might arise between the existing dominant class or set of groups, on the one hand, and the state rulers on the other' (1979: 26). However, she does concede that recent developments in the Marxist theory of the state are cognizant with this problem and that through the debate on the relative autonomy of the state (see, for example, Miliband 1970, 1973; Poulantzas 1969, 1974; P. Anderson 1974; Offe 1975) they have recognized the potential for independent agency by the state from direct control by the dominant class.

Within this literature much attention has been devoted to the range of structural constraints which an existing regime of accumulation places upon the options for state structure and agency. The argument has developed that state elites may at times need to be free from a specific dominant class group in order to forward the long-term interest of an entire dominant class. Marxists, however, have stopped short of asserting that states are potentially autonomous from dominant classes, class structures, or modes of production. Skocpol (1985) thus attempts to move beyond the Marxist assumption that state forms and activities vary in accordance with modes of production and that state rulers cannot possibly act against the basic interests of a dominant class. She thereby explicitly treats the state as autonomous and thus implies that state and civil society co-exist as two separate entities; a clear methodological flaw. Only in this limited sense does Skocpol move beyond the argument of how states vary with, and function for, modes of production and dominant classes.

In summary, Skocpol (1985) develops six key propositions which characterize the statist position:

- The class upheavals and socio-economic transformations which have char-acterized social revolutions have been closely intertwined with the collapse of the state organizations of the old regimes and with the consolidation and functioning of the state organizations of the new regimes. Hence, we can make sense of socio-revolutionary transformations only if we take the state seriously as a macro-structure.
- The administrative and coercive organizations are the basis of state power.
- These state organizations are potentially autonomous from direct dominant-class control.
- State organizations necessarily compete to some extent with the dominant class(es) in appropriating resources from the economy and society.
- Although a state usually functions to preserve existing economic and class structures, it nonetheless has its own distinct interests *vis-à-vis* the dominant class(es).
- States exist in determinant geopolitical environments in interaction with other actual or potential states/geopolitical environments, as well as economic and class structures conditioning and influencing a state structure and the activities of its elite.

This formulation is significant in the sense that it stresses both the role of a powerful state elite and the importance of treating the question of the legitimacy of state elites as a key explanatory concept.

Mann's principal interest lies in what he terms, 'the centralized institutional ensembles called states and the powers of the personnel who staff them' (1988: 4); hence, the 'state elite.' His work confronts the question: what is the nature of the power possessed by states and state elites? He contrasts the power of state elites with power groupings in civil society such as ideological movements, economic classes, and military elites. Mann (1988) emphasizes two meanings of state power, which correspond to the rise in the size and complexity of the state and the decision-making process in advanced industrial societies. These he recognized as two analytically distinct and autonomous dimensions of power. The first, 'despotic power,' relates to the range of actions which the elite is empowered to take without traditional negotiation with civil society, and the second, 'infrastructural power,' refers to the capacity of the state to actually penetrate civil society and to implement political decisions. Mann observes that '[t]he state penetrates everyday life more than did any historical state. Its infrastructural power has increased enormously' (1988: 30)

Crucially, however, Mann (1988) also argues that although the capitalist state has a strong infrastructure it is also despotically weak. Capitalist states with strong infrastructures are powerful in relation to individuals and to the weaker groups in civil society, but feeble in relation to dominant groups, at least in comparison with most historical states. From these two independent dimensions of state power Mann derives the four ideal types of state formation: feudal, bureaucratic, imperial, and authoritarian (1988: 30). The first two he characterizes as low in despotic power but high in infrastructural coordination, the latter two as high in despotic power but low in infrastructural coordination. His typology stresses two major historical tendencies: a developmental tendency in the growth of the infrastructural power of the state; and no general developmental tendency in the despotic powers of the state. Hence, although Mann is in agreement with reductionist theorists that the state is essentially an arena, he locates this as precisely the origin and mechanism of its autonomous powers:

> The state, unlike the principal power actors of civil society, is territorially bounded and centralized. Societies need some of their activities to be regulated over a centralized territory. So do dominant economic classes, churches and other ideological power movements, and military elites. They, therefore, entrust power resources to state elites, which they are incapable of fully recovering, precisely because their own socio-spatial basis of organization is not centralized and territorial. Such state power resources, and the autonomy to which they lead, may not amount to much. If, however, the state's use of the conferred resources generates further power resources – as was, indeed, intended by the civil society groups themselves – these will normally flow through the state's hands, and thus lead to a significant degree of power autonomy. Therefore, autonomous state power is the product of the usefulness of enhanced territorial centralization to social life in general.
>
> (Mann 1988: 31)

In Mann's view this has varied considerably through the history of societies, as has the power of states.

Major criticisms

It would be wrong to exaggerate the novelty of the revival of interest in the state, for, as Bob Jessop has observed, 'the statists have simply rediscovered themes well known to traditional state theorists and not unknown in more recent pluralist, neo-Marxist and structural-functionalist work' (1990a: 283). For example, Domhoff (1987: 160) claims that the statists simply revisited the work of the radical elitists, who were well aware of the potentially autonomous power of the state. Neo-Marxists have been equally critical. Jessop (1990a: 285) draws attention to the statist's crude separation of state and civil society. As Levine puts it, the statist view assumes 'the separation of the state from social and economic forces, analyzes the state in its own right, and then claims that the state influences and directs change in both the economic and social spheres' (1987: 99). Paul Cammack (1989: 271) also argues that structural Marxists are well versed in the statist approach. As Jessop illustrates, 'it is hard to distinguish operationally between a statist approach and structural Marxism, for both see the state as an autonomous actor concerned with long term objectives' (1992: 285).

Four observations can be drawn from these two modern elitist perspectives. First, there is considerable disagreement amongst commentators as to whether there is a distinctive elitist approach (see, for example, Birch 1993: ch.11; Dunleavy and O'Leary 1987: ch.4). Certainly there has been a great deal of convergence, with the distinction between the pluralist, Marxist and elitist positions becoming more blurred as the capitalist state has matured. However, elitism has always been a broad church. Indeed many theorists have treated Marxist theory as an elitist theory due to its emphasis upon the state as an instrument for securing ruling-class domination (Birch 1993: 186). Second, while most authors argue that classical elitism has its roots in Machiavelli, Hobbes, Plato, and others, there is little consensus on which modern theorists can be considered under the elitist banner. Third, the conceptual ambiguity surrounding the elitist position means that, despite the challenge which elitist thought poses to the main premises of the liberal democratic model, there exists no adequate elitist theory that demonstrates satisfactorily that the distribution of political power can be ascribed as elitist. As such, elite theory provides only a partial understanding of the relationship between the state and civil society. Fourth, the genealogy of its theoretical development relates directly to the changing concerns of both Western European and American political science.

Case study: contemporary variants of elite theory and the study of Irish public policy

In this section we highlight the role that elite theory performs in an explanation of policy development in Ireland, through an exploration of two related policy areas: agri-environmental and food safety policies. In relation to the former, an examination of Irish agri-environmental policy illustrates the existence of a privileged agricultural policy community which has been able to shape the trajectory of reform significantly to suit its own interests. In relation to the latter, an examination of Irish food safety policy illustrates the emergence of an epistemic elite exercising privileged influence on the development of food safety policy in Ireland.

Agri-environmental policy in Ireland

This policy area has already been subject to a number of policy network studies, which seek to explain the continuity and stability in policy development through the promotion and maintenance of political access (Collins 1993; Adshead 1996; Taylor and Millar 2002a, 2002b). According to Marsh and Rhodes (1992:4), policy network studies are useful insofar as they recognize that 'in most policy areas a limited number of people are involved in the policy making process' and that, as a consequence, 'many fields are characterized by continuity, not necessarily as far as policy outcomes are concerned, but in terms of the groups involved in policy making' (for a more detailed discussion of policy networks, see Chapter 7). Within this framework a policy community represents a network with a limited number of participants and capable of consciously excluding some actors. There are frequent and high levels of interaction and consensus between policy community members, and the relationships between them are based on exchange, such that each member of the community perceives him- or herself to be part of a 'positive-sum' game (Marsh and Rhodes 1992: 251).

Characterizing the Irish agricultural policy arena as a policy community, both Collins (1993) and Adshead (1996) note that the close relationships – between the main farmers' representative organizations and the Department of Agriculture – within this network allow privileged access for the community to continue, but, more importantly, often limit or restrict access for outsiders. While personnel within the network may change positions, they rarely move outside its immediate orbit. Indeed, in many instances senior Irish Farmers' Association (IFA) members have been former civil servants, both at national and European level, while IFA members have been actively co-opted into the department as special advisers (Collins 1993: 115). Granting access to organized interest groups in this way is seen as making the system more effective in supplying public needs (Richardson and Jordan 1982). The ability of the Irish agricultural policy community to maintain a stable network capable of limiting access to outsiders has proved crucial in the agricultural community's capacity to shape the pace and trajectory of reform.

Thus, for example, the IFA's ability to gain access to government has enabled it to play a significant role in the construction and maintenance of Irish agricultural policy – in the maintenance of agreed policy agendas and, where necessary, in ensuring that its own objections to certain policy ideas and/or developments receive a favourable hearing (Adshead 1996: 593–8). The same can be said in relation to environmental legislation, where it is clear that the more traditional and better established farming interests have stymied a number of attempts to deal on an overall basis with the problems of agricultural by-products and water pollution (Taylor 2001). Indeed, from as far back as the Fisheries Act of 1959–62 the agricultural policy community has been able to resist moves aimed at providing more stringent regulation (Taylor 2001). This situation continued into the 1970s with the introduction of the 1977 Water Pollution Act, which offered a defence to the polluter on the grounds that prosecution would not take place provided that s/he had taken 'all reasonable care' to prevent entry. Since its inception, the Irish farming lobby and the Department of Agriculture Fisheries and Forestry have always resisted attempts to remove this form of defence. For legal purposes, the phrase 'all reasonable care' was usually equated with procedures that accorded with 'good agricultural practice.' What constituted 'good agricultural practice' was, of course, defined by the Department of Agriculture and not by those charged with preventing water pollution (Taylor 2001: 17–18).

The importance of political access in sustaining reforms that were beneficial to agriculture was also evident in attempts to bring agriculture within the regulatory grasp of the Environmental Protection Agency (EPA). The EPA has both direct and indirect responsibilities for regulating pollution arising from agriculture. It is directly responsible for licensing large-scale pig and poultry operations, and, once licensed, operators are expected to have in place a self-monitoring plan that is checked on a random basis by the EPA (Sherwood, cited in Taylor 2001). Few would disagree that the regulation of pig and poultry farming was in urgent need of reform, a process in which it was anticipated the EPA would play a significant role. Indeed, in one of its earlier sets of forecasts the EPA suggested that new pig and poultry operations would be licensable by the end of 1994 and that existing operations would be brought into the system within twelve months (Sherwood, cited in Taylor 2001). It was a prediction that proved to be quite optimistic yet difficult to sustain, largely due to the agency's naivety in underestimating the incisive and well-organized opposition of the farming lobby. The introduction of Integrated Pollution Control (IPC) licences for pig and poultry units emerged only in September 1996 and licensing for existing operations did not commence for a further year (Taylor 2001: 74).

From the outset, the agricultural community's attitude to any kind of licensing scheme was one of open hostility rather than controlled opposition (Taylor 2001). In an attempt to placate the vociferous objections of the IFA, the Minister for the Environment acceded to requests that the licences would be open-ended, with no need for renewal after a specified period (*Farmers Journal*, 10 August 1996). Still the matter was not resolved. The IFA was suspicious that this concession only temporarily addressed the issue and anxious that the government had not made any serious attempt to negotiate change within the industry, and as a consequence it decided to bring the licensing issue into its negotiations on the *Programme for Competitiveness and Work* (PCW). The result of this was that the IFA successfully delayed the extension of the 1997 Ministerial Order to existing pig farm operations until March 1998 (Taylor 2001: 75).

Another area of agri-environmental policy that reflects the predominant influence of the agricultural policy community described above is in relation to the implementation of regulatory reform introduced by the Rural Environmental Protection Scheme (REPS). The REPS is a critical element of Ireland's agri-environmental policy and forms part of a wider package of reforms set out by provisions in the EU's Common Agricultural Policy (CAP). The key aim of the REPS is to aid in the 'reconstruction of the farmer as both producer and custodian of the countryside' (Regan, cited in Taylor 2001). In doing so, it is intended to reconcile the need to maintain income transfers to farmers and yet assuage the environmental lobby's demands for greater regulation of agriculture. The REPS has three principal objectives: first, to establish farming practices which reflect a concern for conservation, landscape protection, and wider environmental problems; second, to protect wildlife habitats and endangered species of flora and fauna; and, third, to promote environmentally friendly production of quality food.

Once more, however, we can see that the predominant influence of the farming lobby has managed to militate against the REPS' success as an effective instrument for environmental protection (Taylor 2001). This has been achieved, first and foremost, by the farming lobby's success in reducing the inspection rates of participants in REPS, a move which has cast doubt on its credibility as a bona fide pollution control programme. Originally, the intention had been to check all cases for compliance – action that the former Minister for Agriculture, Food and Forestry, Ivan Yates, suggested was in everyone's best interests – since the 'enhancement of the agri-environment could be served only by operating effective control and monitoring arrangements' (Yates, in Houses of the Oireachtas, *Dáil Debates*, 1996/467: 1,870). Opposing what it saw as unnecessarily stringent regulation, the IFA called on the minister to halve the rate of inspection in order to speed up payments to farmers. It was a 'request' to which the minister duly complied, suggesting in defence of his policy 'U-turn' that most farmers were complying with their obligations under the scheme already.

Whether or not this is the case, it is clear that the agricultural policy community has been successful in maintaining a largely *self-regulatory* environmental regime and, when challenged, has successfully thwarted attempts at a radical overhaul, sustaining a situation in which voluntary compliance predominates. This enduring strength was convincingly encapsulated by the former Minister of the Environment, Brendan Howlin, during the passage of the Waste Management Act, when he stated that attempts to subject slurry spreading to an IPC licence 'would not be appropriate or practical…we must be realistic about that. The *agricultural community* would not be able to bear that type of imposition' (Howlin, in Houses of the Oireachtas, *Dáil Debates*, 1995/ 460: 85; emphasis added) (for further details, see Taylor 2001: 88).

Food safety policy

Developments in food safety policy in Ireland lend themselves easily to the use of mapping out of epistemic communities as a framework for analysis. Certainly, within the Irish policy process the establishment of the Food Safety Authority in Ireland (FSAI) indicated a move towards the use of science as a political tool and policy instrument. At the time of the establishment of the FSAI, public health and safety were in doubt following a flurry of well-publicized food-contamination scares and occurrences. Widely publicized incidences of salmonella and bovine spongiform encephalopathy (BSE) had not only heightened public distrust in food standards, but also the public's belief in the ability of politicians to solve these problems (Taylor and Millar 2002a). As a consequence, the then Minister for

Health, Brian Cowen, announced that the government's preference would be to establish a 'science-based authority' which would offer advice for all policy-makers concerning food safety (Taylor and Millar 2002b: 14).

From the outset, the government made it clear that it would be relying heavily upon the technical and scientific expertise of the newly established authority to cover a wide expanse of 'food policy,' including labelling, industrial practices, and food technology. Within the Oireachtas, however, opposition parties became quite perturbed at the lack of transparency in the workings of the authority. A particular point of contention was the inability of the minister to clarify the exact *modus operandi* of the scientific committees established by the FSAI (Taylor and Millar 2002b: 15). In response, a government spokesman declared his belief that it was not the job of the government to enforce structural elements upon the FSAI which might compel scientific committees to share information with all elements of the authority (Taylor and Millar 2002b: 18). This attitude of govern-ment serves to illustrate how an Irish epistemic community centered on food safety policy was positively sheltered from the public's and even the opposition's scrutiny, whilst other pertinent interests were completely excluded from the entire organization.

The creation of the FSAI represents a political watershed, in that it severed a longstanding relationship between the Department of Agriculture and the farming community, one which had only served to alienate the consumer from the process in the past (Taylor and Millar 2002b: 15–16). With the establishment of the FSAI it was assumed that consumer organizations would work in conjunc-tion with the farming community to improve food safety, not just production. The minister openly advocated a primary role for the consumer within the authority, yet 'in practice...seemed reluctant to establish precisely the role or numbers of consumer organisations on the FSAI's consultative council' (Taylor and Millar 2002b: 19). Moreover, while Minister Cowen reiterated his view that the authority should have a broad consensual work base, the absence of accurate statutory protection for the consumer equivalent to the position held by the scientific community within the consultative council served effectively to priori-tize one sectional interest over another (Taylor and Millar 2002b: 19). While alleviating public fear was a factor in establishing the FSAI, interest group consultation was not a method of doing so.

While there is little doubt that the establishment of the FSAI was progressive in terms of public health policy, its creation has set an ambiguous precedent for other European countries. The ability of administrations to exclude those who are recognized as having a role to play within policy construction in favour of a community who can only enhance one side of the debate has led many to argue that 'democratic control and accountability are concepts in search of new mean-ings even at a national level' (Majone, cited in Radaelli 1999: 770). Public policy is continually fashioned in a manner that aims to protect all – without necessarily consulting or conferring with all on the issues involved. So long as this is the case, democracy is challenged: 'Democracy is all about conflict, and perhaps a certain degree of inefficiency in the policy process is the price that has to be paid for a wider participation and a more mature debate' (Radaelli 1999: 770).

Summary review of theoretical utility

Three main conclusions may be drawn from this exposition of elite theory. First, elitism still provides an important focus for the work of political scientists and political sociologists, particularly in the United States, and presents a compelling critique of the liberal democratic model. Second, when contrasted with other theories of the state, contemporary elite theory tends to be preoccupied with the nature and role of privileged elites in (specific) decision-making centres and pays less attention to developing a broader understanding of the relationship between the state and civil society. This is because elite theory as a grand narrative remains difficult to sustain in an empirical sense, for, as Birch reminds us, 'there is no adequate and convincing theory showing that democratic systems must always be elitist in practice' (1993: 202). Moreover, it could easily be argued that elite theory also offers an insufficient conceptualization of the relationship between elite circulation and the nature of state crisis and legitimation. Third, it is clear that the credibility of the elitist approach has increased in response to the dramatic rise in the size and complexity of the capitalist state: its future development is likely to reflect a concern with the emergence of new social and political forms as a consequence of globalization pressures (see Chapter 12). Analysing how far increased globalization has facilitated changes in state form and the behaviour of state elites must therefore be a key concern for contemporary elite theorists.

Yet, despite this, elite theory continues to contribute much to the tool bag of the political scientist. As Domhoff puts it, with regard to the United States:

> we should continue to remind ourselves that members of an upper class making up less than one per cent of the population own twenty to twenty five per cent of all privately held wealth and forty five to fifty per cent of all privately held corporate stock; they are over represented in seats of formal power from the corporation to the federal government; and they win much more often than they lose on issues ranging from the tax structure to labor law to foreign policy.
>
> (Domhoff, cited in Olsen and Marger 1993: 180)

Further reading

Domhoff, G. (1967) *Who Rules America?*, New York: Prentice-Hall.
Haas, E. (1990) *When Knowledge is Power: Three Models of Change in International Organizations*, Berkeley, CA: University of California Press.
Keohane, R. and Nye, J. (1977) *Power and Interdependence*, Boston, MA: Little Brown.
Krasner, S.D. (ed.) (1983) *International Regimes*, Ithaca, NY: Cornell University Press.
Mann, M. (1988) *States, War and Capitalism*, New York: Basil Blackwell.

Michels, R. (1911) (1962) *Political Parties*, New York: Free Press.
Mills, C.W. (1956) *The Power Elite*, New York: Oxford University Press.
Mosca, G. (1896) (1939) *The Ruling Class*, New York: McGraw Hill.
Pareto, V. (1935) *The Mind and Society*, London: Cape.
Skocpol, T. (1979) *States and Social Revolutions*, Cambridge: Cambridge University Press.

2 Pluralism and the politics of morality

Gary Murphy

Introduction

Interest groups are central to the political process and their existence places constraints on government, as much of the process of governance can be seen as the management of the 'interface between governments and groups' (Richardson 1993: 10). An essential element of Western European democracy has been the so-called 'co-option' of interest groups into the policy process, in which the interrelationship between governments and interest groups, depending on the specific policy area, can often be of greater significance for policy outcomes than general elections (Richardson 1993: 12).

In essence, pluralist theories offer the most positive image of group politics, emphasising the capacity of groups both to defend the individual from the government and to promote democratic responsiveness. The core expression of pluralism is that political power is fragmented and widely dispersed, with decisions made through a complex process of bargaining and interaction that ensures that the views and interests of a large number of groups are taken into account (Heywood 1997: 255). However, as one group of commentators has pointed out, in practice pluralism has tended to occupy an uneasy 'no man's-land between being a "normative" theory of how politics ought to be conducted and a "positive" theory of how groups actually do operate' (Gallagher *et al.* 2001: 407). A useful definition of pluralism for our purposes is:

> a system of interest representation in which the constituent units are organised into an unspecified number of multiple, voluntary, competitive, non-hierarchically ordered and self-determined (as to type or scope of interest) categories which are not specifically licensed, recognised, subsidised, created or otherwise controlled in leadership selection or interest articulation by the state, and which do not exercise a monopoly of representational activity within their respective categories.
>
> (Schmitter 1974: 96)

The pluralist model of interest group behaviour is open to activity in any sphere of political engagement, unlike corporatism, which exclusively refers to the management of the economy and the roles of the unions and employers. To this extent this chapter concentrates on certain non-economic interests, namely moral interest groups, and examines how successful (and to what extent) these groups have been in putting pressure on the decision-making system.

Brief review of the evolution of pluralism

Pluralism as a normative theory has its origins in the early liberal political philosophy of Locke and Montesquieu. Its first systematic development can be traced back to the contribution of James Madison to *The Federalist Papers*, in which he argued that the multiplicity of interests and groups in society needed to find expression in a political voice so that stability and order in society would be ensured. He thus proposed a system of divided government based on the separation of powers that would offer a variety of access points to competing groups and interests (Heywood 1997: 76). In essence, multiple lines of division would weaken the possibility of majority tyranny, hence the setting-up of a republic including heterogeneous social groups and territorial areas so that political factions which arose would be numerous and diverse (Dahl 1956: 4–33; Dunleavy and O'Leary 1987: 14–15). Thus a whole strand of liberal thought considers interest groups to be a fundamental element of pluralist democracy.

Academic recognition of interest group behaviour dates to the early twentieth century and Arthur Bentley's *The Process of Government* (1908), but widespread interest in such a phenomenon can be traced to David Truman's post-war classic study *The Governmental Process* (1951). The study of groups is now fully incorporated into wider analyses of the distribution of political power and the nature of the state to the extent that interaction of groups with the state is crucial to any understanding of the nature of modern governance (Ball and Peters 2000: 126–7). In its modern form, the most influential modern exponent of pluralism is the American political scientist Robert Dahl (1961), who argued that although the politically privileged and economically powerful exerted greater power than ordinary citizens, no ruling or political elite was able to dominate the political process. The key feature for Dahl (1961), and his colleague Charles Lindblom (1977, 1980), was that the competition between parties at election time and the ability of interest groups to articulate their views freely established a reliable link between the government and the governed and created an effective channel of communication between the two (Dahl 1961: 311). Thus a sufficient level of accountability and popular responsiveness was in place for the political system to be regarded as democratic.

Mainstream variants in current usage

Different pluralist conceptions of interest group behaviour show that individual interest groups apply pressure on political elites in a competitive manner. Power in policy-making is attributed to individual groups operating in particular areas at particular times. This competition is usually disorganised and its main essence is to exclude other interest groups from the policy process. Pluralism offers no formal institutional role to interest groups in decision-making or the implementation of policy. Interest groups are assumed to be self-generating and voluntary, which allows the critical role for government in mediating between groups who are competing with each other to represent the interests of the same classes of people in similar areas of economic and social activity. Indeed, group activity may be fragmented and group membership may only be a small proportion of the possible total. Moreover, groups in the same field of interest may be poorly co-ordinated by peak organisations, resulting in a pluralist rather than a corporatist model of behaviour emerging. This can mean that better organised interest groups with more resources and more strategic social, economic and political positions than others can be relatively powerful influences on government in such a pluralist model (Budge and Newton 1997: 159).

In theory, although not all groups have equal levels of power or resources, the fact that it is relatively easy to form a group should ensure at least some access to the levers of political power (Smith 1990: 309). In a pluralist system new groups can emerge and be accommodated within the system by other groups adapting and by the very nature of pluralist democracy allowing such groups to form. The key question to be answered, however, is what influence such groups can have. Most pluralists accept that the market in political influence is imperfect and contains actors with differing capacities to alter public policies. Economically, for instance, many pluralists accept that business interests have held a dominant interest in influencing government since the early 1980s in most Western European states and that the state is most definitely not neutral. The effect of this is that on some grand economic issues the state and business interests combine to remove the issue from public debate, with the result that pluralistic politics resides in secondary non-economic issues (Lindblom 1977: 142; Gallagher *et al.* 2001: 408). To that extent it has been argued that the single most distinctive feature of the pluralist account of decision-making is that it is characterised by conflict rather than consensus (Gallagher *et al.* 2001: 409).

Major criticisms

Despite recognising the inevitability of conflict between groups, the optimistic nature of pluralism suggests that the outcome of political activity in a pluralist system is a product of the balance between the various forces involved. However, because of its disorganised nature pluralism has been heavily criticised for being a vague and incomplete theory of political activity (Jordan 1990). Other critics of pluralist theory point out that pluralist explanations of power relationships between groups and the state are based on the admittance of safe political issues into the political arena to the exclusion of conflict-laden issues. Moreover, there is evidence that groups which share in the ideological bias of a government are more likely to be admitted into the policy-making process and that those groups which do not conform to the dominant set of values are likely to be excluded from the policy domain. Classic examples here would be the exclusion of trade unions and groups arguing for state intervention in the economy during the dominant new right economic thinking of the 1980s in a number of Western European democracies and, a decade earlier, the exclusion of groups with a conservative viewpoint from the dominance of liberal ideology in western democracies (Galligan 1998: 17).

Mancur Olson, in his *The Logic of Collective Action: Public Goods and the Theory of Groups* (1965a), was one of the sternest critics of the economic view of pluralism. He challenged the main tenet of the theory that economic groups take action to defend the interests of the group and the individuals of whom it is composed, to the personal benefit of those individuals. Olson maintained that in large groups individuals are not usually prepared to make sacrifices in order that the group as a whole should attain its objectives, even if the result in the long run proves to be to the advantage of each individual member. In the economic context Olson argued that large economic groups such as consumers were much less powerful than small groups of industrialists that were organised and well structured to influence policy-makers. Thus the common interest is of itself not enough in the case of consumers to set up a group that comprises all or virtually all those who would be potential members and be capable of taking collective action. Another example of this would be in the case of trade unions, where, although their actions can help to win advantages for all wage-earners, most unions attract the membership of only a small percentage of their potential supporters (Olson 1965a; Mény and Knapp 1998: 146). In an Irish context evidence exists that business interests have regular access to policy-makers and that they enjoy a relationship with government similar to that of major business representatives in other Western European states (McCann 1993: 37–54).

Pluralism and cause-centred groups in the Irish context

As we have seen, pluralism resides both outside and within economic interest groups. To the extent that corporatism entails only such sectional groups, this chapter focuses on pluralism in cause-centred groups, most notably within those groups operating within the sphere of moral politics.[1] In general, groups which are formed to promote a cause are generally classed as outsiders, with little access to policy-makers and a minimal influence on public policy. In reality, however, not all cause-oriented groups are destined to remain outside the policy process (Galligan 1998: 18). In the Irish context cause-centred groups have been significant players in the Irish policy process since the early 1980s and their activities and influence have become much more visible. Groups formed in the hope of getting a single piece of legislation enacted have become quite vocal in recent years, particularly in the area of moral politics, and there can be little doubt that such political engagement has been conducted in the domain of the interest group (G. Murphy 1999: 279). Moreover, such group activity in moral politics is highly conflictual, and the engagement within this domain suits our pluralist definition as the interest representation does organise into an unspecified number of multiple, voluntary, competitive, non-hierarchically ordered and self-determined categories. Moreover, these groups are subsequently not specifically licensed, recognised, subsidised, created or otherwise controlled in leadership selection or interest articulation by the state. Finally, in this area of moral politics in particular, groups do not exercise a monopoly of representational activity within their respective categories. Indeed, the tale of interest group behaviour in the moral domain is one of high factionalism among groups, often among those who are theoretically on the same side.

Case study: pluralism and the politics of morality in Ireland

Our case study dealing with pluralism and moral issues in Ireland can be traced back to the early 1980s and the lead up to the referendum on abortion in 1983 under the then *Fine Gael*/Labour coalition government. The sequence of constitutional amendments dealing with moral issues began with the abortion referendum of 1983 and continued up to, and included, the abortion referendum of March 2002. The first question we might ask is how did it come about that referendums would become the vehicle through which moral interest groups would attempt to influence public policy in this area? In Ireland restrictive abortion legislation had remained intact and virtually unchallenged since 1861 under section 58 of the Offences against the Person Act. Section 59 of the same act also provided that anyone helping a woman having an abortion would be liable to considerable pressures (Hesketh 1990: 1–2). In its pluralist context Ireland was unusual, in that in both Britain and the United States the abortion issue became salient as a result of the activities of pro-choice groups, who were campaigning to liberalise restrictive abortion legislation, whereas in Ireland the issue was politicised through the activities of anti-abortion groups.

The restrictiveness of the 1861 Act and the virtual absence of any calls for its repeal, up to the early 1980s at least, gives us a classic study of a pluralistic nature. Why, if such a situation prevailed, did the government of the day put a deeply divisive referendum to the people in 1983, when up to just a few years previously there had been virtually no calls for any repeal of the existing legislation? In essence the so-called pro-life campaign was anticipative in that its aim was to prevent the future legislation of abortion in Ireland. It anticipated that abortion might become legal through either parliamentary action or court activity or both. It feared that a simple amendment of the existing act through a new act could legalise abortion, notwithstanding the fact that the idea of replacing the existing act with a more permissive or liberal act was simply not an option that any government would be willing, or even want, to do. Second, the pro-life campaign feared that if abortion was not constitutionally prohibited there was a danger that an action could be taken in the Irish courts to challenge the then existing legislative prohibition of abortion in an attempt to have it declared unconstitutional.

Thus it was those groups who wished to impose a distinctly Catholic view of morality on the Irish state who would become the acknowledged kingpins in the field of pressure group politics. Indeed, the Society for the Protection of the Unborn Child sprang up completely unannounced in 1981 and within two years had, along with other like-minded groups under the umbrella of the Pro-Life Amendment Campaign (PLAC), successfully persuaded the government of the day to call a referendum with the purpose of introducing an amendment which would in effect guarantee the rights of the unborn child and constitutionally outlaw abortion (Girvin 1986: 61–81). Pluralistically speaking, how did this happen? In April 1981 the leader of Fine Gael, Dr Garret Fitzgerald, then in opposition, was approached by a group of people who said that they were concerned about the possibility that the Irish Supreme Court might copy its American counterpart's decision in *Roe vs Wade*, which had declared state legislation against abortion to be unconstitutional. The Fianna Fáil government of Charles Haughey had also been approached by the same people. Dr Fitzgerald has since written that it seemed highly improbable to him that the Irish Supreme Court would ever challenge the existing abortion legislation. Nevertheless, such was his personal antipathy to abortion, and conscious as he was of the opposition of the vast majority of the people of Ireland, that he was willing to support a constitutional amendment that would limit the court's functions in this matter (G. Fitzgerald 1991: 416). Rather confusingly, over a decade later Dr Fitzgerald would write:

> as it seemed to me sensible that this complex matter be left to the legislative power of the Oireachtas, I agreed that an amendment along such lines should be introduced and later confirmed that it would be included with other constitutional changes which I proposed to introduce with a view to removing sectarian elements from our 1937 Constitution.
>
> (*Irish Times*, 2 March 2002: 14)

If Dr Fitzgerald believed that such a matter be left to the Oireachtas then why would he be supporting any new insertion to the Constitution, which by its very nature removes power from the Oireachtas and places it explicitly in the hands of the people at the ballot box? The answer probably lies in the pluralistic nature of pressure group politics. In the hectic political atmosphere of 1981–2, which saw three governments elected in the space of eighteen months, the question of an anti-abortion amendment forced its way on to the political agenda. Fitzgerald has stated that he had no time to deal with the issue in the short period of his first government, from July 1981 to February 1982. Yet the Charles Haughey government of February–November 1982 announced that they would, if re-elected in the election of November, introduce a constitutional amendment on abortion. A year earlier Dr Fitzgerald, as Taoiseach, had met the PLAC to tell them that a constitutional change in relation to abortion would be incorporated into a general constitutional review that he had proposed. They were dissatisfied with his response and continued their representations on this issue through both elections in 1982, with the result that both major political parties, Fianna Fáil and Fine Gael, had by late 1982 undertaken to introduce a pro-life abortion amendment into the Irish Constitution. Nowhere in Dr Fitzgerald's memoirs, *All in a Life* (1991), does he state what sorts of pressure tactic were brought to bear on him by such groups. Yet the reality is that his government, and indeed that of Charles Haughey in the same period, was hopelessly ill equipped to deal with such a highly organised pressure group as the PLAC. Haughey wrote to the PLAC thus:

> I am glad to be able to confirm to your executive committee that when elected to office the new Fianna Fáil Government will arrange to have the necessary legislation for a proposed constitutional amendment to guarantee the right of the life of the foetus initiated in Dáil Eireann during the course of this year, 1982, without reference to any other aspect of constitutional change.
>
> (Haughey, quoted in O'Reilly 1992: 75)

The singularity of this proposal was in direct contrast to the Fitzgerald view on the amendment as part of a constitutional package.

In essence, the original referendum on abortion came about quite simply due to the incessant lobbying of a number of highly vocal interest groups who argued that the legal ban on abortion could be overturned in the courts and that a constitutional ban on abortion was imperative. Eventually the wording that Fianna Fáil put forward, which was acceptable to PLAC, was forced through against the advice of the then Attorney-General, Peter Sutherland.

The divorce referendum of 1986 is another extremely relevant example of the politics of pluralism and the impact of groups in influencing government decision-making. Women's interest groups had been active in Irish politics since the early 1970s. Organisations such as Action, Information and Motivation (AIM) and Cherish (a single mothers' organisation) became important lobbying agencies for changes in family law and the status of women. Moreover, the National Women's Council of Ireland, which represented a range of established women's organisations, also sought to influence government policy in a wide range of areas affecting women (Galligan 1998: 54). While AIM was very influential in placing specific and narrowly defined reforms in the field of family policy on the political agenda, it had much greater difficulty in finding parliamentary and governmental approval of the need for the introduction of divorce legislation. AIM joined with the Divorce Action Group (DAG) and the Irish Council for Civil Liberties in lobbying for divorce from 1981 onwards. With the election of the Fine Gael/Labour coalition government in 1982 such lobbying held out the hope of success, as the introduction of divorce was one of the tenets of Garret Fitzgerald's constitutional crusade. Moreover, the issue had been a live one within Fine Gael since the late 1970s, when strong support was given at the Fine Gael *Ard Fheis* of 1978 for the removal of the constitutional ban on divorce (G. Fitzgerald 1991: 623). Any success would, however, entail the use of a constitutional referendum, which by its very nature would be much more public and controversial than the reform agenda pushed by AIM up to that point.

In July 1983 the Fine Gael/Labour government established an all-party joint committee on marital breakdown with a view to obtaining cross-party consensus on a family law reform agenda that would include divorce. This committee received over 700 written and twenty-four oral submissions, including the views of AIM, DAG, the Free Legal Aid Centres, the Catholic Marriage Advisory Council and the Irish Council for Civil Liberties (Galligan 1998: 102). When the committee finally reported in 1995 it stopped short of recommending the removal of the ban on divorce as the then opposition Fianna Fáil members opposed such a move. Such opposition notwithstanding, the government, buoyed by a series of opinion polls, decided that the time was right to tackle the issue of divorce. Yet after the decision to hold a referendum was taken the Taoiseach, Garret Fitzgerald, procrastinated for months while he attempted to convince the churches, particularly the Catholic Church, that the time was right to introduce a modest measure of reform. The delaying of the referendum, however, also delayed the preparation of the necessary background papers to enable the government to deal with any issues that might arise in the course of a referendum campaign. The result was that when the referendum was called, with little advance public or political discussion, the government was woefully unprepared (Finlay 1998: 33).

The campaign itself was deeply divisive and bitter, and resulted in defeat for the government's proposed removal of the ban on divorce by 63 per cent to 37 per cent (Girvin 1987). A poll carried out at the beginning of the campaign showed 57 per cent in favour of the amendment and 36 per cent against (Girvin 1987: 93–8). The opposition of the Catholic Church had proved crucial. Rather naively, at the outset of the campaign Fitzgerald had assumed that, given the Catholic Church's stated position that it did not seek to impose its theological views on the civil law of the state, the only relevant consideration would be whether the balance of social good would or would not be served by a restricted form of divorce:

> I recognised that there could of course be divided views on this issue – it was essentially a matter of judgement – but the fact that the two sides of this crucial question were never addressed by the church during the course of the campaign disturbed me.
>
> (G. Fitzgerald 1991: 631)

Furthermore, in a country where ownership of property means so much, doubts raised in the public mind by those on the 'no' side regarding the equitable distribution of property after divorce proved hugely influential in returning a 'no' vote. As one commentator who was involved in the 'yes' campaign has written:

> The opponents of divorce were able to rely on a mixture of fear about property and land, and a message that this was a government which couldn't be trusted. I came to believe in the course of that campaign that a

great many women, who had been prepared to vote for divorce before it started, began to see divorce as a reward for philandering husbands.

(Finlay 1998: 33)

A decade later saw another referendum on divorce, when, after a concerted campaign of persuasion by those groups wishing to see the constitutional ban on divorce removed, all the main political parties assented and a referendum was eventually held in November 1995.

The campaign was primarily fought by concerned interest groups as the government deliberately pursued a low-key approach, with one minister claiming that by it doing so the hysteria associated with the 1986 divorce campaign would be avoided (Girvin 1996: 179). Given the nature of the various moral campaigns of abortion and divorce in the 1980s and early 1990s, it is hardly credible that any campaign on a moral issue in Ireland could not be without elements of hysteria. Although the reasoning of the government could be considered suspect, the fact that it took a back seat meant that the various interest groups involved could come to the fore in the debate about divorce. While the forces of moral conservatism had shown themselves to be far better skilled in modern pressure group techniques than those who sought to modernise Irish society in the abortion and divorce referendums of the 1980s, by the 1995 divorce referendum those groups in favour of the amendment such as DAG and the Right to Remarry Group had proved themselves to be efficient operators in the game of pressure politics. In the words of one journalist who followed the campaign closely, 'without the efforts of members of voluntary organizations with direct experience of marriage breakdown who…felt it was necessary to campaign for divorce independently of the Government, the amendment would have been lost' (*Irish Times*, 27 November 1995: 11).

The passing of the divorce referendum, however, does not mean that pressure groups associated with a traditionally Catholic view of morality are on the decline. It is in fact a tribute to the effectiveness of these groups that the result in the divorce referendum was so narrow. Polls taken just four months before the referendum showed that 69 per cent of those questioned favoured changing the Constitution to allow for divorce (Girvin 1996: 175). That there was only a margin of just over 9,000 votes in favour of the referendum at the end can be attributed to the professional strategy of those involved in the 'no' campaign, who associated traditional Irish and Catholic values to their cause. Indeed the No-Divorce campaign had established a steering committee in December 1994, which from then on had worked on a 'comprehensive and professional plan to defeat the referendum' (*Irish Times*, 27 November 1995: 1). Another anti-amendment group, the Anti-Divorce campaign, was formed in the months prior to the campaign and consisted of a core group who had steered through the 1983 abortion amendment and formed the Anti-Divorce campaign of 1986.

What is interesting about those groups who campaign on a conservative view of morality is that they garner a risible amount of support when they enter the mainstream political arena. After the referendum defeat both the then No-

Divorce campaign vice-chairman and Christian Solidarity Party chairman Dr Gerard Casey and Richard Greene of *Muintir na hEireann* stated that they would be looking at the next general election for the 50 per cent of voters whose views were now no longer represented in the Dáil (*Irish Times*, 27 November 1995). Yet in the 1997 election, held just over eighteen months later, Greene lost his deposit in Dublin South, polling 1,431 first preferences and 2.47 per cent of the first-preference vote; while Casey, running in the generally liberal Dun Laoghaire constituency, also lost his deposit, receiving 2,000 first preferences and 3.69 per cent of the first-preference vote. Two years later, in the 1999 European elections, Casey again lost his deposit running on a generally conservative Catholic agenda, receiving 3.3 per cent of the first-preference vote. What this shows is that individuals who play major roles in mobilising large sections of the population to vote a certain way in morality-based referendums struggle at national election time, when the issue base is obviously much wider.

On the abortion front, the 1983 referendum ended up having the exact opposite effect to that anticipated by those groups who advocated the introduction of an amendment (and probably all those who voted for it), when in 1992 the Supreme Court found that the threat of suicide provided grounds for having an abortion in Ireland within the meaning of the Eighth Amendment. It was the famous 'X case', where the High Court had prohibited a 14-year-old rape victim from travelling to Britain for an abortion, even though she had the support of her family, which gave rise to the Supreme Court challenge and the ultimate legalisation of abortion in Ireland, although there is no record of an abortion actually having been carried out in Ireland on grounds of potential suicide of the mother. The Supreme Court did, however, also decide that there could be no absolute right to travel if the sole intention was to procure an abortion. Both decisions caused a storm of protest, with both the Catholic Church and the various anti-abortion groups demanding that a new referendum be held. The former argued for an absolute ban on abortion in the Constitution, while liberals criticised the infringements of the right to travel (Girvin 1993: 118).

At a political level the question of how the Supreme Court decision should be addressed proved to be contentious. With the exception of Fianna Fáil, all political parties wanted a legislative response in order that the protocol attached to the Draft Treaty on European Union (the Maastricht Treaty), copper-fastening the provisions of the Eighth Amendment (which had now been so controversially interpreted by the Supreme Court), would not become synonymous with the abortion issue in the eyes of the public, thus leading to confusion over the substantive provisions of the Maastricht Treaty as a whole. The pro-life groups were insisting that the abortion issue be dealt with first, but on this occasion the Fianna Fáil government, under its new Taoiseach Albert Reynolds, refused. While clearly personally anti-abortion, Reynolds was eager to show that his government would not bow to the pressure of the anti-abortion groups, and he took particular care to distance himself and his government from the major anti-abortion interest groups: 'The objective of the Government, one shared by the opposition parties, was to retain control of the agenda on abortion and not let it slip into the hands of the extra-parliamentary reform groups as had happened in 1982–83' (Girvin 1993: 120). The dismissal of the President of the Law Reform Commission, Justice Rory O'Hanlon, a mainstay of the 1983 and 1986 referendums, was the most obvious public expression of this.

The government's balanced approach in standing up to the anti-abortion groups was actually quite successful, and of course it begs the question why other governments did not adopt a similar attitude. However, the sheer mobilising power of such groups was looked upon by the main political parties as being something that should be treated with extreme caution, as they did not want such groups impinging directly on the electoral system. Ironically enough, as we have seen, when such groups did mobilise politically they ended up being categorical failures. Moreover, during the Maastricht referendum the various anti-abortion groups who actively campaigned against ratifying the treaty were, in many parts of the country, the only groups canvassing against the treaty, and this can again be interpreted as a significant defeat for the anti-abortion groups (Kennelly and Ward 1993: 118). Once they moved out beyond their rigid morality domain, their influence, electorally at least, waned significantly. Nevertheless, the Fianna Fáil/Progressive Democrat coalition government decided that another amendment was probably the best way to deal with the issue. This approach was largely driven by Fianna Fáil with the Progressive Democrats acquiescing. When the amendment wording was finally issued, dividing the proposed constitutional amendment into three areas – the first regarding the life and health of the mother, the second on the right to travel and the third on the right to obtain information about services legally available in other EU states – the Progressive Democrats were critical of the so-called substantive issue concerning the distinction made between the 'life' and the 'health' of the mother but supported the travel and information amendments.

What of the interest groups and their influence? The pro-life campaign opposed the amendment on the grounds that it would in essence permit abortion and demanded yet another referendum to return the situation to the 1983 position. They then put forward their own wording. The government, however, stood firm and refused to take the pro-life wording as its own. Then the pro-life movement split. Professor Cornelius O'Leary, one of the founding members of the Pro-Life Amendment Campaign in 1983, advocated a 'yes' vote on the grounds that a defeat would leave the Supreme Court decision in place and would thus be considered a victory for those advocating abortion in Ireland. In diametric opposition to this view, Senator Des Hanafin, another stalwart of the 1983 campaign, argued that a principled anti-abortion stand necessitated a 'no' vote. Moreover, the pro-life campaign believed that if there was a 'no' vote they would then be in a strong position to influence subsequent legislation. This, of course, was to ignore the government's dismissal of their arguments in relation to the referendum itself, and can be interpreted as a sign that the pro-life campaign believed, probably naively, that their pluralistic pressure advocacy on the government would work again. In the midst of all this the government fell, and a caretaker Fianna Fáil administration saw the amendment on the substantive issue defeated and those on the right to travel and information passed on the day of the general election. In a pluralistic context the main lesson to be learned from the abortion referendums of 1992 is that the government took a much more hard-line position in relation to the pressure exerted on it by the pro-life groups than it had in 1983 and, indeed, only a few months earlier in relation to the Maastricht protocol. This can be put down to the personal belief of the Taoiseach, Albert Reynolds, that it was the duty of the government to lead in such areas and that it was the political parties rather than the interest groups who should take the lead on such issues. The government had resisted the pressure placed on it by pluralistic interest groups, but of course by dint of the result in the referendum it had not resolved the issue of abortion.

After the defeat of the amendment in relation to the first so-called 'substantive issue', the two governments that were in office during the 27th Dáil (the Fianna Fáil/Labour coalition of 1992–4 and the 'Rainbow' government, comprising a coalition between Fine Gael, Labour and Democratic Left from 1994 to 1997) parked the issue of abortion. In the first coalition, most Fianna Fáil members remained opposed to legislation, and the Labour Party, while generally favouring a more liberal approach, was unwilling to destabilise the coalition over the issue. The second 'Rainbow' coalition, on taking office, simply decided to maintain the status quo as laid down by the Supreme Court decision in 1992. Yet, in the last months of that coalition, Fianna Fáil opposition, under the new leadership of Bertie Ahern, began to make strong noises on how legislation should be framed to regulate the ambiguous status of abortion. Abortion did not figure in the June 1997 election campaign and, more significantly, was not mentioned in the subsequent Fianna Fáil and Progressive Democrat agreement for government *An Action Programme for the New Millennium* (Government of Ireland 1997). Still, however, Ahern had given a personal commitment to deal with the issue if he became Taoiseach and, more significantly, he had given specific commitments to independent TDs (members of the Dáil) Mildred Fox, Jackie Healy Rae, Harry Blaney and Tom Gildea in order to ensure their support for his minority government. Each of these politicians had also played pluralistic politics in their constituencies by stating explicitly in the election campaign that they would strive to get an abortion referendum in place, although later Mr Healy-Rae denied that he had personally sought an abortion poll (*Irish Times*, 8 March 2002: 8).

Five years later, in March 2002, the Irish people faced yet another referendum on abortion designed in essence to limit the capacity of the Oireachtas to legislate on a complex issue. Why the government went down this road when experience would seem to have shown that the complexities of the abortion issue were not capable of being definitively settled by constitutional action is unclear, but it seems that in the final decision, made by the Taoiseach himself, his view was that a constitutional amendment was the only way to solve the issue. In a pluralistic context the proposal itself followed an extensive consultation process with a whole variety of lobby groups including the medical profession, the Catholic Church, and both pro-life and pro-choice groups. The main pro-life

groups, the Pro-Life Campaign and the Pro-Life Movement, gave the amendment their enthusiastic support but there is no evidence, as there was for the
1983 referendum in particular, of their ability to bring significant pressure to
bear on the government of the day. Indeed the government itself was somewhat
divided, with the minority Progressive Democrat coalition partner showing no
great enthusiasm for the amendment. Once again, however, the pro-life ranks
split in a classically pluralist way. Both Youth Defence and its ally the Mother
and Child campaign opposed the amendment because they argued that it failed
to protect the unborn *from the moment of conception*. In terms of pluralist politics,
then, after split in the pro-life ranks the interest representation of the constituent
units had shown themselves once more to be organised in an unspecified number
of multiple, voluntary, competitive, non-hierarchically ordered and self-determined categories – none of which was able to exercise a monopoly of
representational activity within its respective category. This, of course, then split
the vote in the referendum itself. Furthermore, in a clear sign of voter disen-
chantment with the politics of morality being fought out via referendum, the
2002 turnout, at 42.89 per cent, was significantly lower than in 1992 (68.16 per
cent) and 1983 (53.67 per cent).

Summary review of theoretical utility

The politics of morality tells us much about the theory of pluralism in its cause-
centred context. The 1983 referendum is an exemplar case. Garret Fitzgerald
has written that he should never have accepted the original referendum proposal,
'however harmless it may have appeared at the time, for that commitment to
introduce a constitutional amendment on the issue led me into a position that,
while intellectually defensible, was much too complicated to secure public understanding or acceptance' (G. Fitzgerald 1991: 446). Then why did he do it? His
reaction to his first meeting with the PLAC was reported by one PLAC member
present as 'grovelling' (O'Reilly 1992: 68):

> It seems extraordinary that a man of Fitzgerald's intelligence, with his
> pluralist outlook, his much vaunted academic interest in theology and other
> religions, his antipathy to the sectarian nature of much of the state's laws
> and constitutional provisions, should have bowed the knee so quickly and so
> unthinkingly to those people. The most cursory enquiries about the attitude
> of non-catholic churches to abortion would have demonstrated the lack of
> absoluteness in their positions, with a greater weighting accorded to both the
> life and the liberty of the woman.
>
> (O'Reilly 1992: 69)

While the reference to 'those people' identifies the author's own bias in this
particular sphere, the charge in essence remains convincing. The reference to
pluralism is in its social context of shared difference, but it is in pluralism in its
political context that the answer lies. The perceived electoral influence that such

groups might well have seems to have been the main reason behind such acqui-
escence to the PLAC's demands. While such groups have had a negligent effect
electorally when they have presented themselves to the electorate, to have been
perceived as 'soft on abortion', as Fitzgerald himself alluded to a rumour then
doing the rounds about him (G. Fitzgerald 1991: 416), would have been enough
to have been electorally suicidal in the fluid political situation of the early 1980s.
The reason why such an amendment was eventually accepted is in essence a
classic case of pluralistic politics. The PLAC was an umbrella group which
formed with the intention of getting a single piece of legislation enacted and did
everything in its power to ensure such an outcome. It did this in conflict with
other groups, and its influence on the then government and indeed main opposition party in detriment to those on the other side of the equation is
quintessentially pluralist. What Irish society got out of this referendum was a
decade and more of social division that, judging by the referendum of March
2002, is still with us today.

What does the divorce referendum of 1986 tell us about the theoretical utility
of pluralism? In the first instance, it points to the effectiveness of various pro-
family reform legislation groups who were able to force their concerns into the
legislative arena. DAG, formed in 1980, for instance, proved very effective in
attracting support from the Labour Party and the liberal wing of Fine Gael
(Girvin 1987: 94). Again, in much the same way as with the abortion referendum, though in relation to a different moral issue, group activity in relation to
divorce was highly conflictual, with interest representation organising in a
number of multiple, voluntary, competitive, non-hierarchically ordered and self-
determined categories, so that none of the groups was able to exercise a
monopoly of representational activity within its respective category. Finally,
however, the outcome of pluralist lobbying was a victory for those who advocated reform.

At a fundamental level, the defeated amendment had for the first time placed
the issue of marital breakdown firmly on the political agenda; in particular the
need to develop a humane response to such breakdown, making adequate financial and material provisions for those in family separation cases. Although the
Anti-Divorce campaign had proved successful in mobilising opinion against the
amendment, political debate after the referendum concentrated on reforming
family policies and the policy process reverted to routine procedure in the
Department of Justice, with AIM once more lobbying on equality-focused issues.
Pluralistically speaking this is important, as it shows how cause-centred groups
can have an impact on governmental bureaucracy. Eventually in 1989 the then
Fianna Fáil minority government adopted Fine Gael Deputy Alan Shatter's judicial separation initiative, first introduced as a Private Member's Bill in the Dáil in
1987, and passed the Judicial Separation and Family Law Reform Act (Galligan
1998: 103). To the extent that this statute broadened the grounds for judicial
separation to include a 'no-fault' provision and more explicit measures on financial settlements and protection for children, it set the scene for a rerun of the
divorce referendum. After the 1992 election, the Fianna Fáil/Labour government

in its programme for government explicitly committed itself to 'a major programme of family law reform, culminating in a referendum on divorce in 1994' (Fianna Fáil/Labour, *Partnership for Government*, 1993: 1).

The theoretical utility of the case study is also shown to great effect by the insertion into the Draft Treaty on European Union (the Maastricht Treaty) of a special protocol to protect the Eighth Amendment, the aim of which was to secure indefinitely the outlawing of abortion in Ireland. In a pluralistic context this is important, as there is evidence to suggest that the then Taoiseach, Charles Haughey, and the then Minister for Foreign Affairs, Gerard Collins, were convinced by anti-abortion activists that without such a protocol the Constitution would not be able to protect the original amendment. If this was the case there was a fear that opponents of abortion in Ireland would oppose the Maastricht Treaty unless specific safeguards were put in place. Given the recorded mobilising power of these groups in previous referendums, this was not a threat to be taken lightly by the government. In December 1991 Collins persuaded his European colleagues to take the protocol on board. It was a decision which had come about through the lobbying of the pro-life groups. And here is one of the key problems with pluralism: the level of influence some groups can have on governments, while other groups and even political parties do not know what is going on. As one commentator pointed out about the protocol decision:

> The key issue here of course was that such a private debate should ever have been conducted by the Government with the non-elected lobbyists. What right did they have to make demands and seek consultations when the elected representatives of the people, the opposition parties, did not even know what was going on?
>
> (O'Reilly 1992: 139)

Albert Reynolds' subsequent refusal to allow the pro-life lobby to dictate to his government on this question shows that pressure group politics can only work if the government allows it to work by acceding to pressure group influence.

Conclusions

What does the politics of morality tell us about pluralism in the Irish context? Pluralism, at its heart, is about emphasising the positive image of groups both to defend the individual from the government and to promote democratic responsiveness. Yet, as we have seen, it would be naive simply to treat pluralism in this way. Pluralism in the context of political power is supposed to be fragmented and widely dispersed, with decisions made through a complex process of bargaining and interaction that ensures that the views and interests of a large number of groups are taken into account. However, pluralist conceptions of interest group behaviour show that individual interest groups apply pressure on political elites in a competitive manner. In the Irish case this is true of groups on both sides of the conservative/liberal divide in relation to moral politics. Pluralist competition is usually disorganised and its main essence is to exclude other interest groups from the policy process. Again, this can be seen to be substantially true in our case study. Those groups advocating an abortion referendum in 1983 were successful in their attempt to exclude those groups with a diametrically opposite view to them from influencing government. The competition between these groups was disorganised and group activity was fragmented, so that ultimately it was the PLAC which came to the fore as the major success in the game of moral pressure politics at this time.

In essence, pluralist theory offers no formal institutional role to interest groups in decision-making or implementation of policy, but points to the critical role of government in mediating between groups who are competing with each other to represent the interests of the same classes of people in similar areas of social activity. Nevertheless, our case study shows that some interest groups can be better organised than others, with more resources and more strategic social, economic and political positions. Thus they can be relatively powerful influences on government in such a pluralist model. This is what happened in particular in the abortion referendum of 1983 and the Maastricht protocol of 1992, but not in 1992 or 2002, when the political elites made the running and also acted in a pluralist manner by mediating between groups. This was also the case for both divorce referendums. If one examines pluralism in Ireland today from a cause-centred group perspective it is clear that moral interest groups on both sides of the conservative/liberal divide have played a central role both by ensuring that referendum amendments get put to the people and by playing an active part in the campaigns. At the beginning of the chapter it was argued that an essential element of Western European democracy was the co-option of interest groups into the policy process, in which the interrelationship between governments and interest groups, depending on the specific policy area, could often be of greater significance for policy outcomes than general elections. In terms of moral politics in Ireland there can be little doubt that this statement holds. Primarily it was interest groups who managed to persuade governments of various hues to get amendments put to the people, and it was the interest groups who campaigned hardest to get the referendums passed or defeated. While the question of divorce has been settled, it is clear that the abortion issue has not. Future governments can expect to come under pluralist pressure from a variety of interest groups seeking either to get legislation passed or to have another amendment put to the people. Whether governments will be able to resist such pressure remains open to question; what is not, is that, for the interest groups involved, morality politics in Ireland will remain aggressively pluralistic.

Note

1   Moral politics has been an increasingly important issue in Ireland since the 1980s. The 1937 Constitution was particularly Catholic in orientation and, while the special position that the Catholic Church held was removed from the Constitution in 1972, there has nevertheless continued to be a strong link between Church and state in Ireland. The 1983 referendum on abortion was seen by its opponents as strengthening this link

between Church and state, and in essence the various referenda on abortion and divorce in Ireland since 1983 have been to some extent about the influence of the Catholic Church on the state's moral politics. Inserting such moral issues into the Constitution extrinsically links Church and state in the area of sexual morality, and interest groups on both sides have been to the fore in these referenda.

Further reading

Dahl, R.A. (1961) *Who Governs? Democracy and Power in an American City*, New Haven, CT: Yale University Press.

Hug, C. (1999) *The Politics of Sexual Morality in Ireland*, London: Macmillan.

Jordan, A.G. and Richardson, J.J. (1987) *Government and Pressure Groups in Britain*, Oxford: Clarendon Press.

Murphy, G. (1999) 'The Role of Interest Groups in the Policy Process', in J. Coakley and M. Gallagher (eds) *Politics in the Republic of Ireland*, 3rd edn, London: Routledge.

Smith, M.J. (1990) 'Pluralism, Reformed Pluralism and Neopluralism: The Role of Pressure Groups in Policy-Making', *Political Studies* 38: 302–22.

3 Marxism, the state and homelessness in Ireland

Eoin O'Sullivan

Introduction

For Marx, the economic system that emerged with the transition from an agri-cultural-based society to an industrial-based one was conceptualized as capitalism. Capitalism, for Marx, was an economic system based on the produc-tion and exchange of privately owned commodities within an unconstrained market. Within this market, the *value* (as opposed to the price) of any commodity or good was an expression of the amount of human labour power expended on its production. From this starting point, Marx develops an account of capitalism as a necessarily exploitative and class-based system, one in which the *price* of labour in an unconstrained market may easily be set below its *value*. As such, *unpaid* labour is extracted from the sellers of labour power, the proletariat (or workers), by the owners of capital, the bourgeoisie (or capitalists), under the form of 'free and equal exchange' in the marketplace (see Pierson 1998; M. O'Brien and Penna 1998; Gamble *et al.* 1999 for further detail). Despite (often substantial) variations in emphasis amongst Marxist analysts of the state, under-pinning their analyses is the belief that the primary function of the capitalist state or the state under capitalism is the reproduction and maintenance of capi-talist social relations. How this is achieved and maintained has, however, been the subject of much debate.

Brief review of the evolution of Marxist approaches

It is a truism that one of the few areas that Marxist theoreticians of the state can agree on is that neither Karl Marx himself nor his co-author Fredrick Engels left any coherent and unified theory of the capitalist state. Rather, as Bob Jessop, a leading contemporary Marxist theoretician of the state, observes, 'their work comprises a loose and often irreconcilable series of philosophical, theoretical, journalistic, partisan, *ad hominem*, or purely *ad hoc* comments' (Jessop 2001: 149). This difficulty has not eased with the passing of time and despite voluminous and detailed attempts by Marxist-inspired social and political scientists to define and interpret the illusive capitalist state or the state in capitalist society. Jessop (1990a: 249) suggests that 'there is no really convincing and easily accessible

Marxist theory of the capitalist state' and that many of the more satisfactory accounts 'remain accessible only to those initiated into the higher mysteries of Marxist theory' (Jessop 1990a: 249).

Despite this rather discouraging start, the chapter sets out to introduce students to various Marxist theories of the state in order that we can begin to understand how Marxists have interpreted public policy-making (see also Pierson 1996; Kelly 1999; Hay 1999; D. Marsh 2002 for similar overviews). We will then examine the nature and extent of homelessness in Ireland and see what insight Marxist analyses provide to our understanding of the existence of homelessness in a wealthy society such as Ireland, and competing explanations of homelessness will be reviewed and debated.

Mainstream variants of Marxism in contemporary usage

For the purposes of this chapter, two broad categories of Marx-inspired theories of the state can be identified. 'Instrumental' approaches generally derive from Marx and Engels' position in the Communist Manifesto that the state is nothing but an executive committee for the bourgeoisie. On the other hand, 'Structural' Marxists, see the state as having a degree of autonomy from the bourgeoisie, and as able to ensure the accumulation of capital with greater effectiveness than private capitalists themselves. Structural Marxists argue that the relative autonomy of the state is necessary to ensure the long-term interest of the capitalist class. In both versions, the state is seen as distinct from society, with the state essentially a superstructure that serves to rationalize more fundamental forces stemming from class relations based on the means of production. In general, for Marxists the state is a mechanism that reproduces the normative social order so that particular, not general, interests are protected and enhanced. In a capitalist society, no matter what level of economic development and what form of state, the particular interests are those of the capitalist class. These two Marxian approaches have been augmented in recent years by Jessop's (1990a, 1990b, 2001) 'strategic-relational theory of the state', which posits a more structurated relationship between 'the state' as executive and 'the state' as society (see Hay 1995, 1999).

Instrumentalist views

The instrumentalist view of the state takes its starting point from the claim in the Communist Manifesto that 'the executive of the modern state is but a committee for managing the common affairs of the bourgeoisie' (Marx and Engels 1967 [1848]: 82). Thus, from this perspective, policy formulated by the state will reflect the needs and interests of the minority bourgeoisie to maintain their rate of profit and no policies will be implemented that would fundamentally affect the class division of society. Until the early 1970s, this view of the state was dominant in Marxist thinking and the instrumentalist view became accepted as the Marxian theory of the state. This reflected in large part the dominance of Leninism in the period after the First World War. For Lenin 'the State is an organ of class domination, an organ of oppression of one class by another; its aim is the creation of "order" which legalizes and perpetuates this oppression by moderating the collisions between classes' (Lenin 1943 [1918]: 9).

Neo-Marxist instrumentalists such as Miliband (1969) elaborated this classical Marxist analysis of the state in the late 1960s and early 1970s, arguing that the state is an 'instrument for the domination of society' (Miliband 1969: 22). Those in the ultimate positions of power in the state apparatus, such as cabinet ministers, higher-ranking judges, senior civil servants, etc., are, according to Miliband (1977: 73–4), recruited predominantly from the ranks of the upper class and upper middle class. For Miliband, the state will always act in the interests of capital, because of 'the character of its leading personnel, the pressures exercised by the economically dominant class and the structural constraints imposed by the mode of production' (Miliband 1977: 74).

The instrumentalist view of the state, based on classic Marxist views of the singular importance of the economy in dominating all social relations, was gradually undermined as the influence of the Italian Marxist Gramsci (1971, 1977) became more pronounced in the early 1970s. Although his work was written during the 1930s, it was not widely translated and disseminated until the late 1960s. The essential innovative concept introduced by Gramsci was the notion of *hegemony*. Gramsci defined the state as 'the entire complex of practical and theoretical activities with which the ruling class not only justifies and maintains their domination, but manages to win the active consent of those over whom it rules' (Gramsci 1971: 244). A key question for Gramsci was how the capitalist state is able to obtain the active consent of the proletariat despite its exploitation of them. One obvious method is coercion. The capitalist state controls both the military and the police and any attempt by the proletariat to overthrow the existing capitalist order would be met with by repression. However, for Gramsci, coercion by itself was not sufficient to maintain capitalism; it also required consent. By consent, he meant the manner in which the proletariat accepted the structures of capitalism. This consent was achieved through the institutions of civil society such as the mass media, the family, voluntary agencies, churches, educational agencies, etc, which, he argued, were responsible for inculcating in the proletariat the dominant values and ideology of capitalism and rendering them natural or inevitable. Thus, rather than simply using coercive strategies to maintain its domination, the bourgeoisie could achieve this through 'manufactured consent backed by coercion', or, in other words, *hegemony*.

Structuralist views

Drawing both on Gramsci's work and the concept of 'relative autonomy' devised by the French Marxist Louis Althusser (1970), the state, according to neo-Marxist structuralists, can not be fully understood as the instrument of the ruling class. They assert that the social class of those managing the state is of less significance than the class structure of a society, which ensures that the state serves the capitalist class. Social classes and the state are, according to Poulantzas (1973, 1975, 1976, 1978), objective structures, and their relations must be taken as an objective system of regular connections. Since class relations create the state, the state is a condensation of class-based relations. And, in as much as the state reflects objective power structures, the state cannot be independent: it can only be *relatively autonomous*. As such, it is given the capacity to act independently of individual capitalists while remaining unavoidably the state of the owning ruling class. The state 'takes charge, as it were, of the bourgeoisie's political interests and realizes the function of political hegemony which the bourgeoisie is unable to achieve. But in order to do this, the capitalist state assumes a relative autonomy with regard to the bourgeoisie' (Poulantzas 1978: 12).

For Poulantzas, the capitalist state is characterized by 'the unity proper to institutionalized political power and its relative autonomy [from economic classes]' (1978: 31). The state's relative autonomy from social classes is crucial to the stability of capitalist societies, since the state acts as a 'factor of cohesion between the levels of a social formation…and as the regulating factor of its global equilibrium as a system' (1978: 66). Poulantzas's (1978) argument is that this autonomy allows the state to intervene to arrange compromises with the dominated and dominant classes when the long-term interests of the dominant classes are threatened. The state is able to arrange such compromises because of its ability to manipulate social actors' perceptions of its goals. Although the state claims to advance the general interests of society, it is really advancing the long-term interest of the hegemonic class. In other words, in understanding the nature of the state under capitalism, the state might not act in the interests of particular capitalists, but in the long-term interests of capitalism.

In a variant on this theme, Block (1977, 1980) argued that the state is not reducible to class interests and power. For Block, 'State power is *sui generis*, not reducible to class power' and 'each social formation determines that particular way in which state power will be exercised within that society' (Block 1980: 229). Block introduces the concept of 'state managers', who, he contends, are independent from the capitalist class insofar as they are not involved in the relations of production (even if they were proper members of that class before they became state managers). 'State managers' are Block's solution to the problem of 'relative state autonomy', which he argues reduces state power to class power. Since the state managers are independent of and not controlled by the capitalist class and are responsible for maintaining 'business confidence', the reduction of state power to class power implied in the qualification 'relative' is inappropriate and unnecessary. State managers are dependent on a healthy capitalist economy materially, for financial resources, and ideologically, for purposes of continued legitimacy (Block 1987: 58). Thus, state managers act to maintain favourable conditions for capital accumulation, or what Block labels 'business confidence' (1987: 59), because it is typically in their own specific interests to do so. State managers have substantial leeway in terms of what political and economic interests are met with respect to particular policies and activities. The state thus has discretion in terms of what concessions are to be made with respect to various capitalist or working-class demands. Second, state managers may at times be in a position to pursue their own strategic agenda, but such occasions are rare. State managers maintain capitalism, not because they are themselves part of the bourgeoisie or because they are instrumental pawns of the dominant class. Rather, the power and position of state managers themselves are contingent on the continuation of the existing capitalist system.

Strategic-relational theory of the state

The previous two interpretations of the functions of the state, acting in the interests of the ruling class or in the long-term interests of capital, are rejected in Jessop's (1990a, 2002) strategic-relational theory of the state (Kelly 1999; M. Kenny 1999). Jessop (1990a) is less concerned about what the state is and more about how it comes to be a concrete, societal force. For Jessop, 'the state can be defined as a relatively unified ensemble of socially embedded, socially regularized, and strategically selective institutions, organizations, social forces and activities organized around (or at least involved in) making collectively binding decisions for an imagined political community' (Jessop 2002: 40). Different actors undertake purposeful action, albeit constrained by the capitalist structure, pursuing particular 'state projects', which make and remake the state. By 'state project', Jessop refers to the political agenda of a particular group of state actors as they engage in 'explicit attempts to coordinate the action of different organizations, structures and systems to produce specific results' (Jessop 1990a: 360). Ultimately, then, state projects give the state 'a certain organizational unity and cohesiveness of purpose', effectively bonding together the 'institutional building blocks' of the state system and setting them in motion (Jessop 1990a: 353). Only with this coupling of state structures and a particular strategic state project can the state be described as an actor with the potential to impact on other societal spheres. At any given time there are multiple state projects in existence, each trying to unite and mobilize political resources in particular directions.

These *strategies* are constantly in flux, and consequently so too are the boundaries of the state, resulting in a 'dynamic and constantly unfolding system' (Hay 1999: 170). Whilst the attributes of the state at any particular point in time are structured by these strategies, the realization of such strategies

> depends on the structural ties between the State and its encompassing political system, the strategic links among state managers and other political forces, and the complex web of interdependencies and social networks linking the State and political system to its broader environment.
>
> (Jessop 2001: 167)

Ultimately, for Jessop, the state is a paradox in that it is responsible for ensuring the cohesion of the society of which it is also a part. As a consequence of this paradoxical position, it is continually called upon by diverse social forces to resolve society's problems and is equally continually doomed to generate 'state failure' since so many of society's problems lie well beyond its control and can even be aggravated by attempted intervention.

(Jessop 2001: 167)

Overall, Jessop is of the view that we can only ever understand the role of the state in particular institutional, historical and strategic contexts. On this basis, unlike earlier accounts, there can be no general theory of the capitalist state, only specific ones.

Criticisms of Marxist approaches

The various Marxist theories of the state, described briefly above, have been subject to considerable criticism, both from the internecine arguments amongst Marxists themselves and also, more significantly, from non-Marxist analysts of public policy. First, Marxist analyses have been accused of 'economism'; that is, reducing all possible explanations to economic factors. As Howlett and Ramesh argue:

the problem of economic determinism continues to haunt the theory, notwithstanding efforts to avoid it. No matter how hard neo-Marxists try to overcome the problem by devising concepts such as 'relative autonomy of the State' or 'ideological hegemony' to take non-economic factors into account, they cannot entirely avoid reducing social and economic phenomena to an economic base. This is because of the nature of the theory whose fundamental unit of analysis is the largely economically-based 'class'. To remain Marxist, no theory can dispense totally with these assumptions, even if it is recognized that policy makers are affected by factors other than economic imperative.

(Howlett and Ramesh 1995: 25)

Second, there is the inadequacy of Marxist theory to explain the complexity and detail of public policy. Ideas which at a theoretical level offer a degree of plausibility have often come unstuck when applied to a particular policy in a particular context. For example, in the case of Ireland, those who occupy positions of power in the civil service, judiciary, military, police, cabinet, etc. are not recruited only from the upper classes, but are representative of a broader range of classes (see Daly 1999). Likewise, those who have made substantial profits in property development and building in Ireland in recent years have tended to come from impoverished rural backgrounds rather than being the sons of the bourgeoisie. Even if we believe that the state acts in the interests of capital, specifying the mechanisms by which these objectives are actually achieved has proved problematic for Marxists. While Jessop has attempted to deal with some of these issues by his insistence that we understand the role of the state in particular institutional, historical and strategic contexts and provide 'detailed accounts of the complex interplay of social struggles and institutions' (2002: 41), few concrete studies inspired by this perspective have emerged.

Third, if we accept the view that in the final analysis the state always operates in the interest of capital, and if the specific mechanism by which the state acts in the interest of capital is specified, how do particular social and public policies serve the interests of capital? For example, as Pierson has noted:

> some Marxists have argued that the welfare state provides the indispensable underpinning for a market-based social and economic order, whilst others have seen it as incompatible with the long-run integrity of a capitalist economy. A number of Marxist and neo-Marxist commentators have managed to affirm all of these principles more or less simultaneously!
>
> (Pierson 1999: 175)

Thus we are left with the difficulty of explaining how public and social policies simultaneously both sustain and undermine capitalism. The answer in part depends on the variant of neo-Marxism you subscribe to, but it nonetheless exposes a key difficulty for Marxist analysts of public policy.

Case study: homelessness in Ireland

Althoughs difficult to quantify, most agencies working with the homeless identified an increase in homelessness from the early 1970s onwards. Furthermore, they highlighted that homelessness was not the preserve of middle-aged alcoholic men, as is often popularly perceived. Rather, homelessness embraced men, women and children. Although a range of voluntary agencies provided an array of services, there was a lack of co-ordination between them and the statutory agencies. More significantly, statutory responsibility for the provision of services for the homeless was allocated to two different state agencies (Health Boards and Local Authorities), neither of which expressed any great interest in developing and expanding services for the homeless. As Harvey has argued, '[u]ntil the 1980s, homeless people were at best a marginal concern to the Irish administrative and political system. Homeless people were seen as drop-outs, vagrants, tramps, anti-social people, for the most part unwanted elderly men' (Harvey 1995: 76).

Although a number of estimates of the extent of homelessness had been produced during the 1970s and 1980s, they were either localized or 'guestimates'. The figure of 5,000 homeless persons was the estimate most commonly cited by voluntary and campaigning agencies in the late 1980s and early 1990s. It was not until 1991 that (as a consequence of provisions in the 1988 Housing Act) the first statutory national count of homelessness since 1925 took place (E. O'Sullivan 1996). It comprised a snapshot of those who were deemed homeless by statutory bodies on the night of 31 March 1991. The results of this survey suggested that there were 2,751 homeless persons in Ireland. This exercise was repeated in 1993 and saw a slight decrease in the number of homeless persons, to 2,667. These figures were considerably lower than the estimates put forward by the voluntary sectors, which were swift to criticize the methodology and administration of the assessment. In light of these criticisms, and the housing assessment methodology more generally, the Department of Environment commissioned the Economic and Social Research Institute (ESRI) to explore the meaning and adequacy of these assessments; they concluded that, whilst 'some undercount had taken place', they were not in a position to quantify the degree of undercount (Fahey and Watson 1995: 104). They also highlighted the inconsistencies in the methods of recording homeless persons of different local authorities.

By the mid-1990s it was becoming increasingly apparent that the legacy of disinvestment in social housing in the late 1980s and early 1990s, coupled with the various sales policies and exacerbated by demographic trends, was leading to a housing crisis in Ireland (E. Fitzgerald 1990). The numbers on the housing waiting list had more than doubled between 1988 and 1996, but, somewhat surprisingly, as measured by the local authorities homelessness had not increased.

In March 1999, the local authorities undertook a further assessment of housing need and homelessness.[1] The results of these assessments showed an ongoing increase in households on the housing waiting lists, rising from over 36,000 in 1996 to nearly 50,000 in 1999,[2] with all indications suggesting a similar increase between 1999 and 2002. The number of homeless households, which had remained at approximately 2,500 between 1991 and 1996, showed a dramatic increase, more than doubling, to 5,234 households. Of the 5,234 assessed, 2,947 were single-person households. The 1999 assessment of homelessness provided, for the first time, a breakdown by gender of homeless adults assessed and the children of homeless adults disaggregated. Of those 5,234 assessed as homeless, virtually half were adult males (49.5 per cent), 26.7 per cent were female adults and the remaining 27 per cent were children (O'Sullivan and Higgins 2001).

With this apparent substantial increase in homelessness and the increasing number of households on the local-authority waiting lists, still relatively little attention was devoted to housing policy issues. When housing did appear on the policy agenda, from 1996 onwards, the focus was on the increased costs to the middle classes of purchasing private homes (Downey 1998; O'Sullivan 1998).

Traditional explanations for homelessness in Ireland

Much of the research on homelessness over the past two decades or so has been polarized between the work of those who privilege either structural (macro-level) or individual (micro-level) factors in their explanations (see, for example, Elliot and Krivo 1991; Thorns 1991; Jencks 1994; Neale 1997). Broadly, structural accounts suggest that homelessness is a consequence of broad factors such as poverty, unemployment and, most importantly, lack of access to affordable

housing. Individual-level accounts suggest that homelessness occurs as a consequence of personal problems, such as various forms of addiction and mental
illness, which make it difficult for individuals to maintain a home and lead to
homelessness. On the whole, Irish government responses have tended to favour
more micro-level explanations of homelessness.

Homelessness – An Integrated Strategy, the first comprehensive policy document
published by the Irish state to address homelessness, concluded that, while 'the
dynamics of homelessness involve a complex interrelationship of social and
economic factors', those leaving institutional care of various kinds were most
vulnerable to homelessness (Department of the Environment and Local
Government 2000a: 7). In the *Homeless Preventative Strategy*, it was claimed that the
earlier strategy recognized

> that a solution to homelessness is not just about the provision of housing or
> shelter and that there is a need for a comprehensive approach involving
> health, care and welfare, education, training and support, as well as accom-
> modation, to enable homeless persons to re-integrate into society and to
> prevent others from becoming homeless.
>
> (Government of Ireland 2002: 5)

It then went on to state:

> There are many reasons why people become homeless, including
> behavioural or other problems or social phobias which inhibit them making
> proper use of existing services. Homeless persons may have mental health,
> alcohol, drug-related problems or multiple needs, which are not met effec-
> tively either by homeless or mainstream services.
>
> (Government of Ireland 2002: 8)

This document reiterated the belief that those most at risk of homelessness were
those leaving institutional care. What is of note in these two official analyses is
the relative absence of housing availability as an explanation for homelessness.[3]

Downplaying the role of housing as a factor in the creation of homelessness is
not unique to the Irish government: explanations of homelessness in the US and
Europe have also downplayed the role of housing affordability, placing greater
emphasis on de-institutionalization and addictions (Jencks 1994; Fitzpatrick
1998). The more popular (though not necessarily more accurate) explanations
for homelessness suggest that mental illness, alcohol abuse, drug use and changes
in society's treatment of these problems are the principal determinants of homelessness. The tendency is to neglect explanations that focus on increases in
housing costs relative to personal income, which can drive low-income households out of the housing market and into the streets and shelters (see, for
example, Marcuse 1988: 72 in relation to the US).

Still, as Quigley and Raphael (2001) observe, this form of analysis appears to
be justified by the traits of the homeless population. Research, both in Ireland

and internationally, describes the homeless population as suffering disproportionately from mental illness, drug and alcohol addiction and extreme social isolation, with high proportions of the homeless having been institutionalized at different periods of their lives. Homeless women, in particular, in addition to the above characteristics are often recorded as having histories of domestic violence and/or sexual abuse. In addition, counts of the homeless population suggest that they constitute a small fraction of the population (between 0.1 and 0.2 per cent in the Irish case). Given this confluence of personal problems and the relatively low incidence of homelessness, it is tempting explain homelessness in terms of personal pathologies and to dismiss explanations of homelessness that focus on structural factors such as housing market conditions.

Nevertheless, a number of recent international studies of homelessness suggest that tighter housing markets are positively associated with higher levels of homelessness (O'Flaherty 1996; Kemp *et al.* 2001; Quigley and Raphael 2001). For O'Flaherty, the rental vacancy rate exerts a negative and statistically significant effect on homelessness, while measures of housing costs such as median rents and rent-to-income ratios exert positive and significant effects. It seems likely that many of those who are currently vulnerable with respect to homelessness would be capable of accessing and retaining secure accommodation if affordable and appropriate dwellings were available. Given this, the key underlying cause of homelessness can be seen to lie in the interaction of the labour and housing markets. In Kemp *et al.*'s (2001) study in Scotland, unemployment exerted a more significant force on homelessness than did the housing market, but housing affordability and de-institutionalization were still important factors. Quigley and Raphael (2001) argue that relatively minor shifts in housing market conditions can have substantial effects upon rates of homelessness and that homelessness can be reduced by attention to the better functioning of housing markets.

Marxist interpretations of Irish homelessness

Marxists, not surprisingly, stress structural factors over individual ones as explanations for homelessness. While the extent of homelessness recorded in the various assessments between 1991 and 1996 may have been underestimated, thus exaggerating the 1999 figure, when it is combined with other sources there is evidence of a strong rate of increase in homelessness during the second half of the 1990s in Ireland. Despite this increase, homelessness has been primarily interpreted as a consequence of personal pathologies rather than as relating to changes in the housing system.

In the second half of the 1990s a crisis of housing affordability emerged in Ireland (Duffy 2002). However, rather than restructuring the operation of the housing market, all public policies in this area have continued to promote home-ownership as the most desirable tenure form, irrespective of the cost and the consequences. This was largely because the housing crisis was portrayed as an affordability issue for the middle classes rather than as a more generalized crisis in overall housing policy in Ireland (O'Sullivan 1998). There is nothing particularly new about this. As Engels perceptively noted in 1870:

> What is meant today by housing shortage is the peculiar intensification of the bad housing conditions of the workers as the result of the sudden rush of population to the big towns; a colossal increase in rents, a still further aggravation of overcrowding in the individual houses, and, for some, the impossibility of finding a place to live in at all. And this housing shortage gets talked of so much only because it does not limit itself to the working class but has affected the petty bourgeoisie also.
>
> (Engles 1942 [1887]: 3)

On this interpretation, housing affordability and availability only became a public policy issue when they began to affect the middle-classes' ability to purchase their own homes from the mid-1990s onwards and with their consequent increasing dependence on the private rented sector. The flurry of policy activity, such as the Bacon Reports (Bacon 1998, 1999, 2000)[4] and the *Report of the Commission on the Private Rented Sector* (Department of the Environment and Local Government 2000c), emerged from demands from the petite bourgeoisie. Substandard conditions in the private rented sector, in addition to the lack of security of tenure, had existed well before the mid-1990s (L. O'Brien and Dillon 1982). In addition, unless the legitimacy of home-ownership was reaffirmed, substantial sections of the capitalist class would lose out, particularly developers, speculators and their 'friends'. Although some of the measures proposed had the effect of temporarily reducing their rate of profit, those that did so were relatively quickly reversed. Indeed, the unhealthily close links between some politicians and developers had, since the 1970s, been the subject of much speculation and controversy, and in recent years was finally exposed (Cullen 2002; Flood 2002). What has emerged is the manner in which legislation and actions by politicians have enriched a minority at public expense through the re-zoning of land for housing. Windfall profits for well-connected developers and builders were the result, together with an increase in the cost to the state of building local-authority housing (Drudy 2001).

These arguments notwithstanding, you do not have to be a Marxist to note that some 'obvious' policy responses – the acquisition of land in order to provide public housing, and regulation of the private rented sector – although not formally excluded from the policy agenda, have not been implemented or enforced. This was not, however, due to ignorance of the problem. As far back as January 1971, a committee was appointed by the Minister for Local Government to consider

> in the interests of the common good, measures for controlling the price of land required for housing and other forms of development, ensuring that all or a substantial part of the increase in the value of land attributable to the

decisions and operations of public authorities shall be secured for the benefit of the community.

(Committee on the Price of Building Land 1973: 1)

The committee eventually published its deliberations in 1973, but it was divided over the main recommendations. Whereas the majority of members recommended that local authorities should be enabled to purchase potential development land at the existing land-use value plus 25 per cent, the two representatives from the Department of Local Government argued that there was no 'justification for a radical departure from the basic compensation principle on which the present code is founded' (Committee on the Price of Building Land 1973: 83). They argued that the majority proposal would give rise to 'insuperable Constitutional difficulties' (Committee on the Price of Building Land 1973: 83) but, more fundamentally, it would be tantamount to a 'severe attack on private property rights' (Committee on the Price of Building Land 1973: 85), which could not be justified.

This upholding of the right to private property has strongly influenced housing policy in Ireland. In 1981 the limited form of rent control that existed in Ireland was deemed unconstitutional, and current attempts to make landlords register with local authorities have also been constitutionally challenged (De Blacam 1992; Department of the Environment and Local Government 2000b: 94, 95). Private property is of course crucial to capitalism, but it is also an essential doctrine of Catholic social thinking (Dorr 1992). Again, Marxists might argue that in Ireland the Catholic Church still retains a strong hegemonic role, though this view is equally substantiated by non-Marxists also (see Chapters 4 and 8). The conclusions that Marxists reach over what to do about this problem are, however, perhaps more radical. Engels was clear on what needed to be done.

There are already in existence sufficient buildings for dwellings in the big towns to remedy immediately any real 'housing shortage', given rational utilization of them. This can naturally only take place by the expropriation of the present owners and by quartering in their houses the homeless or those workers excessively overcrowded in their former houses. Immediately the proletariat has conquered political power such a measure dictated in the public interests will be just as easy to carry out as other expropriations and billetings are by the existing state.

(Engels 1942 [1887]: 4)

Summary review of theoretical utility

Since independence, the stated housing objectives of successive Irish governments have been to ensure that, as far as the resources of the economy permit, every family can obtain for their occupation a house of good standard at a price or rent they can afford, located in an acceptable environment (Department of the Environment 1995). In practice, as Fahey and Watson have argued, one could make the case that the goal of home ownership has been advanced to such a degree that it has come into conflict with the goal of adequate housing for all and, until the recent past at least, has sometimes seemed to occupy the primary rather than the secondary position in housing policy.

(Fahey and Watson 1995: 20)

(see also National Economic and Social Council 1988; L. Murphy 1994, 1995).

This core statement of housing policy has been expanded in recent years, so that future housing strategies aim to 'develop and implement responses appropriate to changing social housing needs and mitigate the extent and effects of social segregation in housing' (Department of the Environment and Local Government 1991: 1; see also Redmond 2001 for a critique of social housing in Ireland). The various Housing Acts place responsibility on the individual housing authorities for the delivery of services on the ground, while the Department of the Environment provides the legislative framework for housing provision, funding as necessary, the monitoring of the national housing situation and the development of appropriate policy responses.

As the above statements and the earlier discussion imply, the Irish housing system is strongly biased in favour of home-ownership. A range of subsidies and incentives have facilitated the expansion of home-ownership from the foundation of the state,[5] which in turn has residualized other tenures and constructed the belief that the tenure of preference is home-ownership. Indeed, in most advanced capitalist countries home-ownership has become the dominant tenure form, eclipsing, in particular, the rental tenure (Doling 1997).

Marxists have generally interpreted this trend as a hegemonic strategy where the state drives a home-ownership ideology which, by offering most households a stake in a 'property owning democracy', acts as a 'bulwark to Bolshevism' (Kemeny 1992). Home-ownership, from this interpretation, attaches individuals to wage labour, private property and the maintenance of prevailing socio-capital relations. Thus, the desire for home-ownership is not an innate preference, as suggested by some (see P. Saunders 1990); rather, 'current tenure preferences are the product and not the cause of tenure systems' (Kemeny 1981: 63). This occurs because, in the conceptual framework devised by Kemeny (1995), Ireland's rental market is highly 'dualistic', divided between a high-rent unregulated profit market offering no security of tenure and a 'command economy' public rental system with heavily restricted 'poor law' access. Consequently, high rates of home-ownership are the norm for most people, because the way housing provision is structured means that no housing offering security of tenure is available other than through owner-occupation.

In addition to the various financial incentives to home-owners – which include no residential property tax, no capital gains tax on sale of principal residence, no stamp duty on new housing for owner-occupation, mortgage interest relief, and cash subsidies to first-time buyers (see Drudy and Punch 2001, 2002 for further details) – public housing in Ireland is sold (or privatized) to sitting tenants at heavily discounted rates. From the time that local-authority housing was first provided in the late 19th century to the present, nearly three-quarters of the stock, amounting to nearly a quarter of a million units, has been sold to tenants (Fahey 1999a). Unlike other countries, particularly the United Kingdom, this policy of privatization has its origins in the land agitation of the 19th century (Fraser 1996) and was only introduced in urban areas from the 1960s (Fahey 2002). Thus, the thrust of housing policy in Ireland has been to ensure a 'property owning democracy', but the origins of this policy are more complex than is generally perceived.

Until the early 1990s this policy was largely sustainable: a relatively stable housing market existed in Ireland, with comparatively easy access to home-ownership. From 1995 onwards, however, this rapidly began to change as a consequence of changing household formation patterns, increasing economic prosperity and net inward migration, leading to demand outstripping supply in all tenures, despite record levels of housing construction output. The cost of new and second-hand houses in the private market rose rapidly, local-authority waiting lists doubled and rents in the private rented sector tripled between 1990 and 2000 (O'Sullivan 2001). In this context, it is hardly surprising that the number of homeless persons doubled between 1996 and 1999, with all indications suggesting that this figure is rising.

These changes are interrelated, with increased house prices leading to a higher demand for private rented accommodation, as purchasing a home has been postponed for longer periods of time. Moreover, with demand for private rented accommodation outstripping supply, the unregulated market has responded with higher rents. Higher rents in the private rented sector and rapidly increasing prices for new houses, coupled with sluggish local-authority housing output, have led to an estimated nearly 5,000 new additions on to the local-authority housing waiting list each year. As house prices increased, a shift occurred in the profile of borrowers. In 1988 professionals, managers and employers accounted for just over one-third of the new mortgages in Ireland; by the late 1990s they had increased their share of the market to nearly half. Skilled and semi-skilled workers held their share of new mortgages at just under 30 per cent, but the group that lost out significantly were salaried non-manual workers, who saw their share drop from 27 per cent to 13 per cent (O'Sullivan 2002).

These salaried non-manual households now found themselves primarily dependent on the private rented sector for independent accommodation, as their incomes were insufficient to purchase from the market but too high in most cases to qualify for social or affordable housing (Fahey 1999b). The number of units in the private rented sector had increased in absolute terms by over 60 per cent between 1991 and 1997 (McCashin 2000), partly in response to various urban renewal incentives and other fiscal incentives, which increased the number of individuals purchasing a second home for investment purposes (Department of the Environment and Local Government 2000c; Memery and Kerrins 2000). Negative real deposit interest rates during the latter half of the 1990s would also have exerted a powerful pressure on those with surplus financial resources to invest in the private rented sector with its high rate of return compared to other investments. Despite this increase in overall supply, however, with an increasing number of salaried non-manual workers seeking accommodation in this sector, and for longer periods of time than was the norm in the 1980s and early 1990s, demand quickly exceeded supply and rents rose steeply and rapidly.

As the private rented sector increasingly became the only option for households that had traditionally purchased their own homes via the market, this resulted in increased rent levels for existing tenants. In 1999 a commission was established by government to see how particular concerns over the sector could be addressed. These concerns largely focused on the issue of security of tenure and rent controls. A number of recommendations were put forward, which are in the process of being implemented, but the considerable disagreements that existed within the commission did not ease this task (Department of Environment and Local Government 2000c: 164–76).

The persistence of these problems may in part be explained by any of the three major Marxist variants discussed earlier. From an instrumentalist point of view, this is explicable by reference to the fact that the state acts in the interest of the capitalists and devises policies to ensure that their profitability is maintained at the expense of the proletariat. Key personnel in politics and the civil service manipulate policies to suit these interests. Thus, we can expect to see no fundamental changes in the housing market that would diminish the rate of profitability of the capitalist class. From a structuralist point of view, maintaining the stability of the existing class structure and the long-term profitability of capitalism results in policies that support these objectives. Housing policies, particularly the nature of the tenure system, are part of this process. The state intervenes in the housing market to maintain existing policy patterns rather than to challenge them, particularly if the capitalist class is disrupting traditional expectations. Thus, the various Bacon Reports can be seen as instruments whereby traditional class structures would be maintained even if this meant temporary restrictions on the profitability of the capitalist class in this area.

From a strategic-relational point of view, we see that the state is called upon by diverse social forces to resolve the housing problem, but that the problem is interpreted in different ways by different social forces. Private tenants wish for security of tenure and others wish to be able to purchase their own homes at affordable prices, but others see such policies as detrimental to their profitability. Consequently failure will result, as the state cannot simultaneously satisfy all interests. The balance of power between these societal forces is constantly in flux and the outcome is contingent on the strategy employed by the state at different periods for different reasons.

The existing responses to homelessness in Ireland via the abovementioned action plans etc. have a restricted understanding of the nature of homelessness in Ireland and relate homelessness primarily to administrative defects and the absence of specialized programmes to reintegrate the homeless. Such a perspective acknowledges to a limited degree that structural factors may contribute to homelessness, but ultimately sees the solutions as involving specialist rather than generic solutions. Potentially, such a perspective may see homeless services evolving away from mainstream public policies on housing etc. and create the perception that homelessness is a matter of individual responsibility, resulting in more specialist and rehabilitative schemes that aim to normalize the homeless. While these strategies, at a superficial level at any rate, are inclusionary, the state also operates exclusionary strategies. The number of arrests by the *Gardai* under the Vagrancy Acts increased by over 300 per cent and arrests under the Public Order Act 1994 by 130 per cent between 1996 and 2000, as Ireland adopted elements of a 'zero-tolerance' policing policy (O'Donnell and O'Sullivan 2001; for a Marxist account of the function of vagrancy laws, see Chambliss 1964). As a consequence, Irish public policy-making with regard to homelessness is para-doxical. Strategies of inclusion via *Homelessness – An Integrated Strategy*, though formally inclusionary, are in fact subtly exclusionary, since the explanations that they offer for homelessness lead to a focusing of public policy on the develop-ment of specialist and normalizing services to meet the needs of homeless individuals rather than engaging with the structural question of housing reform. Whilst Marxist interpretations of state behaviour may prove too extreme for many, they do present a positive antidote to the virtual absence of macro-level or structural variables in most explanations of homelessness in Ireland and else-where.

Notes

1 A further assessment took place in March 2002, but at the time of writing the results were not available.
2 Considerable confusion exists concerning the numbers on the housing waiting list, particularly since 1996, and how social housing need is conceptualized and measured. Essentially, three different figures can be used: first, households which apply to local authorities to have their housing need met and are deemed to require local-authority housing; second, households which apply for local-authority housing but are deemed best suited for other social-housing measures; third, households which are in the private rented sector in receipt of a rent allowance under the Supplementary Welfare Allowance (SWA) scheme. In the 1999 assessment of housing need, 39,176 house-holds fell into the first category, a further 8,257 households fell into the second category and approximately 40,000 were in the third category. In all official commu-nication from the Department of Environment and Local Government it is the first figure, rather than the cumulative total of first and second figure, that is utilized. The issue of rent-supplemented tenants is more complex. It would appear that only a small number of rent-allowance recipients are registered on the local-authority housing waiting list. The assessment of housing need conducted in March 1999 suggested that 29 per cent of those assessed as in need of local-authority housing were in receipt of SWA rent allowance. Thus, depending on the measure used and how housing need is conceptualized, the number of households which require social housing (within the existing allocation criteria) can range from just under 40,000 to just under 80,000 if those in receipt of rent allowances are also included.
3 *Homelessness – An Integrated Strategy* does fleetingly acknowledge that 'the key difficulty in tackling homelessness is the scarcity of more appropriate accommodation' (Department of the Environment and Local Government 2000b: 34).
4 The newly formed Fianna Fáil–Progressive Democrat Government in 1997 promised action on the rapid rise in house prices as a part of their election campaign. In this

regard, the first of what are known as the Bacon Reports (after the key author Peter Bacon) were commissioned and the first report was delivered in April 1998. The proposals outlined in the report called for massive intervention in the housing markets by the government designed to calm the housing markets, particularly the market geared toward first-time buyers. A second report, commissioned to assess the success of the changes imposed by the first report and to make further recommendations, was published in 1999. The government introduced no major changes in the demand side, but introduced several changes regarding the supply of land and infrastructure, including a phased repeal of the lower capital gains tax on development land. The third Bacon Report was delivered in mid-June 2000. This report recommended wide-ranging changes to the property taxation system in relation to investors and first-time buyers, as well as changes in planning and development procedures. Outlining some of the infrastructure initiatives contained in the previous two reports, an update on the status of specific projects was included in order to assess the need for future intervention in the housing markets.

5   Rates of home-ownership grew from 60 per cent of housing stock in 1961 to nearly 80 per cent in 1991.

Further reading

Hay, C. (1999) 'Marxism and the State', in A. Gamble, D. Marsh and T. Tant (eds) *Marxism and Social Science*, Basingstoke: Macmillan.

Jessop, B. (1990a) *State Theory: Putting Capitalist States in their Place*, Cambridge: Polity.

Jessop, B. (2001) 'Bringing the State Back In (Yet Again): Reviews, Revisions, Rejections, and Redirections', *International Review of Sociology* 11(2): 149–73.

Jessop, B. (2002) *The Future of the Capitalist State*, London: Blackwell.

Kelly, D. (1999) 'The Strategic-Relational View of the State', *Politics* 19(2): 109–15.

4 Feminism and politics of gender

Pat O'Connor

Introduction

Many people today are reluctant to define themselves as feminists, the word 'feminism' frequently evoking 'an image of strident, unattractive women' (Kourany *et al.* 1993: 1). However, at its simplest, feminism is concerned with the value of women and their lives. In a national poll, nine out of ten Irish women said they had heard of feminism. Four out of five of these women said they knew what it meant: 87 per cent seeing it as developing women's confidence in themselves; 76 per cent as developing society so that women play a greater part; and 84 per cent as ensuring that the things that women value influence the development of the society and economy (MRBI 1992). It is possible to identify analytically different kinds of feminism, reflecting different priorities as regards action, different ideas about the state and different kinds of mechanisms as regards change. Initially, attention will be focused on three of these: liberal, radical and socialist feminism.

Liberal feminism has typically marshalled arguments about organizational efficiency and effectiveness, as well as broader ideas about democratic representation involving women's rights as citizens (Lovenduski 1997). Traditionally, equality in this perspective is defined very much in male terms: the 'normal' citizen is male, has no need for maternity leave and few responsibilities as regards childcare or unpaid work in the home. There is an implicit acceptance of a male model of work–life balance, a 'male' organizational culture, hierarchical styles of management, etc. Classical liberal feminism (e.g. Friedan 1963) was particularly concerned with the removal of legal and educational barriers in the context of paid employment. In an Irish context, the existence of the Marriage Bar and of differential wage rates for men and women (which persisted up to 1973) were targets for this kind of liberal feminism. However, by the 1980s liberal feminism internationally recognized that the removal of such barriers was not in itself sufficient, because of women's greater responsibilities for childcare (and consequent vulnerability to part-time employment, poverty, lack of promotion, etc). Liberal feminists, such as Friedan (1981) in her later work, argued for greater state involvement in mediating between paid employment and family responsibilities. Overall, liberal feminists see the state as a potentially neutral arbiter which has been captured by one group (viz. men). The solution, as they see it, is through education, first, to increase the proportion of women in state structures and, second, to reduce or eliminate men's prejudicial attitudes. The question as to whether this is sufficient to change the wider societal context, organizational ethos, or work/family balance is typically ignored by liberal feminism. Quite simply, liberal feminism suggests that if women want to succeed in the world of paid employment they must do so on male terms, within organizations based on the male as the norm. Thus: 'Liberal feminism has brought to the surface the suppressed truth that the state is gendered, and has used this truth to inspire a formidable and sustained politics of access' (Connell 1994: 142).

For radical feminists, gender is an institutional reality. Some radical feminists see this as related to biology, while others see it as related to social and cultural factors. The historical existence of male dominance is referred to as patriarchy, i.e. culturally constructed ideas about male supremacy and privileging that are embedded in procedures and processes inside and outside the workplace, as well as in attitudes about what is 'natural', 'inevitable', 'what women want'. Connell suggested that the majority of men benefited from what he called 'the patriarchal dividend' in terms of 'honour, prestige and the right to command. They [men] also gain a material dividend' (Connell 1995a: 82). Connell (1995b) was at pains to suggest that most men do not want to oppress or exploit women. However, they are reluctant to forego privileging, being most comfortable if it appears that it is 'given to them by an external force, by nature or convention, or even by women themselves, rather than by an active social subordination going on here and now' (Connell 1995b: 215). Because men wished to be men, patriarchal privileging persists.

Internationally, key issues for radical feminists have included sexuality and violence. MacKinnon (1982) focused on the way that rape law in the US was framed, arguing that so-called legal objectivity was in fact the institutionalization of men's interests. Equally, it has been noted that in Australia job evaluation schemas created by the state reflected its systemic patriarchal bias by valuing 'male' skills, attributes and activities more than 'female' ones. For radical feminists, the state in its practices, procedures and organizational culture is a patriarchal power structure. Organizational culture is the concept used to refer to the complicated fabric of myths and values that legitimize women's position at the lower levels of the hierarchy, and the concept which 'chills' women out when they attempt to step out of their 'proper' place into 'men's place' in managerial structures. Radical feminism stresses that real equality must be based on recognition and valuing of difference, whether this is biological difference or socially and culturally created difference. It is frequently pessimistic about the possibilities of organizational transformation in male-dominated and male-controlled organizational structures:

> You may find a place, as long as you simulate the norm and hide your difference. We will know you are different and continue ultimately to treat you as

different, but if you yourself specify your difference, your claim to equality will be nil.

(Cockburn 1991: 219)

Attempts by liberal feminists to be accepted in such organizations are, they suggest, conditional on women's adjustment to a male norm. When women themselves assert their difference (for example, through pregnancy) this will be used to justify disadvantaging them.

Socialist feminists are concerned with a fundamental restructuring of society in terms of both class and gender hierarchies. They are concerned with the nature and effect of the – at least analytically separate – systems of capitalism and patriarchy. As Hartmann (1981, 1994) notes, a purely class analysis fails to explain why women are subordinate to men within and outside the family and, indeed, why the reverse is not true. A socialist feminist restructuring of society involves a change in the value of women's work – whether this is unpaid work done by women in the home or the valuing of predominantly female work outside it. For socialist feminists, the state represents patriarchal and capitalist interests. Some have emphasized the way in which state policies are underpinned by ideas about masculinity and femininity (e.g. the idea in the 1960s and 1970s that girls were 'naturally' not able to do honours maths). The situation of lone parents, who are frequently dependent on social welfare because of the absence of childcare and are expected both to be in paid employment and to care for their children twenty-four hours a day, highlights the contractions in the state's position. Socialist feminists are concerned with the diversity of women's experiences (e.g. the experiences of poverty amongst working-class women or the discrimination experienced by Traveller or refugee women). They differ from radical feminists insofar as they do not see gender as the most fundamental, most widespread and most devastating model of oppression. They point out that, although the state assumes that men's interests are the norm, in fact it privileges middle-class (white, heterosexual) men. Thus, socialist feminists see women, working-class men, gay men, etc. as potentially making common cause.

Brief review of the evolution of feminism in Ireland

In Ireland a concern with feminism is rooted in a number of intellectual traditions, including the history of the Irish Women's Movement (Mahon 1995; Smyth 1993; Connolly 1996, 2001), international studies of equality policies (Gardiner 1997), the impact of the women's movement on aspects of state policies (Good 2001) and an exploration of women and social policy in an Irish context (Kennedy 1999; U. Barry 1998).

Feminist activity in the late 1960s and early 1970s emerged in what has been described as the (second) Women's Movement. It was an attempt to promote change within patriarchal power structures (such as the economy and the political and legal structure) and cultural systems that reflected and reinforced a differential valuation of men and women. Very early on, we see the utilization of international pressure by an ad-hoc committee of ten women's organizations in Ireland so as to bring about the establishment of the First Commission on the Status of Women in 1970. This sort of strategy is typical of liberal feminism. In Ireland in the early 1970s, typical liberal feminist concerns were equal pay and equal access to paid employment. However, the strategies used by the Women's Movement included a variety of grassroots mobilization – something which is much more typical of radical feminism. Such strategies included the public launch of the Irish Women's Liberation Movement on the most popular television programme of the time (*The Late Late Show*). Such strategies generated questioning of patriarchal control that legitimated the response by the state to European Union (EU) Directives in the area of paid employment in the 1970s. In Ireland radical feminism was concerned with family and sexual issues: radical action centring mainly on the three abortion referenda (1983, 1992 and 2002), two divorce referenda (1986 and 1996) and legal initiatives around crisis pregnancies. In the 1970s and 1980s a wide range of organizations, reflecting both radical and liberal feminist influences, emerged from within the Women's Movement to provide support and services for women that were not provided by the wider institutional structures. They included fertility guidance clinics; Cherish, to support pregnant single women; the Women's Political Association; rape crisis centres; the Irish Women's Aid Committee, etc.

The 1990s saw three very different kinds of developments. First, although the phrase has not been generally used in Irish feminism, the 1980s and 1990s were characterized by an increase in what Australian work has called 'femocrats', or bureaucrats committed to advancing a feminist agenda (Franzway *et al.* 1989; Mazur 2001). Some of these were activists in service organizations that became increasingly institutionalized. Others were in the expanded and increasingly professionalized Council for the Status of Women (now the National Women's Council). Still others were in organizations and agencies that became 'embedded within the state' – for example through the social partnership process, in the Department of Equality and Law Reform, etc. (Good 2001). Their existence needs to be located in a wider institutional context characterized by the election of Mary Robinson, the first woman President of Ireland, the establishment of the Second Commission on the Status of Women and the creation of a separate Department of Equality and Law Reform (1993–7) which monitored the implementation of the recommendations of that Commission. Second, the 1990s also saw the rapid growth of locally based (mainly working-class) women's groups concerned with women's poverty and with empowering women in their families and communities. One might regard such developments as reflective of socialist feminism, although they typically did not describe themselves in these terms. These groups typically used non-hierarchical methods of organization. Their work was facilitated by funding from a variety of state and EU resources (such as the EU's New Opportunities for Women (NOW) programme, Doyle 1999). Third, the 1990s also saw the strengthening of a feminist intellectual critique of Irish society. Up to then, with a small number of notable exceptions, little was written about the Women's Movement and its importance in Irish society. This was perhaps not surprising given the hierarchically and numerically male-dominated nature of Irish universities (O'Connor 2002). In the early 1990s all of the universities in Ireland had women's studies programmes at undergraduate and/or postgraduate level, with a total of approximately forty Women's Studies courses in existence (albeit under-resourced and with inadequate staffing levels). Feminist publishing also flourished, in the shape of Attic Press, the *Irish Journal of Feminist Studies* and university publishing initiatives by the Women's Studies staff and students. These developments stimulated a wider ideological challenge, including a critique of the social policy area for its exclusion of a gendered analysis of citizenship (see, for example, Kennedy 1999), a critique of employment equality and broader welfare and sex equality policies (Gardiner 1997; Mahon 1998). The universities' obligations in the equality area, the importance of role models for that half of the undergraduate and postgraduate student populations who are women, and a major anonymous university-wide funding initiative on behalf of Women's Studies, premised on increased mainstreaming, offer some hope for the continuance of an intellectual critique of those structures which create and transmit knowledge.

Mainstream variants of feminism in current use

In Ireland, by far the most common variant is liberal feminism. Implicit in it is a concern with access and representation, reflecting a concern with legitimacy, democratic deficits and imperfect citizenship. This perspective 'treats patriarchy as an accident, an imperfection that needs to be ironed out' (Franzway *et al.* 1989: 15). The assumption is that once awareness has been created and stereotypical thinking changed, the state and other structures will be gender neutral. In the meantime an attempt needs to be made 'to level the playing pitch', with positive action being allowed in the 1998 Equality Act. Radical feminism has also had an influence (O'Connor 1996, 1998, 2000a; Department of Justice, Equality and Law Reform 1999; Humphreys *et al.* 1999), particularly in terms of a critique of gendered organizational procedures and cultures, sexual harassment, the devaluing of 'women's work', the peripheral location of 'women's units' and the underlying relationship between masculinity and management.

Psychoanalytical feminism, postmodern feminism and global feminism are mainstream variants, although they are less prevalent in Ireland. Psychoanalytical feminism recognizes that work, whether paid or unpaid, is also about meaning and identity. Thus it opens up the whole question of what women want and value, and the way this is affected by their early experiences within particular societies. Thus, for example, it is arguable that there is a cultural expectation that 'love labour' (Lynch 1989; Lynch and McLaughlin 1995) should be embedded in women's identity in Irish society. Equally, one might suggest that some men's underlying fear of and hostility towards women (see Clare 2000) reflects the traditional pattern of women's dominant responsibility for childrearing (Chodorow 1978; Dinnerstein 1977). Preference theory (Hakim 1995) has become one of the most popular contemporary faces of this broad area in the UK. Hakim argues that women are responsible adults who chose to be either home-centred uncommitted workers or committed workers. This perspective pays little attention to the context in which that choice is made. Thus, for example, in 1971, when the Marriage Bar was in existence, only 7 per cent of married women were in paid employment in Ireland. To assume, as preference theory does, that this pattern simply reflected women's commitment seems very problematic.

Postmodern feminism has been concerned with deconstructing all unitary explanations and with understanding and valuing the position of 'Other' (the marginal, the devalued, etc.). Theorists such as Irigaray (1993) have challenged us to reflect on how we can know what it is to be a woman since language itself is patriarchal. Postmodern feminism arguably ignores the fact that in countries such as Ireland gender is the frame within which adults are seen and evaluated. In such a context behaviour and achievements are not gender neutral: thus, for example, the ambition and single mindedness of a chief executive have quite a different flavour depending on whether that person is a man or a woman. Similarly, promiscuous sexual behaviour is seen very differently for the same reason. The area that is 'mapped' by gender varies, of course, between different societies. However, in Ireland, regardless of how we see ourselves, we are seen as women. New feminism, which has emerged as a reaction to postmodern feminism, 'concentrates on the material realm of inequality' (Walter 1998: 5–6). It stresses the reorganization of paid work so as to achieve a better balance between work and family; comprehensive childcare (free) for all children whose parents want it; tackling poverty and violence; and men wanting to, and taking on, the same responsibilities as women in the home. Also part of a new feminist agenda are issues related to the importance of increasing the number of women in public positions of power and providing education and training for women in what Walter calls 'dead-end' jobs. Essentially, however, this is simply a selective version of the agendas of liberal and radical feminism.

Global feminism has highlighted the extent to which gender is affected by lines of social cleavage apart from class and race within an increasingly globalized world – such cleavages arising from imperialism, colonialism, etc. It is particularly concerned with the oppression experienced by Third World women, and seeks to challenge the implicit ethnocentrism in much First World feminist thought. It can be seen as lying within the broad tradition of socialist feminism since it is concerned with 'the oppressive results of colonial and nationalist policies and practices, how Big Government and Big Business divide the world into the so-called First World (the realm of the haves) and the so-called Third World (the realm of the have-nots)' (Tong 1998: 226).

Feminism has been compared to other social movements, such as environmental or civil rights movements, which also rely on popular awareness and mobilization. However, implicit in feminism is a fundamental challenge to the patriarchal order that underlies the main institutional structures (whether these are the institutional Church, the economic system, the legal or political system, etc.). This is arguably related to a certain coyness surrounding individuals' identification of themselves as feminists. A further consequence is that the elements in a feminist agenda that will be taken up by these institutional structures are those that are most compatible with other agendas and least disruptive of the patriarchal order. Thus for example, job-sharing initiatives, which are predominantly taken by women and used to reduce their opportunities as regards promotion are likely to attract more support than fundamental changes in promotional mechanisms, re-evaluation of the value of women's work or challenging male organizational cultures and styles of management.

Major criticisms

There are four main types of criticism. First, there are those who argue that institutions, including the state, are gender neutral, so that feminism as a gendered explanatory framework is irrelevant. Second, there are those who are critical of the two most common frameworks, arguing that liberal feminism is concerned with women who are already privileged and that radical feminism is an extreme view endorsed only by those who are 'man-haters'. Third, there are those who argue that women's position ultimately reflects their preferences and/or their biological make-up, and thus that it is inevitable or what women want. Fourth, there are those who see a focus on feminism as unacceptably challenging male authority.

The first argument, namely that organizations in general, and the state in particular, are gender neutral, is one that is implicit in much popular thinking and in the views of classical sociologists (such as Weber). However, since the late 1980s increasing attention has been paid to the 'gendered process internal to the bureaucratic process of the State' (Witz and Savage 1992: 6). Increasingly it is accepted that once one accepts that 'staff bring their personal interests into organisations and that these shape the way they discharge their functions, [one] must also accept that gendered perceptions, practices and attitudes will be present too' (Halford 1992: 172). In terms of authority and division of labour, it is difficult to see how an argument that gender is not relevant can be sustained. In Ireland, almost three-quarters of administrative, executive and managerial positions are held by men; areas of predominantly female employment tend to be lower paid than areas of predominantly male employment; women's hourly earnings in the industrial sector are roughly three-quarters of men's; the tiny proportion of executives in the private sector who are women earn 75 per cent of what their male counterparts earn – and this is not due to lower levels of education for women (O'Connor 2000a; Government of Ireland 2001).

The second criticism is rather different. There are two specific elements to it. Criticisms of liberal feminism focus on its concern with middle-class, well-educated women (i.e. women who are relatively advantaged by comparison with other women). This criticism implicitly endorses a rather colonial view of women. It implies that insofar as such women have a 'comfortable' if subordinate place within the structure, this is, or should be, sufficient. This would be seen by many as a highly offensive view of women. In addition, underlying this criticism is a concern with the failure of liberal feminism to explore all possible sources of discrimination, oppression, etc. Attempts have been made to develop frameworks that incorporate multiple axes (for example socialist feminism or global feminism). This is a very difficult exercise, and raises the question of the relationship between these elements (for example, is a black, working-class, lesbian woman four times more oppressed, or do these forms of oppression interact other than in an additive way). Class as an analytical concept has long faced similar difficulties, although in Ireland these have not diminished an academic acceptance of the concept. Hence, the question as to why the partiality argument is used in the case of liberal feminism needs to be raised. The second part of this criticism focuses on radical feminism and implies that the name itself is sufficient to indicate that it is an extreme perspective, and hence by definition unacceptable. Some suggest that all radical feminists are biological essentialists and/or man-haters. This is simply not true. Radical feminism does, as the word 'radical' implies, go to the root of the issue. At the heart of radical feminism is a challenge to the relatively lower public value attached to women. It questions the societal value reflected in the wages and working conditions of those in areas of predominantly male activity (such as engineering) and predominantly female activity (such as nursing or primary teaching); and the relative importance of expenditure in such predominantly 'male' or 'female' areas. In a world where both women and women do roughly the same total amount of paid and unpaid work, it looks at the implications of the fact that, internationally, women undertake disproportionate amounts of unpaid work (United Nations Report 2000). Indeed, many writers and dramatists have depicted Irish women as strong, coping and courageous, while Irish men have been presented as weak, sometimes over-dependent on maternal approval and often rather pathetic figures. This view, however, ignores the increasing importance of the machinery of the state, and the subordinate position of women within it and in the wider public arena.

The third criticism suggests that women's position ultimately reflects their preferences and/or their biological make-up. Given the rapidity of change in Irish society over the past thirty years it is difficult to sustain an argument that biology is destiny. Thus, for example, the middle-aged grew up hearing that it was not 'natural' for women to be paid as much as men, that married women did not want to be in paid employment, etc. Such views are now seen clearly as (quaint) social and cultural constructions. The question as to whose interests such views serve is increasingly seen as crucial.

The fourth criticism specifically focuses on feminism as a challenge to male authority and is quite visible in contemporary Irish society. Thus, for example, feminism is depicted as emasculating men; it is seen as in some way responsible for boys' underperformance at school and for male suicides. Situations where women are promoted over their male counterparts are seen as indicating that the candidate is unqualified other than in terms of gender, with promotion of women by women being seen as particularly problematic (in stark contrast to promotion of men by men). The devaluation of childcare by a patriarchal legal system, and hence its allocation to women, is resented by some men who want to share custody of their children. Incoherent rage and a twisted sense of protectiveness sometimes appear to have been reflected in the murder of wives and children. Civil rights for blacks in the US in the 1960s were bitterly opposed – as indeed was the end of slavery in the nineteenth century. At the heart of such attitudes lies a failure to accept societal and cultural change – change which is also politically and economically necessary and morally desirable.

Overwhelmingly, the changes that have occurred in Irish society since the Women's Movement in the late 1960s and 1970s have been in individual behaviour (e.g. in family size, paid employment, etc.). In many cases they have occurred despite, rather than because of, institutional support from the patriarchal structures of the institutional Church, state, economic system, etc. What is required is a reframing of gender relations within this changed society. For the most part such institutional structures have been strikingly unwilling to do this. This is despite the fact that every day we see individual men making such adjustments in their day-to-day lives – because of their ties to wives, lovers, daughters and mothers.

Case study: feminism and civil service reform in Ireland

The state is not, of course, a unitary phenomenon; nor is its position in gender politics fixed. The state is typically seen as including not only the Houses of the Oireachtas but also the civil service, judiciary, police, army and state-run enterprises. In this section we will look at the impact of feminism on one particular part of the state apparatus, viz. the civil service. It will be suggested that the civil service has been affected by feminism, both indirectly (i.e. through the influence of the EU Directives and financial requirements) and directly (through the influence of grassroots feminism and/or femocrats). It will be argued that the main influence has been liberal feminism, and the effect of this has been greatest when it has coincided with other agendas (whether these have been those of the EU, trade unions, etc.). Prior to looking at this, some key aspects of the legislative situation and policy context will be outlined. These are seen as part of the context for, and to some extent the effect of, civil service action.

The introduction of the European Economic Community (EEC) Directive on equal pay in 1975 was at the insistence of France, which already had legislation and which did not wish to be at an international disadvantage within an economically integrated Europe. Ireland's compliance with this directive was prompt, reflecting the fact that European pressure at that time was combined with grassroots feminist influences. However, the 1974 Anti-Discrimination (Pay) Act and 1977 Employment Equality Act had a limited effect on the male/female wage gap because women and men continued to do different kinds of jobs and men continued to be disproportionately represented in senior positions. Indeed, the very way in which the 1977 Employment Equality Act was phrased and interpreted by the courts implicitly endorsed a subtle acceptance of the differential treatment of men and women. The *Nathan v. Bailey Gibson* case, drawing on legal precedents from the European Court of Justice, clearly established that if a practice affected one sex more than another, then indirect discrimination was an issue. Thus, taken-for-granted differential treatment of women became problematic. In some arenas, however, it continued to occur because indirect discrimination had become so embedded in state practices. Thus, for example, the overwhelming majority of state-funded *Foras Asiseanna Saothair* (FAS, national training and employment authority) programmes continued to be targeted at those on the Live Register, although it was recognized that since women were less likely than men to be on this register this 'suggests indirect discrimination in access to vocational training' (Fourth Report of the Oireachtas Fourth Joint Committee on Women's Rights 1996: 22). Provisions for positive action were included in the EU Amsterdam Treaty (1998). Under the 1998 Employment Equality Act positive action is permitted: 'removing existing inequalities which affect women's opportunities in the areas of access to employment, vocational training and promotion, and working conditions' (Section 24). However, such measures targeted at compensating women for existing disadvantage 'remain largely untried' here (Doyle 1999: 137). Case law in the European Court of Justice has further clarified the issue where both candidates are equally qualified but one sex is underrepresented in posts at that level (the *Kalanke v. Bremen* (1995) and the *Marschall v. Land Nordrhein Westfalen* (1997) cases). In Ireland, debate about this kind of positive action has not even begun. It is also well established that Ireland has one of the least-developed systems for state-subsidized non-stigmatizing childcare in the EU. Maternity leave was introduced in 1981, although it was not particularly generous by comparison with other EU countries. Parental leave was introduced in conformity with an EU Directive in 1998 and is unpaid (and the EU has already had to instruct the state to extend its coverage). 'Family-friendly' policies are promoted, but such policies, although they facilitate individual women's attempts to reconcile work and family, frequently militate in practice against their promotion. There is an EU Code of Practice (1996) recognizing the implicit gender bias in job classifications, but this has received almost no attention.

In addition to its influence at a legislative level, the influence of the EU has also been important in terms of financial pressure. In 1996 the European Commission noted that, although limited targeted funding initiatives for women were important, they were not sufficient. Thus, regulations governing the Structural Funds placed a legal obligation on member states to gender mainstream policies and programmes receiving Structural Funds: first, by analysing their implications for women and men (gender impact assessment); and, second, by checking that the gender dimension has been taken into account at every level of decision-making (gender-proofing). Hence, gender mainstreaming was adopted in the National Development Plan (NDP) (2000–6) and an NDP Equality Unit was established to address mainstreaming issues (thus providing some in-house femocrat influence). The five-year review process after the United Nations Fourth World Conference on Women (1995) indicated that major challenges remained. International pressures, combined with femocrat influences and grassroots feminism, led to the formulation of a *Draft National Plan for Women* (Department of Justice, Equality and Law Reform 2001). The main focus is on what Mazur (2001: 5) has called descriptive representation (i.e. the presence of women) as opposed to substantive representation (i.e. activities or ideas 'that favour women's interests in their full complexity'), with the mechanisms to improve women's underrepresentation in senior positions being particularly vague.

Overall, there has been a consistent pattern of moving forward on gender initiatives in response to legal and/or financial pressure from Europe. Broadly similar patterns can be seen in the case of equality policy within the civil service itself. The accession of Ireland to what was then the EEC necessitated the removal of the Marriage Bar in the civil service in 1973 and the ending of the practice of having different wage scales for men and women doing identical work. In 1986 the civil service announced its commitment 'to employment policies, procedures and practices which do not discriminate on the grounds of sex or marital status, and which promote full equality of opportunity between men and women' (Civil Service, Circular: 15/86). Its Code of Practice referred to recruitment and training practices and procedures, and stressed that single-sex training programmes should continue to be provided and encouraged as laid down under Section 15 of the 1977 Employment Equality Act. References to promotion were more vague, with no reference being made to the various rules and arrangements existing within particular grades and departments. The impression that the commitment of the civil service to liberal equality measures was, until very recently indeed, mainly rhetorical is suggested by a number of phenomena. We will focus on three of these: legal cases taken by civil servants themselves; the relative lack of change in the proportion of women at senior level; and the attitudes emerging from a study of civil servants commissioned by the general secretaries themselves.

First, then, despite the monitoring mechanisms established in the mid-1980s, practices which were fundamentally discriminatory continued to exist and only came to light through legal action – typically taken by the union. The hollowness of the 1986 Code of Practice as regards job-sharing became apparent in 1997, when employees in the Department of Finance took a successful case against that department when it would not allow them to job-share. Job-sharers (who were predominantly women) were also credited with less service than full-time workers when they were being considered for promotion (which was widely affected by seniority). This was seen as discriminatory by the European Court of Justice in 1997. A number of other cases have been taken and won, including one where the Irish High Court found that there was systematic discrimination against female clerical assistants, who were put at a lower level than their male counterparts in the paper keeper grade when both groups were included in the clerical officer grade.

Second, despite the (second) Women's Movement and the civil service commitment to gender equality, positional authority has remained very much in male hands. This is clearly recognized in its new Gender Equality Policy (Department of the Taoiseach 2001). This noted that although women made up 69 per cent of the total civil service staff at the lower levels (i.e. clerical officer to higher executive officer), they only constituted 23 per cent of those at the higher level (assistant principal to secretary general). The percentage of women in the principal officer grade increased by only 1 per cent between 1987 and 1997 (from 23 per cent to 24 per cent), although the proportion of women in the next grade (principal officer) increased from 5 per cent to 12 per cent over the same ten-year period. However, the representation of women at the very top is still very low, 91 per cent of general secretaries and 88 per cent of assistant general secretaries being men (Department of Justice, Equality and Law Reform 2001). These trends are not peculiar to the Irish civil service (Levinson *et al.* 1992; Canadian Government 1990). Very similar trends also exist in the UK civil service, although the 'Marriage Bar' was removed there in the 1940s (Hansard Society 1990).

Third, then, in 1997 the Co-Coordinating Group of General Secretaries at the top of the civil service commissioned research to investigate the imbalance in the representation of women in the higher grades. One of the most important themes to emerge from this multifaceted study involved promotional mechanisms. The authors noted that the existing arrangements were 'complex, highly variable...and all too often opaque' (Humphreys *et al.* 1999: 182). Roughly half of both the men and women saw change in promotional procedures as key. When asked to recommend future improvements, promotion was also most often mentioned by both men and women (Humphreys *et al.* 1999: 128–9). There was also clear evidence of gender variation in the experience of discrimination. Thus, 9 per cent of men at higher executive officer (HEO) level or above but 25 per cent of women stated that they had been unfairly treated or discriminated against because of their gender (Humphreys *et al.* 1999: 131). Amongst the women, this increased dramatically with level: up to 40 per cent of women principal officers/assistant principals stated that they had been unfairly treated because of gender; two-thirds of women who were at general/assistant secretary level said that they knew of colleagues who had been treated unfairly because of their gender (Humphreys *et al.* 1999: 131–2). The most common area where discrimination was considered to have occurred was as regards promotion (Humphreys *et al.* 1999: 131–2).

Humphreys *et al.* highlight their concern about the gender implications of a reliance on seniority as a basis for promotion and recommend that affirmative action needs to be taken 'if women are not to be discouraged in their promotional prospects by the double burden of work and caring, the gender stereotyped attitudes of management' (Humphreys *et al.* 1999: 190–1). They noted that although women were less likely than men to enter promotional competitions, they were as willing as men to allow their name to go forward for promotion in their own department. Departments are now required to set goals for the participation of women in promotion processes and actively to seek their increased participation (Department of Finance 2001b: 11). Such goals are, of course, entirely legal and no more problematic than other strategic management goals. Across the civil service as a whole there is a specific goal of having one-third of posts at assistant principal level held by women by 2005 (Department of Finance 2001a: 7). Reference is made to the development of an organizational culture which maximizes the potential of all civil servants, although no mechanisms seem to have been put in place to tackle the reliance on seniority or the promotional implications of differentially valued 'male' and 'female' areas of work. The effectiveness of this new policy remains to be seen.

Thus, the civil service can be seen as illustrative of a context where a (diluted) liberal feminist influence has come into play, under the influence of the EU, particularly in those areas where a feminist agenda has coincided with that of major stakeholders and has marginal effects on patriarchal control. Interestingly, there has been no discussion of the relevance of the attempts made to tackle religious discrimination in the Northern Ireland Police Force (viz. 50/50 selection of those above a merit level) to tackling gender imbalance in the civil service. Equally, contract compliance and grant denial for employers who fail to meet their statutory obligations – the very measures long advocated by the sex, race and disability lobbies in Northern Ireland – have not been considered.

It is important to stress that the patterns that have emerged in the civil service are by no means atypical. Broadly similar trends occur in the representative arm of the state: 80 per cent of full government ministers are male, as are 76 per cent of junior ministers (and 87 per cent of TDs and 82 per cent of senators). These patterns, of course, are not peculiar to the state but also occur in the semi-state structures, in the private commercial sector and in academia, etc. (O'Connor 1998, 2000b, 2002; Department of Justice, Equality and Law Reform 1999). Thus the patterns in the civil service can be seen as reflecting a wider Irish cultural pattern. In the US, on the other hand, 44 per cent of managers and administrators are women; the 26 per cent in Ireland places us below Spain (32 per cent) and the UK (33 per cent) and above Greece (22 per cent) on this indicator (United Nations Report 2000: 165). Interestingly, however, although Irish women constitute only 26 per cent of managers and administrators, they constitute two-thirds of those in the professions. Thus their relative absence from such positions cannot be explained by their educational level.

Summary review of theoretical utility

The relationship between feminist ideas, rooted in an inchoate social movement, and their impact on policy-making (whether at the level of defining the problem, of setting agendas or of formulating policies and implementing them) is by no means clear cut. Like any unidimensional explanatory framework, its importance is difficult to prove, all the more so since the elements of a feminist agenda which are most likely to be adopted are those which are compatible with the agendas of other stakeholders. In Ireland, with a small number of exceptions, the whole question of the influence of gendered thinking on Irish policy has been little discussed, despite the fact that it is widely assumed that adult men and women have different interests, priorities and lifestyles. Internationally, the dominance of postmodern feminism in the 1980s and 1990s moved feminism away from a concern with very real social inequalities to more esoteric concerns with language and literature. The increasing recognition of ethnic and racial difference and of differences between First and Third World women's experiences posed further challenges – challenges with which feminism is still struggling. Such challenges are typical of all major explanatory frameworks. However, within a country such as Ireland, which is still racially/ethnically largely homogenous and where being male/female is still crucially important in social and cultural terms, the relevance of feminism as a framework for understanding policy remains important. It is worth stressing that recognition of a gendered reality does not assume that this is simply created by biological differences between men and women. Rather, in a society where gender is a socially and culturally constructed reality, certain policies and priorities will seem obvious to those in hierarchically and numerically male-dominated structures (for example, childcare measures may well appear less important to those in these structures than the provision of international-level sporting facilities).

The influence of feminism on public policy is debatable. On the one hand, on the assumption that feminism is a very powerful institution it is sometimes seen as 'causing' a wide variety of undesirable social patterns (ranging from marital breakdown to male suicide). On the other hand, major institutions, such as the state (whether its representative or administrative arms), the institutional Roman Catholic Church, the economic system, the legal system, etc., do not unequivocally underpin and support a feminist vision. Feminism can be seen to have an effect particularly and insofar as its interests have coincided at particular moments with those of other major (predominantly patriarchal) stakeholders. Feminist strength is arguably important in influencing the definition of problems and the setting and maintaining of a feminist agenda. This can be reflected, first, in a grassroots women's movement; second, in a feminist intellectual elite; and, third, in terms of the positioning and strength of 'femocrats', whether in the state apparatus or more broadly in organizations concerned with women's issues. Of course, a radical grassroots sector may actually provide alternative organizations (e.g. rape crisis centres in Ireland in the 1970s). These combined factors accounted for the prioritization of legislation in the equality area in the early 1970s and for the stress on job-sharing, which was seen as simultaneously reducing women's possibilities as regards promotion and providing much needed increases in the labour force in the 1990s.

Connell has suggested that '[t]oo close an alignment with feminism gives offence to patriarchal ideology as mobilised in the churches, and to men's employment interests as mobilised in corporate management and male-dominated unions' (1994: 161). In Ireland the (predominantly female) service sector is the main source of current and future employment, women are doing better educationally than men and including women in decision-making positions within the economic system is seen by the EU as crucial to economic viability and political stability. For the most part, the actual policies that are formulated and implemented reflect the nature of the strategic alliances that are possible at any one moment in time. The net effect has been incremental change in those areas that are least corrosive of male authority and most compatible with other social objectives. However, the perceived legitimacy of voices which articulate women's needs and perspectives in all their diversity is still problematic.

Further reading

Cockburn, C. (1991) *In the Way of Women*, London: Macmillan.

Connell, R.W. (1995a) (1987) *Gender and Power*, Oxford: Blackwell.

Connell, R.W. (1995b) *Masculinities*, Cambridge: Polity Press.

Connolly, L. (2001) *The Irish Women's Movement: From Revolution to Devolution*, London: Palgrave.

O'Connor, P. (2000a) 'Ireland: A Man's World?', *Economic and Social Review* 31(1): 81–102.

Franzway, S., Court, D. and Connell, R.W. (1989) *Staking a Claim: Feminism, Bureaucracy and the State*, London: Allen & Unwin.

5 Neo-corporatism and social partnership

William K. Roche and Terry Cradden

Introduction

We can outline three broad ways in which advanced liberal democratic states have sought to influence pay determination and the wider conduct of industrial relations. These models are useful in describing and contrasting the roles of governments in the employment relationship, in European countries in particular.

The auxiliary state

As the trade union movement in the United Kingdom developed into a major social force, the idea of an auxiliary and largely residual role for the state became central to the British tradition of 'free collective bargaining'. In this tradition it was held that the settlement of pay and other terms and conditions of employees should be left to negotiations between employers and independent trade unions representing the employees. In line with the tradition of free collective bargaining, the parties to industrial relations, and in particular the unions, insisted on settling their affairs without interference from governments. It was experience of the consequences of early state attempts at intervention that gave rise to this view; and legislative initiatives to reform union structure or control industrial action were similarly vehemently opposed.

The role envisaged for the state, and largely accepted by the state, thus involved it acting in a purely *auxiliary* capacity: by, for example, making available publicly funded institutions, such as labour courts and dispute resolution services to which unions and employers might resort when conflict between them could not be resolved by negotiation. The key philosophical premise (and the key working assumption) of the auxiliary state approach was that political stability, economic progress and social peace were best fostered by 'industrial self-government', and especially by free collective bargaining.

Neo-liberalism

Neo-liberalism will not be central to our analysis of change in industrial relations in Ireland. It is discussed here briefly, however, for two reasons: first, because of its influence in other countries; and, second, because neo-liberalism emerged in the 1980s as part of the philosophy of a newly emergent political party, the Progressive Democrats (PDs). The neo-liberal or 'neo-laissez-faire' approach sees no merit in state policies supportive of collective bargaining or dialogue with interest groups. Indeed, neo-liberalism's major defining feature is an insistence that only the freest possible operation of labour markets will ensure macro-economically benign industrial relations outcomes – particularly as regards pay determination.

Neo-liberalism thus demands the systematic elimination by government of influences believed to impede the free market. Pay agreements negotiated at national level are seen as inflexible; worse still, they draw unions and other orga-nized interests into public policy-making, with inevitably damaging increases in public expenditure. Pay determination at enterprise, establishment and site level is favoured as being most likely to reflect the 'economic realities' of different sectors of industry and of different regions. In industrial relations terms the emphasis in neo-liberal policy is on curbing trade union organization and power, by legislative changes if necessary. These focus, in the first place, on making strikes and other forms of industrial action by workers more difficult to under-take; and, second, on enhancing the ability of employers and employees to resist unionization.

With respect to labour market policy, the emphasis is on deregulation and on the reconstitution of competitive labour markets eroded by earlier government intervention. Important among the mechanisms used to achieve this 'freeing up' are the removal of legal minimum wage-setting mechanisms and the dilution of employees' rights to employment security, especially legal protections against unfair dismissal. Dialogue at national level with employers and trade unions is avoided, and government intervention intended to control incomes is disavowed as self-defeating. At the same time, quasi-market devices of various kinds are introduced into the public sector to 'proxy' the market disciplines endured by the private sector (see Farnham and Horton 1993). Strongly espoused also is individ-ualized performance-related pay, which means rewarding each employee in accordance with his or her measurable output of work.

Neo-liberalism is underpinned by right-wing political thinking, and an approach incorporating the elements described above has characterized the poli-cies of successive Conservative administrations in the United Kingdom from 1979 to 1997, those of Republican Presidents of the United States in the 1980s and early 1990s, and the outlook of governments of varying political labels in New Zealand since the 1980s.

Neo-corporatism

From the 1970s onwards, industrial relations scholars, political scientists and historians began to use the concept of 'bargained corporatism' or 'neo-corporatism' to comprehend a major direction of change in the role of governments in industrial relations in Western Europe (Schmitter 1979; Maier 1984). As a normative theory of effective economic governance, neo-corporatism calls for states to become *active parties* to the conduct of industrial relations and pay bargaining – to become, in effect, 'deal-makers'. Collective bargaining is thus no longer the preserve of autonomous unions, employers and/or employers' associations, guarding their dealings against encroachment by the state.

Rather, the spheres of politics and industrial relations overlap, and collective bargaining becomes directly tied to government decision-making, especially in the areas of economic and social policy. Unions and employers admit the government as a negotiating partner in what then becomes a tripartite process of bargaining, and one in which the state seeks to gain direct influence over pay determination as a key lever in its management of the economy. As a quid pro quo, unions and employers participate in the formation of public policy in areas such as taxation, employment creation and social programmes like welfare, housing and education. In return for an influence on public policy, union and employer leaders are expected to co-operate by 'delivering' their members' support for jointly agreed policies, including the limits on pay increases typically specified in such agreements (Panitch 1980; Goldthorpe 1984).

Writers on neo-corporatism employ the prefix 'neo' to distinguish tripartite bargaining arrangements of the 1960s and 1970s from the 'pure' corporatism of countries like Germany and Italy under earlier Nazi and Fascist regimes. In these instances, independent unions and employers' associations were abolished and replaced by organizations controlled by the state – which were then simply utilized as instruments of state policy. We might also note in passing that corporatist theory, with its search for a *via media* between liberal capitalism and state socialism, exerted some influence in Ireland during the 1930s and early 1940s. By the 1960s, however, when a drift towards neo-corporatism had become evident, 'vocationalism', as it was called, no longer retained even a vestigial influence in Irish politics (O'Leary 2000).

A brief review of the evolution of neo-corporatism

As a normative theory, neo-corporatist thinking would usually be considered to have a left-wing, equalitarian pedigree, and empirical cases of strongly institutionalized neo-corporatism during the 1970s and 1980s were to be found mainly under social democratic governments in the Scandinavian countries. But neo-corporatism featured too in the smaller democracies of Western Europe, especially Denmark, Austria and Switzerland – sometimes under governments of a slightly more rightist, Christian Democratic hue (see Goldthorpe 1984; Katzenstein 1985). Responsible for the drift towards neo-corporatism from the 1960s onwards were rising inflation, increased industrial militancy, flagging productivity growth and a slowdown in the long post-war capitalist boom. These problems led governments in a number of European countries to explore new ways of influencing the behaviour of unions and employers, by according their organizations the kind of role in public policy formulation described above (Crouch and Pizzorno 1978). However, it is possible to discern two subtypes of the neo-corporatist model.

Mainstream variants in current usage

This chapter considers two main variants of corporatism: 'classical neo-corporatism' and 'competitive corporatism'. Both are discussed below.

Classical neo-corporatism

During the 1960s and 1970s, which some commentators now refer to as the 'golden age of European neo-corporatism' (M. Rhodes 1998: 212), such arrangements involved governments pursuing incomes policies (perhaps more accurately titled 'incomes-*control* policies') in the context of broadly Keynesian programmes of demand management and macro-economic stability (M. Rhodes 1998; Pochet and Fajertag 2000; Traxler 2000). Under this model, 'fairness' typically featured as an objective, so incomes policies often included the equalitarian or 'solidaristic' aim of reducing income inequality. A reflection of the influence on unions, and sometimes on governments, of ideals of social justice, this was usually allied with a more pragmatic concern to curtail wage militancy by seeking to legitimize income distributions in the economies affected.

It was standard practice for public and social spending, often financed by public borrowing, to be harnessed to 'classical' neo-corporatist agreements. In acknowledgment of union strength and assertiveness, states were also willing to make concessions to organized labour in the shape of new modes of labour market regulation. The possibilities here included the curtailment of the right of employers to lay off or dismiss workers, and the extension of 'industrial democracy', by which employees might be granted an input into organizational decision-making as it affected their vital interests.

Competitive corporatism

Neo-corporatism withered in many European countries during the 1980s. Recession and pressures emanating from more globalized product and capital markets, often allied with shifts to the right in political ideology, began to have their effects. The result was the undermining of neo-corporatist institutions and a move by governments in a number of countries – including some with strong neo-corporatist traditions – towards neo-liberalism. Indeed, some commentators were moved to write of the *demise* of neo-corporatism.

Yet the 1990s witnessed a resurgence of neo-corporatist 'social pacts' across Europe. The basic features of these pacts were similar to those of classical neo-corporatist arrangements, in particular in that they involved tripartite agreements concluded jointly by unions, employers and governments. These new agreements, however, often differed greatly in their priorities as compared with earlier neo-corporatist accords. During the 1990s they began to focus on pay deals consistent with the enhancement of national competitiveness; on competitively sustainable levels of public expenditure, involving the reform of tax, pension and social security systems; and on promoting measures to increase the flexibility, skill and sometimes the quantity of the labour supply. Noticeable too was that unions often now sought to justify their involvement less in terms of beneficial negotiating 'breakthroughs' than on the grounds that the concessions available represented the 'least bad' outcome for their members (M. Rhodes 1998). Baccaro has aptly described this feature of neo-corporatism in the 1990s as 'macro-economic concession bargaining' (Baccaro 2001: 3).

Significant also was the jettisoning of the Keynesian frameworks of demand management that had been a feature of earlier pacts. This reflected the sharply curtailed latitude that now existed for using public spending to prime or control economic activity. For member countries of the European Union (EU), the Maastricht Treaty convergence criteria for entry to European Monetary Union (EMU) further restricted the use of demand-side measures, by imposing tight strictures on levels of public debt and budget deficits. Eurozone members also lost control over the core economic management mechanisms of interest and exchange rate policies – which were transferred to the European Central Bank (Pochet and Fajertag 2000; Goetschy 2000). What also happened was that equalitarian concerns about managing the income distribution, or eliminating want, receded in priority (M. Rhodes 1998). Labour market *deregulation* in the interest of competitiveness and flexibility rose to the top of the list instead. And industrial democracy measures, focused in the 1960s and 1970s on workers' rights, gave way to employee and union involvement linked to the promotion of *company* objectives, especially the achievement of competitive advantage. Hence have resurgent 'social partnership' pacts during the 1990s been portrayed as instances of 'competitive', 'supply-side' or even 'lean' corporatism (M. Rhodes 1998: Pochet and Fajertag 2000; Traxler 2000; Traxler *et al.* 2001). It is of some significance that nine of the fifteen member states of the EU – Belgium, Finland, Germany, Greece, Ireland, Italy, the Netherlands, Portugal and Spain – arrived at social pacts of this competitive neo-corporatist kind during the 1980s and 1990s (Visser and Hemerijck 1997; Pochet and Fajertag 2000).

Major criticisms

Though important as a normative theory of economic governance and widely applied in the analysis of the politics of industrial relations in Europe during the 1970s, and again during the 1990s, the theory of neo-corporatism is marked by a series of debates, unanswered questions and explanatory problems.

Undemocratic?

The theorists of classical neo-corporatism argue that the interest groups involved in its operation, particularly trade unions, operate in a centralized, bureaucratic and hierarchical – and thus inherently undemocratic – way. The institutional arrangements supporting neo-corporatism might be similarly described, and governments may thus be seen to be reinforcing these unattractive features by seeking to operate in neo-corporatist mode (for a discussion, see Baccaro 2001). This view resonates with the claim of critics of social partnership that it is elitist and fundamentally undemocratic (for examples of this line of criticism in the Irish case, see C. McCarthy 1977: ch. 14; O'Cinneide 1998; Allen 2000). It is also seen to be undemocratic in elevating the influence of interest groups in economic policy-making over that of the elected parliament. This has been an important strand of commentary on the Irish experience; but as social partnership seemed to prove its economic worth as the1990s proceeded, this view was pressed less forcefully.

More democratic?

The criticism of social partnership as undemocratic, in both of the senses outlined, has met with theoretical and empirical rejoinders. For some commentators, social pacts are seen to carry the potential for an expanded 'associational' or 'deliberative' democracy and for the *enhanced* involvement of members of interest groups – who are, after all, also citizens – in economic and political governance (see Hirst 1993). We return to this below when we consider rival portrayals of social partnership in Ireland to those provided by neo-corporatist thinking. Other analysts have used the resurgence of neo-corporatism in Italy during the 1990s to criticize the received view of it as undemocratic; the Italian case, they say, points to the potential to create a 'democratic corporatism' based on intensive dialogue with the rank and file, and a decentralization of union deliberative and decision-making processes (Baccaro 2000, 2001).

Supportive institutions

Attempts to explain the varying effects of classical neo-corporatism during the 1960s and 1970s, particularly with respect to inflation, economic growth and unemployment, relied mainly on the existence of 'supportive institutional arrangements'. It was widely held that centralized union and employer confederations, based on industrial-type union structures (versus 'fragmented' structures involving occupational, general and craft unions), greatly enhanced the probability that the parties to partnership deals would deliver on their respective commitments (Roche 1997). In the same vein, political systems and governments with union-supported class-based parties and political representation were seen further to enhance the success of neo-corporatism – by providing unions with a trusted state ally and favouring consistent and longer-term economic and social policies. The absence of these supporting institutions was used to explain the ultimate failure of neo-corporatist agreements in Ireland during the 1970s (described below, to meet the objectives of any of the parties involved (Hardiman 1988).

However, this view was criticized as overly simplistic. In particular, it seemed to ignore how economic crisis, threats to the security of the parties to centralized deals, and hard-headed assessments of the balance of advantage might have equivalent effects to centralization or government dominance by social democratic parties (see Roche 1997: 153). The emergence of apparently durable social pacts in countries like Ireland, Italy, Spain and Portugal, which possess few of the institutional features that were believed to provide the cement for neo-corporatism, has added further to the search for different mechanisms and contexts supportive of social partnership (Traxler 2000; Traxler *et al.* 2001; Baccaro 2001).

Economic and social effects

Classical neo-corporatism was seen by many commentators as providing a more effective basis for macro-economic management than any other politico-institutional arrangements. Then it emerged that strongly institutionalized neo-corporatism (such as that in Ireland since the late 1980s) *and* strong neo-liberal regimes (like that in the US in the 1980s and 1990s) might *each* be compatible with economic stability and relatively high performance (Calmfors and Driffill 1988). In contrasting the two approaches, however, neo-corporatism was seen to involve lower levels of economic and social inequality and less emphasis on gaining competitive advantage through low labour costs and lower levels of social protection (see Roche 1997: 154–7). In the light of the priority accorded to supply-side measures under competitive corporatism, the question arises as to whether neo-corporatism can be identified any longer with relatively equalitarian outcomes, or with a search for competitive advantage based on maintaining economic and social inclusion. Certainly some Irish commentators have suggested otherwise, in straightforwardly equating Irish social partnership from the late 1980s with policy priorities more commonly associated with neo-liberalism (see von Prondzynski 1992; O'Hearn 1998; Kirby 2002).

The attempt to contrast the genesis and features of the 'classical' neo-corporatism of the 1970s with those of 'competitive' neo-corporatism during the 1990s actually confronts a complex reality – one which involves some degree of empirical overlap between priorities and arrangements prevailing under both variants, and some common roots. This is apparent in three main areas. First, the recent emphasis on globalization and recession having triggered co-operative dealings between unions, employers and states – dealings focused on handling economic pressures to mutual advantage – closely parallels earlier judgements on the origins of 1970s neo-corporatism (see Katzenstein 1985). Second, the idea that the 1970s version was most pronounced and durable in small European states is consistent with recent interest in the apparently durable and economically benign cases of competitive neo-corporatism in small states also. Third, contrasts between the priorities of competitive neo-corporatism and earlier versions confront another conundrum: in reality no *single* classical neo-corporatist model existed; rather, there was a range of different institutional features, according to different degrees of priority to equalitarian objectives. On the one hand we can identify the relatively highly equalitarian 'social corporatist' models of the Scandinavian countries and Austria (M. Rhodes 1998). In other cases, the Irish one included, equalitarian objectives were more muted; hence the contrast in this respect with social pacts during the 1990s is less marked.

There has been little sustained and detailed study of the dynamics and durability of competitive neo-corporatism. Indeed, the question of whether it brings into being and is sustained by different institutional mechanisms, or is undermined by different tensions and conflicts than characterized earlier neo-corporatist arrangements, remains open (see Baccaro 2000, 2001). So too does the question of whether recent social pacts may be more pragmatic and contingent than the neo-corporatist deals of earlier decades (see M. Rhodes 1998). The fact that Ireland since 1987 has witnessed the longest era of centralized tripartite bargaining in its history might appear to belie such a view. At the same time, there is growing speculation as to whether Irish social partnership, which originated in a deep economic, labour market and social crisis, can be sustained in conditions of strong economic growth, low unemployment and increasing economic uncertainty.

Case study: the development of neo-corporatist approaches in Ireland

The auxiliary state and the pay rounds system

The practices of collective bargaining as well as non-intervention by the state were already firmly embedded in the Irish industrial relations system by the time the Irish Free State was set up in 1921.[1] A four-year departure from non-interventionism began with the issue of the Emergency Powers (No. 83) Order in 1941 – better known as the Wages Standstill Order. But what came to be the principal identifying mark of Irish industrial relations in the 1950s and 1960s actually arose from the lifting of the Order in 1945. This effectively created a single 'starting line' for all groups of workers, and began a process of 'synchronized' pay bargaining that was to last until 1970 (Roche 1997). The resulting intensive, concentrated, periodic negotiations between employers and trade unions were called 'rounds', and were eventually given numbers – as in 'the fourth round'. The broad outcome of a round was highly influential in economic terms, all the more so since it was often used also as the basis for the pay rates of workers in non-unionized employment.

The weightiest factors bearing on pay negotiation during this period were increases in the cost of living and 'comparability' or pay rate comparisons between one group of workers and another (W. McCarthy *et al.* 1975). This reinforced the notion of a 'going rate', which was essentially driven by the

bargaining achievements of certain large groups of workers with a strong negotiating hand – and which ignored the effects on small enterprises in price-sensitive
sectors. This obliged the government, against the grain of the auxiliary state
model, to intervene on three occasions (1948, 1964 and 1970) and threaten to
impose legally enforceable pay norms.

The drift to neo-corporatism

Yet the most remarkable thing about the 'patterned' free collective bargaining
that characterized the early stages of the rounds system is that the state played
such a limited role. This differentiated Ireland quite distinctly from the developing post-war neo-corporatism of the other European countries noted above.
But it was becoming more commonplace to view pay determination under the
rounds system as inherently inflationary, and to consider the absence of a state
input into wage bargaining as manifestly disabling in terms of the kind of
Keynesian macro-economic management in which Irish governments aspired to
engage. As it happens, very little was done immediately to address that issue, but
some foundations upon which to build change were being laid.

Sean Lemass of Fianna Fáil, though showing little sympathy towards 'vocationalism', had displayed some corporatist inclinations in the 1940s, and set
much store by the need to keep the trade unions in a 'democratic partnership'
with government (Bew and Patterson 1982; Cradden 1993). With his party back
in power after the defeat of the first Coalition government, and with his appointment as Minister for Industry and Commerce, Lemass set up a number of
tripartite consultative institutions that enabled employers, unions and the state to
engage in regular dialogue about the development of public policy. These,
together with a joint forum, the Employer–Labour Conference (ELC), set up by
the Irish Congress of Trade Unions (ICTU) and the Federated Union of
Employers (FUE), was important in enabling the parties to build up experience
of working with each other on economic matters.

Although for most of the 1960s the majority of trade union leaders remained
devoted to the auxiliary state model, and especially to free collective bargaining,
there was nevertheless an evident drift towards neo-corporatism. A prolonged
and damaging strike by key maintenance workers across Irish industry in 1969
was just one manifestation of a serious deterioration in the industrial relations
climate, and added considerably to the pressure for change. Tangible evidence of
a new direction was the initiation in 1970 of a decade of centralized bargaining,
on a bipartite ELC basis to begin with, but later with the full participation of the
government.

National agreements 1970–80: classical neo-corporatism?

The most important milestone on the road to neo-corporatism was reached in the
mid-1970s when budgetary policy began to be used explicitly to obtain wage
moderation. National deals now began more and more to rely on neo-corporatist

'*tri*partism' – in particular on the availability from government of tax and social welfare concessions in exchange for wage moderation. As time went on the agreements also began to cover issues such as reducing unemployment and improving state health and educational provision.

But things did not always proceed smoothly, mainly because the unions were internally divided. While there seemed to be a majority in favour of national agreements and understandings, a significant number of unions wanted a return to decentralized free collective bargaining. The 'antis' were well organized and almost succeeded in killing off the 1979 National Understanding. It was only when government reverted to threatening a legally enforceable pay norm that an ICTU Special Conference agreed to the deal. A year later it was the employers, represented by the FUE, who formed the awkward squad; they strongly resented what was described as 'undue political pressure' on them by the government to sign up to the 1980 agreement, and only relented when provided with specific promises on items to be included in the next budget by the Minister for Finance.

What can we conclude about this decade of centralized bargaining, which seemed so much to fit the 'classical' neo-corporatist model? Instead of generating a virtuous circle in which pay restraint contributed to positive economic outcomes which in turn provided further support for tripartite bargaining, a vicious circle was set in train. Trends in disposable pay and trends in unemployment both worsened; employers in many sectors faced intensifying competitive pressures and increasingly uncertain trading conditions; and the state was forced simultaneously to raise taxes and to resort to borrowing to fund government spending. Worthy of note also, however, is that on display were both equalitarian and economic objectives. For while the objectives of the unions were, if not entirely equalitarian, predominantly to do with 'economic fairness', Irish governments in the 1980s were set on rescuing the economy from 'excess', and the employers had a roughly similar focus on competitiveness. This perhaps adds weight to the argument that it is difficult to distinguish neo-corporatist agreements or phases in any clear-cut way, the agreements in question here having an emphasis on reducing inequality, but also on increasing economic performance by containing pay costs. Be that as it may, at the beginning of a new decade the fate of neo-corporatist centralized bargaining was sealed – at least for a time.

1980–7: free collective bargaining restored

The collapse of neo-corporatism in the early 1980s might best be put down mainly to government and employer resistance, based on their conclusion that the trade unions had done better out of ten years of pacts than they had. The unions had also become disillusioned with the capacity of national agreements to meet their objectives. As a result, the edifice of neo-corporatism collapsed under the weight of cumulative disillusionment on all sides. The outcome was a reversion to the auxiliary state model, which lasted for some six years. It seemed, to begin with, that there would also be a reversion to the 'rounds' system. However, there were soon such significant divergences in both levels of wage increases and settlement dates that the notion of the round was increasingly rendered redundant.

What of the ground-level effects of this period of free collective bargaining? The 'winners' and 'losers' were evident enough. While public-sector workers gradually fell behind the rest of the field, those employed by foreign-owned, export-oriented high-technology firms tended to do relatively well – with manufacturing generally doing better than services. More worrying than these distributional difficulties, however, was that between 1980 and 1986 hourly earnings increased at a higher rate in Ireland than in all other European Monetary System countries. While all this was going on, however, the tripartite bodies referred to earlier continued to function, and the National Economic and Social Council (NESC), which replaced an earlier body with roughly the same consultative and advisory functions, was to play a key role in a revival of neo-corporatism.

The advent of social partnership

In a report issued in 1986 with the support of all three participant bodies, the NESC had outlined a comprehensive programme for economic recovery. Particularly noteworthy was that it recommended the cutting of public expenditure, something traditionally abominated by the trade union movement and something that would have been well nigh impossible even to discuss under the neo-corporatism of the 1970s. Implementation of the plan would, of course, only be possible by agreement between the social partners. But why should the parties want to go back to tripartism?

For the unions there were several considerations. First, under tripartism their lowest-paid members had been protected by minimum pay increases. Second, the early to mid-1980s 'free-for-alls', combined with increases in the income-tax burden, had led to declining real living standards for many trade union members and had widened the gap between top and bottom levels of pay of unionized workers, threatening the solidarity of the trade union movement. Third, the most serious and prolonged declines in trade union membership and organization since the 1920s and increasing unemployment made union leaders wary that what was happening in Britain under the Conservative's neo-liberal regime might also occur in Ireland. Allied to this, a possible realignment of Irish politics towards the centre-right of the political spectrum was also on the cards following the retirement of Garret Fitzgerald as leader of Fine Gael and early electoral impact of the nascent Progressive Democrat Party. A return to social partnership seemed to promise help on all these fronts.

Decentralized bargaining had been a mixed blessing for the employers. The number of strikes had fallen, but most other indicators were negative: governments of all hues had relied on borrowing rather than cutting expenditure to meet current spending commitments, and the national debt had reached truly alarming levels. Although pay increases were beginning to moderate, they had outstripped inflation during the six years of decentralized bargaining; and the burden represented by the 'social costs' of employment – taxation, pensions and social security contributions – had also increased. Though the employers were not especially inspired by the idea, therefore, tripartite bargaining seemed to hold out the prospect of linking pay restraint with economic and fiscal reform.

The foundations of competitive corporatism

Conscious that it would inherit a very difficult economic situation if it succeeded the Fine Gael/Labour Coalition in office, the Fianna Fáil Shadow Cabinet began wooing the unions in advance. This ensured that they, at any rate, were already on board for a renewal of social partnership when the new administration was formed in 1987. The FUE, for its part, was finally won over by the possibility of pay moderation. The result was a three-year agreement, entitled the *Programme for National Recovery* (PNR) – and one that differed, furthermore, in some key respects from the national agreements of the 1970s.

It set the expected sharp limits on pay: a 3 per cent increase per annum on the first £120 per week of earnings and 2 per cent thereafter, with an underpinning minimum of £4. The PNR also included some broad expressions of intent: to promote increased employment; to improve social welfare provision; and to reduce direct taxation – in other words, income tax and pay-related social insurance (PRSI) contributions – on lower-paid workers. But the PNR's most portentous features were commitments to the control of public expenditure and a reduction in government borrowing. An era of competitive neo-corporatism seemed to have arrived.

There was widespread recognition of the PNR's beneficial effects, and this ensured that it was followed by the *Programme for Economic and Social Progress* (PESP), covering the period up to 1993. This allowed much the same percentage increases (though these now varied year upon year) but also permitted an additional and 'exceptional' provision for an extra amount to be negotiated at enterprise or plant level. But there were some serious economic retreats during the period of the PESP, including a devaluation of the punt. As well as several pay-related crises, there were also major rows over income-tax increases and cuts in social welfare – argued by the unions to be in breach of the PESP. But the programme still held together. It also weathered a change of government after Fianna Fáil failed to achieve a majority in a snap election in 1989 and was obliged to coalesce with the Progressive Democrats. The Progressive Democrats had, of course, a neo-liberal agenda, but this had no discernible effect on the government's approach to the PESP.

In 1992, after a change of leadership, that government was succeeded by a more left-leaning Fianna Fáil/Labour Coalition. Against the background of a recovering economy a new agreement was inevitable. So the PESP was succeeded by the *Programme for Competitiveness and Work* (PCW), which ran until 1996. Its pay provisions followed much the same pattern as in the two previous pacts, with another local bargaining clause, but with more attention being given to non-pay issues.

At ICTU insistence, the PNR and the PESP both contained references to the desirability of worker participation, which had sometimes been an element of classical neo-corporatist agreements in other countries. However, an important union report on new management methods seemed to endorse employee involvement with a 'competitive advantage' component (ICTU 1993). What was being sought with increasing insistence was for partnership at national level to be complemented by partnership in the enterprise, plant and office.

As regards non-pay issues of interest to more than just the unions, what was notable about the PESP and the PCW was the incorporation of further and deeper commitments to improving Irish fiscal and macro-economic conditions. While there had been huge cuts in public expenditure and a reduction in the national debt during the period of the PNR, in the subsequent two programmes very explicit targets were agreed for spending and debt repayments. Such a degree of consensus between unions and employers – the latter now represented by the Irish Business and Employers' Confederation (IBEC), the successor body to the FUE – had certainly not been forthcoming in the 1970s. Moreover, economic and industrial relations trends since 1987 had shown clear improvements over those recorded during the return to decentralized bargaining in the 1980s.

The PCW ended on a sour note, with negotiations still dragging on a large number of claims under its 'local bargaining' clause, and with public-service workers complaining that they had done poorly out of it in comparison with other groups. While this made the negotiation of a new agreement more difficult, the continuing economic success that attended the period of the PCW ensured that a new deal would be done. Negotiated this time with a Fine Gael/Labour/Democratic Left government, the new agreement was the most ambitious yet, and the name was intended to capture its essential tone. Called '*Partnership 2000*' (sometimes just P2000), it provided for generally higher pay increases and tax reductions than in the previous agreements, plus another clause – more tightly written this time – allowing for a degree of local bargaining beyond the general norm. But it also included commitments to 'promoting enterprise' and the setting up of what came to be named the National Competitiveness Council, as well as an explicit endorsement that 'developing partnership in the workplace' was a key to building a more competitive Ireland. A National Centre for Partnership was established to promote partnership in enterprises and workplaces. Private-sector companies were also encouraged to reward employees for their contribution by means of profit-sharing. Finally, a vexed labour market regulation/deregulation question, concerning legal procedures for the recognition by employers of trade unions for collective bargaining purposes, was passed for resolution to a tripartite 'High Level Group'.

It was becoming clear also that economic growth in Ireland had accelerated in a context marked by increasing income inequality, high levels of low pay and persistently high levels of relative income poverty (see Allen 2000; Kirby 2002). Adding a more clearly classical neo-corporatist dimension, P2000 laid stronger emphasis than earlier on dealing with inequality, long-term unemployment and social exclusion. No doubt this was also a reflection of a new development: the participation in negotiations for the first time of the so-called 'social pillar', comprised of bodies such as the National Youth Council, the National Women's Council, the Irish National Organization for the Unemployed and the Conference of Religious of Ireland.

By the time P2000 was agreed, then, there was an effective all-party consensus on the suitability to Irish circumstances of tripartite negotiations and neo-corporatist agreements. Fine Gael and the PDs, while less favourably disposed to social partnership to begin with than Fianna Fáil, now fully supported the model. In the case of the PDs the focus had shifted from mild hostility to a resolve that social partnership deals should reflect an appropriate balance between enterprise-focused (broadly supply-side) and social/redistributive priorities – the so-called 'Boston or Berlin' debate. Lest there be any doubt about the PDs' position, in the run-up to the 1997 general election, which brought a new Fianna Fáil/PD Coalition to power, they made it very clear that they were fully signed up to Partnership 2000.

As the first few years of P2000 progressed, there were a number of other things to cheer supporters of social partnership. While anecdotal evidence suggested that by mid-1999 there was wage drift beyond the agreed norms, a survey of 1,000 settlements confirmed that the level of adherence was 'remarkably strong'. Agreement in broad terms to a procedure for union recognition was arrived at. Unemployment dropped sharply. The number of days lost due to industrial disputes fell to an all-time low. A survey of IBEC members showed strong support for a continuation of social partnership. An opinion poll in late 1999 indicated that 78 per cent of the public thought that social partnership was 'very important' or 'quite important' to economic development. Finally, it was reported by a union enthusiast for partnership that expenditure in real terms on health, education and social welfare had increased by 117 per cent, 71 per cent and 45 per cent, respectively, since 1987 (*Industrial Relations News* 1999, nos. 9, 18, 24 and 42).

Negotiations on a successor to P2000 started in late 1999, but did not really begin in earnest until January 2000. After much posturing, scrambling for advantage and spinning to the media, an agreement was reached on 26 January. On offer under the new *Programme for Prosperity and Fairness* (PPF) was a 15 per cent increase in pay over a period of thirty-three months, plus another 10 per cent in tax cuts. Workers on the national minimum wage, which was to take effect in April, and others on low wages were to do even better; and a new Social Welfare Bill would provide increases worth another £5 a week to those earning under £200 a week, through PRSI and health-levy exemptions.

The PPF sought to deepen and extend the workplace partnership process begun under P2000, and it also built on earlier programmes by involving the social partners in a range of areas of public policy, under the aegis of five 'frameworks'. Arising from these public policy frameworks, in excess of twenty working groups came into existence to address policy development and implementation in such areas as childcare, family-friendly work, housing and gain-sharing. Small wonder that some of those involved in the intensive follow-up to the agreement began to complain of 'partnership fatigue'.

An important development under the PPF was perhaps a testimony to the resilience of social partnership. Despite a general conviction that inflation would remain below 3 per cent, the consumer price index for the twelve months to June 2000 rose by 5.5 per cent. The unions argued that the PPF had been negotiated on the basis of a continuation of low inflation, and demanded a review of the agreement. The employers at first bluntly refused to reopen discussion on the grounds that there was no provision in the PPF to permit this. It took until December to agree an additional 5 per cent increase in pay over the rest of the life of the PPF. IBEC's price for this was a strengthened 'industrial peace' clause. A seasoned observer was moved to suggest that if inflation remained high and industrial action put further pressure on pay, 'it is highly unlikely that partnership will survive' (*Industrial Relations News* 2000, no. 47: 12). By the spring of 2001, moreover, observers were beginning to comment that the pay agreement at the core of social partnership was becoming a fiction. Private-sector increases began to exceed the national pay norm, not infrequently by a substantial amount, and pay militancy was also increasing in the public sector. The recession in the US economy from the summer of 2001, deepened by the terrorist attacks of that September, was reflected in increased uncertainty and mounting job losses in the Irish economy. The agreement may indeed have been saved by the economic slowdown, and this too may have shortened the odds on a successor to the PPF when the agreement expires in early 2003. Some employer leaders have nevertheless expressed considerable doubt as to the advisability of negotiating another partnership agreement, and have stressed that any agreement that might emerge should be 'leaner', on the pattern of the original PNR (*Industrial Relations News* 2002, no. 6).

Summary review of theoretical utility

It will be apparent from the account above of social partnership in Ireland that the theory of neo-corporatism has considerable utility in accounting for the genesis, features and effects of important developments in Irish industrial relations, and in accounting for changes in the process of economic governance more generally. In particular, we have suggested that the concept of competitive corporatism is broadly faithful to developments in social partnership since 1987. To identify social partnership, as we have done, as a part of a wider European trend involving social pacts focused on competitiveness and supply-side priorities nevertheless opens up a series of questions which this short chapter cannot consider in any detail. These include whether the dynamics of Irish social partnership during the 1990s differ in important respects from those associated with classical neo-corporatism, and in ways that render partnership 1990s style more robust and durable than earlier social partnership arrangements (see Hardiman 1988). This question becomes particularly interesting when we recall that social partnership since 1987 has accommodated deep economic crisis, unprecedented economic growth and a sharp economic slowdown from mid-2001. In doing so, social partnership has also focused in a broadly sequential manner around a spectrum of priorities: the handling of economic and fiscal crisis; European integration and EMU; competitive advantage; workplace innovation and labour supply problems. Equally relevant is the related question of whether neo-corporatism since 1987 has given rise to new strains and contradictions, for example between leadership within the social partner groups and their respective constituencies, or perhaps arising from the effects of growing economic inequality on wage moderation. Relatively little is known about the micro-level effects of social partnership on the functioning of the organizations representing the social partners, or on public management and public policy-making processes.

Notwithstanding the relevance and utility of neo-corporatist theory to the Irish case, some commentators have sought to present alternative accounts of social partnership, and we assess two such accounts in conclusion.

Social partnership as incorporation

Kieran Allen has presented a trenchant critique of Irish economic development during the 1990s in his book *The Celtic Tiger: The Myth of Social Partnership in Ireland* (2000). Here we consider mainly Allen's portrayal of the functioning of social partnership arrangements. Allen claims that the exceptional performance of the Irish economy during the 1990s can be explained largely in terms of a booming US economy, associated US foreign direct investment flows, and massive EU transfers through the 'structural' and 'cohesion' funds programmes (Allen 2000). The benefits of economic growth are seen mainly to have advantaged business and well-paid occupations groups, an argument sustained by pointing to the rising share of profits in gross domestic product, growing earnings inequality and under-investment in public and social services (Allen 2000: chs 3 and 4).

For Allen, social partnership has functioned primarily as a means of sustaining gross differences in the outcomes of growth by incorporating union leaders and reinforcing their control over rank-and-file members. Through their involvement in social partnership agreements and institutions union leaders have looked after their own interests by securing relatively orderly industrial relations – an outcome also desired by employers and the state. Rank-and-file trade union members have thus been denied independent and vigorous representation (Allen 2000). Union co-operation with workplace change under social partnership has also resulted in work intensification for many employees (Allen 2000). Allen nevertheless views this state of affairs as unsustainable: economic growth and rising inequality have fuelled workers' expectations and fostered social discontent. In consequence, an increasingly assertive and militant working class will sooner or later challenge and destroy social partnership (Allen 2000).

Allen's 'incorporation thesis' is open to a series of criticisms. First, research points to a high level of support for social partnership from the late 1980s among union members and the general population (ICTU 1998, 2001; Jones

2001: 90–3; R. Fitzgerald and Girvin 2000: 282–4; *Business and Finance* 1996: 24–5). This support is found in spite of a realization that the benefits of economic growth accompanying social partnership have been highly unequally distributed (IMS 1997). These survey data hardly point towards a 'discontented majority' (Allen 2000) or incipient class struggle. What is striking, on the contrary, is the historically low level of industrial conflict recorded during the 1990s in spite of modest year-on-year rises in nominal and real wages, unprecedented economic growth and the advent of near-full employment. Second, far from union incorporation at the workplace having led to more onerous work regimes, the best evidence available points to only the most modest incidence of workplace partnership involving unions during the 1990s (Roche and Geary 2000). Third, survey data again show that union members welcome more involvement by their unions in workplace partnership, and that they favour this kind of representation over traditional adversarial postures (ICTU 2001: 2).

Fourth, while it can be accepted that union leaders may have different priorities to rank-and-file members and that they enjoy a capacity to mobilize resources in support of favoured policies, the view that they can *impose* these favoured policies on members is untenable. Allen supports his argument by pointing towards the split votes on the terms of social partnership agreements that have been common *within* unions, in comparison to the general support for social partnership among union leaders (Allen 2000). Social partnership has not, however, met with generalized or uncritical support from union leaders. Some of them have withdrawn from social partnership agreements because they had failed to deliver particular concessions for union members. Others have threatened to do so to win concessions: for example, the threat by the Scientific, Industrial, Professional Technical Union (SIPTU) – the largest union in Ireland – in response to details of tax reforms announced in the 2000 budget to which it objected. Others still have been forced to pull out of social partnership in response to intra-union factionalism or rank-and-file dissent: for example, the opposition of the Association of Secondary Teachers Ireland (ASTI) to the PPF. It has, moreover, been more common in research on trade union government to view close or split membership votes as an indicator of union *democracy* than of *oligarchy* (Hemingway 1978: ch.1).

Social partnership as post-corporatist concertation

A different interpretation of the evolution and functioning of Irish social partnership from the late 1980s has been proposed by O'Donnell (see R. O'Donnell and O'Riordan 2000). This questions the application to social partnership of theoretical categories and ideas 'found in earlier studies of classical North European neo-corporatism', and suggests that the 'Irish case might assist the formulation of a new concept of post-corporatist concertation' ('working together') better able to portray arrangements emerging in several European countries (R. O'Donnell and O'Riordan 2000: 252). The 'post-corporatism thesis' is supported by highlighting a number of features of the Irish case. First, 'deliberation' and 'problem-solving', with the capacity to shape and reshape the parties' preferences, are seen to be prominent features of the dealings between the social partners, interwoven into a process that also involves '("hard-headed") bargaining' (R. O'Donnell and O'Riordan 2000: 250). Second, the range of interests represented in social partnership is seen to go beyond those arising from functional interdependence between labour and capital, and to challenge the representational monopoly of confederations on each side (R. O'Donnell and O'Riordan 2000: 251). Third, new relationships are seen to be emerging between government policy-making institutions and interest groups at various levels, from national to local. Thus, it is argued that 'traditional conceptions of neo-corporatism seem premised on an outdated view of the power, autonomy and effectiveness of central government' (R. O'Donnell and O'Riordan 2000: 251–2).

The 'post-corporatism thesis' thesis confronts a number of problems. First, many of the central arguments advanced are so abstract as to be compatible with many different patterns of interaction between social interest groups, or to be without clear and direct empirical reference points. Second, no empirical data has been adduced to illustrate these ideas, much less to subject them to empirical testing. Third, the relevant theoretical context for a 'post-corporatist' interpretation of recent social pacts should include 'competitive corporatism', rather than focusing solely on the categories and ideas in earlier studies of North European neo-corporatism. As outlined above, the literature on neo-corporatism has moved on; a post-corporatist critique should at least keep pace. Fourth, the stress on dialogue and problem-solving as key attributes of social partnership neglects the degree to which attributes such as these are long-familiar and indeed quite banal features of negotiations under neo-corporatism (Schmitter and Lehmbruch 1979) – as indeed they are under pre-corporatist and non-corporatist arrangements of various kinds (see Walton and McKersie 1965). Equally longstanding and familiar is another attribute muted in the post-corporatism thesis: the determined pursuit of sectional interests. That this remains a feature of relationships between the parties to social partnership is clear, for example, from union withdrawals or threatened withdrawals from social partnership to seek or win concessions; from employer threats to withhold concessions agreed in social partnership, when economic circumstances are seen to warrant a tough line; and from government tax reforms focused on electoral advantage rather than on agreements entered into under social partnership (on the issue of taxation, see Hardiman 2000). Fifth, the stress on the involvement of a wide range of interests under social partnership neglects the degree to which a hierarchy of representation and influence is apparent, in particular separating the 'social pillar' from the more significant and functionally interdependent interests of business and labour (see R. O'Donnell and Thomas 1998). It is clear that under social partnership the pivotal and influential interlocutors remain the employers and unions.

Finally, 'traditional conceptions' of neo-corporatism, far from being based on an 'outdated view of the power, autonomy and effectiveness of central government', explicitly recognized that the power of central government had to be heavily compromised in order that it might be effective (Schmitter and Lehmbruch 1979: 189). International commentary on recent social pacts clearly sees no need to conclude that the task of governing has become more complex in the manner suggested by proponents of post-corporatism – that is, arising from the 'complexity, volatility and diversity of economic and social problems and of social groups' (R. O'Donnell and O'Riordan 2000: 251). Rather, what is seen to shape governments' agendas and modes of engagement with interest groups are acute economic and fiscal problems and the search for competitive advantage in a more globalized international economic order (see M. Rhodes 1998).

Whether qualitative change in a 'post-corporatist' direction may thus be said to have occurred in the manner in which interests are defined, represented and compromised under social partnership remains open to considerable doubt. The onus must be on those committed to such an interpretation to report empirical evidence consistent with their viewpoint. In the absence of such evidence, and on the basis of what we know of its functioning and effects, it seems clear that social partnership in Ireland since 1987 can best be understood in terms of the theory of competitive corporatism.

Note

1   The history of Irish public policy in the industrial relations arena that follows relies heavily on Roche (1997) and to a lesser extent on Cradden (1999). For the period after 1999, *Industrial Relations News* and the *Irish Times* archive at www.Ireland.com have been the principal sources.

Further reading

Calmfors, L. and Driffill, J. (1988) 'Bargaining Structure, Corporatism and Macroeconomic Performance', *Economic Policy: A European Forum* 6: 13–61.

Cradden T. (1999) 'Social Partnership in Ireland: Against the Trend', in N. Collins (ed.) *Political Issues in Ireland Today*, Manchester: Manchester University Press.

Hardiman, N. (1988) *Pay, Politics and Economic Performance in Ireland 1970–1987*, Oxford: Clarendon Press.

Rhodes, M. (1998) 'Globalization, Labour Markets and Welfare States: A Future of "Competitive Corporatism"?', in M. Rhodes and Y. Meny (eds) *The Future of European Welfare: A New Social Contract?*, London: Sage.

Roche, W.K. (1997): 'Pay Determination, the State and the Politics of Industrial Relations', in T.V. Murphy and W.K. Roche (eds) *Irish Industrial Relations in Practice*, Dublin: Oak Tree Press.

Schmitter, P.C. and Lehmbruch, G. (eds) (1979) *Trends Towards Corporatist Intermediation*, London and Beverly Hills: Sage.

6 Clientelism: facilitating rights and favours

Neil Collins and Mary O'Shea

Introduction

Theories of public policy address the core question of political science that was popularly summarised by Lasswell (1936) as 'who gets what, when and where?' In other words, what sections of society are routinely favoured in the distribution of public goods and services? Many explanations focus on social class, regional distinctiveness, religious affiliation and other forms of group identity. The power of some groups is reflected in their electoral strength, strategic skill or centrality to the economy. At broader levels, the place of individual states in the international capitalist system has been offered as an important factor in determining public policy. Clientelism is of quite a different order of explanation. It is about the relationships between individual citizens and politicians, though it too seeks to answer Lasswell's question. Clientelist models of politics must, therefore, be understood as highlighting how resources are allocated within the parameters of much bigger systems. They are nevertheless interesting and, for understanding the particular politics of allocation at the micro level, potentially very powerful.

Ireland's political system has shown an ability to incorporate significant pressure groups through corporatist arrangements by which tangible benefits are received by 'privileged' interests (for a fuller discussion on corporatism, see Chapter 5). Individual citizens also seek to gain advantage or overcome disadvantage via privileged access through the intervention of their local representatives. Both of these types of political understanding have been described in the literature on other countries as clientelism and this dual use has led to some confusion about the concept in the Irish context. Following the established Irish understanding, this chapter will look primarily at the second type of clientelism. Nevertheless, some of the features of the more general model are instructive and it will also be examined.

Introduction to the main concepts and concerns of the approach

The literature on clientelism is diverse, but some common elements in how it is understood are important. Brachet-Marquez has usefully defined clientelism as:

the structuring of political power through networks of informal dyadic [two-person] relations that link individuals of unequal power in relationships of exchange. In clientelistic structures of authority, power is vested in the top individual (the boss, sovereign, or head of clan) who personally decides how to distribute resources according to personal preferences.

(Brachet-Marquez 1992: 94)

Clientelism in this sense is often associated with a corporatist form of government. In Mexico, for example, the leaders of the dominant party, the *Partido Revolucionario Institucional* (PRI), distribute economic benefits in a personalistic way through patronage networks. As De La Pena explains:

In Mexico, functionaries become visible to the public as inaugurators of beneficial works: schools, hospitals, markets, multifamily apartment complexes…. Among the popular classes many have memories of benefits effectively given to them or some close family…that did not derive from the impersonal operation of a system but of the personalised benevolence of – the PRI.

(De La Pena, cited in Cross 1997: 170)

The crucial difference between this form of clientelism and the concept as applied to Ireland is that the politician rarely has direct control of the resources sought by the client. For this reason, Gallagher and Komito suggest that Irish clientelism may be more accurately described as *brokerage*, whereby 'politicians' brokerage activities are similar to the activities of a range of professional mediators; the difference derives from their special access to the state bureaucracy and their specific motives in carrying out brokerage functions' (Gallagher and Komito 1999: 212).

An important definition of the core relationship between patron and client used in the general literature is provided by Clapham:

The patron–client relationship – an exchange relationship between roles – may be defined as a special case of dyadic…ties involving a largely instrumental friendship in which an individual of higher socio-economic status (patron) uses his own influences and resources to provide protection or benefits, or both, for a person of lower status (client) who, for his part, reciprocates by offering general support and assistance, including personal services, to the patron…. This relationship need not be illegal or illegitimate, at variance with the formal rules or moral expectations governing the operation of the hierarchy within which it takes place.

(Clapham 1982: 61)

Table 6.1 summarises this definition and points to the main modifications that may be made to it, as suggested by the use of the term 'clientelism' in the literature on Ireland.

Table 6.1 The patron–client relationship in the general and Irish literature

Definitions	General	Ireland
Instrumental friendship	Yes	Yes
Unequal social status	Yes	Unequal political access
Use by patron of own influences and resources	Yes	Rarely; usually brokerage
Client reciprocates by offering general support	Yes	Usually electoral
Relationship need not be at variance with formal rules or moral expectations	Yes	Boundaries unclear; corruption possible

It can be seen that Ireland appears to exhibit many of the features identified by the general literature, though in a distinctive form. It is important to stress, however, that clientelism offers only partial explanations of the pattern of Irish public policy. It should not, for example, be confused with the phenomenon of 'pork-barrel politics', i.e. government spending that is primarily for the benefit of local interests in a particular constituency rather than the state as a whole. Similarly, the manipulation of the 'business/electoral' cycle by inflating government spending before an election is not clientelism. On the other hand, patronage, rewarding individuals with appointments to official bodies may be clientelistic depending on the circumstances (see the case study on privilege below, pp. 000–00).

Brief review of the evolution of clientelism

Rostow (1971) suggested five stages through which states develop: traditional society; preconditions for take-off; take-off; sustained growth; and mass consumption. Traditional society is deemed to encompass all societies prior to the seventeenth century. It had few of the structural characteristics of contemporary Western society. The preconditions for take-off and take-off itself are a steady rate of change in the political, social and manufacturing sectors. This allows growth within all aspects of society. Finally, a modern, typically capitalist, civilisation emerges. In the age of high mass consumption, the final stage, a country is in a stable situation, i.e. little or no growth is necessary to maintain it. Each stage had been experienced by America by the 1950s and has been associated with different forms of political organisation. In other states the different stages emerged at a slower pace. For Rostow (1971), modernity implied liberal democracy and pluralism. Though this school of thought has become more nuanced, modernisation theorists still tend to see traditionalism and modernity as juxtaposed. Clientelism is for them an anachronistic form of politics for a liberal democracy and will inevitably decline.

Brusco *et al.* (2001), in a study of Argentina, provide a clear example of the assumption that clientelism is a temporary phenomenon whose demise is associated with modernisation or democratic maturity, a notion that influenced Irish political science greatly in the 1960s (Chubb 1963). In reporting their empirical work, they see the purpose of their research as identifying 'the conditions under which democracies undergo a transition from clientelist to programmatic politics…. Under clientelism, electoral support is the sole criterion on which politicians give goods to voters… .Clientelism is a *problem* for developing democracies' (Brusco *et al.* 2001: 2; emphasis added).

For Brusco *et al.* (2001: 3–6) clientelism exhibits the following features:

- it targets the poor for clientelist pay-offs;
- it takes advantage of clients' need for immediate benefits;
- it limits voters' information and autonomy;
- it discourages the provision of public goods;
- it deters the entry of political challengers;
- it is associated with local political monopolies;
- it encourages pockets of authoritarianism in transitional democracies;
- it keeps voters' incomes low;
- it feeds on poverty;
- it creates an interest among politicians in economic stagnation.

This list of indictments is based on the idea that public political discourse should concern policy choices that apply universally – that is, to every member of a society and consistently as a right or duty. Each citizen gets or gives from or to the state exactly what is formally agreed through the public political process. The patron–client bond, in contrast,

> [is] based on a personal or private morality of obligations between individuals, which is necessarily at variance with a public morality based on the goals which an organisation is intended to achieve or the internal virtues which it is intended to exhibit.
>
> (Clapham 1982: 1)

Thus, in a modern state modernisation theorists would claim that clientelism has no place since its existence depends primarily on the fact that the patron–client bond derives from the notion of responsibility to one's family, which is characteristic of traditional society and so is immediately understood by all parties to a transaction (Calvert and Calvert 2001: 145). In such societies, the danger of clientelism is that it may flourish unrestrained as individuals enter private relationships and arrangements that are not open to scrutiny by modern state structures (Calvert and Calvert 2001: 145). Still, however, modernisation need not completely preclude clientelist tendencies. Vlachos-Dengler (2000) noted that while Greece was economically vibrant and well on the path to modernisation, following the example of other modern Western democracies, it ended up with a political culture of clientelism and inertia to reform.

Similar criticisms are also made of other European states. The 1999 successes of the Freedom Party of Austria (FPÖe) were in part explained by disgruntlement with the clientelism of the Social Democrats and the People's Party, the two parties that had dominated Austrian politics since 1945. Their electoral losses helped the extreme right-wing political leader Jörg Haider into power, much to the disapproval of other members of the EU. In Ireland, the denunciation of clientelism is rather less severe, though some still view it as a form of political immaturity that dampens collective political action (M.D. Higgins 1982; Hazelkorn 1986).

Mainstream variants in current usage

Much of the theoretical work on clientelism is derived from observations in Africa, Asia, South America and southern Europe (Clapham 1982) and shows that clientelist links between citizens and elites tend to have similar features. Most usually they are: voluntary; connecting people of unequal socio-economic status; personal and face to face; and long lasting. Although neither party is forced to take part in clientelist relations, each feels some sense of obligation to the other, which may likely be a response to impersonal or alienating bureaucratic structures. Thus, clientelist exchanges are private rather than public, lacking the permanence and public legitimacy that characterise formal authority structures, and are often the key to understanding how people obtain the resources that they need (Komito 1985). For all of these reasons, so-called 'modernisation theorists' tend to associate the incidence and prevailing existence of clientelism and clientelist relations with traditional societies.

Still, however, other aspects of clientelist relationships have confounded the predictions of modernisation theorists. Clientelist relationships are neither simple economic domination and exploitation nor egalitarianism in a democratic sense. Neither are they intrinsically improper. They do, however, imply competitiveness among politicians. They obtain when scarce resources controlled by the state are accessed through the political elite in return for electoral and related support. The persistence of clientelism in successful globally participating economies, such as the United States, weighs against modernisation theorists' accounts of clientelist relations. Toinet and Glenn (1982: 212) observe that, though 'awkwardly at odds with official rhetoric', clientelism is part of the American system and 'a Carter or Reagan attacking "those politicians in Washington"…finds that once in power they have to work through the system'.

Asserting the incidence of clientelism in modern Western democracies, Toinet and Glenn identify three more specific, though often overlapping and connected, forms of patronage or clientelism in America. The first is clientelism stemming from the federal system, whereby:

> [the] distributive relationship between the central government and the
> peripheral areas [is] governed by representative institutions which make the
> representative responsible for the well-being of his district or State, and

which are organised so as to favour the power of certain individuals or areas.

(Toinet and Glenn 1982: 213)

The second is traditional boss or machine politics, and the third, clientelism of the electoral system. 'Machine politics' represents a particular form of electoral clientelism, one which received its prototypical expression in urban America around the turn of the last century. By virtue of the political co-ordination of favours, patronage and public contracts, such parties created formidable electoral majorities which repeatedly swept into power (J.C. Scott 1977: 493). It is possibly this form of clientelism, together with clientelism of the electoral system, which resonates more in an Irish context because of its role in integrating immigrants into American politics.

In many other contexts, clientelism may be found in social arenas where a patron provides benefits that are not otherwise available. For example, in peasant communities landowners may provide land, security and other assistance and, in return, receive food, labour, military service and social acknowledgement – remnants of a feudal society. In such circumstances, the patron's role is often to act as a bridge between the local and national systems of power, so that 'by recognising private interests and using the machinery of the state to purvey private benefits to groups and individuals' the patron accords the client 'a vested – and purely instrumental – interest in the maintenance of the state itself' (Clapham 1982: 16).

Like many approaches to clientelism, this bridging role suggests that, as the national system develops, patrons become brokers dependent on privileged access to external resources. In this role, they compete with other 'providers' such as priests, teachers, agricultural advisers and others with access to the state. Once their monopoly over resources is gone, patrons may leave the market because there is no longer any advantage to them. Thus, Martin observes that a whole class of landed patrons left the political arena in the late nineteenth century and that their replacements 'did not control...[the majority's] votes like the old landed ascendancy had prior to the Secret Ballot Act of 1872' (M. Martin 2003: in press). As a consequence clientelism, as it is understood in contemporary Ireland, usually refers to exchanges between politicians and voters so that the transactions involved centre on influence over state benefits and electoral support.

Case study: establishing the boundaries of clientelism – the Irish experience

The Irish experience is often seen as anomalous in the literature on clientelism because it defies the theme of modernisation (M.D. Higgins 1982). Garvin places Ireland in a pattern of developing political systems similar to that of the modernisation theorists, noting that, in common with other newly independent states, in Ireland the state machine was 'an island of relative modernity'. Still, however, he acknowledged that many politicians 'often owe their power to popular forces and organisations which are less than wedded to the idea that government should be "rational-bureaucratic", impersonal, even-handed or tolerant' (Garvin 1981: 190). For this reason, Garvin described Ireland as 'a periphery dominated centre', in other words, a political system in which the central government is captured by provincial interests. This phrase captures a great deal about Irish politics but, in the context of clientelism, it may focus too much attention on the politics of *rural* Ireland. The concentration on rural local politics was reinforced by two very important research monographs on Cork (Bax 1976) and Donegal (Sacks 1976) that provided detailed insights into Irish clientelism and were able to reveal similar patterns of political competition in diverse parts of rural Ireland. Still, the potential rural bias was redressed by Komito's (1985) study of clientelism in an Irish urban setting, which confirmed that 'clientelism exists in Dublin' and exhibits a similar pattern to that in other parts of the Republic.

In both urban and rural Ireland, politicians hold 'clinics', regular scheduled sessions to which constituents can come to discuss personal or other issues. It is also common today for problems to be presented by the telephone, letter or e-mail. By the same token, politicians have also begun to use technology to record and track representations. Although private research by one Labour Deputy has sought to answer the question, it is still not clear what proportion of representations are made to more than one politician, whether those making their case are usually party supporters or whether they give their first-preference vote to the Deputy or councillor they approach.

In Ireland, politicians have been described as specialists helping the 'bureaucratically illiterate' (Gallagher and Komito 1999: 211). It is the working class who use the clientelist system most: it is the cases relating to social welfare, housing and medical entitlements that dominate deputies' and local councillors' caseloads. The perception is that these 'customer' complaints may not be heard unless they are facilitated by politicians. This perception has persisted despite public management reforms under the Strategic Management Initiative (SMI),[1] which have encouraged a customer focus by government departments. Similarly, the ombudsman system introduced in 1984 has done little to reduce clientelism.

It is important to note that the evidence from case studies offers a picture of brokerage that is low key and routine. Major allocative decisions are not involved. Rather, the politician is 'like a lawyer, who operates not by bribing the judge, but by ensuring that the case is presented better than the citizen would be able to present it' (Gallagher and Komito1999: 212). Former Taoiseach Garret Fitzgerald gives an example from his own experience:

> in the 1970s when as a TD I held clinics…. A couple with one child came to see me because the wife could not have any more children and they wanted to adopt a second child. The adoption society could not help them because, due to the housing shortage of that time, they lived in a one-room, privately-rented apartment. Because of that shortage, Dublin Corporation

could not provide them with a two-room apartment when they had only one child: families with two or more children had precedence.... Each of these bureaucratic rules was reasonable in itself; together they added up to a piece of inhumanity that could be removed only by an intervention in the system to break the nexus between the two rules – which I eventually succeeded in doing.

(*Irish Times*, 20 April 2002: 14)

A reputation for effective presentation of a case is an asset as important for Irish politicians as it is for barristers and lawyers. Ironically, however, the politician must eschew any sense of social distance. This requirement dates from the early years of Irish democracy. As Martin notes:

The new leaders came from the same classes as the majority of the people.... The result was that the bargaining power of the voters *vis-a-vis* the political elite increased considerably. The introduction of PRSTV [proportional representation on the single transferable vote system] was also instrumental in this increase. [I]t increased the accessibility to the leaders by those who had voted for them.

(M. Martin 2003: in press)

Much of Martin's evidence is taken from Cork city in the early years of the state when 'the fellow-workers and neighbours of voters were now the new political elite both at national and local level' (M. Martin 2003: in press). Still, however, most of the literature on Ireland highlights the rural dimension and portrays the politician as 'the countryman's personal emissary to an anonymous state' (Sacks 1976: 50–1). Thus, when O'Carroll referred to Irish politicians as 'cute hoors', he was reflecting on the 'appreciation [in rural Irish communities] of the skill of the "fixer"' (O'Carroll 1987: 81):

to be successful in politics aspirants to office have to be able to show they have power. Those who can deliver material favours are said to have 'pull'...[which] indicates an ability to 'deliver' more than other competitors for political office.... In local parlance the actions which most strikingly demonstrate power, however, are termed 'strokes'.

(O'Carroll 1987: 82)

Today, the politician is afforded a less 'heroic' role, even in rural Ireland. Still, a reputation for 'effectiveness' is a significant electoral advantage, especially since 'the state is rarely seen as impartial or impersonal; special contacts and influence are believed to be more relevant than need or qualifications in obtaining state benefits' (Komito 1985). Taking up this theme of electoral advantage, Collins and Cradden's (2001) discussion of clientelism in Ireland points to several supportive features within the Irish political system, which is why elections are won or lost by relatively few voters switching their support. These include: the stability of the party system; the lack of serious ideological divisions between the main parties; a tradition of strict party discipline in the Oireachtas; and the high partisan loyalty of Irish electors. They highlight, however, that one of the strongest influences on the 'constituency behaviour' of politicians is the single transferable vote (STV) system of proportional representation (PR) voting in multi-member constituencies. This in effect obliges politicians to compete not only against the candidates of other parties, but also against fellow party nominees. Fianna Fáil or Fine Gael may win or lose, but the main priority for each politician is that he or she is personally successful. Any analysis of Irish elections, therefore, must account for the intra-party competition. As O'Sullivan notes:

> An exclusive focus on parties as the principal democratic actors…ignores the fact that the Irish electoral system…presents voters with a choice not only among parties but also among candidates of the same party, since even the most staunchly partisan voter is obliged to rank individuals within a party list.
>
> (M.C. O'Sullivan 1999: 181)

To ensure success regardless of party fortunes, a politician must have some basis of support among the electorate other than party allegiance. Clearly, because the parties do not allow open displays of disagreement at election time, candidates of the same party cannot compete for support based on policy considerations. Irish politicians, therefore, emphasise their local, social and personal links with the electorate. Cultivating a substantial personal following is seen as a sure way of guaranteeing an adequate share of first-preference votes; and the way to ensure such a following seems to be to offer a better 'service' to constituents than any other TD, including fellow party members. It sometimes seems that the term 'hard worker' is the best accolade that a politician can possess.

Parties similarly wish to select a candidate with a good chance of winning a seat. Galligan's study of the 1997 general election in Ireland highlights the continuing importance of localism in Irish politics:

> Political experience and family connections are two components of localism, long identified as an important feature of candidate selection…. Localism…remained a central feature of the main-party candidates…through family ties, networks based on a record of local involvement, local council representation, or a combination of these factors.
>
> (Galligan 1999: 77)

Knowing someone through family or local ties assists the transactions at the centre of the clientelist political system. To maximise their advantage, particularly in rural areas, parties will try to avoid having candidates from the same part of a constituency so that the local networks of their standard-bearers do not overlap.

To be in a position to help clients, politicians at all levels cultivate contacts in the various bureaucracies of the state. Clearly political seniority helps. As Dooney and O'Toole describe, ministerial office is a major advantage in the mechanics of representations:

> A politician belonging to a government party makes a request by letter on behalf of his constituent to the minister responsible. Those in the opposition parties who have previously held office write personally to the secretary general of the department, while ordinary backbenchers write to him formally or to an official whom they have got to know. Letters to the minister are, in the first instance, acknowledged by the minister himself, with an additional copy of his reply to the politician to send to his constituent. The original letter is then sent from the minister's private office to the appropriate section of the department for preparation of a final reply.
>
> (Dooney and O'Toole 1998: 236)

Many ministers use a team of civil servants to deal with representations, as the former Taoiseach Garret Fitzgerald noted when he first took office:

> I recall my astonishment when I became *Taoiseach* and discovered that the personal secretary who came with me into my Department, and who alone helped me to look after constituents' problems, was about to replace a General Office that was staffed by no less than 16 civil servants, who had been servicing my predecessor's constituency work. Something similar happened after a change of minister in the late 1970s in the Department of Foreign Affairs.
>
> (*Irish Times*, 20 April 2002: 14)

Local authority membership is also particularly important to a strategy of access to the bureaucracy, because, not only are local councils themselves significant service providers, they also nominate from their members to the governing bodies of other state agencies such as health boards, vocational educational committees and so on. M.C. O'Sullivan notes that the proportion of TDs in recent Dala with local authority experience has fluctuated between 85 and 90 cent; 75 per cent of TDs were members of a local authority before their initial election and a further 11 per cent were elected to a local authority following their first election to the Dáil (M.C. O'Sullivan 1999: 191).

Though the parties at local level dominate candidate selection, Marsh and Sinnott explain that central party strategy can also favour well-grounded local candidates who are 'often expressing the hope that even if things were going badly for them in the national opinion polls, their candidate strength on the ground would save the day' (1999: 173). They also emphasise the importance of brokerage and localism in analyses of Irish voting behaviour, where 'competition among candidates, especially among candidates of the same party, contributes to the localisation of electoral competition' (Marsh and Sinnott 1999: 173).

Irish politicians today are seen by many as useful agents to guarantee the receipt of state benefits. But a question remains as to when this attitude developed. According to M. Martin brokerage-style politics emerged at the very beginning of the modern Irish party political system and '*Dáil* deputies were expected to act as intermediaries for their constituents and did so. The followers of both *Cumann na nGaedheal* and *Fianna Fáil* expected rewards and "prizes" from their respective elites' (M. Martin 2003: in press).

After independence, the Free State bureaucracy retained the features of its British predecessor. The enormous importance of the civil service and local authorities and, to a lesser extent, the state-sponsored bodies was heightened by the dominance of the public sector in the rather underdeveloped post-independence economy. Because of its political indispensability, the civil service was able to retain its corporate integrity and identity and to resist pressures towards politicisation. The recruitment and promotion procedures of the Irish public service are formally and rigorously meritocratic. Nevertheless, M. Martin (2003) notes that the party grassroots also felt that they would be 'looked after' once Fianna Fáil had attained power (in 1932) and that a number of *cumainn* also called for the abolition of the Local Appointments Commission and the restoration to local authorities of the powers taken from them by the commission.

Such pressure was vigorously and successfully resisted for posts under the remit of the Central and Local Appointments Commissions. At other levels, however, Manning (1999) suggests that the extent of Fianna Fáil patronage, especially during the governments of the 1930s and 1940s, was extensive – albeit hard to quantify:

> Opposition TDs complained loudly and frequently that representations by them to government departments were sidelined in favour of government Deputies, giving a clear message to voters that if you wanted something done the only effective route was through the *Fianna Fáil* organisation. Increasingly it seemed that party membership was the key to many public appointments, whether it was as a road ganger, a CIE [*Cora Iompair Eireann*] worker, or to the judiciary.
>
> (Manning 1999: 202)

Whether or not Fianna Fáil began this trend is unclear. Manning argues that clientelism was well established in the early years of the state and Garvin (1981) suggests that clientelism in independent Ireland was simply a continuation of a much older pattern. Arguing that by the end of the nineteenth century Ireland had one of the most advanced, centralised and rationalised administrative machines in Europe, Garvin suggests that 'the contrast between Irish administrative development on the one hand and Irish social and economic development on the other was stark; government was, over most of the island, the only large modern organisation that existed' (1981: 190). The alienation between the state and the majority of its subjects was so profound, it is argued, that intermediaries of various types became essential to the political system (Martin 2003).

This argument is countered by Komito (1985), who points out that Ireland is not simply a European version of the 'non-Western developing, post-colonial state'. Komito argues that Ireland's difference lies in the fact that the independence gained in 1922 represented more a change in regime than a revolution. Moreover, the civil service remained largely Irish and was unchanged; economic power was diffuse rather than centralised; there was no flight of capital after independence; and independent Ireland lacked the ethnic and cultural diversity associated with other post-colonial states. Still, however, although Komito may underestimate the divisiveness of the Civil War, his argument is consonant with those accounts that date Ireland's pattern of clientelism as of longer standing than independence. Despite consensus on the longevity of the phenomenon, its practice in both rural and urban settings, as well as its contextual underpinnings in characteristics of Irish electoral competition, there is some lack of clarity about the types of transactions involved.

In order to help differentiate the different kinds of clientelist exchanges cited in the literature, Figure 6.1 sets out a typology of Irish clientelism. It begins by juxtaposing 'rights' and 'favours'. Rights are taken to mean public policy entitlements that citizens have by virtue of their circumstances. For example, all senior citizens are permitted to travel on the bus free of charge. Such rights may be inhibited because the wrong department was contacted, an appropriate social security number omitted or some other supporting material not enclosed when a claim was made. This sort of clientelism is predominantly enabling or facilitative; as the former Taoiseach Garret Fitzgerald explains, it often 'involves people seeking their rights from an administrative system whose rules are often too complex and rigid to accommodate the hugely differentiated legitimate needs of citizens' (*Irish Times*, 20 April 2002: 14).

Figure 6.1: Typology of Irish clientelism

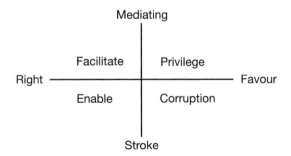

Favours are benefits that are subject to some discretion or judgement. The criteria for third-level student grants, for example, allows for latitude and discretion at local authority level. Some legislation allows considerable discretion to ministers. For example, Section 6 of the Urban Renewal Act 1986 states that:

> The Minister may, with the consent of the Minister for Finance, for the purposes of this section, by order declare an area to be a designated area where he is satisfied that there is a special need to promote urban renewal therein, and may by such order describe such area in whatever manner he thinks fit.
>
> (Urban Renewal Act 1986: sect. 6)

The involvement of politicians in obtaining rights and favours can be seen as part of a continuum. Similarly, the actions of the politician may be contrasted if they involve mediating or brokering as opposed to adding benefit or 'pulling a stroke'. Sacks puts forward a picture of imaginary patronage because politicians' 'control over the distributive institution is quite limited' (1976: 7). For Chubb, the 'intervention or good offices of a "man in the know"' (Chubb 1963: 273) is considered important by some citizens to obtain state services to which they may in fact be entitled. In this case, the politician is facilitating access to a right and in cases such as these Chubb suggests that politicians deliberately exaggerate their influence.

In some cases, however, politicians can enable clients to obtain benefits that they would not obtain independently. As Gallagher and Komito put it, 'the value of contacting a TD lies in the fact that this can enable people to find out about the existence of – and/or how to obtain – benefits, grants or rights of which they would otherwise have been unaware' (1999: 210). Such a bonus may be gained by the politician causing an official to use discretion in a way that would normally be denied even though a basis could be found within the regulations. In other cases, the client may benefit from corruption, i.e. the misuse of public office to gain an individual benefit outside the framework of established policy or permitted discretion.

Collins (1987) notes that the literature on clientelism in Ireland provides a relatively shallow explanation of the role of the public official in the process of exchange. Taking issue with Bax's (1976) assertion that local bureaucrats in particular are dependent on politicians for career advancement and are influenced by their promotion prospects, Collins's (1987) explanation stresses the autonomy afforded to local government managers and their staff in the area of policy formation by the focus of politicians on detailed implementation. Central to this explanation is a divergence of interests in relation to power: politicians seek influence over the details of delivery; bureaucrats wish to guide broad policy. This pattern runs counter to formal distinctions between policy and administration but, argues Collins (1987), provides the basis of a stable *modus operandi* for public policy-making in Ireland. Still, the extent of Irish clientelist relations is variable. Some civil service departments are more vulnerable to political pressure than others, some state benefits are less costly to deliver than others, and some politicians are able to exert greater pressure than others (Komito 1985). In order to explore these differences, the case studies below illustrate four different – and fictional – examples of Irish clientelist relations, according to the typology outlined in Figure 6.1.

Case study: mapping the spectrum of Irish clientelist relations

The topic of clientelism does not lend itself easily to a case study approach because of the inherent confidentiality at its core. Below four fictional examples are presented that illustrate the categories summarised in Figure 6.1.

Facilitate

Mary Murphy applies for a medical card. Her application is sent to her local health board. She is refused on the grounds that she is just above the financial threshold. She visits the clinic of her local TD, who is a member of the health board in her capacity as a local county councillor and is one of the county council nominees. Having spoken to Mary Murphy, the TD identifies that in her application she did not include the medical evidence of an aspect of her daughter's illness which required medication. The TD wrote to the health board and by providing the information with regard to her daughter Mary Murphy gets a medical card for her daughter.

Comment

The TD, by knowing how to apply and providing the correct information, facilitated Mary Murphy in getting a medical card for her daughter to which she was entitled. This is a typical example of mediation on behalf of a constituent to facilitate the delivery of a right.

Enable

The government has introduced a measure with regard to a business expansion scheme for the tourist sector in the budget. Patrick Murphy is a hotel owner whose hotel is on the border of the geographic boundary limit of the scheme. He applied for the scheme but was refused. He went to the clinic of his local TD, a government backbencher. He discussed his proposal and the TD checked with the minister's office. He was given the name of the relevant official administering the scheme and, having discussed the particular case, the TD identified how Patrick Murphy should apply to fit into the regulations. The information provided enabled Murphy to submit an eligible application. The hotel postal address was outside the boundary but the land on which he wished to build the self-catering apartments was within the geographic area. After the TD had spoken to the relevant official it was agreed Patrick Murphy could resubmit his application using the postal address of the forthcoming scheme.

Comment

The hotel owner was refused on his initial application. The intervention of the TD enabled a valid application to be made. The detail of regulations may not be distributed with application forms, but there are instances where the intervention of a public representative and the relevant official checking the regulations can identify a route to 'enable' a successful application. In enabling this right there is an element of a stroke, identifying a way of making the regulations 'fit'.

Privilege

Johanna O'Brien is a party activist and a member of the National Executive of her party. She is a businesswoman and her curriculum vitae includes active involvement in a number of business organisations. She is a director of a number of companies and is a recognised expert, speaking at many conferences on companies in crisis, issues of change, etc. She indicates to her local TD, a government backbencher, that she would appreciate some recognition and an appointment to a state board would give her additional credibility and business recognition. She is appointed to a state board.

Comment

Johanna O'Brien is very successful in business, but it is through her party involvement that she is nominated to a state board. This is a privilege and a favour that her local TD gets the relevant minister to deliver, i.e. the Deputy mediates to deliver a favour on behalf of a constituent.

Corruption

P.J. Stapleton is a company director of West Satellite, a satellite TV company in the West of Ireland. The Minister for Communications is his local TD and Stapleton is a party supporter.

To establish a satellite TV channel new equipment must be erected, and the preference of West Satellite is to locate the equipment near its broadcasting base in the town where it has land available. Under current regulations it is not possible to locate satellite communications equipment in urban areas. To have to get an alternative site would add significant costs to the venture. P.J. Stapleton arranges to meet the Minister for Communications for lunch. He requests that the minister amend the regulations to allow erection of satellite equipment within a 3-mile zone of government-owned land of 10 acres or more. The site of West Satellite would be covered by this change to the regulations. Stapleton also assures the minister of a contribution. The minister agrees to the request. A cash donation of €50,000 is paid to the minister.

Comment

Political corruption is the abuse of public office for private gain. The above example is blatant corruption. The change of regulation is being made only on the grounds of money. The downside of clientelism is a public perception that policy decisions with regard to companies may be influenced by corrupt overtures.

Summary review of theoretical utility

This section examines the extent to which clientelism provides a valid explanatory framework to explain aspects of Irish public policy. As we have already seen, modernisation theorists argue that clientelism thrives in more traditional societies, and so the obvious question to raise is: to what extent is contemporary Ireland still a traditional society capable of supporting clientelist relations? Leading opinion writers in the Irish media seem to think it is. Fintan O'Toole of the *Irish Times* suggests that 'the core [of the Irish political system] itself is deeply rotten, eaten away by a rampant clientelism in which the political messenger-boy takes no moral responsibility for the message which he is delivering' (*Irish Times*, 13 April 2002).

Strong opinions such as this, however, may not only be 'pointing out the obvious' but equally be a reflection of clientelism's immediacy and cultural acceptance. The activities of Tull MacAdoo, a rural backbencher in the novels of John B. Keane, have caused many a reader to 'chuckle to himself as he enters the web of local intrigue and petty skulduggery among the rural politicians' (1978: 1). Almost all voters, urban dwellers as well as rural, will have some story of a clientelist transaction, whether successful or not. Alternative explanations, based on, for example, structural or class theories, simply do not have the same colour as clientelism and so may be rejected without due consideration. The significance of localism and personalism in Irish politics is a case in point.

Using the Labour Party's election strategy in 1997 to support his case, Holmes (1999) argues that local issues remain very important to Irish politics. In this instance, 'Labour made a strategic decision early on to fight the election on a constituency-by-constituency basis, and its campaign put a very strong emphasis on what the party had done for each locality' (Holmes 1999: 45). This strategy was less benignly interpreted in the *Irish Times*, when Fintan O'Toole suggested that Labour had 'laid all the stress on clientelist politics. The message is simply that the party's TDs are good workers on the ground who deliver tangible benefits to their constituents' (*Irish Times*, 3 June 1997).

The Labour Party's approach is instructive because it illustrates the intra-party nature of competition that is often a feature of the STV system of PR that pertains in Ireland. The All-Party Oireachtas Committee on the Constitution also noted that STV PR had a specific influence over Irish politics, encouraging 'excessive constituency workloads; an absence of encouragement to parties to nominate socially representative slates; internecine local rivalries, leading to a high turnover of deputies and the discouragement of some high quality candidates' (2002: 15). They did, however, see one of its major benefits as promoting constituency service and responsiveness to change.

This points to the second major issue with clientelist explanations of public policy, which lies in the difficulties (as shown by the fictitious examples above) associated with assessing its true extent and significance. According to Gallagher and Komito, 'whichever way their work was measured it was clear that the volume of constituency work had gone up greatly since earlier surveys in the 1960s' (1999: 208). An incident in 2002 revealed that over 14,000 letters were received by the Department of Justice in a year from Oireachtas members (*Sunday Business Post*, 14 April 2002). Other central government departments dealing with health and housing and social welfare issues receive a lot more. Still, much of the evidence used to support clientelist explanations is collected by anthropologists whose research methods favour the reporting of individual experiences. It is for this reason that Bax's (1976) conclusions have been heavily criticised. He may have been over-reliant on stories from individual politicians and clients of 'strokes' pulled and favours secured.

Certainly, if Komito (1985) and others are correct, much of the benefit of politicians' actions is imaginary, though they have a vested interest in presenting their interventions as crucial. Whilst it is clear that politicians are busy making interventions for constituents with the bureaucracy, what is not known is the proportion of administrative decisions on which representations are made, how influential they are and how many electors never seek the help of a politician. Comparative data suggest that politicians everywhere are active on behalf of individual candidates. British Members of Parliament hold 'surgeries' and write letters; French Assembly members are also reported to use their contacts for local people (Knapp and Wright 2001); and even in Scandinavian jurisdictions, where citizen efficacy is high, politicians are active. In Ireland most politicians are backbenchers or local councillors, so that scrutinising or legislating opportunities are relatively few, of limited immediate impact and generally unnoticed by constituents. Given this context, even if electoral, cultural or administrative factors did not underpin a *clientelist* approach, politicians would be likely to be busy on behalf of constituents, especially since research in recent years, across several countries, has indicated that conscientious constituency work can significantly improve the re-election prospects of an incumbent member (Studlar and McAllister 1996: 69).

This is less true in countries with list systems of election because the link between individual parliamentarians and particular localities is less clear. Nevertheless, German members of parliament still spend a high proportion of their time on individual queries. The difference between Ireland and many other political systems is that being active is seen as vital to re-election rather than marginal (Bowler and Farrell 1993; European Commission DG X 1992; Wood and Young 1997). Under the 'first past the post' electoral system in Britain, for example, it may be that no amount of constituency work can insulate a candidate from a significant 'swing' in the popularity of his or her party.

Moreover, even if we ignore the significant impact made by alternative voting systems, the fact still remains that in Ireland personalism is at the heart of politics. As one Irish Deputy explained, helping people can be a rewarding activity in itself: 'I'm fascinated by politics…more people than politics. I learn something new everyday…. Meeting ordinary individuals who don't understand something…I unravel that for them…it's an education for me for the next case' (Noel Davern, Minister of State; interview with Vincent Browne, RTE, 9 April 2002).

Certainly, in the Irish case at least, the view that clientelism is a phase in a country's development from which politics will emerge into a more universalistic, ideological and transparent pattern seems too determinist. It is also based on a model of clear ideological alternatives between parties and high civic competence among voters. Such conditions are in fact receding as ideology has diminished as a mark of distinction between major parties under the weight of the current liberal consensus and citizens have become less participative in politics. Moreover, in Ireland clientelism may indeed be a rational choice for both politicians and electors.

The universalistic ideal under which all citizens are provided for according to their rights and duties presupposes a bureaucratic system that is completely efficient and well informed. There is little evidence to suggest that this condition is often met. Even if they are well intentioned, public officials can make decisions without complete evidence or on too literal or narrow interpretations of the data they possess. Though the recent SMI has sought to change attitudes, traditionally the public servant is not rewarded for being helpful and approachable. For politicians the reverse is true. Similarly, the most junior people are most often the civil servants in direct contact with the public: promotion means escaping the 'front desk'. For politicians seniority brings no such relief. Indeed, for the local government and civil service agencies, politicians may provide a preliminary screening that means many minor queries never reach them. Despite the perfunctory exchanging of letters, clientelism may reduce the burden on the bureaucracy. Gallagher and Komito suggest that 'in return, civil servants may well give special priority to representations from TDs and respond more sympathetically than to letters of complaint…from ordinary members of the public' (1999: 24).

Dooney and O'Toole, on the other hand, are dismissive of this argument, suggesting that 'officials are not impressed by representations, to which they are well accustomed' (1998: 236). The matter may or may not be re-examined, depending on the issue, the nature of the examination already made, and the political standing of the person making the representations. Despite such assertions, the clientelist system may usefully augment official channels in individual cases without necessarily disadvantaging those who only avail themselves of the formal mechanisms. It also provides a source of feedback on policy or a form of 'market intelligence'. As the former Taoiseach Garret Fitzgerald notes:

The system of clinics, at which politicians meet constituents with problems, is thus not merely justifiable: it has a potentially positive role in the process of politicians learning how to do the job for which they are elected – legislation and government administration.

(*Irish Times*, 20 April 2002: 14)

Set against its positive aspects, some observers see the clientelist nature of Irish politics as a source of cynicism among the electorate and as demeaning to politicians. Thus, for example, instead of using parliamentary questions and other privileges to monitor the policy of the executive, many parliamentarians are content to spend most of their time seeking out information about minor details of administration so as to satisfy clients' demands. Paradoxically, therefore, politicians as a body may have relatively little impact on policy-making *per se*. Because of this, Dooney and O'Toole argue that the whole clientelist system is self-defeating even for ministers:

Since ministers demand that priority be given to representation, official resources are diverted away from dealing with the issue which the representations are intended to ameliorate…[T]he system distracts ministers and senior officials from the policy-making activities in which they should more properly be engaged.

(Dooney and O'Toole 1998: 236)

The idea that politics is about policy, in the sense of broad statements of value, while administration is a less charged activity best left to officials is deeply held by most bureaucrats. It is represented in the legal and administrative framework of most states. In practice, however, this view is often contested. In Ireland it appears that politicians are used as a resource by all sections of society. Similarly, while some civil service departments are busier with representations than others, no area of policy is immune. Local authorities are as busy as central government and would presumably be even busier if Ireland were a less centralised state. Since the critical condition needed to support clientelism is control over scarce resources by the state, politicians with a motive to intervene, such as securing re-election, may well continue to regard the allocation of resources in individual cases (perhaps to citizens who feel that there is some barrier to accessing them) as a necessary and important part of their job. So long as these conditions are widespread and prevalent in Ireland, clientelism will continue to be a useful model for explaining public policy outcomes – if only at mundane and low-key levels.

Note

1   Under the 1997 Freedom of Information Act and other measures, the SMI presents an influential programme of public-sector reform in Ireland – one that seems to presuppose that politicians interests are concentrated on the broader policy arena. The SMI is committed to e-government, greater transparency in decision-making

and a 'customer-orientation by civil servants'. In the longer term, it may reduce the need for politicians' assistance in helping citizens to be more self-reliant and inhibit clientelism. As yet this is far from clear.

Further reading

Carty, R.K. (1981) *Party and Parish Pump*, Ontario: Wilfrid Laurier University Press.

Clapham, C. (ed.) (1982) *Private Patronage and Public Power*, London: Frances Pinter.

Collins, Neil and Cradden, Terry (2001) *Irish Politics Today*, Manchester: Manchester University Press.

Gallagher, M. and Komito, L. (1999) 'The Constituency Role of TDs', in J. Coakley and M. Gallagher (eds) *Politics in the Republic of Ireland*, London: Routledge.

Hazelkorn, E. (1986) 'Class, Clientelism and the Political Process in the Republic of Ireland', in P. Clancy, S. Drudy, K. Lynch and L. Dowd (eds) *Ireland: A Sociological Profile*, Dublin: Institute of Public Administration.

O'Carroll, J.P. (1987) 'Strokes, Cute Hoors and Sneaking Regarders: The Influence of Local Culture on Irish Political Style', *Irish Political Studies* 2: 77–92.

O'Sullivan, M.C. (1999), 'The Social and Political Characteristics of the Twenty-eighth Dáil', in M. Marsh and P. Mitchell (eds) *How Ireland Voted 1997*, Boulder, CO: Westview Press.

7   Policy networks and sub-national government in Ireland

Maura Adshead

Introduction

Few people engaged in studies of public policy have managed to avoid consideration of policy networks and the utility of network analysis. A great deal has been written and continues to be written about their capacity to further our understanding of the policy process. So much so that the discussion has grown tiresome, as those of contradictory viewpoints fail to convince one another and those of no firm view are increasingly frustrated by the proliferation of 'new improved' network explanations – all slightly different and yet all essentially the same. This chapter makes no great claims for the network methodology, other than those that everyone can already agree upon, but still it intends to push the debate about the utility of network analysis forward by showing how networks can most profitably be used for cross-national comparison. This approach is both methodologically and practically beneficial. In terms of the former, it advances the utility of policy networks by radically simplifying their use and acknowledging the need for typological heterodoxy. In terms of the latter, it allows us to draw practical insights from policy comparison which improve our understanding of, and facilitate lesson-drawing from, different policy processes.

Simply put, policy network analysis is a means by which to depict the relations between different policy actors in a given policy area without resorting to idiosyncratic descriptions of country-specific institutions and agents. Instead, network analysis allows us to map out the 'key players' in a given policy area by referring to their particular structural, associational or personal relations to each other. The explanatory utility of this approach is subject to debate. For some, it provides a neat way of representing complex policy arenas and policy-making processes in a few key groupings that provide a ready framework for analysis. Thus a network approach to the explanation of policy-making may, instead of providing long descriptive passages about the case study in question, refer instead to a range of key specified interests (governmental, bureaucratic, public, private or voluntary and so on) and the nature of their interactions with each other (Dowding 1994,1995). For others, this approach to policy explanation is more than simple description, since by emphasizing the importance of certain sorts of relationships in the policy arena over others (be they financial, professional, personal, institutional and so on), they claim to have added a qualitative distinction to their analysis (Richardson and Jordan 1979; R.A.W. Rhodes 1981a; Wilkes and Wright 1987; D. Marsh and Rhodes 1992). Much of the work using network analysis in Dutch and German academia goes still further, by suggesting that networks represent a new form of governance, one where central government has either lost or else substantially revised its omnipotent status in the policy process (Mayntz 1994; Klijn 1997; Kickert *et al.* 1997). Some even treat networks as an alternative more significant model for the ordering of interests than hierarchies or markets (Kenis and Schneider 1991). These approaches are discussed in more detail below, and an examination is made of the most usual criticisms made against network analysis, concerning their explanatory utility and the most appropriate level of analysis to which they should be applied.

Brief review of the evolution of this approach

Perhaps the first question we might ask about policy networks is whether they are a new way of *describing* the policy-making process or a new way of *thinking about it* entirely. Jordan (1990b) suggests that the idea of a policy network, if not the term itself, has been part and parcel of American political science for some time. Throughout the 1950s and 1960s, American studies of the policy process discussed the importance of regular contact between interest groups, bureaucratic agencies and government, characterizing the web of relations between these groups as tantamount to 'sub-government' in the policy process. Much of the sub-government literature emphasized the existence of certain 'privileged' groups with close relations to government, who by virtue of their position maintained a predominant influence over policy. In some cases, the superior ability of such groups to organize and control their members meant that they were able successfully to 'capture' the government agency responsible for their regulation – a phenomenon that became known as 'agency capture'. The allegedly *triangular* relationship between such interests, agencies and government was often referred to as the 'iron triangle' of government in much of the sub-government literature (Lowi 1969; Peters and Pierre 1986; Oldersma *et al.* 1999). Although this notion of government was refuted by pluralists such as Heclo and Wildavsky (1974; see also Heclo 1978), still the idea of the triangulation of power continued (McFarland 1987), though the extent of control exerted by such 'iron triangles' was often contested and the existence of alternative countervailing producer or professional interests was often presented as a vindication of pluralist explanations of the policy process (for a more substantive discussion on pluralism, see Chapter 2). Heclo (1978), for example, argued that although iron triangles might occasionally exist it was more normal for fairly open and permeable 'issue networks' or 'policy communities' to develop instead.

In Britain, writers such as Richardson and Jordan (1979) and Wilkes and Wright (1987) developed some of the ideas from the US sub-government literature in their characterization of the British policy process. Their studies of

British policy-making laid emphasis on the interpersonal nature of relations between policy actors, stressing the existence of disaggregated governmental sub-systems, which together with certain recognized interests form separate policy communities in their own field or interest. These 'policy communities' are characterized by three key features. First, there is a disintegration of central policy-making authority, whereby policy-making is divided into sub-systems within which the government, or government agencies, and pressure groups negotiate:

> The central point is that policy-making is fragmented into sub-systems and the main boundaries are between sub-systems rather than between component units of government, agencies and pressure groups, and interpenetration of department and client group, an osmosis in personnel terms with ex-civil servants appearing in groups (and less so, vice versa).
>
> (Richardson and Jordan 1979: 44)

Second, this organization of the policy-making process results in highly personalized relations between policy actors – it is increasingly difficult to differentiate groups, agencies and departments because they are players in the same game:

> Boundaries are unclear; 'government' and 'governed' is difficult to maintain as a distinction. Matching this complex network of organizations is a complex network of personnel. In effect, policy is now made between an internal and an external bureaucracy. So similar are both sides that transfer is relatively easy.
>
> (Richardson and Jordan 1979: 61)

The third and final feature of the policy community is its negotiated order and negotiated environment achieved through pragmatic improvisation and accommodation. 'Negotiated order' refers to the processes of give and take, of diplomacy and of bargaining, implying that social order must be continually 'worked at' (Richardson and Jordan 1979: 101). It also refers to the process of continuous reappraisal of problems whereby 'order is conceived in terms of a complex relationship between the daily negotiative process and a periodic appraisal process' (Richardson and Jordan 1979: 102). This is possible as a consequence of government's 'pragmatic improvisation', whereby new structures are created to ensure that policy authority is shared with private and semi-private institutions (Richardson and Jordan 1979: 59). Pragmatic solutions may be forged for all types of problems by means of 'accommodation'.[1]

Around the same time that Richardson and Jordan developed their ideas about sub-governmental systems and the development of policy networks, a second set of British scholars, associated primarily with Rhodes, were also deploying the notion of policy networks, but with a different analytical emphasis. The key emphasis in R.A.W. Rhodes's (1981a, 1981b) work was on inter-organizational relations and *structural* – as opposed to *personal* – relationships between political institutions.

Following Benson (1982: 148), Rhodes (1988: 77) defines a policy network as a cluster or complex of organizations connected to one another by resource dependencies. Rhodes argues that members of a policy network behave in such a manner that 'each deploys its resources, whether constitutional/legal, organizational, financial, political or informational to maximize influence over outcomes whilst trying to avoid becoming dependent on the other players' (D. Marsh and Rhodes 1992: 11). Networks, he argues, are rooted in resource exchange. As a consequence, the distribution of resources between actors in a specific network remains central to any explanation of the distribution of power in that network. In later work, Rhodes (1986, 1988) began to distinguish between different types of networks along two dimensions: first, according to the pre-eminence of identified interests which make up the network (professional, intergovernmental or producer networks, for example); and, second, according to the cohesiveness within the group. On the one hand, large atomized networks with no close professional, producer or governmental relations, he termed 'issue networks'. On the other hand, closely knit networks characterized by stable relations and restrictive memberships, he termed 'policy communities'.

Rhodes (1997: 9) argues that policy networks matter because of the way that they affect policy outcomes. Policy networks facilitate coordination of public and private interests and resources and, in that respect, may enhance efficiency in the implementation of public policy. In their extreme form, these networks may even become sufficiently concerted and cohesive to resist or even challenge state powers (Pierre and Peters 2000: 20). When they develop in this manner, they are essentially self-regulatory structures within their policy sector (see R.A.W Rhodes 1996a). Because of this, Rhodes (1997: 9–10) argues that the study of policy networks is important for six key reasons:

- they limit participation in the policy process;
- they define the roles of actors;
- they decide which issues will be included and excluded from the policy agenda;
- through the rules of the game, they shape the behaviour of actors;
- they privilege certain interests, not only by according them access but also by favouring their preferred policy outcomes;
- they substitute private government for public accountability.

Much of Rhodes's work draws upon continental European literature on inter-organizational theory (Hanf and Scharpf 1978; B. Martin and Mayntz 1991; Jordan and Schubert 1992). Both approaches are concerned with the development of modern society that is characterized by functional differentiation, whereby private organizations or quasi-governmental agencies have an increasingly important role to play in the policy process and often control key resources. Rhodes' (1994) work on the 'hollowing out of the state', for example, refers to the declining ability of central government to retain its 'control capacity' over policy outcomes (see also R.A.W. Rhodes 1996a). German and Dutch network analysts have gone even further, by suggesting that policy network analysis 'does not so much represent a new analytical perspective but rather signals a real change in the structure of the polity' (Mayntz 1994: 5), one where 'government organizations are no longer the central steering actor in policy activities' (Klijn 1997: 33). The idea, prevalent in German literature, is that networks are emerging as a new mode of governance which may be counterposed to alternative modes such as hierarchies and markets.

The idea of governance as *hierarchies* reflects the traditional Weberian model of public service used to characterize most Western democracies at the turn of the last century. This was essentially governance by law, whereby instead of the government seeking to bridge the public–private divide it strictly upheld the differentiation between the two. In this tradition, the state was conceived of as the epitome of collective interest and distinctly separate from the rest of society – governing society by the imposition of law and other forms of regulation. The idea of governance as *hierarchies* has since been dismissed by many, who contend that it only applies to earlier forms of 'Fordist' economy, where state organization was characterized by highly standardized forms of public service and where domestically controlled markets allowed the state unrivalled strength (Pierre and Peters 2000: 15–18). The idea of governance as *markets* reflects more contemporary attitudes about the efficacy of market solutions as opposed to 'big government', whereby markets are seen as the most efficient and just allocative mechanism available since they do not allow politics and politicians to 'interfere' in effective resource allocation.

As well as developing network models for state governance, European scholars have also used network analysis to model the increasingly complex policy arena provided by the European Union (EU) (Heritier 1993; Risse-Kappen 1996; Eising and Kohler-Koch 1999). Eising and Kohler-Koch's (1999; also Kohler-Koch 1996, 1997) theory of network governance in the EU proposes that the development of the EU is best understood as an exercise in *system building*, involving the transformation of European governance from a 'compound of member states, into an overarching transnational political space' (Kohler-Koch 1999: 19). Here, emphasis is given to the segmented and differentiated aspects of the European polity at national and sub-national levels and their capacity for congruent development.

Perhaps the most widely known deployment of the network concepts in European integration studies is Marks and Hooghe's development of multi-level governance theory (Marks *et al.* 1996a; Marks *et al.* 1996b). Multi-level governance approaches to EU policy-making are based on three main assumptions: first, decision-making competencies are *shared* by actors at different levels rather than monopolized by state executives; second, collective decision-making between member states implies some loss of control by individual state executives; and, third, political arenas are interconnected rather than nested. Thus, whilst multi-level governance theorists do not reject the notion that state executives and state arenas are 'the most important pieces of the European puzzle', they nevertheless assert that states have lost their monopoly – both over

European policy-making and over the aggregation of domestic interests (Marks *et al.* 1996b: 346).

The rising tide of network analysis in EU studies points to the obvious heuristic utility of policy network models for studies of EU policy-making (Adshead 2002: 6). By their nature, policy network models are able to portray the intricacy of newly emerging governance systems in the EU. They are able to highlight the interactions and 'networking' between different types of policy interests at supranational, national and, increasingly, sub-national levels of government; within the public and private spheres; and at the interface between traditional government institutions and actors and increasingly significant new governance institutions and actors (such as quangos, para-public bodies and various associations from civil society). In doing so, studies of the EU using network analysis are able to contribute to and help support interpretations of the EU polity as multi-level governance. Indeed, the proliferation of these studies supports

> a growing convergence among international relations and comparative scholars conceptualizing the EU as a multi-level structure of governance where private, governmental, transnational and supranational actors deal with each other in highly complex networks of varying density, as well as horizontal and vertical depth.
>
> (Risse-Kappen 1996: 62)

Mainstream variants in contemporary usage

In order to impose order on a proliferating variety of network definitions, R.A.W. Rhodes and Marsh (1992) constructed a typology based on the distinction between policy communities and networks using 'policy network' as a generic term. The typology proposes a continuum, marked at each end by an ideal-type – at one end the policy community, and at the other the issue network (see Table 7.1). The positioning of individual studies in relation to either ideal-type is a matter for empirical research. According to the Rhodes and Marsh typology, an ideal-type policy community has the following characteristics: a limited number of participants *with some groups consciously excluded*; frequent and high-quality interaction between all members of the community on all matters related to policy communities; consistency in values, membership and policy outcomes, which persist; consensus, with the ideology, values and broad policy preferences shared by all participants; all members of the policy community have resources, so the links between them are exchange relationships. As a result of this last criterion, the basic interaction in the policy community is one involving bargaining between members with resources. Rhodes and Marsh propose that in the ideal-type policy community there is a balance of power which is a positive-sum arrangement, even if all members do not benefit equally. They suggest that the structures of the participating groups are hierarchical, so that leaders can guarantee compliant members. Rhodes and Marsh's characterization of an ideal-type issue network is in many instances the extreme opposite of the policy community: many participants; fluctuating interaction and access for the various members; limited consensus and ever-present conflict; interaction based on consultation rather than negotiation or bargaining; and, finally, an unequal power relationship in which many participants may have few resources, limited access to decision-making fora and scant influence over decision-making.

The Rhodes and Marsh (1992) typology presents a useful set of organizing concepts for comparison because the network concepts described above can be applied in different European states, with different policy-making institutions, organizations and actors. Using this typology not only facilitates uniform characterizations of policy processes in different states, but also allows a range of comparisons along the five suggested dimensions of network analysis: the number of participants and the type of interests they represent; the relations between policy actors in terms of the frequency, quality and continuity of their interactions; the distribution of resources amongst them, in terms of finances, status, access to information or authority; and the distribution of power or policy authority between key policy actors and institutions (Adshead 2002). Still, however, there remains the problem of how to relate the differences found between alternative networks to a common independent variable, for if this cannot be done the comparative utility of network analysis is lost. It is this issue of finding and defining key independent variables in order to explain network differentiation that left network approaches most vulnerable to criticisms over their explanatory utility.

Major criticisms

Critics argue that the difficulty with networks is that once they have been used to characterize the policy process their explanatory utility is exhausted. Dowding (1994, 1995) argues that they are 'merely a set of metaphors' created for the study of British and European politics. Keohane and Hoffman (1990) have made the same claim, though directed more specifically at European-level policy-making. The central argument of this critique is that unless network analysis can explain *why* the differences between certain network types exist, their only use is in positing new ways to characterize different policy-making processes, which are perhaps no better than those that preceded them. If this is the case, then network analysis can add nothing new to characterizations of the policy process since all it offers are 'newfangled' models of policy processes which still resort to standard macro-economic or political theories in order to explain their existence. Dowding (1995: 269) argues that 'network approaches fail because the driving force of the explanation, the independent variables, are not the network characteristics *per se* but rather characteristics of components within the networks'. These components explain both the nature of the network *and* the nature of the policy process'. Referring to the two chief alternative sets of network characterizations in British politics (see above, pp. 116), Dowding argues that:

Table 7.1 The Marsh and Rhodes typology of networks

Dimension	Policy community	Issue network
Membership:		
No. of participants	Very limited number, some groups consciously excluded	Large
Type of interest	Economic and/or professional interests dominate	Encompasses range of affected interests
Integration:		
Frequency of interaction	Frequent, high-quality interaction of all groups on all matters related to policy issue	Contacts fluctuate in frequency and intensity
Continuity	Membership, values and outcomes persistent over time	Access fluctuates significantly
Consensus	All participants share basic values and accept the legitimacy of the outcome	A measure of agreement exists, but conflict is ever present
Resources:		
Distribution of resources within network	All participants have resources; basic relationship is an exchange relationship	Some participants may have resources, but they are limited; basic relationship is consultative
Distribution of resources within participating organizations	Hierarchical; leaders can deliver members	Varied and variable distribution and capacity to regulate members
Power:	There is a balance of power among members; although one group may dominate, it must be a positive-sum game if community is to persist	Unequal powers, reflecting unequal resources and unequal access; it is a zero-sum game

Source: R.A.W. Rhodes (1997: 44).

The network protagonists have tried to answer empirical questions by definitional dogma rather than constructing theories – which often already exist – to explain their empirical observations. Conversely, they try to resolve theoretical disputes by reference to evidence compatible with both theories. Essentially the conflict between Jordan and the Rhodes–Marsh acolytes is over the nature of the state. Both sides use their versions of network theory to try to secure their position, but the empirical evidence they cite is exactly the same.

(Dowding 1994: 66)

Dowding's criticisms regarding the deployment of network concepts raise two contentious issues regularly associated with critiques of network analysis. First, they indicate that if network concepts are to be employed successfully in policy analysis it is paramount to choose an accompanying explanatory theory for which the evidence collected cannot be claimed by opposing theoretical viewpoints. This has most usually been the downfall of network analysis deployed in order to make claims about the nature of the state. Second, and related to the first issue, they indicate the importance of clarifying the level (or levels) of analysis to which the network analysis is being directed.

Outside international relations (IR) literature, policy-making studies are often referred to as middle-range or meso-level analysis, falling midway between macro (or systemic) and micro (or actor-oriented) levels of policy analysis. Taking the EU as an example, a macro-level study of European integration might seek to characterize the collection of entities that together make up the EU as a 'governance regime' in its own right, whereby the sum (the EU as a polity) is bigger than the parts (the constituent states, interests and institutions). This approach is developed by Bulmer's (1994) adaptation of new institutionalism as a way of characterizing the revival of European integration in the mid-1980s. Micro-level studies of European integration, however, would seek to examine particular developments occurring within states or institutions, or amongst interests in the EU (see, for example, Fitzmaurice 1988; Nicoll 1984; Teasdale 1993). Meso-level analysis, by contrast, concentrates on sectoral studies. The intention of this level of analysis is to characterize broader patterns of change than would be possible in single micro-level studies and to give greater explanatory detail than is possible with macro-level studies. Thus meso-level analysis is designed to give explanatory depth by simplifying a complex political system and focusing on one part of that whole without losing sight of the 'bigger picture' (see, for example, Adshead 1996; Bomberg 1994; Ford and Lake 1991; Geyer 1996). The same may be said of state-focused policy studies.

It is in relation to problems over levels of analysis that many network explanations of the policy process have come to grief. By detailing the existence of networks operating within some wider political context and relating the existence of the networks found to other theories, at either the macro or micro level, network analysts are criticized for confusing the *explanandum* (that which needs to be explained, viz. different policy processes) with the *explanans* (the explanation itself, viz. different policy networks).[2] In other words, by developing comprehensive contextualizations of the policy environment within which the networks under study are found, it is not clear whether or not the deployment of network concepts actually adds anything to the study which was not already covered by the description of the network environment. In this respect, it is often argued that network evaluations of policy outcomes in different states rely too heavily on the use of macro-level theories of the state. At worst, this leads scholars to point out that policy networks are configured differently in different states. At best, it enables scholars to agree on the differences between networks observed, but to disagree on the macro-level explanation of the state (corporatism, pluralism, Marxian political economy, etc.) that produces them. It is this observation that brings criticisms about the deployment of network analysis full circle, by suggesting that because network characterizations of the policy process do not clearly identify an independent variable for analysis of policy change they fail to produce anything other than a new way of describing traditional policy processes and problems.

The following case study of Irish sub-national government is presented using network analysis in order to see if these criticisms hold true and whether or not there is anything to be said for network explanations of the policy process.

Case study: sub-national and regional regeneration

For local government purposes, the Irish state is divided into twenty-nine county and five county borough (city) areas of equivalent status, each with a separate elected council. The five county borough corporations represent large urban populations (in Dublin, Cork, Waterford and Limerick) existing within their respective county boundaries. Below this tier of local government is a lower tier of representative authorities in the smaller urban areas of counties and county boroughs: there are five borough corporations, forty-nine urban district councils and twenty-six town commissioners (Government of Ireland 1996: 97). There was originally a set of rural district councils too, but these were abolished and their powers transferred to the county councils in the 1920s (Sinnott 1995: 254).

Although the counties and county boroughs have equivalent legal status as the main units of local government in rural and urban areas respectively, some functions are carried out by county councils throughout the entire county, including the urban areas represented by county boroughs.[3] Similarly, at sub-county level some functions that are legally vested in urban authorities are exercised on their behalf by the county council on foot of local agreements (Government of Ireland 1996). Though the county is the most important unit of local government, its range of functions is limited, relating primarily to physical infrastructure and public recreation facilities (Sinnott 1995: 255). These include the provision and organization of public housing, local road networks, water supply, waste management and sewerage, the maintenance of public amenities and a limited role in environmental protection. County councils also have some secondary functions in the areas of education, health and welfare, though in these areas they are subordinate to the specialized state-sponsored bodies (SSBs) responsible for each of these areas.[4]

SSBs are 'autonomous public bodies, other than universities, neither temporary in character nor purely advisory in function' (IPA 1997: 128). There are five types of SSB: commercial, developmental, health, cultural and regulatory/advisory.[5] The creation of numerous SSBs and the transfer of functions to them that might otherwise be the responsibility of local government typify Irish government attitudes to policy delivery, whereby practical problems are often solved at the expense of democratic accountability. The development of the 'managerial system' in Irish local government further illustrates this point.[6] Under this system, the provision of all local services falls under the direction of a single individual – the city or county manager – answerable to the council, but with a statutory position and statutory powers.[7] The consequence of this is virtually a single administration in each county area (Chubb 1992: 271).

Over time, sub-county districts faced the problem of how to provide an increasing range of public services with a relative scarcity of technical, administrative and financial resources when compared to larger county units. As a result, many gave up some of their functions to county level. Counties and county boroughs (the major cities that have county status) increasingly began to dominate sub-national government, and 'local government in Ireland became and is now primarily county council government' (Chubb 1992: 271). Added to this, the small number of elected authorities at sub-county level (represented by boroughs, urban districts and town commissioners) means that by the standards of comparable small states there are very few locally elected councils (T.J. Barrington 1980: 43). Over the years, despite numerous reports and policy studies instigated by central government (Government of Ireland 1971, 1973, 1985, 1991), no major changes occurred. With the exception of a little tinkering to the system here and there, it could reasonably be argued that Irish local government has changed very little since the foundation of the state.[8]

Despite the lack of any formal institutional reorganization of sub-national government, over time the need to develop policy delivery mechanisms led to the creation of several types of organization operating at sub-national level (Chubb 1992: 262). On the one hand, there are a number of authorities responsible for the administration of some service, whose governing bodies consist both of members of the local authority and of interested associations or groups in the region, such as the eight Area Health Boards or the eight Regional Tourism Organizations. On the other hand, some central authorities have themselves decentralized their business to regional level for administrative, managerial or customer convenience. These include SSBs such as the Electricity Supply Board (ESB), the Industrial Development Authority (IDA) and certain government departments. The authorities with devolved powers and those with decentralized administrations all operate boundaries to suit themselves, and so the regional areas thus far created do not coincide. Chubb notes that since there is also an underlying network of local authorities, 'the result is a jungle of administrative areas that is both impenetrable to the ordinary citizen and frequently inconvenient for any kind of business that involves more than one authority or regional organization' (1992: 263).

Much more could be (and has been) written about the beleaguered state of Irish local government, but even this short review gives an indication of the dense network of organizations operating at ground level and the potentially complex range of interactions between them. This 'administrative jungle' has been further complicated in recent years by an enormous increase in development activities at this level – many driven by EU initiatives – that seek to incorporate an ever wider circle of policy actors into sub-national government. Although these initiatives have varying aims and objectives, it is possible to identify common approaches. There has been an emphasis on the creation of partnerships that have fostered innovation, bringing together actors from statutory, voluntary, public and private sectors in a manner that has gained international recognition (OECD 1996).

New approaches to local development have resulted in local authorities acquiring new functions: instead of operating as administrative agents of central government, with responsibility for a limited number of services, they now act as central coordinators for the ever widening arena of actors in sub-national development. The 1994 Programme for Government stated that 'the local authority must become the focus for working through local partnerships involving local community-based groupings, voluntary bodies, the private sector, and public agencies' (Government of Ireland 1994: 70). In this regard, the Operational Programme for Local Urban and Rural Development 1994–9 (OPLURD) supported this new view of local authorities and provided significant evidence of local authorities taking a new approach to partnership initiatives at local level.

According to the terms outlined earlier in this chapter, these developments in Irish sub-national governance might be construed as evidence of a move away from *governance as hierarchies* to new forms of *network governance*. The challenge, then, is how depict this change so as to interpret the institutional mosaic that comprises Irish sub-national government in some meaningful way. The following account uses interview material and original research from a broader cross-national comparison of sub-national government in Germany, Ireland and Britain (Adshead 2002). In each case study area, having selected a number of 'obvious candidates' for interview, the extent of the policy network was subsequently determined by reputational analysis, so that the final arbiters of who should or should not be included in the policy network were those individuals and institutions involved in the policy process themselves. In this study, the focus was on regional regeneration policy.

Interviews were designed to find out who were the 'main players' in regional policy, and it was not long before a consensus emerged in each case study about who were the most important policy actors: these constituted the network's membership. Network resources and dynamics were investigated by asking each interviewee a series of questions about the operation of regional policy within the network: what function they performed; what they believed to be the most significant developments in the operation of regional policy and how they were affected by them; whether or not they could determine the functional responsibilities of other network members; what links they had with other network members and what was the nature of these associations – formal/informal, personal/institutional, strong/weak, etc.; which network members were best at promoting their aims and objectives. These questions formed the basic interview structure, but the questions were open-ended and interviewees were encouraged to contribute their own views and opinions about the conduct of regional development strategies. Interviews were also designed to ascertain what the trends in regional policy formulation and implementation were and which actors played the most significant role in policy change. The following picture emerged.

Network formation

In contrast to other states, where the autonomy of regional or local government is constitutionally guaranteed, the formation of regional policy networks in Ireland is a much more informal affair. Although the Irish government takes responsibility for guiding and directing regional policy (through the various Operational Programmes of the five-year National Development Plans), it leaves the initiative and details of policy implementation to a range of regional development interests at local level – a practice which has been referred to elsewhere as Irish 'state-sponsored bottom-up development' (Adshead and Quinn 1998: 219). In this sense, the organizational framework for current development strategies represents government attempts to give formal acknowledgement to a range of pre-existing local development borders and boundaries as they have tended to be drawn up in policy practice.

The conversion throughout the 1990s, by Irish policy-makers and practitioners alike, to the 'bottom-up' approach to regional development means that, despite a renewed interest in the reform of local government and even limited moves towards proposals for regional devolution, the small-scale county boundary has remained the most important administrative unit. This has occurred less by design and more by default. The 'administrative jungle' created by the differing regional boundaries of the many various state agencies and SSBs renders them meaningless in terms of their ability to define sub-national administrative or organizational units, further justifying the use of the one administrative unit which has a long history and widespread acceptance (Chubb 1992: 262). Additionally, the strong culture of localism and personalism in Irish politics makes the county boundary the largest meaningful political unit for effective local politicking (Schmidt 1973; Farrell 1983; Gallagher and Komito 1992). Finally, in 1995 the establishment by central government of County Strategy Groups (CSGs) – designed to secure intra-programme linkages and integration of development policy at local level – copper-fastened the importance of the county unit as the primary unit of evaluation in studies of local development. Following a change of government in 1996, CSGs were dropped in favour of Strategic Policy Committees (SPCs). Carrying out a broadly similar role to the CSGs, SPCs were established for all major service areas in each local authority. Their membership is comparable to that of the CSGs, with the addition of a local council member to support the broader inclusion of public representatives. SPCs have been augmented with the creation of City/County Development Boards, charged with the task of preparing integrated strategies for local economic, social and cultural development and taking cognizance of all locally delivered associated public services. Strategies were due for completion in January 2002.

The importance attached to strategic planning and programming of development initiatives compensates for the lack of formally defined administrative boundaries in the formation of development policy networks. Strategic programming at national and sub-national level gives legitimacy to a range of policy actors, helping to set the parameters of policy and the level of involvement between different policy actors. Essentially, development policy networks are formed almost entirely by local consensus. Irish government support for 'bottom-up' development strategies encourages the participation of a wide range of local actors, including public bodies, private interests and community groups. The emphasis on multi-agency responses to regeneration, whereby the same actors are often involved in different projects with different partners, contributes further to the ad-hoc and more informal nature of regional policy networks: there are, for example, no definitive functional or territorial divisions between different network actors, nor any hierarchical relationships between them. Establishing policy coordination in this way means that network boundaries are not formally drawn by any outside agency. The structure and scope of the networks are determined by negotiation and consensus between a range of development actors operating across the county.

Network membership

In Ireland, changed approaches to development policy which place great emphasis on partnership in, and ownership of, the development process have significantly influenced the configuration of regional policy actors. Since the mid-1980s, a series of national concordats between the government and 'Social Partners' – national representative associations from business and trade unions – have provided continued support for area-based development partnerships (Adshead and Quinn 1998: 217). The condition of government support for these partnerships, however, is that 'integrated area action plans should be drawn up in consultation with such other local groups and bodies, public agencies and local representatives of the social partners as appropriate'.[9] Area partnership plans must set out the basic strategy to achieve the objectives of economic and social revitalization in their area (CEC 1993). The Irish government's commitment to partnership approaches to policy-making in general and regional policy in particular has led to the inclusion of the broadest range of development interests in the regional policy process.

Although the number of interests represented is high, they are organized in such a way that regional policy networks can be understood by reference to a few key groupings: the City/County Development Boards, guided by a member of the central government's Local Development Liaison Team and including all of those bodies funded through OPLURD; the local authorities; locally constituted Enterprise Boards; locally based partnership initiatives; and the various state agencies and SSBs that have some role to play in regional development. In many cases membership of one of these groups does not preclude membership of another. The staff of local Enterprise Boards, for example, are often seconded from their local authorities. Similarly, when many local development partnership companies were established they sought experienced officers from other local development agencies. As a result, most partnership companies and LEADER[10] groups throughout Ireland have representatives at board level from a variety of SSBs, their local Enterprise Boards, their local Council and other relevant statutory agencies.

One of the most interesting features of Irish regional policy networks is the non-structured nature of their membership. Typically, relations between network members are functionally, as opposed to hierarchically, determined. Sharing resources on a 'project-to-project basis' prevents the formation of hierarchical relations. This is illustrated by the fact that, although a single agency may be involved in a number of projects, it may lead on only one, whilst other different projects are headed by other different agencies. With such fluid and open network memberships, it is perhaps useful to refer to the ideal-type policy community characterized by Richardson and Jordan (1979). Whereas Marsh and Rhodes emphasized the importance of exclusive memberships, which were often hierarchically organized, Richardson and Jordan emphasized the importance of interpersonal relationships between policy actors. Their model of a policy community is characterized by the disintegration of policy-making authority, with policy-making negotiated amongst sub-systems made up of government and/or government agencies and other interests. Negotiation is achieved through pragmatic improvisation and accommodation. The Irish emphasis on programmatic government, evidenced in the nine Operational Programmes which together made up the National Development Plan 1994–9, supports the notion that in Ireland policy-making has been divided into a series of governmental sub-systems.[11]

Network resources

In Ireland, there is no automatic mechanism to ensure an equitable distribution of resources for development. There is, however, a degree of indicative development planning in the OPLURD framework which stipulates what types and forms of local development are most desirable. There is also a noticeable disposition towards integrated strategic programming and planning in all aspects of policy implementation. Still, development actors and agencies are expected to tender for funding on the basis of concrete development proposals, and partnership bids between public and private interests are encouraged. The Irish budgetary model may be distinguished from others (such as the British, for example) by its explicit support for *community development* and its positive action in favour of *social and economic cohesion*. By attaching conditions to regional aid funding (such as widespread local consultation and representation, and favouring multi-agency initiatives and strategic programming), the Irish government approach to regional policy financing is designed to foster co-operation within and between regional policy networks rather than stimulate damaging competition.

This attitude is further encouraged by the Irish government's heavy reliance on EU Structural Funds assistance in support of regional policies. First and foremost, instead of attempting to substitute EU funding for national public expenditure, the Irish government has levered the maximum amount of financial support available from the EU by providing the matching funding required by the EU principle of additionality. This has helped to eliminate damaging competition for funds within and between regional policy networks. The variety of alternative funding sources also help to prevent direct rivalry between agencies involved in policy implementation. For example, funding for the Enterprise Boards is issued annually through the Department of Trade, Enterprise and Employment. LEADER groups receive their funding through the Department of Agriculture, which administers the EU LEADER programme, whilst Area Partnerships receive funding from the government's Area Based Regeneration (ABR) initiative and as part of the *Partnership 2000* programme for government.

Second, and equally important, the incorporation of EU Community Support Frameworks into national regional policy programmes and initiatives enables the government to integrate its own public expenditure with that provided by the EU in the most cost-effective way. The fact that EU Community Support Frameworks for Ireland are incorporated into the Irish government National Development Plans means that the goals, objectives and targets of national regional policy, together with the policy instruments used to bring them about, coincide exactly with, and are supported by, EU Structural Funded programmes.

Third, Irish government emphasis on the value of integrated strategic planning in general, and in particular the prospect of secured funding for up to five years, promotes joint projects and co-operation across regional policy networks. Thus, despite the absence of institutionally based strategic planning, regional policy integration is the consequence of a deliberate change in policy style – the so-called 'moves towards new governance' expressed through increasing interest in 'government by partnership' and 'bottom-up' approaches to development (Walsh 1995).

In summary, regional policy networks in Ireland and Germany reflect the typical policy community features outlined by Rhodes and Marsh (1992) relating to the distribution of resources. They have adequate finances which are deployed effectively between a variety of agencies who are encouraged to co-operate with each other, supporting Rhodes and Marsh's proposition that in a policy community 'all members of the policy network have resources, so the links between them are exchange relationships'. Thus the basic interaction is 'one involving bargaining between network members with resources, so that there is a balance of power, not necessarily one in which all members equally benefit but one in which all members see themselves as in a positive-sum game' (R.A.W. Rhodes 1997: 43–4).

Network dynamics

Irish regional policy networks are based on a 'partnership model' of politics. In the absence of formal functional and institutional organizations for development policy, which might have been provided by strong local government, the formation of Irish regional policy networks is much more informally based and is a function of locally based personal and functional relationships between regional development interests. This, together with a long history of volunteerism and community activism and successive government initiatives designed to foster partnership and multi-agency approaches to development, has meant that the membership of Irish regional policy networks tends to be open and non-hierarchical.

This approach to policy formulation is further encouraged by the way in which Irish regional policy is funded. Since the resources for any single project may be made up from funds gathered from many different agencies and sources, it is only practical for network members to develop good relations with each other – not only as potential recipients of regional aid, but also as potential sponsors and co-funders. The fact that local government has embraced this new form of policy-making has helped to cement its introduction: by contributing to development projects led by alternative development agencies, local authorities are often able to circumscribe much of the bureaucracy created when the council alone takes on a project using public funding. Moreover, by co-operating with a range of alternative development agencies, the local authorities are able to maximize the impact of their limited resources, whilst the local partnerships and community groups are beginning to recognize the authorities as partners in local development – rather than the political or bureaucratic fiefdoms which they were once assumed to be. The increased use of partnerships in local development initiatives reflects a change of attitude towards the financing of regional development in Ireland as well as a recognition that partnership strategies are often the most effective way to coordinate the regional regeneration (OECD 1996). This attitude to the financing and organization of regional policy in Ireland is best summed up as a positive-sum organization of policy, thus supporting the view that Irish regional policy networks are still best understood as ideal-type policy communities.

Network characterization

We can see from the case study presented above that in Ireland regional policy networks exhibit a 'consistency in policy values, membership and policy outcomes which persists over time', together with a 'consensus over the ideology, values and broad policy preferences shared by all participants', which supports Rhodes and Marsh's (1992) propositions about policy communities. There is

Table 7.2 Locating Irish sub-national policy networks in the Marsh and Rhodes typology

Formation	Responsibility for regional policy is decentralized to local level; network boundaries determined by personal interactions; negotiated order achieved through strategic planning and partnership initiatives
Membership	Wide-ranging and inclusive membership which is non-hierarchically and informally organized into a few key groups, representing a mixture of public, private, community and voluntary organizations
Resources	All participants have equal access to resources, so that basic relationships are exchange relationships
Dynamics	Highly personalized, non-hierarchical relations between policy actors, blurring the distinction between 'government' and 'governed'; negotiated order which is constantly 'worked at' through pragmatic innovation and accommodation
Power	There is a balance of power among members which supports positive-sum outcomes; all members perceive themselves to be sufficiently better off in this set-up to ensure its continuance

success of partnership initiatives across Ireland illustrates the negotiated consensus between policy actors over policy preferences and desired outcomes suggested by Richardson and Jordan's model of a policy community, and there is widespread evidence of highly personalized and informal relations across a range of policy areas (Adshead 1996; Laffan 1989; O'Toole 1995). Moreover, in relation to regional development the adoption of 'bottom-up' approaches to regeneration (where emphasis is placed upon building the capacity of the population through enabling principles such as *partnership* and *subsidiarity*) has brought together actors from statutory, voluntary, public and private sectors in 'a way that blurs familiar distinctions between public and private, national and local, and representative and participative democracy' (OECD 1996: 9). As in the Richardson and Jordan model of policy communities, the distinction between 'government' and 'governed' is often difficult to maintain (Richardson and Jordan 1979: 61). Irish regional policy networks are based on a negotiated order and environment which is achieved through pragmatic improvisation and accommodation, again supporting their interpretation as *policy communities*.

Summary review of theoretical utility

Recapping the arguments and issues raised already about the deployment of network concepts in the explanation of public policy, and specifically in relation to the case study outlined above, we can ask three main questions about the utility of network analysis. First, what is its heuristic utility? Second, does its deployment add any new insights into the analysis? Third, does its deployment give us any greater insight into the nature of the state?

In relation to the first point, it is clear that a network characterization of the range of actors and organizations involved in Irish sub-national government does make for a relatively easy explanation. If we were to list all of the organizations involved in the so-called 'administrative jungle', the list would be a long one and the descriptive narrative commensurately dense. Moreover, by grouping together certain organizational types in the network membership it becomes easier to see how different kinds of network members interact and relate to each other in the policy process. This relates to the second issue about the deployment of network concepts. It could be argued that by presenting the material in this way, this characterization of the policy arena highlights the informal and ad-hoc nature of relations between policy actors. Undoubtedly, other depictions of Irish policy processes that do not use network analysis have made this claim already. Still, however, the network depiction of sub-national government does enable us to characterize the structure and form of the policy-making arena (in this case, as a policy community) despite the absence of formal administrative or organizational boundaries. And in this sense it could be argued that we have developed new insights into the organization of the policy process that traditional institutionalist depictions of the policy process would not have raised or highlighted. Finally, does this new insight into the policy process at sub-national level give us any greater insight into the nature of the state more generally? Certainly, we can see evidence of a move away from *governance as hierarchies* to new more flexible forms of governance. Whether or not this represents an entirely new form of governance or a subtle reorientation of existing forms remains open to debate (see R.A.W. Rhodes 1996a; Adshead and Quinn 1998).

The lesson from this study is that although the Rhodes and Marsh (1992) typology presents us with a useful set of organizing concepts for policy analysis it is a little too restrictive when applied to policy studies outside the UK. Whilst the simplicity of the Rhodes and Marsh (1992) typology revived the analytical utility of network analysis, still the fact that it was so strongly influenced by their own involvement in UK policy studies meant that, despite the obvious heuristic capacities of policy networks, their suitability for cross-national application and/or policy comparison was diminished. The importance, for example, that Marsh and Rhodes attached to structural/financial aspects of UK government organization led them to emphasize these explanatory variables over and above others that might have more explanatory capacity in other states (see, for example, Heclo 1978; Wilkes and Wright 1987; Oldersma *et al.* 1999). This deficiency has since been recognized and explored at length (D. Marsh and Smith

2000), but still the tendency is for single case studies which are mainly concerned with UK policy-making. In this study, the deployment of network analysis to study a non-UK state where the policy environment is quite different to that found in the UK raises questions about the wisdom of preferring certain explanatory variables over others (such as structure over agency) when carrying out empirical research. Thus, for example, the case study on Ireland in particular reaffirms the contribution that earlier scholars, such as Richardson and Jordan (1979), made to the network literature. Moreover, it suggests that, instead of trying to make claims for network analysis that are readily contested (about the nature of the state, for example), networks can claim an explanatory utility all of their own if they are deployed primarily for cross-national policy comparison.

Notes

1   Accommodation is a term coined by Arend Lijphart (1968) to convey the process by which divisive issues and conflicts in the Netherlands are settled despite only a minimal consensus.
2   Dowding (1994: 66).
3   These include motor taxation, library services, fire, building control, emergency planning, generally national and regional roads, and most aspects of pollution control.
4   The Vocational Education Committee (VEC) for education, and the eight regional Health Boards that deal with health and welfare.
5   Examples of SSBs include: *An Bord Trachtala* – The Irish Trade Board; *Bord Fáilte* – the Tourism Board; *Cóillte* – the Forestry Board; *FÁS* (*Foras Aiseanna Sáothair*) – the Training and Employment Authority; *Forbáirt*, providing a range of science and technology services and programmes for enterprise to facilitate the development of Irish business; *Forfás* – the policy advisory and coordination board for industrial development and science technology; the Industrial Development Authority (IDA) – designed to create employment by providing incentives for foreign enterprises to set up in Ireland; and *Teagasc* – the Agriculture and Food Development Authority.
6   The Cork City Management Act (1929) – the consequence of lobbying by businesses and professionals for a more accountable system of local government – marked the introduction in Ireland of the 'managerial system'. It was followed by a series of local Acts for various cities, culminating in the County Management Act of 1940, which extended the system and operationalized it throughout the state by 1942.
7   The main functions reserved for elected members include: the adoption of the annual estimate of expenses; the fixing of annual rates and amounts to be borrowed to meet these expenses; the making of development plans and by-laws, house-building programmes; and assisting other local bodies in providing services and amenities. These various functions can be exercised only on the passing of a resolution. Executive functions, which are the responsibility of the county/city manager, include: arrangements made by the manager in relation to staff; acceptance of tenders; making contracts; fixing rents; making lettings; and deciding on applications for planning permission.
8   The 1963 Local Government (Planning and Development) Act was intended to give local authorities greater freedom to expand their developmental role without the need for constant referral to central government. In practice, however, it served primarily to strengthen the role of the county managers at the expense of elected council officials. In 1991 the area covered by Dublin County Council and Dun Laoghaire Corporation was re-divided into four county authorities: Dublin County Council was reduced and three new county boundaries were created in Fingal, South Dublin and Dun Laoghaire/Rathdown.

9 This condition arises from the mainstreaming of Article 4 in the agreement signed between the Irish government, Area Development Management (the Irish agency responsible for distributing EU Structural Funds assistance) and the European Commission on all regional policy initiatives. This Article also outlines the three main purposes of regional assistance: first, to promote and assist integrated local socio-economic development and make a positive contribution to economic and employment development in local communities, in terms of enterprise creation and development leading to increased employment; second, where possible to bring about an explicit and targeted redistribution of job chances towards the unemployed by providing the training and/or education necessary to enable them to participate in local development programmes; and, third, to support the main forces of local development by contributing to capacity building of local organizations with a view to enabling them to participate as primary movers in local development programmes (see CEC 1993).

10 LEADER (liaisons entre actions de développement de l'économie rurale) is a European Commission-sponsored Community Initiative designed to assist rural development.

11 The National Development Plan 1994–9 comprises the following Operational Programmes: Industry (which includes a Food Sub-programme); Tourism; Transport (roads, sea ports, airports and rail); Environmental Services (water, sanitary and waste services, coastal erosion); Economic Infrastructure (telecommunications, postal services, energy); Agriculture, Rural Development and Forestry; Fisheries; Human Resources; and Local Development (County Enterprise Boards, area-based approach to disadvantaged areas, Community Employment Development Programme and Social Employment Scheme, Urban Renewal) (Government of Ireland 1993: 161).

Further reading

Adshead, M. (2002) *Developing European Regions? Comparative Governance, Policy Networks and European Integration*, Aldershot: Ashgate.

Bomberg, E. (1994) 'Policy Networks on the Periphery: EU Environmental Policy and Scotland', *Regional Politics and Policy* 4: 45–61.

Dowding, K. (1995) 'Model or Metaphor: A Critical Review of the Policy Network Approach', *Political Studies* 43: 265–77.

Marsh, D. and Rhodes, R.A.W. (eds) (1992) *Policy Networks in British Government*, Oxford: Clarendon Press.

Richardson, J.J. and Jordan, G. (1979) *Governing under Pressure. The Policy Process in a Post-parliamentary Democracy*, Oxford: Martin Robertson.

8 Institutionalism 'old' and new: exploring the Mother and Child scheme

Michelle Millar

Introduction

Institutions – both formal and informal – exist all around us: they mould and shape our daily actions, consciously and unconsciously. We are all familiar with formal institutions, such as the government, firms, hospitals, universities, which are all responsible for the organisation of key activities in our lives. Many of us, however, are less familiar with the idea of *informal institutions*, which are equally important in shaping the way our lives are organised. For example, the rules of the road constitute an informal institution: in Ireland, we all know to drive on the left hand side of the road, dip our headlights for oncoming traffic and obey the speed limit; if not, there will be negative consequences for us and other drivers. Just as formal institutions work because they have rules, so too do informal institutions like the rules of the road. Other drivers know what to expect of us and we know what to expect of them. Without the rules of the road there would be chaos.

In this chapter we consider the study of institutions or 'institutionalism' as an approach to understanding the policy process. Koeble argues that the institutional approach goes to the 'heart' of the basic problem of social science because it addresses the balance regarding '[h]ow much weight ought to be given to the individual and to the institutional context within which decisions are made and to the larger environmental factors such as culture, social norms, and conventions' (1995: 231–2). Thus, institutionalism as an approach seeks to discover the role that institutions play in the determination of social and political outcomes (Hall and Taylor 1996: 936), and the basic idea of institutionalist approaches to understanding politics and policy is that 'all participants in a political process understand and accept the rules of that process' (Gorges 2001: 138). As March and Olsen put it:

> The core notion is that life is organised by sets of shared meanings and practices that come to be taken as given for a long time. Political actors act and organise themselves in accordance with the rules and practices which are socially constructed, publicly known, anticipated and accepted. Actions

of individuals and collectives occur within these shared meanings and practices, which can be called institutions and identities.

(March and Olsen 1997: 141)

This chapter begins by considering 'old' institutionalism as a context for the development of 'new' institutionalist approaches. It will review the three 'new institutionalisms' and summarise the major criticisms levelled at them. The case study in this chapter utilises these new institutionalist approaches as a methodology for understanding events surrounding the introduction of the Mother and Child health scheme of 1951. This key example of early developments in Irish health policy is most often cited as a typical example of a clash between Church and state. We will see, however, that by deploying an institutionalist approach to the explanation of events, there appears to be far more to understanding this debacle than a simple case of the Church leaning on the state. Finally, we will review the theoretical utility of institutionalism in understanding policy outcomes.

Main concepts and concerns of institutionalism

Referring to the difference between 'old' and new institutionalist approaches to the study of politics and policy-making, R.A.W. Rhodes (1996b) points out that 'old' institutionalism consisted mainly of detailed studies of the political, administrative and legal structures within a country. Thus an 'old' institutionalist approach refers to a methodology that is primarily descriptive and inductive in style. It may be applied to 'studies which systematically describe and analyse phenomena that have occurred in the past and which explain contemporary political phenomena with reference to past events. The emphasis is on explanation and understanding and not on formulating laws' (Kavanagh 1991: 482). The key focus in this approach was to observe, explain and understand institutions, and in this respect perhaps one of the greatest exponents of the so-called 'historical-comparative approach' was Herman Finer (R.A.W. Rhodes 1996b: 45). In his extensive and detailed work, Finer (1932, 1954) compared the major institutions in various countries by observing their formal structure and operation.

Some would argue that in fact there is no 'old' institutionalism in the sense of there being any clear methodology or approach; it was simply the way politics and public administration used to be studied and taught. As Rhodes points out:

Our forebears in political science were not preoccupied with methodology. Not for them the lengthy discussion on how to do it. They just described, for example, the government of France, starting with the French constitution. The focus on institutions was a matter of common sense, an obvious starting point for studying a country and therefore there was no need to justify it.

(R.A.W. Rhodes 1996b: 42)

By the 1950s, however, this attitude to the study of politics was increasingly challenged by advocates of a more 'scientific' approach. The behaviouralist approach is concerned with why people behave in the manner in they do. As Saunders explains, what 'differentiates' behaviouralists from other social scientists is their 'insistence (a) that observable behaviour, whether it is at the level of the individual or social aggregate, should be the focus of the analysis; and (b) that any explanation of that behaviour should be susceptible to empirical testing' (1995: 58). Institutionalists responded by injecting more analytical rigour into their studies. Whereas traditional organisational studies based on the Weberian conception of authority tended to concentrate on the formal rationale and view of the organisation from the outside, new studies began to examine the role that political institutions play in shaping and determining social and political outcomes. David Selznick's (1949) seminal work on the Tennessee Valley Authority highlighted the disparity between how institutions really work 'on the inside' as opposed to the formal organisational structures they presented 'from the outside'. Selznick looked at the interaction between the organisation and its external environment and how it, in turn, influences decision-making processes (Parsons 1995: 324–5). It was this idea that institutional norms may structure and shape the context in which decisions are made that provided the impetus to devise new ways of looking at the role of institutions and led eventually to the development of new institutionalist approaches, more commonly referred to as 'new institutionalism'.

Institutional analysis is predicated on March and Olsen's dictum that 'what we observe in the world is inconsistent with the ways in which contemporary theories ask us to talk' (1984: 747). That is to say that the 'new' institutionalists believed that the theoretical tools available to them for the study of politics and policy failed to explain what actually occurred in the policy process. It was becoming obvious from studies such as Selznick's that the formal laws, rules and administrative structures of institutions did not explain actual political behaviour or outcome. As a consequence, new institutionalists argued that explanations that focused exclusively on actors and agents in the policy process without taking account of the institutions that shaped their behaviour were, at best, only giving a partial explanation of political outcomes and, at worst, failing to explain the process satisfactorily at all.

Mainstream variants of institutionalism in current use

Key to our understanding of new institutionalism is that it does not constitute one single body of thought. In fact there are three major variants: *historical institutionalism, rational choice institutionalism* and *sociological institutionalism*. In this section we will consider the main concepts underlying each of these approaches in turn. Whilst the collective focus of all three approaches is institutions and their influence on the decision-making process, 'each provides a different window or insight into how institutions shape the way in which decision-making takes place' (Parsons 1995: 324). However, what cannot be understated is the fact that for these theorists all life occurs within an institutional context, and as such has certain rules, procedures and norms which must be adhered to.

> To describe behaviour as driven by rules is to see action matching of a situation to the demands of the position…rules define relationships among roles in terms of what an incumbent of one role owes to incumbents of other roles.
>
> (March and Olsen 1989: 23)

Central to all three variants of new institutionalism is the idea that formal and informal 'rules of the game' tend to specify the duties, obligations and actions of political actors. Much like our rules of the road, whereby other drivers know what to expect of us and us of them, in the policy-making process there are also rules which establish actors' responsibilities to and relationships with other actors. Moreover, these rules tend to remain constant over time as they are embedded in both formal and informal institutional arrangements. As Immergut argues, '[i]nstitutions do not allow one to predict policy outcomes. But by establishing rules of the game, they enable one to predict the ways in which policy conflicts will be played out' (1992: 63).

Historical institutionalism

Central to historical institutionalism is the question: how do institutions affect the behaviour of individuals? This group of theorists are concerned with political decision-making, in particular the manner in which political structures (or institutions) affect political outcomes (DiMaggio and Powell 1991: 4). For this group of institutionalists, as their title suggests, 'history matters' – that is, an historical analysis of institutional variables is utilised to explain outcomes. Unlike the economists, the historical institutionalists do not set out with a hypothesis and a set of assumptions, instead they develop their hypotheses inductively by interpreting the empirical data. Hall and Taylor explain that historical institutionalists define institutions as the 'formal or informal procedures, routines, norms and conventions embedded in the organisational structure of the polity or political economy. They can range from the rules of constitutional order to the standard operating procedures of a bureaucracy' (1996: 938). Much of the work of historical institutionalists involves cross-national comparisons of public policy, with an emphasis on the effect of national political institutions structuring relations among government, interest groups, the electorate and the judiciary. From such investigations, historical institutionalists have argued that social and political causation is *path dependent* – that is, they reject the notion that similar forces operating in similar ways will necessarily produce the same outcome in different organizational contexts.

Thelen and Steinmo argue that historical institutionalism grew out a critique of the behavioural focus of politics in the 1950s and 1960s, which 'often obscured the enduring socio-economic and political structures that mould behaviour in distinctive ways in different national contexts' (1992: 1). They argued that the institutional organisation of any polity is the principal factor structuring collective behaviour and generating distinctive political and policy outcomes, because 'institutions constrain and refract politics'. Thus, 'institutional analyses do not deny the broad political forces that animate various theories of politics: class structure in Marxism, group dynamics in pluralism. Instead, they point to the ways that institutions structure these battles and in so doing, influence their outcomes' (Thelen and Steinmo 1992: 3).

Rational choice institutionalism

Rational choice institutionalism borrows the basic assumptions of all rational choice approaches and applies them to specific organisational contexts. It assumes, therefore, that people choose, within the limits of their knowledge, the best means available to achieve their goals (for a more substantive discussion of rational choice approaches, see Chapter 9). It was primarily developed for studies of US Congressional behaviour in the 1970s, but the scope of rational choice institutionalists has since broadened to consider other areas of political activity, including cross-national coalition behaviour and the development of political institutions (see, for example, Laver and Shepsle 1990; North and Weingast 1989). Since the 1980s most rational choice institutional studies have been influenced by non-cooperative game theory, classically typified by the 'Prisoners' Dilemma' game (see Aspinwall and Schneider 2000). The Prisoners' Dilemma assumes that two prisoners are questioned in separate rooms. Each is offered a free pardon if they turn 'state evidence' against the other. In this game, the rules provide the context in which the prisoners maximise their utility, and more importantly the final outcome of the game is dependent on the actions of the other actors. (Rationally acting, of course, if neither gives any evidence both will go free – but can they assume this level of rationality from each other?)

As with game theory, rational choice institutionalists regard politics as a series of collective action dilemmas where outcomes are sub-optimal. Aspinwall and Schneider explain that rational choice institutionalism sees politics as an arena in which individuals try to maximise their personal gain, and that it assumes that 'actors understand the possibilities and limitations that the diverse decision making rules have created. More particularly…that actors adapt their behaviour to these institutions and use them strategically' (2000: 23).

Going back to our original example, in the 1970s, rational choice analysts began to observe a discrepancy in American Congressional voting behaviour which they could not explain. If rational choice theories about voting behaviours were correct, then it should be difficult to secure stable majorities for bills in the American Congress due to the multi-preference ordering and multidimensional character of the issues brought to Congress. Why on earth, for example, should a Congress member from Texas, with strong policy interests in oil production, vote in support of measures introduced by a Georgian peach farmer to prevent cheap fruit imports? What possible interest could a Texan oil representative have in peach production? The rational choice theorists began to consider the role of 'institutions' in Congress as a means of shaping and forming the preferences of the members of Congress. The institutional factors that they considered include the rules surrounding agenda control and the role of committees. Perhaps, they discovered, if these two senators controlled votes in committees of mutual interest, then it was perfectly rational for them to give a high priority to supporting each other. As Searing explains, the rational choice institutionalists developed models with 'explicit rules of the game that politicians can take into account in calculating how they might best achieve their preferences...rules are the strategic context in which optimising behaviour takes place' (1991: 1,241). They found that many of these structures limited the options that rational actors can choose from and helped to control the range of possible outcomes (Hall and Taylor 1996: 942–3).

Essentially then, rational choice institutionalists believe that *homo economicus* is limited and directed by institutions, so that the actions of 'rational man' are constrained by the rules and conventions of the institution in which he operates. Using approaches such as transaction cost economics (TCE) and the structure–agency approach, rational choice institutionalists observe the role of institutions in shaping preferences and outcomes. The 'transaction' is the primary unit of analysis for this group of theorists. TCE is a model used by rational choice institutionalists based on the assumption that markets involve buying and selling, which in turn involve costs. These would include, for example, the cost of finding customers and suppliers, the cost of negotiating prices with them and the cost of monitoring. Hence those engaged in the market will be concerned with trying to reduce uncertainty and increase control over such transactions. At the core of the model is the belief that lower transaction costs will increase efficiency in the firm. From the rational choice institutional perspective, then, institutions emerge to economise on transaction costs, thereby increasing the number of mutually beneficial transactions that can take place (Parsons 1995: 327–9; Mule 1999).

Sociological institutionalism

The two chief exponents of *sociological institutionalism*, DiMaggio and Powell were responsible for developing the widest possible interpretation of what constitutes an institution: 'whereas most economists and political scientists focus exclusively on economic or political rules of the game, sociologists find institutions every-where from handshakes to marriages to strategic planning departments' (1991: 9). Take the example of something as mundane as a lecture, which can be inter-preted as a kind of informal institution. If we look closely, we can see that there are in fact rules, procedures and norms within the lecture hall. Does it not strike you as odd, for example, that in a room of possibly 200 people 199 should remain silent and listen to a single person when they clearly have only a limited interest in what that person is saying. Accordingly, we can construe that the informal rules associated with student participation in lectures are that, however boring the speaker may be, it is generally accepted that students remain quiet or register their disapproval in more subtle ways than outright protestation. (More students are likely to scribble dismissive notes to each other than they are to stand up and complain that the speaker is dull.) Most likely, as with many other facets of life, you have not conceived of a 'lecture' as an institution. However, if we wish to look at the policy process from a sociological institutional perspective we must remain open-minded as to what constitutes an institution.

Taking this broader sociological view, DiMaggio and Powell (1991) argued that institutions define the actions of rational actors, rather than any objective reasoning or rationale. In explaining this they give the example of an individual seeking a divorce, who cannot seek separation from her spouse by inventing a new divorce procedure but instead must to follow the rules already in place. As a consequence of this approach, DiMaggio and Powell argue that rationality is more often than not institutionally, as opposed to individually, defined:

> Institutionalism in organisation theory and sociology comprises a rejection of rational-actor models, an interest in institutions as independent variables, a turn towards cognitive and cultural expectations, and an interest on properties of supra-individual units of analysis that cannot be reduced to aggregations or direct consequences of an individual's attributes or motives.
>
> (DiMaggio and Powell 1991: 9)

Sociological institutionalists provide cultural explanations based on an understanding of culture as shared attitudes or values. In every organisation or institution there is a prevailing culture. Culture lies at the heart of *sociological institutionalism* because 'it contains the bedrock cognitive similarities that cause people to share perceptions of the world around them' (Aspinwall and Schneider 2000: 8). Jepperson defines institutional culture as 'those rules, procedures and goals without primary representation in formal organisations and without monitoring and sanctioning by some "central" authority' (1991: 150–1). Here, Jepperson is defining 'culture' as something different from the formal institution that conforms to its own rules, in the form of shared values, norms and behaviour. Although it is not written in any formal handbook, there is a culture of casual dress amongst college students; in general students do not come to class in interview attire. Whilst there are no fashion police enforcing this norm in the university, anyone who goes against this culture is likely to be regarded by most as inappropriately dressed in the canteen. In the policy-making process, cultural norms are embedded in the institutional context and persist over time. As Searing notes, 'informal rules are critical to an organisation for it is not possible to operate without them' (1991: 1,241).

Central to *sociological institutionalism* is the notion that institutions help shape legitimacy or 'social appropriateness' – that is, organisations take on specific institutional forms because such forms are valued in a broader cultural environment. DiMaggio and Powell (1991) refer to this as 'institutional isomorphism'.

This can sometimes be a constraining process, as it forces actors to resemble similar organisations:

> Organisations tend to model themselves after similar organisations in their field that they perceive to be more legitimate or successful. The ubiquity of certain kinds of structural arrangements can more likely be credited to the universality of mimetic processes than to any concrete evidence that the adopted models enhance efficiency.
>
> (DiMaggio and Powell 1991: 70)

In some cases 'mimicking' similar organisations might be a dysfunctional move but will be regarded nonetheless as socially appropriate (Hall and Taylor 1996: 949). DiMaggio and Powell utilise the example of Japan's modernisers in the nineteenth century as 'mimickers', sending officers to study the courts, army and police in France, the navy and postal system in Britain and banking in the USA. In an attempt to modernise and legitimise Japanese government, the solution was seen to lie in mimicking Western prototypes (1991: 69).

Criticisms of the approach

Many have asked what is new about new institutionalism. The historical institutionalists themselves would agree that their lineage descends from 'old' institutionalism but also benefits from the behaviouralist theories, which focused on the characteristics, attitudes and behaviours of individuals and groups to explain political outcomes. Still, they distinguish themselves from the behaviouralists, who they argue 'often missed crucial elements of the playing field' and needed to pay 'more explicit attention to the institutional landscape in which interest groups sought to influence' (Thelen and Steinmo 1992: 5). The sociological institutionalists can also trace their roots to the 'old' institutionalism found in the work of Selznick and others. Still, sociological institutionalism

> diverges from that tradition substantially...with the older emphasising the vesting of interests within organisations as a result of political trade-offs and alliances, and the new stressing the relationship between stability and legitimacy and the power of common understandings that are seldom explicitly articulated.
>
> (DiMaggio and Powell 1991: 12)

From an outsider's perspective, one of the main criticisms of new institutionalism has been the inability of the three variants to overlap or learn from each other. As DiMaggio and Powell explain, these three schools are 'united by little but a common scepticism toward atomistic accounts of social processes and a common conviction that institutional arrangements and social processes matter' (1991: 3). This is linked to the fact that all three variants define institutions differently, and for those such as Mule 'confusion abounds about just what new

Institutionalism means, it is a slippery term because it is used to refer to social phenomena at many different levels' (1999: 146).

An additional criticism wielded at all three variants is their apparent inability to explain institutional change. Gorges argues that the utility of new institutionalism 'seems limited if it cannot successfully explain institutional change and institutionalisation without employing a miscellaneous collection of variables in an ad-hoc fashion' (2001: 142). This problem has been also been acknowledged by *historical institutionalist* scholars such as Hall and Taylor (1996: 942), who accept that their approach it is often unable to explain what precipitates change in institutions. Still, however, perhaps this is a spurious complaint: the logic of new institutionalist approaches tells us that all policy-making is a reflection of far more complex social phenomena than the purported actions of given individuals. If this is the case, then perhaps it is more honest to acknowledge that we cannot be clear about the causes of change instead of offering superficial explanations that we know to be untrue.

Case study: healthcare policy in Ireland – the 1951 'Mother and Child' debacle

The Mother and Child scheme has held a unique grip on the Irish public, as Horgan succinctly states: 'with its greedy doctors, its scheming bishops, its vacillating politicians and its Byronic hero. It had all the ingredients of a post-modern fairy tale, especially as it didn't have a happy ending' (2000: 91). Widely referred to as classic example of 'church versus state', there have been a number of academic studies, books and newspaper articles dealing with this story, including Browne's (1986) autobiography – all with a different twist. The purpose of this case study is to show that an exposition of the events using new institutionalist insights illustrates the case to be a far more complex issue than it might at first seem. The summary box below provides a chronology of events surrounding the introduction of the Mother and Child antenatal scheme in Ireland.

Summary review of theoretical utility

As Lee asserts, 'it is an oversimplification to present the mother and child scheme, which can still evoke passionate controversy, as a straight conflict between Church and state' (1989: 318). Instead there were many players in this tragedy. How best can one understand how the Mother and Child scheme fell, and does instituionalism have anything to offer us in this process? Below are three takes on the version of events above, which are developed using alternative new institutionalist explanations.

Chronology of events

1942, UK Beveridge Report recommends social insurance and a universal health service. Perhaps the most significant influence on

---

Irish public opinion after the war, the Beveridge Report proposes that 'comprehensive giants on the road of reconstruction – the others are Disease, Ignorance, Squalor and Idleness"' (R. Barrington 1987: 141). It concludes that all five 'giants' need to be tackled.

1943, Minister for Local Government and Public Health Sean MacEntee prioritises the improvement of the Irish health services as a matter of urgency.

1944, Dr F.C. Ward is given responsibility for health in the department.

1945, Ward drafts Public Health Bill, with measures for controlling infectious diseases, improved medical inspection in schools and free medical services for (ante- and postnatal) mothers and children up to the age of 16 without a means test.

1945, Catholic Hierarchy and medical profession object to the Bill. The Church expresses its discomfort with state interference in the medical inspection of children, particularly adolescent girls, regarding the matter as an infringement on the rights of the family. The Hierarchy's greatest objection is not to the substance of the Bill, but 'to the dangers posed to the morals of women and children by health education' (R. Barrington 1987: 187).

For the medical profession the Bill represents the first step towards 'state medicine' or 'socialised medicine'. In particular, they take exception to the Mother and Child section of the Bill, regarding it as a threat to the income of private practitioners, the majority of which is derived from attending small children. A free service, they surmise, would lead to reduction in the demand for private practitioners. Although the Mother and Child scheme did have negative financial implications for the medical profession, more importantly it was seen as a step in the direction of the National Health Service, which had just been established in the UK. The Irish Medical Association (IMA) believed that 'the strong likelihood was that private practice would gradually be superseded by a salaried state service' (Lee 1989: 316).

1946, Ward, though destined to be the first Minister for Health, resigns over irregularities in his income tax returns.

1946, Dr Jim Ryan is appointed the first Minister for Health and Social Welfare (Lee 1989: 314–15).

31 December 1947, De Valera's government falls. 'The fall of the government enables De Valera to evade the health issue. The new government is

to implement Ryan's Health Act' (Lee 1989: 315).

February 1948, formation of new five-party coalition government. This new government 'ushered a new era in Irish politics'. Fianna Fáil were unable to form a government and were replaced 'by a five-party coalition supported also by independent deputies, the first 'Inter-Party' government' (Coakley 1999: 23). Under the leadership of John A. Costello (Fine Gael), the health portfolio falls to *Clann na Poblachta*, a new Republican Party led by Sean McBride, who nominated his newly elected colleague Dr Noel Browne as Minister for Health at the age of 32.

18 February 1948, Noel Browne assumes responsibility for health. Browne had campaigned on the single issue of tuberculosis (TB), to which he had lost both parents and two siblings; two other siblings and Browne have also suffered from the disease (see Browne 1986). In his capacity as a medical doctor Browne specialised in the treatment of TB and as Minister he worked tirelessly to eradicate the disease. As Barrington observes, 'the effect of this concerted campaign was dramatic. There was a significant reduction in the death rate...the "national epidemic" which had defied earlier attempts at eradication, was under control' (1987: 200). In addition, Browne undertook an ambitious hospital-building programme funded by the Hospital Sweep Stakes.

June 1950, under pressure from Fianna Fáil in opposition, Browne decides to introduce the Mother and Child sections of Ryan's 1947 Act. His first problem is to deal with Fine Gael's opposition to the compulsory and universal nature of the scheme. Browne modifies the scheme, emphasising three things: it was not compulsory, and there would be no means test and no charges for the service (R. Barrington 1987: 200–3). Without formal Cabinet approval for the scheme, he 'relies heavily on government agreement in 1948 to amend the Health Act for authority to act on the Mother and Child Scheme' (R. Barrington 1987: 202).

The IMA also disagrees with his proposals: dispensary doctors state that they will not see poor patients in private surgeries provided for paying patients. Browne infuriates the medical profession and 'seems to have set out deliberately to provoke the profession, in particular the Dublin consultants, by criticising in public their manner of practice and preoccupation with money' (R. Barrington 1987: 205).

October 1950, Archbishop McQuaid of Dublin requests a meeting with Browne at his palace. The Bishops of Ferns and Galway were also in attendance. McQuaid read to Browne from a letter addressed to the Taoiseach outlining Church concerns with the scheme. Amongst other criticisms, the letter stated that

The right to provide for the health of children belongs to parents not tostate. The state has a right to intervene only in a subsidiary capacity, to supplement, not to supplant. It may help indigent or neglectful parents; may not deprive 90% of parents of their rights because of 10% necessitous or negligent parents.
(reprinted in Browne 1986: 158–9)

Browne responds with some concessions to the Bishops and attempts to meet their objections by ensuring that every mother makes a nominal payment to the scheme. Browne outlined these changes in a memorandum and did a whistle-stop tour of many of the Bishops, attempting to gain their support for the scheme personally. However, as Lyons explains, 'through a series of misunderstandings which would have been farcical were not the consequences so tragic, Dr. Browne believed he had satisfied the Hierarchy when in fact he had done nothing of the sort' (1973: 577).

March 1951, Browne attempts to implement the Mother and Child scheme in the absence of explicit Cabinet authorisation or support. Once the Hierarchy had made their views known, Browne's Cabinet colleagues pleaded with him to accept the bishops' ruling. However, Browne's response to them was that he had not made the law and he alone could not make a new one (Browne 1986: 170; Lee 1989: 317).

19 March 1951, McBride calls a meeting of the *Clann na Poblachta* executive, in which he criticises Browne as a minister and member of the party.

6 April 1951, the bishops send another letter to Costello, stating that the scheme is contrary to Catholic social teaching. That night Costello called an emergency Cabinet meeting to withdraw the scheme, with plans to draft one in accordance with the demands of the Hierarchy.

10–11 April 1951, a series of letters is exchanged between Browne and McBride. Under the leader's insistence Browne resigns as minister on 11 April 1951 (Lyons 1973: 578).

As Lee asserts, 'it is an oversimplification to present the mother and child scheme, which can still evoke passionate controversy, as a straight conflict between Church and state' (1989: 318). Instead there were many players in this tragedy. How best can one understand how the Mother and Child scheme fell, and does institutionalism have anything to offer us in this process? The following are three 'takes' on the version of events above, which are developed using alternative new institutionalist explanations.

Historical institutionalism

Immergut (1992), in her study of national health insurance politics, observes how similar proposals for national health insurance and control of doctors' fees in France, Switzerland and Sweden in the 1940s and 1950s led to divergent legislation in each country. These differences, she argues, cannot be explained by differing ideas amongst policy-makers, political partisanship, preferences or organisation of interest groups. Instead, 'these outcomes are better explained by analysing the political institutions in each country. These institutions establish the rules of the game for politicians and interest groups seeking to enact or block policies' (Immergut 1992: 58–9).

More importantly, Immergut stresses that political decisions are not one-off decisions made at a specific point in time. Instead, political decisions involve 'sequences of decisions' made by various actors within different institutional locations. 'Simply put, enacting a law requires agreement and successive affirmative votes at all decision points' (Immergut 1992: 6). Hence, if a political decision is to be successfully enacted, it requires agreement amongst many political actors in different arenas. In understanding the Mother and Child debacle we must consider the different political arenas and actors where the scheme failed to receive the necessary support.

Perhaps the starting point in explaining the crisis was that Dr Browne 'inherited a situation full of possibilities – and of dangers' (Lyons 1973: 576). The legislation underpinning the Mother and Child scheme was enacted prior to his appointment as minister. Objections to the scheme by the Hierarchy and medical profession were also present prior to Browne's appointment. The question remains as to how supportive the inter-party government was to the scheme and to healthcare reform in general. In his memoirs, Browne argues that McBride gave him the health portfolio because Browne 'was an unknown entity appointed to an unimportant position' (1986: 108). It therefore seems legitimate to question whether or not there was agreement amongst the government to oversee healthcare reform and the implementation of the Mother and Child scheme. The fact that the scheme was not the genesis of the inter-party government but of the previous Fianna Fáil government is probably significant in determining the lack of commitment on the part of the coalition to act. It appears that the Minister for Health alone wished to gain the approval of the Church and medical profession for the scheme. Thus, a historical institutionalist approach suggests that Browne was not only struggling against the Church and the medical profession (as is the most usual depiction of the case), but equally against the apathy and inaction of his own colleagues in the coalition government.

Rational choice institutionalism

The conditions of coalition government are an important institutional factor worth considering. In this case, at the heart of the political system was a multiparty coalition including some inexperienced politicians. In this inter-party government, Fine Gael were in the majority, with thirty-one seats, Labour held fourteen, *Clann na Poblachta* ten, *Clann na Talmhan* seven, and National Labour five (Browne 1986: 107). Remarking on this extremely mixed group and the need for all parties to secure some government office, Lyons notes that from the start 'they were dazzled by the possibility of forming among themselves a coalition from which the veterans of so many electoral triumphs would be excluded...an inter-party government emerged to the astonishment of all beholders' (1973: 561). Much of that astonishment lay in the eclectic ideological mix of the coalition: even Browne notes the disbelief amongst some of the *Clann*'s former Republican Party members at McBride's decision to form a coalition with Fine Gael (1986: 107). Browne himself described the problems of coalition government as 'formidable': these 'new radicals had no political experience' and were 'working with people with whom they had little in common' (1986: 108). More important, though, is Browne's conviction that the Fine Gael membership and ministers never fully trusted McBride, 'even though he believed he had captivated and out-foxed them' (Browne 1986: 108). The fact that Cabinet did not act collectively with Browne when the bishops protested against the scheme is one of the main reasons why the scheme fell. Indeed, Costello had already warned Browne in the Dáil that 'whatever about fighting the doctors, I am not going to fight the Bishops and whatever about fighting the Bishops, I am not going to fight the doctors and the Bishops' (cited in R. Barrington 1987: 215).

The Irish system of government ensures that the Cabinet or executive is the decision-making body and to a large extent dominates parliament. The Cabinet is 'collectively responsible' to the Dáil for all of its decisions and actions. Once a decision is made by the Cabinet it then becomes the government position – one to which all Cabinet members must give public support (O'Halpin and Connolly 1998: 255). In this case, however, there appeared to be no specific government position. Indeed, there did not even appear to be a *Clann na Poblachta* position. R. Barrington (1987) and Lee (1989) both contend that Browne failed to secure *explicit* Cabinet approval for the details 'before embarking on his scheme, and thus left himself in an exposed position when the cabinet subsequently disavowed his approach' (Lee 1989: 316). A different version of events is to be found in Browne's memoirs, where he acknowledges that even though Sean McBride believed that he had gone ahead 'impetuously' with the free no-means test component of the scheme and (perhaps more importantly) without the consent of the Cabinet; Browne himself points to a sum of money agreed in the 1948 Book of Estimates between the Departments of Health and Finance, contesting that 'neither of us could or would have gone ahead with a scheme of that magnitude without the consent of the government' (1986: 152). It appears that Browne, for his part, saw this as explicit Cabinet approval – whereas the other coalition government ministers did not.

The misunderstanding outlined above leads us to examine Browne's relation-ship with his party and with its leader, McBride. Immergut's comparative study of healthcare reforms points to the importance of 'veto points' along the chain of decision-making and, more specifically, 'the importance of political parties and party discipline in reducing choice by binding representatives to a particular party line' (1992: 64). That is to say that if the leaders of a party wish to see a policy passed, they are dependent on party support, and in turn upon party discipline, to ensure that all party representatives toe the party line. In this respect, the position of *Clann na Poblachta* was not straightforward: despite being a new party, a large number of 'old republicans' made up the vast majority of party membership; the remainder comprising others who, like Browne, were disillusioned with alternative mainstream parties and so joined this radical group. At the time of the crisis the party was suffering an internal rift and Browne himself became disillusioned with the so-called radical new party, believing that it had been 'corrupted by office' and that it 'was in danger of losing its radical soul' (Lyons 1973: 578).

Throughout the debacle Browne argues that McBride sided with Fine Gael, the medical profession and the bishops. Indeed, McBride's inability to protect, defend, advise, assist or even stop Browne in his endeavours suggests an ineptness on his part as leader: Lee argues that McBride 'failed to provide his movement with the responsible leadership required to translate it from a party of protest into a credible party of government' (1989: 318). In the run-up to Browne's resignation, his relationship with McBride hit rock bottom, with Browne claiming that he was followed by Special Branch or other investigators suspecting him of holding Communist sympathies and plans for a leadership coup (Browne 1986: 179).

In his memoirs Browne (1986) states there were two main personalities in the 'conspiracy to subvert' the implementation of the Mother and Child scheme, which together represented two of the most powerful groups in the country: Dr Tom O'Higgins, Chief Medical Officer for Meath and Minister for Defence, who represented the views of the medical profession at the Cabinet table (albeit not directly); and Archbishop McQuaid, who represented the views of the Hierarchy to the Cabinet. If this is the case, then rational choice institutionalism points to the power of interest groups as part of the institutional framework and to their ability to influence policy outcomes depending upon 'their ability to threaten the passage of the law and, hence, to convince those representatives holding critical votes to block legislation' (Immergut 1992: 63).

Sociological institutionalism

Finally we must consider the pivotal role the Church played, not only in the Irish psyche and society but also in the political culture. Indeed, had the Mother and Child scheme been implemented, it is most likely that Browne would have contravened Catholic social teaching and been denounced by the Church as a Catholic 'who no longer accepts the teaching authority of the Roman Catholic Church' (Browne 1986: 164). This was surely something that no politician with hopes of a future political career could contemplate in 1950s Ireland. As it was, however, events never progressed that far because the 'rules of the game' in Irish politics and policy-making had been established since the foundation of the state. According to these unwritten rules, Irish political institutions accorded a unique role to the Hierarchy and, whether Noel Browne did or did not realise or accept this, the rest of the government did. Up until the 1960s, the Church and its doctrine on all matters concerning the family and society remained unquestioned by society and the political system. Hussey (1993) points to the link between the struggle for religious freedom and political freedom when she argues that when the state gained independence the Catholic Church was seen as the Church of Irish people. She asserts that

> the shared experience of a long and weary fight against Britain gave it a central and pivotal role in the life of the people, who fully identified with it and accepted almost without questions its dominance over every aspect of their lives.

(Hussey 1993: 381)

Clearly, Browne himself did not foresee the level of opposition from the Hierarchy. Dr McQuaid was the Church's key figure in the debacle. From an institutional point of view, when considering the role of the Church in this debate there are three key points. First, the involvement of the Church and members of its religious orders in the provision and management of healthcare gave them a legitimate place in the health policy arena. Even today, many of Ireland's major teaching hospitals, though almost totally funded by the state, are managed and controlled by Catholic Boards of Management and religious orders (Hussey 1993: 373). In the 1950s the state was just beginning to involve itself in the widespread provision of healthcare and the Church controlled all appointments to the hospitals, so much so that Protestant doctors were not employed in Catholic hospitals. Thus, due to its direct involvement in healthcare, the Church was a powerful force in any debate concerning reform.

Moreover, as the guardian of Ireland's moral welfare the Church took issue with two facets of the Mother and Child scheme: the responsibility and rights of the family; and the possibility of exposing Irish women to birth control. The Hierarchy accorded particular importance to the papal encyclical *Quadrageismo Anno* (1931), which criticised the evils of unregulated capitalism and excessive state intervention. Hence, as Lyons explains, 'they were deeply opposed to any contemporary trends which could be interpreted as transferring responsibility for the health and welfare of children from their parents to an impersonal and external authority' (1973: 574–5).

In its opposition to the scheme, the Roman Catholic Church position was further cemented by the prevailing attitudes of the medical profession, who were opposed to what they perceived to be any 'wide scale socialisation of medicine'. As R. Barrington observes, 'the opposition of the medical profession was to be expected since their status, traditions and incomes were threatened' (1987: 247). The doctors were a powerful group organised to resist such a move; they were suspicious of the means tests proposed by Browne, and fearful of excessive political control under a strong minister (Lyons 1973: 577). More importantly, though, the doctors had their preferences represented at the Cabinet in the form of Dr O'Higgins, and Browne has argued that this link between the IMA and the government was significant in the collapse of the Mother and Child scheme (1986: 150).

Conclusions

From institutionalism we learn that policy-making occurs within a context which has rules, procedures, given constitutional arrangements, power relations, norms, values and behaviours. Thus policy-makers wishing to make or implement a policy must be aware of the institutional context. Browne could not change the rules of the game single handed; nor could he have implemented the scheme without Cabinet approval. By utilising institutionalism as an approach to understanding the Mother and Child scheme, we realise that there were many points in the policy process where the policy could and did fail. Any reform of the healthcare system required not only Cabinet approval but explicit Cabinet agreement, something that might prove difficult in a five-party coalition. Moreover, within the minister's own party, support for the scheme was absent. Added to this was the opposition to the scheme from the country's most powerful trade union, the IMA and the Hierarchy, whose values permeated all areas of Irish society and culture. It was no surprise to the more senior members of government when the Hierarchy and the medical profession reacted the way they did, and, being aware of the rules of the game, rather than engage in a policy conflict with these two powerful groups they withdrew the policy. As Mule has succinctly said about institutionalism, 'the real brunt of this standpoint is that actions are not the products of calculated decisions; rather they are embedded in institutional structures of rules, norms, expectations and traditions that severely constrain the behaviour of social actors' (1999: 148).

And what of Browne himself? Inexperienced as he was in Irish political life, he transformed many facets of health policy: the eradication of TB, the hospital-building programme, the establishment of the state's first blood transfusion services. Browne, reflecting in his memoirs, suggests that, 'above all questions, society must ask should politics be left to the amateur?' (1986: 273). Browne was an inexperienced yet idealistic politician who distanced himself from his colleagues but possibly never anticipated the opposition he came up against. As Lee (1989) explains, Browne was probably 'his own worst enemy' in spite of the competition from Costello, McQuaid and McBride. Was he not just naive in the workings of the political system, disrespectful of the dominance of the Church in Irish political culture and caught in the middle of an ineffectual coalition? Browne had anticipated opposition from the medical profession, but, as he wrote in his memoirs, 'I had no reason to believe that there would opposition from the Hierarchy' (1986: 151). Perhaps Browne was not the only naive character in all of this, as he himself quite shrewdly remarks:

neither did the coalition government appreciate that in appointing as Minister for Health a Trinity Catholic educated in a Protestant medical school, they had offered what turned out to be a slight to the Archbishop of Dublin, further compounded by the fact that annually from the pulpit Dr McQuaid forbade Catholics to attend TCD [Trinity College Dublin] under pain of mortal sin.

(Browne 1986: 142)

Shortly after Browne's resignation the coalition fell and Fianna Fáil returned to power. Ironically, Fianna Fáil succeeded in passing some of the Mother and Child scheme provisions into law. Lyons notes that there is clear evidence that 'had it not been for Mr DeValera's expert guidance, Fianna Fail, too might have been involved in a head-on collision with the Bishops' (1973: 578). Institutionalism, and historical institutionalism in particular, is based on the belief that in any given scenario more than one course of action is possible. Had Browne been a more experienced politician, a little more diplomatic in how he treated his enemies, and had he had government support for the scheme, our healthcare system today might be a very different one.

Further reading

Hall, P.A and Taylor, C.R. (1996) 'Political Science and the Three New Institutionalisms', *Political Studies* 44: 936–57.

Kavanagh, D. (1991) 'Why Political Science Needs History', *Political Studies* 39: 479–95.

March, J.G. and Olsen, J.P. (1984) 'The New Institutionalism: Organisational Factors in Political Life', *American Political Science Review* 78: 734–49.

Powell W.W. and DiMaggio, P.J. (eds) (1991) *The New Institutionalism in Organisational Analysis*, Chicago: Chicago University Press.

Rhodes, R.A.W. (1996b) 'The Institutional Approach', in D. Marsh and G. Stoker (eds) *Theory and Methods in Political Science*, Basingstoke: Macmillan.

Steinmo, S., Thelen, K. and Longstreth, F. (eds) (1992) *Structuring Politics: Historical Institutionalism in Comparative Analysis*, Cambridge: Cambridge University Press.

9 Rational actor models, Voting and the Northern Ireland Assembly

Vani K. Boorah

Introduction

Lohmann observed that, in recent decades, rational choice theory (hereafter referred to as RCT)

> has become the rising star of political science...even though rational choice scholars constitute a minority of political scientists, they publish a disproportionate number of articles in the *American Political Science Review* and they are sought after by leading political science departments.
>
> (Lohmann 1995: 127)

If this is indeed the case, then what is this magic formula which gives this minority such power and influence and, conversely, what is the attitude of the majority of political science scholars, who would not describe themselves as 'RCT persons', towards this group? Do they view RCT theorists as redeemers of political science who will place the subject in its rightful place among the panoply of social sciences that like to think of themselves as 'quasi-scientific'? Or is RCT simply a dark art and its practitioners the high priests of an occult faith which, by promoting the worship of Beelzebub, profanes the true deity?

In this context, it is worth pointing out that the RCT literature also travels under a variety of other names: *inter alia*, public choice theory; social choice theory; game theory; rational actor models; positive political economy; the economic approach to politics. However, regardless of the *nom de guerre* adopted by RCT, it always builds on the assumption that people choose, within the limits of their knowledge, the best available means to achieve their goals. They are presumed to be 'instrumentally rational', meaning that they take actions not for their own sake, but only insofar as they secure desired ends[1] (Chong 1995).

More specifically, Green and Shapiro (1994) identify four salient features of RCT. First, RCT involves utility maximisation or, under conditions of uncertainty, expected utility maximisation, which is to say that confronted with an array of options the rational actor chooses the one which affords (or is likely to afford) him/her the greatest welfare. Second, RCT requires that certain consistency requirements must be satisfied: each individual must be capable of ranking options in terms of the welfare they offer him/her and preferences must be transitive.[2] Third, the relevant unit for the study of the political process is the individual: it is the individual, and not groups of individuals, which is the basic building block for the study of politics. Fourth, RCT claims universality in the sense that its models apply to all persons at all times.

The rationale for RCT begins with the observation that in politics, as in economics, individuals compete for scarce resources, and that, therefore, the same methods of analysis used by economists might also serve well in political science. As Tullock observed, 'voters and customers are essentially the same people. Mr. Smith buys and votes; he is the same man in the supermarket and in the voting booth' (1976: 224). Although the incursion of the analytical methods of economics into political science – which is the hallmark of RCT – began in the 1950s, it was not until at least three decades later that the trickle became a flood. Today, not only is RCT disproportionately represented in the pages of leading political science journals but it has also expanded beyond political theory into new fields like international relations and comparative politics (Green and Shapiro 1994).

This application of economic principles to non-market areas, be they in politics or elsewhere, may be viewed in a 'thin' sense, meaning an *inclination* on the part of individuals to satisfy their preferences; alternatively, it may be viewed in a 'thick' sense, meaning that whatever the ends people pursue – deciding on a party for which to vote, deciding on whether or not to start a family – they do so through instrumentally rational behaviour by choosing a course of action which is 'utility maximising' (Ferejohn 1991). The point is that, as Friedman (1995) reminds us, the *possibility* that political behaviour *may* be underpinned by considerations of self-interest is often transformed into the assumption that political behaviour *is* determined by self-interest. For example, one of the founders of public choice theory[3] argued that 'the burden of proof should rest with those who claim that wholly different models of behaviour apply in the political and economic realms of behaviour' (Buchanan 1984: 135).

Mainstream variants of rational choice theory in contemporary usage

In this chapter, the application of RTC to politics is interpreted in the sense of applying RTC to 'public' decisions, where it is assumed that the actors on the political stage base their actions on self-interest. In short, RTC is, for the most part, interpreted as 'public choice' theory, in the sense defined above, or, as Tullock succinctly put it, 'the invasion of politics by economics' (1988: 227). The intellectual foundations of public choice theory lie in five seminal texts: by Arrow (1951), Downs (1957), Olson (1965a), Tullock (1967) and Nordhaus (1975). Each of these is discussed below.

Public choice derives its rationale from the fact that, in many areas, 'political' and 'economic' considerations interact, so that a proper understanding of issues in one field requires a complementary understanding of issues in the other.

Much of economic activity is carried out in a market environment, where the protagonists are households, on the one hand, and firms, on the other. Both sides, according to the rules of economic analysis, have clear objectives: households want to consume goods in quantities that will maximise their utility and firms want to produce goods in quantities that will maximise their profits. The market allows households to reveal their preferences to firms and firms to meet these preferences in such a way that the separate decisions of millions of economic agents, acting independently of one another, are reconciled.

However, a significant part of economic activity involves the state[4] and is therefore carried out in a non-market environment. One reason for the existence of such non-market activities is the existence of 'public goods' or goods supplied by government to its citizens. Of course, the scope of non-market activity depends on the country being considered: in Sweden a range of services – provision of childcare facilities, health and education – are provided by government; in the USA these services are provided by the market.

Another reason for government involvement in the economy is due to the fact that markets do not always operate efficiently. When they do not, because of 'market imperfections' leading to 'market failure', governments have to step in to correct such inefficiencies. These interventions may take the form of corrective taxes and subsidies and/or they may take the form of regulation and directives. At the macroeconomic level, governments are responsible for stabilising, and promoting, the economy's performance with respect to a number of economic variables: unemployment, inflation, the exchange rate, national income, etc.

But, whatever the nature and degree of governmental intervention in the economy, the basic problem that democratically elected governments face is of acting in a manner consistent with what their citizens desire. People express their demands through their votes; if there is a mismatch between the demand for and supply of outcomes, then the political market will take 'corrective action' analogous to the corrective action that economic markets take when the demand for and supply of goods and services is not in harmony.

It was dissatisfaction with the inability and failure of traditional political science methods to address basic issues in political economy that led to the emergence of the new discipline of 'public choice'. These basic issues were, *inter alia*, what factors influence votes? What is the 'best' system of voting for ensuring a correct revelation of preferences? Can the actions of individuals be made more effective when they act collectively? What is the role of re-election concerns in determining the supply of government output? Is there the possibility of conflict between different departments of government? The new discipline of public choice explicitly addressed these issues, and its analysis was explicitly predicated on the assumption that the behaviour of individuals and institutions was motivated by self-interest.

In this way, public choice theory forcefully reminds political scientists of the view held by Machiavelli and Hobbes that many ostensibly public-spirited policies may be motivated by self-interest; with similar force, it reminds economists of the unreality of basing analysis of economic policy on the assumption that the state is a 'benevolent dictator' acting so as to do 'the greatest good for the greatest number'. More generally, the arrival of public choice signalled a shift from a 'normative' to a 'positive' analysis of the political process: the subject matter of public choice was what political actors actually do, not what they should do.

Voting procedures

A major contribution of public choice theory has been to expand our knowledge and understanding of voting procedures. The voting problem is one of selecting, on the basis of the declared preferences of the electorate, one out of an available set of options. Stated in this manner, the voting problem is akin to the problem of social choice, where individual preferences are to be aggregated to arrive at a notion of 'social welfare'.

For example, every individual in society may rank different 'projects' according to the net benefits that they expect to obtain. The problem is that such a ranking by individuals may not lead to a social ranking that is a ranking to which all individuals in society would subscribe. For example, with three individuals (A, B and C) and three projects (X, Y and Z) suppose the rankings are as given in Table 9.1. Then in a sequence of pair-wise comparisons: X versus Y, Y wins, since both A and B prefer X to Y; Y versus Z, Y wins, since both A and C prefer Y to Z; X versus Z, Z wins, since both B and C prefer Z to X. The implied social ordering is that X is preferred to Y; Y is preferred to Z; but Z is preferred to X! The cyclical nature of social preferences arises from the fact that the social ordering is not transitive – or, in the language of electoral studies, there is no *Condorcet winner*. Indeed, the problem of social choice is not unlike that of voting behaviour: in both cases, the issue is one of translating individual preferences into an agenda for collective action that faithfully represents these preferences. This was a point noted by Black (1948).

More generally, the possibility of intransitivity in social rankings – of the sort described above – is not necessarily the result of obtaining such rankings from pair-wise majority rule voting; intransitivity can occur from the application of any rule for creating social rankings which satisfies certain minimal properties. This was demonstrated by Arrow (1951), in his celebrated 'Impossibility Theorem', when he showed that any social rule which satisfied a minimal set of fairness conditions[5] could produce an intransitive ranking when two or more persons had to choose from three or more projects.

Arrow's result rendered all democratic rules of collective action suspect – the idea that the state could act in terms of a well-defined social interest by aggregating individual preferences (Bergson 1938) was now rendered invalid. The work of Black (1948) and Arrow (1951) also drew attention to the potentially unstable nature of majority coalitions. Although the problem of cyclical voting had been known of since Condorcet (see pp. 151), Black's and Arrow's work brought out its relevance to political science. Variations and extensions of Arrow's (1951) result have taken the form of investigating whether the theorem

Table 9.1 Cyclical social preference under pair-wise voting

Preference ordering	A	B	C
First choice	X	Z	Y
Second choice	Y	X	Z
Third choice	Z	Y	X

would continue to be true when one or the other of these axioms was weakened. One line of investigation that has been extensively followed is to relax the requirement that social choice must be based on social *ordering* (complete, reflexive and transitive). Another has been to restrict individual preferences to 'single-peaked' preferences:[6] Arrow showed that if individual preferences are single peaked and the number of voters is odd, then majority decision will yield transitive social preference.[7]

The relevance of the work of Black (1948) and of Arrow (1951) to the voting problem lay in attempting to identify: (a) the desirable conditions that any voting system should satisfy and (b) a voting system that satisfied these conditions. May (1952) showed that when there were only two alternatives, majority voting was unambiguously the best. The problem was to extend this result when there were more than two alternatives. In such situations, different voting systems could be constructed, all of which seemed fair and reasonable – and all of which, in the event of two alternatives, yielded majority rule – but which nevertheless yielded different outcomes.

One possible system is plurality ('first past the post') voting, in which each voter votes for exactly one option and the option receiving the largest number of votes wins. One problem with this system is that it is based on an incomplete revelation of preferences: there is no requirement for a voter to rank the options for which he/she did not vote. As Table 9.2 shows, on the basis of votes cast by 60 voters, A wins by plurality, yet A would lose against B alone (25 to 35) and against C alone (23 to 37). This then points to a second defect of plurality voting, which is the fact that it is subject to agenda manipulation and that the presence, or absence, of options – even if those options cannot win – can affect the outcome. The alternative is for each voter to rank the alternatives in order of preference (as in Table 9.2) and then for the appropriate electoral rule to aggregate these individual rankings into an overall ranking. Such a procedure is termed an 'ordinal procedure'. One possible electoral rule based on an ordinal procedure is the *Borda count*: in the presence of N options, assign N points to the option ranked first, N-1 points to the option ranked second and, finally, 1 point to the option ranked last. A Borda count applied to the data in Table 9.2 sees C a comfortable winner, with 138 points; A coming second, with 105 points; and B finishing last, with 91 points. The Borda count method, however, is also susceptible to false revelation of preferences: voters, irrespective of their true preferences, would be inclined to give the lowest preference vote to the candidate

Table 9.2 Plurality voting

	23 voters	*19 voters*	*16 voters*	*2 voters*
First preference	A	B	C	C
Second preference	C	C	B	A
Third preference	B	A	A	B

they thought was most threatening to their preferred candidate's electoral prospects (Miller 1987).

Both plurality and ordinal procedures may be multi-stage procedures – so that the chosen option only emerges after successive rounds of voting, by combining either of them with the possibility of elimination. Thus, plurality plus run-off eliminates all but the two strongest candidates in the earlier rounds, leaving a simple run-off between the two candidates for the final round. An alternative is to eliminate in each round the weakest candidate and to choose a candidate after N-1 rounds of voting. Although both these voting procedures – and variants thereof – are reasonable, they do not necessarily lead to the same outcome. For example, in Table 9.3: C wins under plurality; A, with 50 points, wins under a Borda count; and B wins against C either under plurality with run-off or with successive elimination of the weakest candidate.

The way out, as proposed by Condorcet in 1785, was to have a pair-wise comparison of alternatives, choosing, at each comparison, the alternative with greater support. An alternative that wins over all the others is then selected as the preferred option and is termed the *Condorcet winner*. Thus, in Table 9.2, the Condorcet winner C beats A 37 to 23, and beats B 41 to 19. However, as Table 9.1 showed and as Table 9.4 shows, a Condorcet winner need not exist: Table 9.3 demonstrates the phenomenon of 'cyclical voting' – also termed the 'paradox of voting' – whereby A beats B (33 to 27), B beats C (42 to 18) and C beats A (35 to 25).

The question, therefore, is whether it is possible to specify conditions under which cyclical voting will not occur. This was addressed by Black (1948) using the concept of 'single-peaked' preferences. Suppose that the set of alternatives can be represented in one dimension – for example choice between different levels of public expenditure – and suppose that for each voter there is a preferred level of expenditure – which may be different for different voters – such that preferences drop monotonically for levels on either side of this optimum. In such a case (see Table 9.1) voter preferences are said to be *single peaked*. Under single-peaked preferences the median voter decides, in the sense that the preferred choice of the median voter is the Condorcet winner. This result, which is the celebrated

Median Voter Theorem, is illustrated in Table 9.1, in which there are five voters – V_1 to V_5 – each with single-peaked preferences. In a pair-wise contest, the preferred choice of the median voter, V_3, will beat the preferred choice of all other voters.

Table 9.3 Multi-stage voting

	4 voters	4 voters	2 voters	9 voters
First preference	A	B	B	C
Second preference	B	A	D	D
Third preference	D	D	A	A
Fourth preference	C	C	C	B

Source: Miller 1987.

Table 9.4 The paradox of voting

	23 voters	17 voters	2 voters	10 voters	8 voters
First preference	A	B	B	C	C
Second preference	B	C	A	A	B
Third preference	C	A	C	B	A

How voters decide

The notion of single-peaked preferences has a certain plausibility in terms of single-issue politics. Although the notion of a single peak can be extended to multidimensional issues, the results are far more complex and will not be reported here. However, if voters distil the complexity of issues facing them into a personal ideological position (extreme left, left, centrist, right, extreme right), then the Median Voter Theorem can be used to predict outcomes in a two-party democracy (Hotelling 1929; Downs 1957). Suppose that voters are distributed along the spectrum of ideological positions from 'left' to 'right' as shown in Table 9.3. Then, if the initial party positions are L and R, R wins: R obtains votes from those to the right of R as well as votes from those between X and R, where X is the mid-point between L and R; L receives votes from voters to its left as well as the votes of those between L and X. However, L can increase its vote, as can R, by moving closer to the centre. Inter-party competition will then ensure that each party will occupy the 'middle ground' – that is, adopt the ideological position of the median voter.

Downs's (1957) book is regarded as one of the cornerstones of contemporary rational actor theory (Monroe 1991) and, not coincidentally, the theory of voting contained within it accords most closely with standard economic theory. In a Downsian world, each voter was rational in the sense that he/she voted for the party that was believed to offer him/her the greatest benefits. Party manifestos were an important way by which voters evaluated these benefits, and consequently, for Downs, such manifestos were a means of winning elections.

However, because collecting information on parties was expensive, no voter would attempt a comprehensive evaluation. Instead, each voter would confine his/her evaluation to those areas where party differences, in the voter's view, were significantly large. When two parties tried to achieve an election-winning position along an ideological position, Downs argued (building upon Hotelling's (1929) result) that they would – as discussed above – converge upon the median voter's ideological position. In summary, therefore, Downs made a seminal contribution towards understanding the nature of party competition, rational ignorance and spatial voting.

Interest groups and collective action

One way that people can reveal their preferences is by voting; another way is by associating with like-minded persons to form 'interest groups' which then lobby government for favourable treatment. The problem is that it does not follow from the fact that a group of people have a common interest that they will form an interest group and bear the cost of collective action. Olson (1965a) pointed out that collective action is vitiated by the 'free rider' problem of public economics: an economically rational person would not participate in (and share the costs of) an interest group because he/she cannot be excluded from any benefits that may accrue from the activities of the group. Consequently, a great deal of potential collective action will not in fact materialise. This view – emphasising as it did the primacy of the individual – flew in the face of those in political science who regarded organised groups as the basic units in politics.

Olson (1965a) argued that two conditions were required for collective action to occur. First, the number of persons acting collectively should be relatively small, so that if one person decided to 'free ride', the group would be rendered ineffective and no benefits would accrue. Second, the group should have access to 'selective incentives' by which it could penalise those who have not, and reward those who have, borne the cost of collective action. Trade union 'closed-shop' arrangements, by which only members can get jobs, are one example of selective incentives. Selective incentives are less often available to potential entrants and to low-income groups. Thus it is the employed rather than the unemployed who are organised, and it is the professional groups – doctors, teachers, lawyers – who are better organised than unskilled occupations. For this reason, Olson (1985) observed that, in the main, collective action would be anti-egalitarian and pro-establishment. Olson's work elevated the 'free rider' problem to a central position in political science. In Mueller's view, 'the free rider problem pervades all of collective choice' (1989: 58).

Collective action and rent-seeking

One of the reasons that collective action would be retrogressive is that it would lead to 'rent-seeking'. Tullock (1967) was the first to analyse rent-seeking. It is a well-known proposition in economics that monopoly price will be higher (and output lower) than price (and output) under competitive conditions. This enables a monopolist to earn 'rent', equivalent to the loss in consumers' surplus from not producing the competitive output at the competitive price.

However, in order to obtain these rents interest groups would be prepared to invest resources to secure a monopoly position. Hence the true cost of monopoly is not just the loss in consumers' surplus but also the total resources invested in 'rent-seeking activities'. Such rent-seeking activities may take the form of airline cartels lobbying for a monopoly over a particular route; less obviously, it may also take the form of a trade union lobbying a firm for 'single-union' recognition. In general, one can categorise three types of expenditure (Buchanan 1980) associated with rent-seeking: expenditure undertaken to secure a monopoly; the efforts of public officials to react to such expenditure; and third-party distortions caused by the rent-seeking activity. For example, in a country with exchange controls, commodities may only be imported with an import licence. Businesses may lobby government to be granted such licences, and the prospect of earning monopoly rents (as businessmen) or of benefiting from the largesse of businessmen (as bureaucrats) may dictate the careers of young persons.

The above analysis raises the question: what is wrong with rent-seeking activities? The answer is that many rent-seeking activities produce profit *without* producing output. Such activities have been described by Bhagwati (1982) as directly unproductive profit-seeking activities. The consequence of contemporary interest in rent-seeking is that a great deal of government activity is regarded with suspicion by conservative economists: the feeling is that much of public-sector activity is concerned with providing rents to special interest groups, and for that, if for no other, reason, small government is good government.

The political business cycle

A key proposition in public choice is that economic activity tends to revolve around election dates, with governments seeking favourable outcomes just before an election and postponing unfavourable outcomes until just after an election. The phenomenon to which this gives rise is known as the political business cycle, and since Nordhaus's (1975) seminal work in formalising and clarifying the nature of these cycles, this has been one of the most researched areas in political economy.

Nordhaus (1975) focused on the short-run trade-off between inflation and unemployment. In his model, the electorate was only concerned about inflation and unemployment, and rewarded or punished its government according to whether it performed well or badly on these two fronts. But, given the existence of the trade-off, it was impossible for a government to do well with respect to both inflation and unemployment. Under these circumstances, Nordhaus (1975) showed that there would be a political business cycle of the following form. Immediately after an election, the government raises the unemployment rate and reduces the inflation rate. This depresses inflationary expectations and moves the Phillips curve[8] closer to the origin. Nearer to the election date, expansionary policies lower the unemployment rate and raise the inflation rate, but – and this is the crucial point – since the government has 'invested' by bringing the Phillips curve closer to the origin, the inflation rate rises, but not by much. The government then fights the election on the basis of both a low unemployment and a low inflation rate.

Major criticisms

In their celebrated book, Green and Shapiro (1994) offered a critique of RCT as it was applied to political science. Their essential point was that, while RCT had led to formidable *analytical* advances in political science, successful empirical applications of rational choice models had been few and far between. In their view, the root of the problem was that RCT had the overwhelming ambition to arrive at nothing less than universal theories of politics – theories that would be true at all times and in all places. It was this major methodological defect that led to a disjunction between theory and reality.

In presenting their critique, Green and Shapiro (1994) were quick to concede the many achievements that have emanated from the application of RCT to political science. But in terms of its consonance with reality RCT contains a number of pathologies. These have been succinctly summarised by Friedman (1995) and his summary is reproduced here:

- RCT scholars engage in 'post-hoc theory development': first they look at the facts and devise a theory to fit them; they often fail to formulate empirically testable hypotheses.
- If data contrary to the theory later appears, the theory is modified to fit the new facts.
- RCT theories often rely on unobservable entities which make them empirically untestable.
- RCT theorists engage in arbitrary 'domain restriction': the theory is applicable whenever it seems to work, and not otherwise.
- RCT theories are vague about the magnitude of the effects being predicted.
- RCT theories often search for confirming, rather than falsifying, evidence.

Case study: vote transfers in the 1998 elections to the Northern Ireland Assembly

As the previous sections have indicated, our understanding of the voting procedures and of the logic of voters has been greatly enhanced by the application of RCT to political science. Yet, according to Green and Shapiro (1994), explaining why people vote remains the Achilles heel of RCT. In a real-world election, with a large number of voters, each voter knows that his/her vote will have an infinitesimally small influence on the final outcome. Given the cost of going to the polling booth, it would be instrumentally rational not to vote. RCT would predict a zero turnout. Yet a substantial number of people do, in fact, vote. The RCT response to this is either to exempt mass elections from the application of RCT on the grounds that instrumental considerations would not apply to voting in such elections (see point 4 in the previous list) or to modify their theory to include the 'psychic' benefits that people obtain from being seen to do their democratic duty (see point 2 in the list). Against this background of the importance of voting both to RCT and its critics, it would be relevant to examine a case study involving voting, and the post-Good Friday elections to Northern Ireland's Assembly are particularly apposite.

Traditionally, voters in Northern Ireland have always voted along community lines: Unionist voters vote for Unionist parties – the larger Ulster Unionist Party (UUP) and the smaller Democratic Unionist Party (DUP) – and Nationalist voters vote for Nationalist parties – the larger Social Democratic Labour Party (SDLP) and the smaller Sinn Fein (SF). But the Assembly elections of June 1998 in Northern Ireland, which involved each of the eighteen Westminster constituencies in the Province electing six members to the Assembly, was the first occasion that voters in the Province were pulled by another force. This was the referendum of May 1998, in which 71 per cent of voters said 'Yes' to the Good Friday Agreement and 29 per cent said 'No'. The referendum has caused a fissure in Unionist politics, with the UUP and its allies supporting the Agreement and the DUP and its allies opposing it bitterly. The result of this fissure was that it was only by a small majority – estimates vary from 52 to 58 per cent – that the Agreement was carried in the Unionist community. On the other hand, since both the Nationalist parties supported it, the Agreement was overwhelmingly endorsed by Nationalists.

The injection of the Agreement into Northern Ireland politics meant that in the Assembly elections Unionist voters were voting along two, opposing, dimensions: traditional community-based voting, which meant sharing their support between the UUP and DUP; and, on the other hand, Agreement-based voting, which meant withholding their support for one, or the other, of the Unionist parties while simultaneously, for pro-Agreement Unionists, crossing the community lines to share their support with the SDLP. The mechanism for sharing or withholding support was the system of Single Transferable Voting (STV) which underpinned the elections. Under this system, each voter writes a number against the name of each candidate listed on the ballot paper and this number expresses the voter's preference for the candidate, the most-preferred candidate having '1' against his/her name. After voting for one's most-preferred candidate, one can extend support to another candidate (perhaps from another party) by giving him/her one's second preference; support can be withheld from a candidate by not giving him/her any preference or by giving a low preference. What makes the system operational is that when a voter's most-preferred candidate is elected, by getting votes above the required 'quota', the votes in excess of this quota (the 'surplus' votes) are transferred to the other candidates using these lower preferences.

A good way of studying some of these transfer patterns is by examining how the surplus of candidates elected at the first count was distributed. The reason is that, under STV, when someone is elected at the first count *all* of his/her votes are examined to determine second preferences. However, if a candidate is elected at a count other than the first, only those votes received *at the count of election* are examined for subsequent preferences. This latter procedure may give a misleading impression of voter preferences, for two reasons. First, it offers only a partial picture – the votes received at earlier counts are ignored for the purposes of transferring votes. Second, it may offer a misleading picture of preferences: an SDLP candidate may be elected and pass on his/her surplus, but if the last transfers to the candidate are from an eliminated SF candidate, then the destination of the surplus will reflect the preferences of SF, not SDLP, voters.

Table 9.5 shows the destination of the surplus of twenty-three candidates who were elected at the first count in the 1998 Northern Ireland Assembly elections. The transfers are classified as follows:

- it is *non-transferable* if no preference, other than a first preference, was expressed on the ballot paper;
- it is an *intra-party* transfer if the second preference was for a candidate from the same party as the elected candidate;
- it is an *intra-community/intra-Agreement* transfer if the second preference was for a candidate from a *different* party, but with the *same* community identity and the *same* views on the Agreement as the party of the elected candidate: transfers from the SDLP to SF (and vice-versa) would fall into this category;
- it is an *intra-community/cross-Agreement* transfer if the second preference was for a candidate from a *different* party and with *different* views on the Agreement, but with the *same* community identity as the party of the elected candidate: transfers from the UUP to the DUP (and vice-versa) would fall into this category;
- it is a *cross-community/intra-Agreement* transfer if the second preference was for a candidate from a *different* party, with a *different* community identity, but with the *same* views on the Agreement as the party of the elected candidate: transfers from the SDLP to the UUP (and vice-versa) would fall into this category;
- it is a *secular transfer* if the second preference was for a candidate from a *different* party which did *not* have a community identity: transfers to the Alliance Party or the Women's Coalition constitute this category of transfers;
- all other second-preference transfers are classed as *other*.

The first thing to note about Table 9.5 is the disparity between the parties in the proportion of second-preference votes that they were able to keep within their party (the intra-party transfers). The least efficient undoubtedly were the UK Unionists in North Down and the Alliance Party in East Belfast: only 57 per cent of those voting for Robert McCartney in North Down and for Lord Alderdice in East Belfast named their respective mates as their second preference. Indeed, 19 per cent of the McCartney surplus votes went to the two DUP candidates (intra-community/intra-Agreement transfer), neither of whom were elected and – this was the cruellest cut – 12 per cent went to the two UUP candidates (intra-community/cross-Agreement transfer), both of whom were elected. For the Alliance Party in East Belfast, the galling fact was that 13 per cent of the Alderdice vote was non-transferable.

Among the Nationalist parties, the party loyalty of SDLP voters was severely tested by the presence of SF candidates: Gallagher in Fermanagh and South Tyrone could only retain 60 per cent of his surplus for his party, losing nearly one-fifth of it to SF, and even Hume, in Foyle, lost 15 per cent of his massive surplus to SF. By contrast, Adams in West Belfast and Neeson in East Antrim retained well over 80 per cent of their surplus for SF, and the only reason for the 12 per cent haemorrhage from Adams's vote was the loyalty of voters towards the SDLP's Joe Hendron.

There was considerable traffic, among Unionist voters, between the 'Yes' and 'No' sides of the Agreement (intra-community/cross-Agreement transfers). From the UUP, 17 per cent of Trimble's vote in Upper Bann, 10 per cent of Taylor's vote in Strangford and 6 per cent of Wilson's vote in South Antrim went to anti-Agreement Unionist candidates.[9] The DUP were no less affected by this cross-Agreement voter mobility: the leakage from the DUP vote to the UUP in North Belfast (Dodds), East Londonderry (Campbell) and Strangford (Iris Robinson) was, respectively, 14, 10 and 9 per cent. Only the Reverend Ian Paisley, in North Antrim, was able to stem this haemorrhage: he passed on 93 per cent of his surplus to his son.

Against this background of intra-community traffic – both among Nationalist and Unionist voters – there was little evidence of cross-community mobility in voter preferences. Hardly any of the vote from Taylor, Trimble and Wilson went to SDLP candidates, and SDLP voters returned the compliment when they restricted their second-preference vote to Nationalist candidates.

So what can one conclude from these results? Mainly that the mould of Northern Ireland politics is firmly intact. Voters in the 1998 elections to the Northern Ireland Assembly were prepared to move between candidates from 'moderate' and 'extremist' parties: the vote transfers between the SDLP and SF was evidence of that. They were prepared to swap between pro-Agreement and anti-Agreement candidates. But, even after the most momentous events in Northern Ireland's short history – events which offered Northern Ireland's voters an alternative to their traditional voting habits – they were not prepared to cross the communal divide. *Plus ça change, plus c'est la même chose.*

Table 9.5 Northern Ireland Assembly elections: June 1998, surplus transfers from candidates elected at the first count

Candidate	Party	Constituency	Surplus	Non-transferable (%)	Intra-party (%)	Intra-community and intra-Agreement (%)	Intra-community and cross-Agreement (%)	Cross-community and intra-Agreement (%)	Secular (%)	Other (%)	TOTAL (%)
McCartney	UKU	N.Down	2,857	2	57	19	12	0	0	10	100
Campbell	DUP	E.Derry	456	8	70	10	11	0	0	1	100
Dodds	DUP	N.Belfast	1,600	3	68	14	14	0	0	1	100
Gibson	DUP	W.Tyrone	1,450	2	0	0	84	0	1	13	100
Paisley	DUP	N.Antrim	3,489	1	93	3	2	0	0	0	100
McCrea	DUP	Mid-Ulster	3,224	1	84	0	14	0	0	1	100
Robinson, I.	DUP	Strangford	3,346	2	84	9	4	0	0	1	100
Robinson, P.	DUP	E.Belfast	5,562	0	82	6	11	0	0	1	100
Alderdice	Alliance	E.Belfast	487	13	57	0	0	23	2	5	100
Neeson	Alliance	E.Antrim	159	4	66	0	0	20	0	10	100
Adams	SF	W.Belfast	3,106	0	84	12	0	0	1	3	100
Doherty	SF	W.Tyrone	462	10	83	5	0	0	0	2	100
Beggs, Jnr	UUP	E.Antrim	676	7	51	5	31	0	3	3	100
Taylor	UUP	Strangford	3,070	2	63	16	10	1	4	4	100
Trimble	UUP	Upper Bann	5,137	0	75	0	17	1	5	2	100
Wilson	UUP	S.Antrim	406	3	82	0	6	1	7	1	100
Gallagher	SDLP	Fermanagh /S.Tyrone	842	6	62	19	0	0	11	2	100
Hendron	SDLP	W.Belfast	168	29	60	7	0	0	0	4	100
Hume	SDLP	Foyle	5,609	1	78	15	0	1	3	2	100
McGrady	SDLP	S.Down	3,036	3	73	8	0	1	8	7	100
Maginness	SDLP	N.Belfast	320	3	78	12	0	1	3	3	100
Mallon	SDLP	Newry /Armagh	5,847	3	73	16	0	1	4	3	100
Rodgers	SDLP	Upper Bann	2,059	3	70	18	0	0	3	6	100

*** *Note*: Figures in parentheses are surpluses.

SF Sinn Fein UKU UK Unionist Party DUP Democratic Unionist Party UUP Ulster Unionist Party SDLP Social Democratic Labour Party

Source: Adapted from *Irish Times*, 29 June 1998.

Summary review of theoretical utility

So how can RCT help us in understanding the outcome of the Northern Ireland Assembly elections? First, in the sense of Downs (1957), parties in Northern Ireland do have manifestos, but, at the most basic level, these amount to no more than appealing to sectarian loyalties: vote for me because I represent a Unionist/Nationalist party and you are Unionist/Nationalist. Underlying this broad sectarian agenda, there is a second, class-based manifesto: as a middle-class/working-class Nationalist, vote for the SDLP/SF; as a middle-class/working-class Unionist, vote for the UUP/DUP. At a primary level, the utility of voters is then determined by sectarian identity, and, given that sectarian identity has been taken account of, at a secondary level utility is determined by class identity. What the results do show is that while voters were willing to cross the class divide they were not prepared to cross the sectarian divide, even though the Good Friday Agreement offered them incentives to do so.

These results can be 'rationalised' by RCT. Politics in Northern Ireland is mostly about distribution: the cake is sent over from Westminster, and what Northern Ireland politicians (earlier civil servants) have to do is decide how to slice it. Given that much of the cake consists of public services, which have a strong geographical dimension, and given that Northern Ireland's two communities are concentrated in different parts of the region, it makes sense to stick with one's sectarian team through thick and thin: enable a Unionist/Nationalist legislator to be elected and he/she will look after you; flirt with the 'other side' and you could end up with nothing.

But what RCT cannot factor into its analysis of elections is two items: the power of individual candidates and the importance of party organisation. As was argued, neither Robert McCartney in North Down nor John Alderdice in East Belfast could convert individual popularity into party popularity. By contrast, the party discipline of Sinn Fein meant its vote leakage was minimal. The interplay between individual and party is a very important part of elections held under an STV system, and here it is imperative that an individual should not get bigger than the party. Yet the desire to stride the political stage like a Colossus (even so modest a political stage as that offered by Northern Ireland) is latent in all our politicians; but those who succumb to its siren call see their party's prospects irrevocably damaged. It is this kind of interplay that RCT, with its emphasis on instrumental rationality, cannot capture.

There can be little doubt that RCT – with its emphasis on the 'instrumentally rational' individual as the foundation of the political process – has significantly enhanced the scope of political science. To list but some of its achievements:

- RCT has raised the possibility that democratic institutions might be dysfunctional in ways not hitherto imagined (see the discussion of Arrow's (1951) Impossibility Theorem, pp. 150 - 2).
- RCT has 'explained' the cyclical nature of the economy in terms of elec

toral exigencies (see the discussion of Nordhaus's political business cycle, pp. 156).

- RCT has 'explained' the tendency for party platforms to converge (see the discussion on Downs (1957) and the Median Voter Theorem, pp. 153 - 5).
- RCT has refined our understanding of the basis on which people vote (Downs 1957; Frey and Schneider 1978; Fiorina 1981).
- RCT has drawn attention to the wasteful nature of activities to which government involvement in the economy gives rise (see the discussion on Tullock (1967) and 'rent-seeking', pp. 155).
- RCT has 'explained' the tendency of governments to get ever larger in terms of the behaviour, and the manipulation of democratic institutions (Peltzman 1980; Meltzer and Richards 1981).
- RCT has brought a fresh look at the behaviour of bureaucracies and bureaucrats (Niskanen 1971).
- RCT has refined our understanding of coalition formation in government through the use of new methods of analysis like game theory (Laver and Schofield 1990; Laver and Shepsle 1996).

But, in the end, RCT in political science raises the same questions that it does in economics. Sen (1977) observed that, in economics, choice and preference are regarded as synonymous: I prefer A to B and therefore I choose A over B; I am observed to choose A over B and therefore it must be that I prefer A to B. Under such a tautological formulation, there is a certain banality in interpreting everyone as acting in a self-seeking manner – by definition, every action is self-seeking since it involves choosing the preferred option. The problem is that in economics no attention is paid to the motivation underlying an action. A person may act for self-seeking reasons, out of sympathy for another person or out of a sense of commitment. Although 'sympathy' can be incorporated into a utility-maximising framework, by allowing external effects (like the welfare of one's child) to affect one's utility, 'commitment' – which involves doing the 'right' thing even at the cost of suffering a reduction in utility[10] – inserts a wedge between choice and preference: I choose to vote not because I prefer, over all the options available to me, queuing in front of a polling booth on a Saturday morning, but because I want to demonstrate my commitment to democracy. Similarly, I choose not to falsely reveal my preferences when it comes to pricing a public good because I have a more overriding commitment to honesty. As Johansen – one of the giants of public-sector economics, which is a subject driven by the free-riding issue – expressed it:

> Economic theory in this, as well as in some other fields, tends to suggest that people are honest only to the extent they have economic incentives for being so. This is a *homo economicus* assumption which is far from being obviously true. No society can be viable without some norms and rules of conduct.

Such norms and rules are necessary for viability in fields where strict economic incentives are absent and cannot be created.

(Johansen 1976: 43)

In economics, a person is given *one* preference ordering and, when all is said and done, this preference ordering represents his *Weltanschauung*. Can one preference do all this? If it does, then, as Sen (1977) expressed it, the purely economic man is indeed close to being a social moron. RCT, notwithstanding its dazzling accomplishments, is in danger of sending the purely political man in the same direction.

Notes

1 One can note parenthetically that an implication of the consequential evaluation of actions, which underlies 'instrumental rationality', is that it is diametrically opposed to a *deontological* approach, which decides whether or not to undertake an action according to its essential 'rightness', irrespective of its consequences (Sen 2001). For example, the deontological insistence of a Mahatma Gandhi (or Martin Luther King or Nelson Mandela) on a non-violent movement – or the deontological refusal of the Democratic Unionist Party in Northern Ireland to have any truck with Sinn Fein – *irrespective of its consequences*, would fly in the face of the consequential approach of RCT. The *Bhagavad Gita* (the sacred book of Hindus, which is generally regarded as constituting the blueprint for the manner in which a 'good' Hindu should lead his/her life) is based upon Krishna recommending a single-minded pursuit of duty without thought for the consequences.
2 A preferred to B and B preferred to C must imply that A is preferred to C.
3 Public choice theory applies the principles of economic analysis to political (that is, 'public') decision-making. It is interpreted in this chapter as being synonymous with RCT.
4 Between one-third and half of gross domestic product in most countries of the Organisation for Economic Co-operation and Development (OECD) is generated through the activities of government.
5 These conditions were the axioms of: *unrestricted domain* (individuals had transitive preferences over all the policy alternatives); *Pareto choice* (if one project made someone better off than another project, without making anyone worse off, then it would be the socially preferred choice); *independence* (the ranking of two choices should not depend on what the other choices were); and *non-dictatorship* (the social ordering should not be imposed).
6 So that the alternatives are arranged in a line such that everyone's intensity of preference has only one peak.
7 This result, earlier discussed in Black (1948), cements the relationship between voting theory and social choice theory.
8 The Phillips curve (due to Phillips 1954) shows a negative relation between inflation and unemployment. The position of the curve depends upon the level of inflationary expectations – lower expectations move the curve in closer to the origin.
9 The fact that 31 per cent of Roy Beggs, Jnr's vote in North Belfast went to anti-Agreement candidates is to be discounted because Beggs, though a UUP candidate, stood on a rejectionist ticket.
10 See note 1.

Further reading

Chong, D. (1995) 'Rational Choice Theory's Mysterious Rivals', *Critical Review* 9: 37–57.

Friedman, J. (1995) 'Economic Approaches to Politics', *Critical Review* 9: 1–24.

Laver, M. and Schofield, N. (1990) *Multiparty Government*, Oxford: Oxford University Press.

Laver, M. and Shepsle, K. (1996) *Making and Breaking Governments: Cabinets and Legislatures in Parliamentary Democracies*, Cambridge: Cambridge University Press.

Sen, A.K. (2001) 'The Discipline of Cost–Benefit Analysis', *Journal of Legal Studies* 29: 931–52.

Tullock, G. (1988), *Wealth, Poverty and Politics*, Oxford: Basil Blackwell.

10 Policy transfer and the Irish university sector

Maura Adshead and Oliver Wall

Introduction

'Policy transfer' is the term used to refer to

> [the] growing body of literature stressing the process by which knowledge about policies, administrative arrangements, institutions *etc.* in one time and/or place is fed into the policy making arena in the development of policies, administrative arrangements and institutions in another time and/or place.
>
> (Dolowitz 1996: 1)

Within this literature there are those whose approach is relatively narrowly focused upon the transfer of *specific policies* as a result of strategic decisions taken by actors inside and outside government (Dolowitz and Marsh 1996). There are also those whose use of the concept is much broader, focusing on *general patterns of convergence* between the policies adopted by states (see, for example, Bennett 1991; Rose 1993). Within both groups, however, the role played by supra-national organisations is an important area for consideration (for a more substantive discussion of the role played by supra-national and external organisations, see Chapters 11 and 12, on Europeanisation and globalisation, respectively). This is because 'intergovernmental and international organisations encourage exchanges of ideas between countries. The European Community and OECD [Organisation for Economic Co-operation and Development] encourage exchanges among advanced industrial nations and the World Bank and the United Nations agencies focus on programs of concern to developing countries' (Rose 1993: 7).

In their review of policy transfer literature Dolowitz and Marsh (1996) identify six main categories of actors who may engage in the process: elected officials; political parties; bureaucrats and civil servants; pressure groups; policy entrepreneurs and experts; and supra-national institutions. The 'lessons' that they draw from alternative policy programmes in existence elsewhere may be positive or negative. Thus, for example, Ireland's decision to develop a more corporatist style of economic management (see Chapter 5) is often explained by successive Irish governments' decisions *not* to copy the prevalent British model of economic management created by stringent control of the money supply and inflation indicators, which is widely associated with 'boom/bust' cycles of economic development (see Bradley 2000). On the other hand, the Strategic Management Initiative (SMI), designed to bring about civil service reform in Ireland, is widely acknowledged as borrowing heavily from the experience of other reform programmes carried out in Canada and New Zealand (McNamara 1995).

Dolowitz and Marsh also point out that there may be different degrees of political emulation, since 'when engaged in policy transfer actors have a range of options on how to incorporate lessons into their political system' (1996: 16). This is because, 'in the real world, we would never expect a programme to transfer from one government to another without history, culture and institutions being taken into account' (Rose 1991: 21). In this respect, Rose outlines a scale of policy emulation, comprising five different degrees of policy transfer: copying, emulation, hybridisation, synthesis and inspiration (1991: 21–2). *Copying* involves the adoption more or less intact of a programme already in effect in another jurisdiction. *Emulation*, while rejecting the option of slavishly copying every detail, accepts that a particular programme elsewhere provides the best standard for designing legislation at home, albeit requiring adaptation to take account of different national circumstances. *Hybridisation* refers to a policy programme that combines recognisable elements from programmes in two different places:

> For example policy makers in a unitary state may want to transfer a programme in use in a federal system. In the absence of a federal structure, the substantive design may be borrowed from one country while the administrative means for delivering it may be based upon a unitary system.
>
> (Rose 1991: 22)

Synthesis is created by combining elements familiar in several different programmes into a whole that is distinctive (Rose 1991: 22). Finally, *inspiration* refers to the use of programmes in existence elsewhere that are used as an intellectual stimulus in order to develop a novel programme without analogue elsewhere (Rose 1991: 22). In this chapter, we examine the adoption of quality assurance mechanisms in the Irish university sector with a view to establishing the extent of policy transfer that occurred in the Irish case, and to see whether or not the policy transfer literature offers us any new insights into the reforms carried out in university management and administration in Ireland. Before doing so, however, we take a brief look at the development of policy transfer concepts and the major criticisms levelled against them.

Brief review of the evolution of this approach

The literature on policy transfer raises a number of themes that are of relevance to studies of public policy change. These include such concepts as policy diffusion, lesson drawing, policy learning, voluntary transfer, coercive transfer and indirect coercive transfer. Amongst these terms, policy diffusion is probably the oldest, and it refers to the mapping out of the process by which policy is transferred, in terms of the timing, geographic proximity, resource similarities and spatial distribution (Walker 1969). These early studies of policy transfer were, however, primarily concerned with policy diffusion across the United States and were more interested in charting the process – as opposed to the content (in terms of implementation and implications) – of policy transfer (Dolowitz and Marsh 1996).

Lesson drawing (or policy learning) addresses the question: 'under what circumstances and to what extent can a programme that is effective in one place transfer to another' (Rose 1991: 3)? The process of lesson drawing starts with scanning programmes in effect elsewhere, and ends with the prospective evaluation of what would happen if a programme already in effect elsewhere was transferred here in the future. Generally speaking, the choice of lessons depends upon a subjective definition of proximity, epistemic[1] communities linking experts together, functional interdependence between governments, and the authority of intergovernmental institutions. In the case of the European Union (EU), Rose has argued that it promotes cross-national comparison 'so that member states can become aware of what their competitors are doing and decide which elements of foreign programs they may wish to copy or adapt' (Rose 1993: 105). In this sense, Rose's concept of lesson drawing is more concerned with the conditions of policy transfer.

Later writers such as Dolowitz and Marsh (1996), who focused more on the agents of policy transfer, used terms such as 'voluntary' and 'coercive transfer' in order to emphasise the process of policy transfer for those actors primarily affected by it. Voluntary transfer refers to policy actors actively searching out 'ready-made solutions' to current policy problems, whereas coercive transfer refers to the imposition of new policies and policy procedures – either directly or indirectly – by the government, by one government over another, by transnational agencies, or by supra-national bodies such as the EU.

Taken together, the policy transfer literature offers us concepts that facilitate charting the process of policy change; outlining the conditions that structure that process; and evaluating the actions of key policy players. This could be viewed as simply 'rich description', falling far short of any grand theoretical design; still, the policy transfer literature does offer useful concepts for empirical studies and cross-national comparisons of public policy change. In this chapter we will present a case study of the evolution of the 1996 Universities Bill, in order to examine what use policy transfer concepts might be in explaining policy change in the Irish university system. Before doing this, however, we provide a few definitions of the terms most commonly used in the policy transfer literature.

Mainstream variants of policy transfer in contemporary usage

There are two major contemporary sets of policy transfer studies: those associated with Richard Rose (1991, 1993) and concerned primarily with 'lesson drawing'; and those associated with Dolowitz and Marsh (1996), which are concerned primarily with the 'who' and 'why' questions of policy transfer. Lesson drawing addresses the question: 'under what circumstances and to what extent can a programme that is effective in one place transfer to another' (Rose 1991: 3)? Thus the term 'lesson drawing' implies that 'political actors or decision makers in one country draw lessons from one or more other countries, which they then apply to their own political system' (Dolowitz and Marsh 1996: 4). The key difference between these two is that Rose suggests that 'lesson drawing tends to be voluntaristic' (1991: 6), whereas Dolowitz and Marsh (1996) see this type of policy transfer as only one variant in a range of possible scenarios – not all of which are necessarily voluntarily entered into.

For Rose, the stimulus to search for lessons is dissatisfaction with current modes of policy operation and implementation (1991: 10–19). At this junction, policy-makers have two alternatives: they may speculate about how a novel programme would work in the future; or they may search (across time or space) for an alternative programme that already exists, with a view to 'importing' a particular policy solution from elsewhere. Lesson drawing implies the latter, and the tendency is for established political values to influence the direction in which the search is undertaken (Rose 1991: 14). As a consequence, 'subjective identification is more important than geographical propinquity in directing the search', and, not unusually, pre-existing informal networks and epistemic communities provide the primary sources when searching for policy programmes and ideas.

For Dolowitz and Marsh, lesson drawing focuses on 'voluntary' policy transfer, which occurs as a result of the free choices of political actors. They are keen to point out, however, that policy transfer may also occur as a consequence of 'one government or supra-national institution pushing, or even forcing, another government to adopt a particular policy' (Dolowitz and Marsh 1996: 4). For them, policy transfer is a term that may refer to both voluntary and involuntary transfers of policy programmes from one place to another. Accordingly, they set out three main types of policy transfer: voluntary transfer, direct coercive transfer and indirect coercive transfer – each of which is discussed below.

Voluntary transfer

Drawing from the work of Rose (1991, 1993) and other writers (Anderson 1978; Polsby 1984), voluntary transfer is usually precipitated by some form of dissatisfaction with current policy practice. It is assumed that when governmental policies are functioning properly there is no need to look to other policy programmes elsewhere. This idea is straightforward enough, but seems to preclude the possibility that states or governments would proactively seek alternative policy solutions before – as a means of pursuing 'best practice' – even if they are relatively satisfied with current modes of policy implementation.

Direct coercive transfer

The most direct method of coercive policy transfer is when one government forces another to adopt a policy, but this kind of transfer from one country to another is rare. More usually, coercive policy transfer arises as a consequence of the influence or intervention of supra-national institutions, such as the World Bank or EU. In Ireland, for example, the establishment of the Food Safety Authority of Ireland (FSAI) was in no small part a response to the EU's *White Paper on Food Safety* (CEC 1999), which contained a detailed set of proposals designed to raise consumer confidence in the food industry when it had reached an all time low after the BSE ('mad cow' disease) crisis (see Taylor and Millar 2002a). Indirect coercive transfer may also arise as a consequence of the influence of large multinational corporations (MNCs), which may force governments to pursue certain policies over others if they are deemed to be more favourable to the MNCs concerned.

Indirect coercive transfer

Drawing on the work of E. Haas (1989), Majone (1990) and Bennett (1991), indirect coercive transfer points to the increasing interdependence of states and governments, which pushes them to work together to find policy solutions to common problems. The impetus for policy transfer here may come from the indirect effect of shared externalities (acid rain, AIDS, environmental pollution, etc.). In this respect, Haas (1990) demonstrated how such interdependence was responsible for policy transfer and the development of common environmental policies between the Mediterranean countries. On a wider scale, we can see the same logic driving broader environmental legislation taken up by EU member states. The evolution of EU environmental policy through the incorporation of successive Environmental Action Programmes (EAPs) in each of the member states is a clear example of how increasing interdependence, acknowledged and developed by the institutions of the EU, led to the emergence of an international consensus which resulted in the policy transfer of common environmental approaches and policies (Peterson and Bomberg 1999; see also Lenschow 1999).

Major criticisms

Clearly, the major problem with the policy transfer literature is the tendency found in policy transfer studies to offer post-hoc rationalisations of the likely factors that may have been influential in facilitating transfer. This is very different, however, from offering a satisfactory account of causal processes. As a consequence, critics of policy transfer would argue that, at best, all policy transfer studies can offer are 'rich descriptions' of policy change, which are not, however, underpinned by any serious methodological approach or rigorous framework for analysis.

Moreover, the transfer literature often has an implicitly rationalistic assumption that policy-makers go out searching for solutions to problems. In fact, the process of policy transfer rarely proceeds from a scenario in which political actors identify a problem, engage in an exhaustive search of all the models that exist, and respond with an objective evaluation of the 'best' policy. It is often the case that the political actors are drawn to particular types of policy in particular countries. Rose acknowledges this when he suggests that 'the tendency is for established political values to influence the direction in which the search is undertaken' (1991: 14); nevertheless, since the basis of the explanation offered in the transfer literature is primarily actor oriented it remains vulnerable to all the usual arguments about the relative importance of structure versus agency in accounts of policy change.

In addition, given that there is rarely pure policy emulation, it is likely that certain governance regimes are more capable of political learning/policy importation and adaptation than others. We need therefore to establish how the agenda becomes set in favour of some policy options over others: what, for example, were the other available options under consideration (if any), and why was the chosen policy option selected as the 'successful policy'? Such an approach would seem to demand that more attention be paid to the institutions and architecture of the political system than is currently the case in most transfer literature (for an expanded discussion of these issues, see Chapters 8 and 9, on new institutionalist and rational choice theory approaches, respectively).

Finally, in addition to certain structural constraints and conditions that mediate the process of transfer, it may be that some policy concepts are more susceptible to transfer and diffusion than others. Perhaps there are specific features associated with some policy options that seem to make them more eligible for adoption than other possible alternatives. If this is the case, then the policy transfer literature could be accused of missing the point – instead of focusing exclusively on the *who* and *why* of policy transfer (identifying the main actors in the policy process and the particular circumstances that shaped their policy choices), perhaps the real focus should be upon what types of policy are most easily transferred and how the configuration of alternative policy environments affects the potential for political learning. Before any policy is transferred, there must be the structural, ideological and institutional conditions that support such transfers. Assuming that this is the case, studies of policy transfer should concentrate as much on policy content and on institutional architectures as on - anything else.

Case study: policy learning and policy transfer the example of 'quality' in the Irish university system

This case study looks at how 'policy learning' helped shape the system of 'Quality Assurance and Quality Improvement' currently in use in the Irish university system. It begins by taking a look at the broader European context within which the Irish university sector must operate. There follows a brief review of the development of quality-audit procedures in the UK – Ireland's closest neighbour, in terms of the historical and institutional evolution of Irish universities, as well as the more obvious geopolitical and linguistic links between the two states. The study concludes with an examination of the development of Irish university 'quality-audit' systems and illustrates that they are both an example of *indirect coercive transfer* in response to European-wide developments and of *policy learning* in reaction against audit procedures developed in the UK.

The European Pilot Project

Under the Dutch Presidency of the European Council in late 1991, a Council of the Ministers of Education put forward a plan to examine ways in which a 'Trans European Model for Quality Assurance' could be designed and implemented. The Council invited the recently appointed Director-General Thomas O'Dwyer of the newly reformed Directorate-General XXII: Education, Training and Youth[2] to 'undertake a comparative study of the methods used in the Member States to evaluate the quality of Higher Education' (CEC 1998: 1). The Commission was also asked to take a further step and 'examine the possibility of developing a limited number of pilot projects in quality assessment in higher education with a view to strengthening co-operation in this field at the European level, taking into account concrete experiences acquired by the Member States in this area' (CEC 1998: 1).

The European Pilot Project (the Project) was initiated in November 1994 and involved all fifteen member states, as well as two members of the European Free Trade Association (EFTA), Norway and Iceland. In total, forty-six institutions were involved with this report. The Project was finally completed in December 1995 and the 'European Report' presenting the findings of the study was published. In order to carry out this project, the Commission established a Management Group made up of experts from the countries which had already initiated assessment exercises (France, Denmark, the United Kingdom and the Netherlands, and also a national representative from Norway, Germany and Portugal). The Management Group delegated the day-to-day management of the Project to a joint secretariat of the French *Comité National d'Evaluation* (CNE) and the Danish Centre for Evaluation. The methodology used by the Commission to carry out the project was to focus on teaching and learning[3] under agreed common guidelines in a number of disciplines (see Thune 1998: 20).

Once the information-gathering period of the Project was complete the Commission took full responsibility for the follow-up stage, assisted by an Advisory Group made up from two members selected from each of the countries involved in the Project. Following this, each country had to institute a National Committee, which would take responsibility for executing the recommendations for the Project, and for analysing the results of the Project within the participating state and presenting them through a European Committee (comprised of the chairmen and secretaries of each National Committee), in order to collate and produce the final 'European Report'. According to Thune, the Pilot Project had two key outcomes: 'firstly the recognition by all the participants of the relevance and intensity of collaboration made possible within the framework of the projects and secondly the resulting strong support by all for the continuation of the collaboration' (1998: 18).

The Bologna Declaration

The Bologna Declaration is perhaps the most important element in mapping out a path for the future direction of higher education policy in Europe. The foundations for the Bologna Declaration were laid down in Paris on 25 May 1998 with the signing of the Sorbonne Declaration by the Ministers of Education of four European countries, UK, France, Denmark and the Netherlands. The Sorbonne Declaration acknowledged as paramount the importance of education, and in particular educational co-operation, in 'the development and strengthening of stable, peaceful and democratic societies' (European Ministers of Education 1998: 5). The following year in Bologna, on 19 June 1999, a full meeting of the EU Education Ministers took place and resulted in the *Joint Declaration of the European Ministers of Education*, better known as the Bologna Declaration. The chief aim of the Bologna Declaration was to 'reach more readability, comparability, compatibility and transparency in European higher education, while preserving institutional diversity and autonomy' (CRE 2001: 3). Thus the Declaration committed itself to the principles of autonomy and independence, while at the same time encouraging the signatories to 'look at the objective of increasing the international competitiveness of the European system of higher education' (European Ministers of Education 1999: 1.

With regard to the specific area of 'quality', the Bologna Declaration seeks the '[p]romotion of European co-operation in quality assurance with a view to developing comparable criteria and methodologies', aiming at the creation of a 'European higher education space' by 2010 (European Ministers of Education 1999: 2). Thus the general focus of the Bologna Declaration is to increase the comparability of European qualifications on a basic level, without attempting to establish a uniform 'European Quality'. Instead, this is to be achieved through the creation of a broad framework, which will guarantee quality by guaranteeing the quality assurance systems already in place or proposed by the member states.

In March 2000, following a recommendation from the Council of Ministers, the European Network for Quality Assurance (ENQA) was established by the European Commission. ENQA already carries out a monitoring function of the different systems in place in Europe as well as acting as a European hub to exchange information on best practice in the area, and in the future it may signal the type of framework that will develop at a European level (Garvie 2001). The development of ENQA is not without its critics: some member states fear that the system will in many ways mirror what happened in the UK and become far

too bureaucratic. Still, most believed that some positive response would be necessary before the official follow-up to the Bologna Declaration scheduled for
Prague in 2001.

Promotion of European co-operation in quality assurance

In early March 2000 the Conference of Rectors in Europe (CRE) – which was
shortly to evolve into the European University Association – with the support of
the European Commission through the SOCRATES Programme, launched a
project to 'explore the context and the feasibility of accreditation across national
borders in Europe' (CRE 2001: 3). Its main motivation was 'to contribute to the
clarification of the key concepts and issues related to this topic as well as the
discussion of possible collaborative accreditation schemes in Europe' (CRE
2001: 3). The process was completed in May 2001, the tight timescale in place in
order for 'a policy statement to be placed on the Prague agenda' (CRE 2001: 4).
The project encompassed a total of four main meetings: in Paris in September,
Vienna in November, Brussels in December and, finally, a seminar in the Oeiras
University in Lisbon in February 2001. This seminar had almost 200 participants, who 'reviewed and tested the concepts, definitions and possible scenarios
for accreditation' (CRE 2001: 4).

Shortly after the CRE meetings, in late March 2001, the Salamanca
Convention on European Higher Education Institutions was held, gathering
together officials from over 300 higher education institutions, members of their
representative organisations, as well as other interested stakeholders, such as
student unions, members of international organisations and so on. The main
purpose of the Convention was to establish a common response to the Bologna
Declaration and to prepare a contribution to the forthcoming summit of the
Education Ministers in Prague. The Convention defined its two main objectives as:

- the mobilisation of European higher education institutions on a transnational basis, in order that they might play a full role in the Bologna
  process, on the understanding that the only real opportunity they would
  have to influence the future would be using their collective clout;
- the mobilisation of European higher education institutions on a national
  basis, in order that they would be able to tell their own government ministers what brand of higher education they wanted and would be willing to
  support.

The Convention commissioned Guy Haug, who was the senior adviser to the
Association of European Universities (EUA), and Christian Tauch, Head of
External Relations with the German Rectors Conference, to examine the
Bologna process and report their findings to the Convention. They presented
their paper, 'Towards a Coherent European Higher Education Space: From
Bologna to Prague' (otherwise known as the Salamanca Convention), and
concluded that '[q]uality is the basic underlying condition for trust, employa-

bility, mobility, compatibility and competitiveness in the European Higher Education Area' (Haug and Tauch 2001: 1).

Prague Communiqué

In May 2001, as an official follow-up to the Bologna Declaration, thirty-two European Ministers of Education met in Prague to 'review the progress achieved and to set directions and priorities for the coming years of the [Bologna] process' (European Ministers of Education 2001: 2). Discussing all the areas set down in the Bologna Declaration, the ministers called upon the universities and other higher educational institutions, national agencies and ENQA, in co-operation with corresponding bodies from countries which are not members of ENQA, to collaborate in establishing a common framework of reference and to disseminate best practice (European Ministers of Education 2001).

Clearly, developments in Europe point to the significance of what Dolowitz and Marsh (1996) have termed *coercive policy transfer*, as an impetus for developing common policy solutions. To what extent this was reflected in subsequent Irish university policy will be examined in the concluding section of this case study. First, however, we look to developments in the UK for further evidence of alternative types of policy transfer in the Irish case.

Contemporary developments in quality-audit procedures in the UK

The links between Irish academics and their British counterparts have always been strong. The diminutive size of Ireland's university sector has often necessitated a more outward-looking approach – in terms of academic recruitment, external examiners, and assessors and so on. Moreover, the tradition of bachelor's degree, progressing to master's degree and finally doctoral degree is also common to the two countries. Not only has contact between academics in Ireland and the UK been close, but so too have links between Irish and British ministers and civil servants – contacts that have increased dramatically in recent times through external bodies such as the Council of the Isles and the longer-standing fora and institutions of the EU. As a consequence, developments in relation to quality-audit procedures in the UK were of particular interest to Irish university heads and academics in general.

The question of 'quality', how to assure it and, more importantly, how best to measure it, had occupied the British public-service psyche since the late 1970s and was brought into force with the introduction of the Financial Management Initiative in 1982. Increasing State control of the universities in the UK was brought about amidst a general tide of public-sector reforms, but also in response to the blanket legislation introduced by the Thatcher government that upgraded all the polytechnics to university status.

The current body with responsibility for reviewing and ensuring quality in the UK is the Quality Assurance Agency for Higher Education, more commonly know as the QAA, which was established in 1991. It is an independent organisation, whose board is comprised of representatives of the institutions, members of the different government funding agencies, government representatives, plus a number of independent members. The QAA reviews all universities and higher education institutes (HEIs) in the UK, as well as providing a 'collaborative' role for some transnational education provided by UK-based institutions.

In line with many other 'watchdog' agencies in the UK, the role of the QAA is to promote public confidence in the quality of educational provision and ensure that the standard of awards is being safeguarded and enhanced. It performs its legislative tasks through both audit and assessment. With regard to audit, the QAA conducts reviews at the institutional level, with particular reference to the degree/diploma-awarding function of the university. Assessments take place on a more micro level of review, usually at programme level, though a more integrated approach is currently under discussion. (www.qaa.ac.uk).

Developments in the Irish university sector

The concept of New Public Management was not unique to the UK; buzzwords such as 'openness and accountability' had started to creep into many areas of the Irish public sector by the early 1990s. Albert Reynolds's intention to streamline the public sector and make it more efficient was brought about with the eventual publication of the Strategic Management Initiative in 1994. Changes in policy before and after the SMI were influenced by it or by the discussions and mood that existed in the lead-up to its inception (for details, see Department of Education 1995).

Traditionally the Irish Department of Education exercised significant control over all areas of education *except* the university sector. Primary and secondary school curriculums were set at a national level, and even the regional technical college (RTC) or information technology (IT) sector was heavily regulated by the centre. The first sign that a more intrusive system of control was possibly going to be imposed on the university sector was the publication of the Department of Education's Green Paper *Education for a Changing World* in 1992. This paper looked at all areas of Irish education, but its comments on the potential change with regard to 'quality assurance' in the universities constituted one of the more intriguing in terms of a change of policy. The chapter on 'Higher education' contains a section on quality assurance which sets out the Department's aims:

> The approach to quality assurance in higher education will be a combination of the development of performance indicators and of internal quality review procedures within the colleges, together with appropriate external monitoring and assistance through a proposed academic audit unit within the Higher Education Authority.
>
> (Department of Education 1992: 191)

Following on from the Green Paper's submission 'there has been wide-ranging debate, in many countries, about the development and use of appropriate indicators' (Department of Education 1992: 191). In April 1995, the Department published a White Paper, *Charting our Education Future*, which, for the first time formally introduced the term 'accountability' to the vocabulary of the university sector, stating that its policy approach would 'seek to balance institutional autonomy with the needs of public policy and accountability, having due regard to the respective rights and responsibilities of the institutions and the State' (Department of Education 1995: 88).

The White Paper sought to extend the remit of the higher education authority (HEA) to include (in both university and non-university institutions) a number of key functions:

- ensuring that systems and processes are in place which will facilitate the necessary public accountability and provide for evaluation of cost-effectiveness, within individual institutions and through the system as a whole;
- ensuring that quality assurance procedures are in place in all institutions and throughout the system as a whole (Department of Education 1995: 94).

The section on 'Accountability' contained four headings: 'Quality assurance', 'Funding', 'University legislation' and 'Research'. The paper once again promised the introduction of comprehensive legislation for the university sector and reconstitution of the university governing authorities. A new unit would be established in the HEA with responsibility for the 'co-ordination of the development of financial management and accounting procedures and management information systems' within the universities under the heading of 'Funding' (Department of Education 1995: 105).

Finally, in 1996 the Minister for Education, Niamh Bhreathnach[4] announced the publication of the Universities Bill, heralding it as the result of 'a lengthy process of consultation and dialogue between the Department of Education and all the interested parties' (Walshe 1999: 142; see also *Irish Times*, 31 July 1996). The Bill had three main objectives: to restructure the National University of Ireland; to provide revised governance structures; and to provide a framework for interaction between the universities and central government and for the universities' accountability to society. In order to achieve these aims, the powers of the HEA were to be extended: all universities would be required to submit a strategic plan to the HEA for approval; and the HEA would be responsible for establishing 'guidelines' for the spending of all university budgets.

Despite the scepticism of some, the HEA stated in a announcement which they had published in the *Irish Times* on 30 October 1996 that its aim was 'to have the highest possible level of institutional autonomy for universities consistent with safeguarding the public interest'. Finally, after a good deal more consultation (see *Irish Times*, 1 November 1996, 11 December 1996; Houses of the Oireachtas, *Seanad* Debates, 1995/145: 113), the amended Bill (with a total of 315 amendments, 100 of which came from the government itself) was passed on

7 May 1997. Chapter VII, Section 35, entitled 'Planning and evaluation', contained the quality-audit provisions devised for the Irish university system. These included provisions for a new Governing Authority, established under the Act, to establish procedures for quality assurance in each university. These procedures would include:

- evaluation of quality, at regular intervals and in any case not less than once in every ten years or such longer period as may be determined by the university in agreement with the Governing Authority (*An tÚdarás*).
- the establishment of provisions for the implementation of evaluation recommendations;
- arrangements for the review of procedures at least every fifteen years, 'having regard to the resources available to the university and having consulted with *An tÚdarás*';
- the publication of evaluation results and recommendations.

Clearly, the quality-audit system instituted by the Irish government was nowhere near as strict or stringent as those operated in the UK and elsewhere in Europe. An examination of why this was the case is provided in the section below.

Lesson drawing and policy transfer in the Irish university sector

The policy influences that resulted in the introduction of quality-audit mechanisms in the Irish university sector came from three areas: 'Europe', the UK, and domestically in terms of New Public Management and the SMI. In this sense, Irish university policy reflects Rose's (1991: 22) idea of policy *hybridisation* – that is, a policy that combines recognisable elements from programmes in several places. We can, however, see elements of both positive and negative policy learning. The general thrust of the reforms represents positive policy transfer from several states, in line with broader developments across continental Europe and at the behest of the EU in particular. This was acknowledged by the Minister for Education, Niamh Bhreathnach when, during her speech introducing the Universities Bill to the *Seanad*, she argued that 'Ireland's development is now linked in an integral way with the development of Europe' (Houses of the Oireachtas, *Seanad* Debates, 1995/145: 113). The widespread introduction of quality-audit mechanisms in European universities was therefore one of the main driving forces behind the introduction of similar legislation in Ireland. Still, however, the explicit intention not to go 'as far as the UK has gone' represents negative policy transfer, in the sense that no Irish government had the same degree of enthusiasm for regulation as its UK counterparts, and as a result few wished to introduce a system as comprehensive and complex as that in UK. As one senior university official explained: 'at the time when the Green Paper came out, and the White Paper and the '97 Act were being drafted, the systems were just coming into place in the UK and their very many negative aspects were very much in people's minds' (interview, 21 September 2002).

The Conference of Heads of Irish Universities (CHIU), realising that legislation in the area was inevitable, decided not to follow the same road as the UK, but instead to make 'a pre-emptive strike' with the publication of their own proposals (CHIU 1995). This document has subsequently shown itself to be the cornerstone on which all the Irish universities have based their quality initiatives.

Following receipt of a CHIU submission to the National Education Convention (NEC) in November 1993, the Chairman of the HEA attempted to acknowledge the interests of all third-level stakeholders in its position paper *Quality and Equity and their Correlation in Higher Education* (1994). In it, the HEA outlined the three perspectives from which quality needed to be considered:

- *the meritocratic view* – that is, in relation to institutional conformity to universalistic professional and scholarly norms and uses of the academic profession as a preference group;
- *the social view*, which considers the degree to which the institution satisfies the needs of important collective constituents;
- *the individualistic view*, emphasising the contribution that the institution makes to the personal growth of students.

In addition, a number of elements in the HEA report reflected the particularistic interests of Irish governmental attitudes to third-level education. Foremost amongst these was the Irish government's view of third-level education as a training ground and primary resource for economic development, reflected in the HEA's claim that 'scholastic' excellence should not be the sole criterion for quality and its opting instead for the creation of quality assurance and evaluation systems in terms of 'quality' and '*relevance*'. The HEA also noted the increasing difficulties associated with implementing any quality assurance system in an era of growing student numbers in higher education. The report also mooted the idea of enhanced availability of data relating to performance in each institution under the authority of the HEA – something which had never been considered by the universities themselves. Finally, the HEA outlined those elements that it viewed as essential to the creation of any quality assurance system:

- institutional self-assessment as the core activity;
- peer review through institutional visits and reporting;
- validation and monitoring the process by a meta-agency.

Developments since the 1997 Universities Bill

The development of performance indicators has never really got off the starting blocks in Ireland. Still, however, the CHIU Working Party proposals on performance indicators make for interesting reading and can be said to encapsulate much of the universities' thinking with regard to the whole 'quality movement'.

Acknowledging the almost inevitable setting of certain standards or benchmarks by the government, the CHIU decided that involvement rather than non-involvement in the process represented 'the lesser of two evils': instead of having quality standards imposed from outside, the CHIU argued that, 'in line with international trends, government introduction of performance indicators is almost inevitable. It is clearly to our advantage to be involved in their formulation' (CHIU 1995: 2).

The involvement of the CHIU in the development of these indicators can be traced back to their initial submission in the first government concordat, the *Programme for National Recovery*. Still, it was really with the publication of the Department of Education's Green Paper that their involvement in the process began in earnest. In January 1995 the CHIU organised a seminar on 'Quality Assurance' at Trinity College Dublin, attended by representatives from all seven universities in the state as well as a delegation from the Irish Federation of University Teachers. This seminar was closely followed, in February 1995, by a one-day seminar at Queens University Belfast that focused on Queens' experience of the quality process.

As a consequence of the Trinity seminar, a working party was established to write a discussion document, which would form the basis of the CHIU position on quality assurance/quality improvement proposals.[5] The subsequent document refers to the importance of European developments in this area as a basis for Irish policy, referring explicitly to the European Pilot Projects for the Evaluation of Quality in Higher Education and the CRE, both of which were significant influences in the determination of the CHIU position. In addition to this, a general and pervasive feeling of distaste for the UK audit system certainly galvanised Irish universities into taking the policy initiative. One senior quality officer in an Irish university articulated the general feeling of Irish academics in this regard when he explained that 'people would have a lot of contacts with colleagues in Britain and would have said, "Oh God, are we going to end up with this system"…you know that in general there was a uniform loathing of it from everybody' (research interview, 10 September 2002).

As a consequence, when the CHIU made its draft proposals for a process of quality improvement and quality assurance mechanisms in Irish universities, *policy learning* was evident from a number of sources:

> The proposal derives from an extensive review of the literature covering quality-related matters in the universities of Europe, North America and the Antipodes.…The proposal also takes into account the way quality-related issues are developing in Ireland. The proposal is therefore not an attempt to re-invent the wheel of quality-related activities. It is rather an effort to learn from those who have gone before, building on their success, avoiding their weaknesses and adapting their exercises to what we believe is appropriate for and needed in Ireland.
>
> (CHIU 1995: 5)

Summary review of theoretical utility

Prior to the 1960s, 'the Irish government did not interfere to any significant extent in the internal affairs of the universities and did not openly raise questions about academic decisions and standards' (Garvie 2001: 3). As a result, the word 'quality' did not enter the legislative vocabulary of the Irish universities until 1997. Up to this point, Irish academics argued that quality was achieved and standards maintained by means of the idea of professional self-regulation in the guise of 'self-assessment' through formal and informal student feedback, peer review of research for publication in learned journals and on competitive funding boards, and, finally, the use of 'external examiners' to check undergraduate exam papers, as well as conducting oral examinations on postgraduate work.

By contrast, practically all fifteen member states of the EU have had some form of formalised quality assurance system in their universities for some time. The first member states to introduce systems to measure and implement quality systems in higher education were France in 1986, the Netherlands in 1988, and the United Kingdom and Denmark, both in 1992. These countries' systems had much in common with each other: the governments all established audit agencies independent of government and the universities, and sought to review all programmes and institutions within a defined cycle. From the beginning, all of these systems agreed on the importance of a four-stage process comprising self-assessment, peer review, site visits and publication of final evaluation reports. 'Within this general consensus', however, 'European discussions have been fed by differences in national interpretations and experiences of the operational implications of setting up procedures' (Thune 1998: 10).

While accreditation systems were not confined to those countries within the EU or EFTA (Australia, New Zealand and America all had 'quality' or accreditation systems in place long before Ireland took a similar step), it was Europe that provided the greatest influence for the development of the Irish third-level quality-audit systems. Free movement of persons – one of the fundamental principles on which the EU is based – is obviously particularly significant for European students and academics. The EU-funded ERASMUS and SOCRATES programmes have set out to promote exchanges between these groups, and all Irish universities have been enthusiastic supporters of these schemes. As a consequence, even though the relationship between Irish academics and their counterparts in the UK has traditionally been strong for reasons of history and language, increased mobility and communications have inevitably led to a greater exchange of ideas between the Irish systems of higher education and their continental counterparts.

The question remains, however: what does the policy transfer literature add to our understanding of new trends in Irish university policy and practice? At its best, the policy transfer literature provides us with a useful typology for the ordering of empirical material in policy studies. In this case, for example, the policy transfer literature does provide a clear framework for analysis and enable us to develop a comprehensive understanding of the evolution of quality-audit procedures in the Irish university sector. At worst, however, this provides us with a neat way to carry out rich description – a useful and necessary pursuit in many studies of public administration, but one that is usually found wanting in any critical exposition of power in the policy arena and, by extension, the process of policy change. This is because the policy transfer literature points to those who successfully engage in policy-making but ignores the interests or influence of those who are excluded from the policy process.

Notes

1 For a more detailed discussion of epistemic communities, see Chapter 1, on elitism.
2 This Directorate-General has been renamed, under the Prodi Commission, Directorate-General for Education and Culture (DG EAC).
3 It is interesting to note that, while the Project did take account of the impact of research in the institutions on the teaching there, it did not evaluate research as a specific entity.
4 Niamh Bhreathnach was a Dáil newcomer when she was appointed as Minister for Education following the 1992 election. She remained in the post when the Labour Party formed the new government.
5 This paper drew heavily on papers already written on the question of quality assurance/quality improvement by Dr Caroline Hussey of University College Dublin (UCD) and Professor Carroll of Dublin City University (DCU).

Further reading

Dolowitz, D.P. and Marsh, D. (1996) 'Who Learns What from Whom? A Review of the Policy Transfer Literature', *Political Studies* 44: 343–57.

McNamara, T. (1995) 'Strategic Management in the Irish Civil Service', *Administration* 43: 4–152.

Polsby, N. (1984) *Political Innovation in America*, New Haven: Yale University Press.

Radaelli, C. (2000) 'Policy Transfer in the European Union: Institutional Isomorphism as a Source of Legitimacy'; *Governance* 13: 25–43.

Rose, R. (1991) 'What is Lesson Drawing?', *Journal of Public Policy* 11: 3–30.

Rose, R. (1993) *Lesson Drawing in Public Policy: A Guide to Learning across Time and Space*, New Jersey: Chatham House.

11 Europeanisation and the Irish experience

Lee McGowan and Mary Murphy

Introduction

Domestic public policy-making is more than ever exposed to external stimuli and pressures. One of the most significant of these has been the European Union (EU). The creation of the EU will undoubtedly go down as one of the major achievements of the twentieth century. From modest beginnings in the early 1950s, successive generations of European governments have agreed a set of treaties and laws and created a set of institutions which have altered the political, economic and social landscape of Western Europe (McCormick 2002; Nugent 2002; Pinder 2001). The EU has changed the way states and peoples relate to one another, redefined the balance of global power and contributed to the longest uninterrupted spell of peace between its member states in their recorded history. It represents a new tier of governance at the European level and a puissant one that increasingly impacts upon many issues of contemporary domestic public policy.

This reality raises a number of highly salient issues on the very nature of the accountability, legitimacy and transparency of the structure and nature of European governance (Neunreither and Wiener 2000b; Peterson and Shackleton 2002). The complexity of this system makes public engagement and, more importantly, attachment to the EU often both difficult and precarious. Nevertheless, there exist a substantial number of policy networks which have developed expertise in specific policy sectors, although their ability to penetrate and influence the EU institutions varies widely from policy area to policy area. An extensive literature on many aspects of EU policy-making now exists (S.S. Anderson and Eliassen 2001; Cini 2003; Richardson 2001; Wallace and Wallace 2000), and it seeks to explain how and why certain policy areas are regulated at the European level; how decisions are made between the EU institutions at the European level; and how effective the wider non-governmental organisations and lobbyists are at helping to set policy agendas and determine policy outcomes.

This chapter does not intend to explore these avenues, but rather to affirm that this tier of European governance is influencing and shaping much of Irish public policy. It is estimated that decision-making at the European level shapes around 60 per cent of current domestic legislation across all EU states. In other words, Ireland is subject to a process of Europeanisation, driven by membership of the EU, that impacts upon domestic policy-making and its actors. Understanding, therefore, the processes by which policies are made at the EU level (in terms of design, decision-making and implementation) is essential for all actors at the national level if they are to advance and even to thwart certain policy outcomes. The EU presents both a challenge, as states adjust to EU commitments, but also an opportunity for member states to espouse a much more proactive role in the direction and design of the EU. Indeed, is Ireland's ability, as one of the EU's smallest states, more limited?

In assessing the impact of the EU and Europeanisation on Ireland, this chapter has been divided into five separate sections. It begins by providing a brief introduction to the concept and meaning of Europeanisation, before going to examine the expanding EU policy base and the different types of EU policies. The subsequent sections sketch a brief overview of Ireland in the EU and, in particular, focus on Ireland's adoption of and participation in the Euro-zone. The penultimate section considers public opinion in Ireland towards the EU, while the last section considers the extent of Europeanisation in the new institutional arrangements in Northern Ireland, with specific reference to institutionalised cross border co-operation.

Brief review of the evolution of 'Europeanisation' approaches

In retrospect, Ladrech unintentionally opened the floodgates of what has become a wide-ranging debate on Europeanisation when he defined this as a 'process reorientating the direction and shape of politics to the degree that the EU political and economic dynamics become part of the organisational logic of national politics and policymaking' (1994: 69). The concept of Europeanisation, in the same way as globalisation, has become highly fashionable and given rise to the emergence of a growing literature in political science and legal circles.[1] Although many write about and use the term 'Europeanisation', there has been little in the way of any serious effort to actually develop a conceptual framework for its empirical application, and different authors have approached the subject from different viewpoints and have placed different emphasis on whom and how it impacts. Indeed, in one overview article Harmsen and Wilson (2000) list as many as eight different types of Europeanisation to be found in the literature pertaining to this concept: new forms of European governance; national adaptation; policy isomorphism; problem and opportunity for domestic political management; modernisation; joining Europe; reconstruction of identities; and transnationalism and cultural integration. The absence of any precise or single definition of Europeanisation has led some (Kassim 2000: 238) to question its usefulness. This may be a rather extreme position, because, despite the very many different definitions, a certain consensus has emerged where most works on Europeanisation identify the EU as the external determinant influencing change at the member-state and also other national (e.g. EU applicant states) levels.

In contrast, however, some authors are more cautious and argue that this approach is perhaps too restrictive (Wallace and Wallace 2000). There is clearly a degree of reality behind such assertions, and it is easy to identify examples of Europeanisation such as the debates on ethnic minorities outside the EU framework (Soysal 1994) to illustrate this. There is also another school of international relations scholars who regard Europeanisation as a regional reaction to globalisation, and as such as having little or nothing to do with the EU (Hirst and Thompson 1999). While acknowledging these positions, it remains true that for the most part the EU is the central core of most Europeanisation debates. Indeed, in some works 'Europeanisation' is frequently used as a synonym for European integration. This said, we also approach with some caution one view of Europeanisation as just the emergence of distinct structures of governance at the European level (Risse *et al.* 2000), as it tends to overlook the key dynamic that is the penetration of the European dimension of the national arena, which is the focus of this chapter.

One of the most interesting issues to arise from all the studies on Europeanisation is whether it is possible to locate and explain instances of convergence or harmonisation, as opposed to lasting divergence and a preservation of national arrangements. Clearly the national context matters. How the European dimension is channelled or refracted through prevailing institutions is an important question. Much, of course, depends on the kind of European influence being exerted. It is strongest when EU directives have to be transposed into national law, but Europeanisation also impacts by influencing opportunity structures, and here the impact depends on the constellation of national actors, and the pressure is weaker.

Most of the existing literature of the Europeanisation theme remains highly specialised. Many analyses focus on particular member states, such as France, Germany, smaller EU states, and exclude Ireland (Soetendorp and Hanf 1998) and the countries of Central and Eastern Europe (Featherstone and Kazamias 2001). Other works have examined specific domestic institutions (Moravscik 1998). Moravscik's work has attempted to show how Europeanisation of domestic policy issues came to strengthen national executives in comparison with other national actors. 'Integration redistributes political resources by shifting control over domestic agendas (initiative), altering decision making procedures (institutions), magnifying informational asymmetries in their favour (information), and multiplying the potential domestic ideological justifications for policies and ideas' (Moravscik 1998: 1). This position is rather problematic, as it overlooks differences and rivalries within the core executive and tends to ignore the financial aspect and EU budgetary issues, which for countries like Ireland have been of particular resonance.

R.A.W. Rhodes's (1997) contribution, moreover, develops Moravscik's (1998) work by locating the Europeanisation process within a new framework under five headings – namely constitutional, organisational, financial, political and informational. His work on policy networks remains an integral component in the study of policy-making, for he correctly argues that in order to fully understand the study of power and dependence one must appreciate the distribution of resources within networks. This feeds directly into numerous EU policy areas, most notably agriculture and fisheries. Peterson and Bomberg (1999) have explored the notion of Europeanisation as policy transfer from one state to another.

Mainstream variants of Europeanisation in contemporary usage

The one common link between the overwhelming majority of writers on Europeanisation (or Europification, according to Andersen and Eliassen 2001) is the association with the EU. The concept of Europeanisation is being used to describe a process whereby EU institutions evolve and member states adjust to EU membership. How and where they are doing so is becoming the subject of closer investigation. But how does Europeanisation manifest itself at the national level? Bulmer and Burch (2000) have done considerable work on the United Kingdom and specify the existence of three domains which are useful to test the degree of Europeanisation. These are:

- policies – for example, how policies set at the EU level impact on the member states, particularly agriculture, fisheries, competition, environment, cohesion and now EMU;
- politics – the Europeanisation of national parties and interest groups;
- polity, or national institutions – that is, the effect of European integration on political and administrative structures in the member states and how these states (and their sub-national regions) organise themselves to handle EU affairs.

However, this very solid approach neglects one highly important aspect, namely the Europeanisation of the citizen. According to Peterson and Bomberg (1999), this fourth domain includes notions of community, culture, identity and citizenship, and very much lies at the core of the Convention's work in the run-up to the next Inter-Governmental Conference (IGC) in 2004. This cultural aspect deserves inclusion and again casts a wide net over a whole range of highly significant questions, none more so than the degree to which Europeanisation is regarded as a 'set of processes through which EU political, social and economic dynamics become part of the logic of domestic discourse, identities, political structure and public policies' (Radaelli 2000: 25). The Europeanisation of EU citizens has been widely neglected in the literature. Hix (1999) is one of the few authors to consider the issue of public opinion in the continued construction of the European project. How EU citizens are to connect with the EU and understand how and why it operates remains a sizeable challenge, but this is an absolutely crucial consideration for the ongoing 'future of Europe' debate. This will be returned to below.

These four domains provide scope for considerable potential scrutiny. Featherstone and Kazamias (2001) have further contributed to the debate by maintaining that Europeanisation has three dimensions or strands which it is useful to separate and which display overlaps with Bulmer and Burch's (2000) work. Europeanisation necessitates the following:

- An increase and expansion of institutionalisation at the EU level – giving greater political co-ordination and coherence. (It also involves the territorial reach of the European 'polity'.)
- The adjustment evident in the institutional setting – incorporating norms, rules and interests of actors within a structured set of relationships; Europeanisation as central penetration (Olsen 2002: 3) of national and sub-national systems of governance. This fits the island of Ireland very well. It refers to the direction of responsibilities and powers between the different levels of governance and focuses on adaptation to the EU.
- The adjustment evident in states that are not members.

These three strands do complement each other. This chapter focuses on the second of these by focusing on Irish experience and the degree to which Ireland has adapted. But how is this adaptation to be measured? Writing on new institutionalism focuses largely on gauging processes of domestic adaptation. There are various branches to this approach, including rational choice institutionalism, social constructivism and historical institutionalism. Each possesses its own distinct slant. All three forms concern themselves with notions of agency and structure in the Europeanisation process. According to Featherstone and Kazamias, they 'posit different types of constraint on actors and have different understandings of how preferences are formed. These differences which stem from contrasting conceptions of what "institutions" are, also suggest distinct interpretations of what the EU institutional setting is' (2001: 9). This chapter now focuses on the Europeanisation of Irish policy-making.

Europeanisation and the expanding EU policy base

Before turning to the Irish case it may be useful to examine the overall context in which the EU operates. The EU's origins lie in three founding treaties – the European Coal and Steel Community (ECSC), the European Economic Community (EEC) and the European Atomic Energy Community (EURATOM) – signed by the six governments of Belgium, France, Germany, Italy, Luxembourg and the Netherlands in the 1950s. Of the three, the EEC Treaty, which set out to create a common market among the six, was by far the most significant. Almost half a century later a succession of treaties – most significantly, the Single European Act (1987), the Maastricht Treaty (1993), the

Amsterdam Treaty (1999) and more recently the Treaty of Nice (2003) – have helped to establish not only a single market for the free movement of goods, services, capital and people, but also a substantial political system at the European level that is governed by a set of supranational (European Commission, European Parliament and the European Courts) and inter-governmental (Council of the European Union) actors making decisions on many aspects of European public policy.

These treaties are the product of bargaining and eventual agreement between the member states (now fifteen) in a series of IGCs that essentially determine EU policy competences. These have expanded considerably from the more limited areas of activity under the ECSC, with the addition of policy areas such as agriculture, competition, transport and the beginnings of a social policy in the EEC Treaty such as to cover most areas of European public policy – including economic and monetary union (EMU), the environment, energy, telecommunications and technology. True, certain sensitive and high-spending areas – such as social security, education, direct taxation and health – remain firmly under the control of the member states, but these are increasingly the exception (Pollack 2000). Most other areas now have a European dimension (including foreign and security policy, immigration policy and policing). The central question remains to what extent is it possible to argue that the process of Europeanisation explains these developments or whether common EU approaches reflect the pressures stemming from globalisation. There exists a considerable degree of overlap between the two.

Public policy studies broadly identify four different types of policy: namely distributive policy, redistributive policy, regulatory policy and constituent policy (Lowi 1972). At the national level the state assumes the responsibility, alongside its direct activities of taxing and distributing benefits and services, of regulating the activities of private actors. With the exception of tax-raising powers, the EU supplies these same policies. In designing a policy typology for the EU (see Table 11.1) Hix (1999) has slightly modified the policy headings, and lists five broad policy headings at the European level: namely regulatory policy, redistributive policy, macro-economic stabilisation policies (e.g. EMU), global policies and citizens' policies. By far the most significant has been the regulatory role of the EU (Majone 1996, 2000), which has affected a range of policies at the national level.

In short, the more EU power and policy competences have grown, the more impact the European level of governance has had on the member states. *How* this impacts is more disputed. Authors like Ladrech (1994) and Radaelli (2000) see the EU member states as passive actors, simply responding to the EU by adapting their own domestic structures or practices to conform to European ones. This view is rather too negative, for Europeanisation is a two-way process and these authors have overlooked or underplayed the more proactive position that EU member states can adopt towards the policy formulation process. Bulmer and Burch (2000) recognise this possibility and maintain that EU integration offers the potential not simply to import norms and ideas, but to export

Table 11.1 Policy typology of the European Union

Regulatory	Redistribution	Macro-economic	Global	Citizens
Single market	Agriculture	EMU	Environment	Citizenship
Competition	Fisheries	Fiscal harmonisation	Competition	
Environment	Cohesion		Trade	
Social policy			Foreign policy	
Telecoms			Defence	

Note: This table has not been designed to provide readers with a comprehensive account of which policy operates under which heading, but rather to illustrate the wide-ranging nature and subject matter of EU policies in 2003.

alternative priorities and ideas on to the European stage. In other words, European integration must be recognised, to a certain extent, as the product of member-state governments' wishes. In short, national governments – and this also includes sub-national governments – often seek to export either their own domestic priorities or also 'policy models, ideas and detail to the EU level' (Bulmer and Burch 2000: 6). Naturally, this gives rise to a degree of compromise and convergence among the states as regards policy outcomes.

This is fundamental if we are to fully understand policy evolution and development. Increasingly since the mid-1990s there has been a distinct move away from the earlier 'Monnet method' or partnership model of EU decision-making – where power was effectively shared between the EU institutions and placed the Commission solely in the driving seat in terms of initiating new policy – to a new position where the main driving force in policy development and policy transfer has centred on member-state governments. Today the Community model has been superseded by the forces of inter-governmentalism, which exerts a much stronger influence than in the past and, to a degree, has marginalised the supra-national EU actors.

Given all these assumptions, this chapter now turns to examine how far Europeanisation impacts on Ireland. Is Ireland a proactive EU state in terms of policy development? In other words, does Dublin pursue a dual strategy of both importing and exporting policy ideas? What are Ireland's policy priorities? These are some of the issues addressed in the following section.

Case study: Europeanisation and Ireland – setting the context

Ireland joined the EU in 1973, at the same time as the UK and Denmark. Irish motivations for achieving membership of the Union were strongly influenced by the UK's decision to join. The two countries were closely connected in terms of trade patterns, and the impact of the UK joining and Ireland not would likely have led to difficulties for the Irish economy. Additionally, however, Ireland's EU membership bid was also based on a desire to improve the economic performance of the country. In the context of EU policies, this translated into a specific Irish emphasis on maximising receipts from the EU budget and strengthening the Common Agricultural Policy (CAP) (Laffan 2001: 3). In later years, Ireland continued to support and endorse the economic context of EU integration. A keen supporter of the 1992 single market programme and a participant in the Euro, Ireland has been a proactive player in furthering EU economic integration.

One of the poorer EU member states throughout the 1970s and 1980s, its economic fortunes began to change in the 1990s, when economic growth reached unprecedented levels and the country began to lose its label of poor relation in the EU family. Its membership of the European club and its receipts from the EU's Structural Funds are oft-cited reasons for the extraordinary performance of the Celtic Tiger. There is no doubting that this funding, taken together with a more outward-looking economic policy in the 1990s, helped to transform the fortunes of the Irish state.

Support for economic integration, however, has not been reflected elsewhere. Indeed, the political dimension of Irish EU membership has been considerably less harmonious than its economic counterpart. Questions of increased political integration, opening up Irish borders to neighbouring member states, the creation of a Common Foreign and Security Policy, the establishment of a Rapid Reaction Force (RRF), and southern and eastern enlargement have all prompted controversy and disputes at home.

Ireland's image within the EU has traditionally been one of passive supporter of the EU and European integration. The history of EU integration has been one of a process driven by economic and political elites that reflected a general permissive consensus among the public. This position has changed considerably in some member states. Public opinion in Ireland (at least up until the first Treaty of Nice referendum of June 2001) remained persistently pro-European, a reality encouraged by the relatively universal cross-party consensus on Irish membership of the EU. In this context Ireland has generally been viewed as 'conditionally integrationist' (D. Scott 1994: 8).

In recent years Ireland's position on Europe has become less clear cut. Ambiguous ministerial statements, policy positions at odds with EU guidelines and the initial rejection by the Irish electorate of the Treaty of Nice have all served to tarnish Ireland's one-time very positive EU image.[2] This point, however, needs a degree of qualification. Since the early 1990s *Eurobarometer* has indicated that in most EU states there has been a fall in support for EU integration among the public at large. The uncorking of the anti-European bottle in the 1990s owes much to the problems surrounding the ratification of the Maastricht Treaty in several member states, the recession of the 1990s and the tough economic measures introduced to ensure that the qualification targets for entry into EMU were met.

The recent Treaty of Nice referenda in Ireland have served vividly to illustrate the extent to which EU membership affects the Irish state. In June 2001 the Irish electorate, on a turnout of 34.8 per cent (the lowest ever for a European integration referendum), rejected ratification of the Treaty of Nice by a margin of 53.9 per cent to 46.1 per cent. The factors which led to the negative referendum outcome were numerous. Primarily, however, Irish voters voiced concerns about the economic and political impact of enlargement on Ireland as a small EU member state, the position of Irish neutrality in the context of an emerging EU Common Foreign and Security Policy, and Irish representation and power within the institutions of the EU. In addition, and crucially, a perceived lack of public information, understanding and knowledge of matters European further hardened voter positions.

By its very nature, the EU involves a pooling of national sovereignty at the EU level. In this way, no EU member state exercises sole sovereign power in the formulation, management and implementation of policies with an EU dimension. The number of public policies which now fall into this category is significant. In effect, the policy base of the EU has increased substantially since the early days of Irish EU membership. Arguably, agriculture was the key concern of Irish politicians and officials during the initial years of participation in the EU. In domestic terms, agriculture was (and remains) of significant economic and political importance in Ireland. As demands for reform of the CAP intensified in the late 1990s, and with Franz Fischler's (Agricultural Commissioner since 1995) mid-term review calling for a radical overhaul of the policy in 2002, Ireland has engaged proactively to defend its farming priorities on the European stage by aligning with France to successfully resist the more substantial cuts in agricultural support being pushed by the United Kingdom, the Netherlands and Sweden. This area is one positive example, from an Irish perspective, of where tactical alliances can be used to promote domestic interests.

Today, Ireland's interests in the expanding policy remit of the EU are considerable. The result is that there is a large EU dimension to the remit of the majority of Irish government departments. In effect, much of their policy domain originates in Brussels, having been decided by the Council of the EU, increasingly with the assistance of the European Parliament (EP) under the co-decision procedure, with the notable exception of making agricultural policy. This transnational making of public policy is directly applicable in the member states and confers immediate obligations on member states and legal rights on citizens. The result is EU legislation and policy which are 'deeply enmeshed in the national public policy of the member-state' (Cox 2001).

The policy process in this context is, therefore, somewhat unconventional. The pervasive impact of policy originating in Brussels has implications for the member state, both in terms of seeking adequately to influence the initial stages of policy formulation and also in the context of responding to policy obligations emanating from Brussels once agreed. The Irish government, like those of all EU member states, has many points of entry into the EU policy-making process. First, it can influence the articulation and development of any given policy; second, it plays a role in the policy decision-making process; and, third, it has some responsibility for the policy implementation stage. Although the European Commission exercises the sole right of initiative in terms of proposing policies and policy developments in the EU arena, it does so having consulted relevant sectoral, regional and national interests. And it is here that Irish interests can initially participate, albeit informally, in the policy process.

Decisions on policies are not the responsibility of the European Commission, but of the Council of the EU, acting either alone or in co-operation with the EP. In the EP Ireland has fifteen members (MEPs) – including the current President of the EP, Pat Cox – each of whom votes according to his/her own ideologies and beliefs, as opposed to nationality. Irish ministers sit on the Council and take their place alongside the other fourteen member-state representatives in debating and agreeing policies. It is only on highly contentious and politically sensitive issues that unanimity is required, and these are fast decreasing. For all other policy decisions, agreement is reached on the basis of majority voting or qualified majority voting. This latter system accords differing voting strengths to member states, based loosely on their relative size. Due to Ireland's status as a small EU member it is necessary for Dublin to build policy coalitions in order to advance and achieve Irish policy preferences.

The implementation phase of the policy process is largely managed and monitored by national authorities. In the Irish case, European directives and regulations are transposed into Irish law by the Oireachtas. Depending on the legal tool, there is some level of discretion in the implementation of policies by national authorities. Participation within this institutional framework is complex. In response, Irish authorities have adapted policy instruments and tools at the national level to accommodate the intricacies and demands of participation in the EU policy process. To illustrate this role, we focus now on one of the most salient aspects of EU policy-making, namely EMU.

Policy example: EMU

Ireland's decision to participate in EMU dates back to the 1991 IGC at Maastricht and the signing of the Treaty on European Union (TEU) in February 1992.[3] The Irish electorate subsequently endorsed this position in the 1992 referendum on the ratification of the TEU.[4] In terms of EMU, the treaty contained provisions for the creation of a single currency, the establishment of a European Central Bank (ECB) and the closer co-ordination of member states' economic policies.

In January 1999, Ireland, along with ten of its EU neighbours, introduced the single currency. For three years the Euro existed in virtual form, until 1 January 2002, when notes and coins were introduced and national currencies were phased out in twelve EU states (Greece had joined the other eleven in 2001). The creation of the Euro involved a significant loss of state sovereignty, and in policy terms saw member states relinquishing control of their national monetary policies. The management of monetary policy is now the responsibility of the ECB, which sets interest rates, controls the supply and production of the new currency, and attempts to control inflation. The significance of the loss of national monetary policy for member-state economies is an issue which stimulates some debate. There is no clear consensus on the importance of monetary policy as an effective tool in the management of a national economy. In the case of Ireland, however, there is some level of consensus that the monetary policy instrument 'was never fully effective in the past' (J. Fitzgerald 2001: 1,368).

The Stability and Growth Pact agreed by the European Council in 1995 subjects Euro-zone states to EU-imposed constraints. The conduct of national economic policy must be relatively uniform within the single currency zone to reduce the potential for inflationary pressures and to ensure currency stability. Effectively, what this requires of national authorities is that government borrowing does not exceed 3 percentage points of gross domestic product (GDP) in any individual year. In addition, EU member states are subject to further Broad Economic Policy Guidelines designed to direct national economic policy-makers.

In 2000, however, the Irish government effectively ignored these provisions and adopted an expansionary national budget which flouted agreed EU guidelines. The budget contained significant direct and indirect tax cuts and large increases in current and capital expenditure, which it was feared would fuel inflationary pressures and destabilise the Euro-zone. The result was a reprimand by the European Commission, followed by censure from the Economic and Finance Council of Ministers (Ecofin). In effect, all fourteen of Ireland's fellow EU member states endorsed the Commission reprimand and demanded that Ireland rectify its budgetary provisions to take more prudent account of EU economic policy guidelines. The Irish government, led primarily by the Minister for Finance, Charlie McCreevy, rejected the criticisms of the EU and vowed to continue with his proposed budget. The rationale for this approach was based on national considerations linked to the need to secure social partnership arrangements (see Chapter 5). The minister argued that the rebuke was unwarranted. He questioned its economic logic and suggested it was evidence that other EU member states were jealous of the Irish economic success story.

The implications of this fallout between the Irish government and the EU are apparent at a number of levels. In the first instance, the episode is an example of the poor fit between Irish public policy and EU public policy. Second, the poor management of the issue by both EU and Irish authorities has led to a certain amount of antagonism between Ireland and its EU neighbours. Third, the issue arguably contributed to a reduction in Irish public and political confidence in the European project. Any suggestions that Ireland, as a small EU member state, was in any way unfairly treated must be cast aside, as Germany, the essential architect of the EMU project (Dyson and Featherstone 1999; Dyson 2002), was itself censored by the Commission in autumn 2001 over the handling of its economic policy.

Clearly, the increasing and intensifying levels of monetary and economic integration between member states mark a new departure in EU policy processes and practices. The EU is generally considered a *sui generis* organisation with no historical precedent. There is thus no adequately comparable model for the management of a monetary union which is not complemented by a political union. The process of achieving, maintaining and ensuring the success of the single currency is a project which cannot be predicted or planned with any high degree of certainty. The institutions and member states of the EU are thus negotiating uncharted waters, and clearly there is the very real potential for mistakes to be made. The EU is also an evolving entity, ever changing in terms of political hue, policy scope, institutional structure and geographic extent. Its operating principles are largely based on consensus-building and problem-solving. In this way the process of EU policy-making is 'gradual, experimental and open-ended' (Teague and Donaghey 2003). Nowhere is this perhaps more evident than in the case of EMU.

The success of the EU monetary union depends, to a large extent, on the concept of trust between member-state governments. The European Commission and the EU member states adopt the view that national economic policies need to be tightly co-ordinated in the Euro-zone. The EU has therefore agreed guidelines by which member states will conduct their national economic programmes. However, these arrangements are based on voluntary compliance by the member states, who are not in fact legally obliged to accept them. In the Irish case, the European Commission and Ecofin reprimand sought to embarrass and coerce the Irish government into compliance because, ultimately, they did not have the capacity to embark on any more emphatic course of action. The outcome of the Irish case study is that the loose and informal policy co-ordination mechanism relied upon proved undependable for both Ireland and the EU. The whole issue of the Stability Pact came under intense pressure in the autumn of 2002 as some of the larger states, notably France and Germany, sought to spend more than the Maastricht criteria allowed.

The irony of the encounter, however, is that there is broad agreement that the 'best national interests of most member states [including Ireland] will normally produce a domestic economic policy stance consistent with the needs of EMU' (J. Fitzgerald 2001: 1,370). This would suggest that the Irish government and the EU system are ultimately at one in terms of their overall objectives. The problem in this case, however, was the poor level and quality of policy co-ordination between the Irish and EU authorities. Reliance within the EU system on informal, ad-hoc arrangements for the co-ordination of policy is not conducive to effective policy outcomes. The construction of 'symbiotic relationships between the European and national levels' has been repeatedly shown to be a difficult means of achieving mutually agreeable ends (Teague and Donaghey 2003). In this instance there is also some evidence of a 'gung-ho' attitude by a European Commission eager to put its mark on and establish legitimacy for the policy regime in which it was intimately involved.

The weaknesses of the EU system, however, are likewise visible at the national level. The Irish public administration response to EU issues can be characterised in terms of centralisation, socialisation and formalisation (Laffan 2001: 88–101). According to Laffan, its performance on the first two is largely satisfactory. The question of formalisation, however, reveals the weakness of the Irish response to the EU public policy process and this is apparent in the case study discussed here. The characteristics of the Irish administrative system place an emphasis on informal, ad-hoc mechanisms of operation (see Chapter 7). There is little in the way of formal written guidelines on actions and practices to be undertaken in relation to EU matters. Meetings of officials and ministers are informal, unstructured and sporadic. Relations between departments are based on casual and unofficial contacts. This lax approach to the EU policy process leaves the Irish system open to criticism. The disagreement between the Irish government and the EU on the issue of economic policy co-ordination is an example of weak and informal operating systems at the national level resulting in difficulties. The Irish government's preoccupation with domestic political concerns was not checked by formal, effective EU-related operating practices at the domestic level, which may potentially have alleviated or overcome the debacle which ensued. In the event, however, the Irish administration was left somewhat blinded to the demands of membership of a single currency zone. A more informed, holistic, formal and less insular view might possibly have averted the crisis.

Identification with the EU: public and political

The political implications of the dispute between the Irish government and the EU were arguably far reaching. Ireland was left somewhat isolated within the EU. The sense of being dictated to by other European governments did not sit well with a public which had previously strongly supported EU institutions and the integration process. Indeed, the Irish Finance Minister suggested that the censure issue had been a contributing factor in the 'No' vote in the Treaty of Nice referendum in Ireland (O'Mahony 2001: 210; Hodson and Maher 2001: 736). This may be true, but it could be argued that the rejection of the Nice Treaty owed much more to the low turnout at the referendum, which itself was the product of the main political parties' inability to sell the treaty to the people.

Traditionally, Ireland has enjoyed a relatively harmonious relationship with the EU and the public has, from the mid-1980s, continually strongly supported moves towards closer European integration.[5] The benefits of Irish EU member-ship are numerous. Irish farmers enjoyed increased prosperity under the provisions of the CAP, Structural Fund and cohesion fund receipts to Ireland were high, inward direct investment (from both the EU and the US) grew, while dependence on the British market fell, from over 60 per cent in the early years of EU membership to just 26 per cent in 1995 (George and Bache 2001: 202–3). Arguably, all of these developments played a contributory role in the unprece-dented success of the Irish economy during the 1990s and beyond. In recent years, however, a distinct shift in debate is discernible in Ireland's relationship with the EU. The censure issue discussed above, continued reform of the CAP, the reduction in Structural Fund assistance, moves towards the creation of a more coherent Common Foreign and Security Policy, the prospect of enlarge-ment to Central and Eastern Europe and growing fears about immigration have all changed Irish perceptions of the EU. These politically charged issues, many with serious implications for Ireland and the Irish economy, have led some to consider a re-examination of the Irish–EU relationship.

On the one hand, however, support for European integration in Ireland continues to show no signs of retreat according to *Eurobarometer* surveys from the early 1990s. On the contrary, support for EU membership is typically high in Ireland, and 78 per cent of the Irish people stated that they 'felt that Ireland's membership of the Union is a good thing', while 86 per cent of respondents stated that Ireland had benefited from membership (European Commission 2002: 8–10), whereas the corresponding figure for the EU as a whole was a full 25 percentage points lower. On the other hand, it can be argued that these statistics underestimate a considerable degree of – seemingly growing – scepticism towards the EU.

The result of the first Treaty of Nice referendum gives further weight to the latter point. Given the general pro-EU stance of the electorate, the question remains, however, what prompted the Irish electorate to reject the treaty? The outcome is all the more dramatic for the fact that the 'Yes' campaign was supported by a cross-section of Ireland's economic and political elites and included the political world, trade unions, farmers, employers and the Catholic Church. All the main Irish political parties bar Sinn Fein and the Green Party supported the referendum 'Yes' campaign. All of the mainstream Irish parties – Fianna Fáil, Fine Gael, the Labour Party and the Progressive Democrats – have traditionally been pro-European and displayed a broad level of consensus in support of European integration. This, however, appears to be strained in recent times, particularly within the ranks of Fianna Fáil, where the emergence of a Eurosceptic camp is becoming more visible.

In the absence of any substantive and conclusive analysis of the referendum outcome, initial observations suggest that the primary concern of voters was the perceived loss of Irish sovereignty and independence which the Treaty of Nice entailed (*Irish Times*, 2 June 2001). The low turnout was clearly an important factor in the rejection of the treaty. Other factors were also important, including the impact of treaty revision on Irish neutrality, the diminution of Irish voting powers within a reformed EU institutional structure, the lack of information and the perceived presumptuous approach of the political establishment to the referendum.

Alongside the economic disagreements between Ireland and the EU, the result of the referendum has changed European attitudes to Ireland. Continental EU observers interpreted the referendum outcome as evidence of the conditionality of Irish support for EU integration, based primarily on direct (financial) benefits. Ireland was perceived as retreating to a selfish national position at the expense of the European project.

Despite the animosity, however, and conscious of the concerns of Irish voters, member states agreed to make some concessions to alleviate specific Irish fears, and issued a declaration, for example, at the European Council summit in Seville in June 2002 stating that Nice did not in any way undermine Irish neutrality: still they refused to renegotiate the Treaty of Nice. The immediate response of the

Irish government to the referendum outcome was to convene a National Forum on Europe. The Forum was a large-scale consultation exercise taking oral and written submissions from interested organisations and individuals. The aim of the initiative was to analyse the reasons for Ireland's rejection of the treaty and to give citizens a stake in Ireland's future within the EU. This initiative is being matched at the EU level by the Convention on the Future of Europe, launched in late February 2002 under the chairmanship of the former French president, Valéry Giscard d'Estaing.

The Irish rejection of the Treaty of Nice could be interpreted as a dramatic illustration of this new sensitivity to all things European, but this apparent blip in EU–Irish relations was easily overturned in a second referendum on the issue in October 2002.[6] Few would have dared to predict the outcome of the latter poll in the final days of campaigning, but the 'Yes' vote returned Ireland to the EU fold, was warmly welcomed in Brussels and greeted with enthusiasm and even 'rejoicing' in the capitals of the applicant states, and, of course, saved Ahern's premiership. Indeed, a further referendum defeat would almost certainly have compelled his resignation. The Nice Treaty came into force in January 2003. In retrospect, the outcome of the first referendum may have been a blessing and even a decisive turning point in the history of the EU (although it certainly did not appear so at the time to EU member-state governments), for it reinforced the need to incorporate and bring on board public concerns, fears and aspirations in the ongoing evolution of the EU project. How the EU and its member-state governments adapt to this challenge will determine future speed and direction.

Northern Ireland

Northern Ireland, although constitutionally separate from the Republic of Ireland, is of some political importance in any discussion of the EU policy process. A region within the UK, its relationship with the EU was traditionally shaped and determined at the national level. Recent developments in Northern Ireland, however, have slightly changed the axis of that relationship. The introduction of devolution and the creation of new regional political institutions have altered the UK and also the Irish political landscape.

The 1998 Belfast Agreement provided for the creation of a 108-member locally elected Northern Ireland Assembly with responsibility for policy-making and implementation in a wide range of defined policy areas. Although European affairs are a reserved power for Westminster, much of the Assembly's work, estimated to be in the region of 60–80 per cent, will be influenced by directives and regulations from Brussels, for example on the environment or on agricultural issues. European issues were one of over a dozen areas assigned to the Office of the First Minister and Deputy First Minister (OFMDFM). Additionally, individual Northern Ireland government departments have policy responsibilities with a significant EU dimension, with notable examples including agriculture, environment and finance.

Within the Northern Ireland Assembly, OFMDFM is shadowed by the Committee of the Centre. This committee scrutinises the work of the department, which includes the co-ordination of EU matters. The pervasive nature of EU policies and the growing extent of their reach have resulted in proposals for the creation of a statutory Assembly devoted exclusively to European matters. Prior to suspension of the Northern Ireland political institutions in October 2002, the Committee of the Centre was in the process of conducting an inquiry in this regard. This followed an earlier inquiry in 2002 which sought to streamline and improve the regional co-ordination of EU policy in Northern Ireland. The Northern Ireland administration was thus beginning to acknowledge the significance and importance of the EU at the regional level, and was consequently attempting to introduce mechanisms via which the region might usefully and effectively have tapped into networks and processes at the EU level.

The Northern Ireland Assembly represents just one aspect of the new political arrangements introduced by the 1998 Belfast Agreement. The North–South Ministerial Council (NSMC) and six complementary cross-border implementation bodies were further institutional developments. The purpose of the NSMC is 'to bring together those with executive responsibilities in Northern Ireland and the Irish Government, to develop consultation, co-operation and action within the island of Ireland – including through implementation on an all-island and cross-border basis – on matters of mutual interest within the competence of the administrations North and South' (Government of Ireland 1998: strand 2, para. 1). The NSMC has a general remit to 'consider the European Union dimension of relevant matters, including the implementation of EU policies and programmes and proposals under consideration in the EU framework'. The Agreement also lays down that arrangements are made to ensure that the views of the NSMC are taken into account and represented appropriately at relevant EU meetings (Government of Ireland 1998: strand 2, para. 17). The NSMC is a novel institution by European standards. It operates between two sovereign states, involves a distinct form of joint decision-making and does not have an obvious counterpart elsewhere in the EU. It raises a series of fundamentally unique issues for exploration.

The Special EU Programmes Body is one of the six implementation bodies. Specifically dedicated to EU issues, it is charged with the cross-border co-ordination of community financial initiatives, including the second Peace Programme, Interreg III, Leader+, Equal and Urban II. The remaining implementation bodies, though less explicitly European, all cover policies with a strong EU focus, including food safety, trade and business development, language, inland waterways, and aquaculture and marine matters.

The British–Irish Council is the third institution created by the Belfast Agreement. It is to meet at summit level twice a year, and in specific sectoral formats on a regular basis at the ministerial level. 'Approaches to EU issues' are listed among the matters of mutual interest which might be discussed at the British–Irish Council, which brings together representatives of the two national governments and of the devolved institutions in Northern Ireland, Scotland and

Wales, plus the Isle of Man and the Channel Islands, and 'elsewhere in the British Isles', if appropriate. A less political animal than the NSMC, it nevertheless broadens the arena within which EU matters may be discussed and is a possible useful future source of influence.

The creation of the above institutions clearly changed the environment within which both governments, north and south of the Irish border; conduct their respective EU policy agendas. There is now a legal obligation for both jurisdictions to be aware of, and where possible to incorporate, each other's interests when devising and negotiating EU policy matters. This political development is relatively new and its evolution has been affected by periodic suspensions of the new institutions. It is hoped that the current difficulties can be resolved speedily to allow the region and the island to develop a common position on and approach to many areas of EU policy where interests are similar. It will require time for the institutions' operation to bed down and establish itself within an increasingly complex institutional environment on the island of Ireland. Time will reveal the extent to which they are successful or not.

Summary review of theoretical utility

In examining the concept of Europeanisation it has become clear that its integral component is the EU, or more specifically the impact of the EU on four arenas outlined above: on domestic politics and policy-making, on political parties and interest representation, on national institutions and on the citizen. Using this concept, we can see that the impact of the EU in Ireland has been monumental, and has helped to transform the country in economic, political and social terms from a backwater state on the periphery of Europe into one of the most solid and 'good European' states in less than thirty years. The engagement has been almost totally positive. Ireland has prospered and has benefited financially from the EU's focus on redistributive policies (CAP and the Structural Funds), has adapted to challenges brought about by the single market programme, shown determination to pursue the EMU project and has brought her own domestic policies (e.g. competition policy) easily into line to conform to European laws while at the same time helping to establish or even prevent stringent new European rules on issues like the environment. National institutions have likewise adapted to the EU. The Europeanisation process and the benefits have even touched Irish (and of course EU) citizens more so than their counterparts in the UK, although much has still to be done (across all member states) to develop and foster the connection between EU institutions, the European project and the citizen.

Being a small state, questions immediately arise as to how successfully Ireland is able to advance its causes and to what extent it is, as a peripheral (in terms of population size and wealth) EU member state, more realistically pulled along by the more powerful larger and core EU states such as France, Germany and the United Kingdom. This reality presents a challenge to all smaller states and one that Ireland has responded to. It is clear that member-state alliances form and dissolve from policy area to policy area. Ireland must make the most out of EU membership by projecting itself on to the European stage, and the best means of doing this successfully is by aligning herself with other states also set on the same priorities, and building a presence in Brussels.

Dublin has recorded considerable success on a variety of fronts, but ultimately her position is largely based on goodwill from the other larger states. This goodwill has been affected by a number of factors in recent years, not least the Irish rejection of the Treaty of Nice referendum in 2001 and the European Commission censure of Ireland in relation to EU economic policy. Many factors were at play in these specific examples. Importantly, however, they point to certain failings in the Irish political system. A lack of policy co-ordination at the domestic level, a reliance on informality and a certain complacency on the part of Irish political leaders have served to expose the potential and often unnecessary difficulties which EU integration can entail. Clear vision and both strong leadership and commitment to the EU all assist Ireland's cause and her European credentials. She must maintain these; otherwise it might be more apt to portray Ireland as 'a taker rather than a shaper of EU policy' and to view Ireland as operating 'in a defensive rather than a proactive manner' (Laffan 2001: 101). Ultimately, Ireland's status as the EU's 'favourite child' may diminish in an enlarged union of some twenty-five states, where Dublin will need to be able to present and defend its policy priorities.

Notes

1   See, for example, the series of Queens' papers on Europeanisation at http: www.qub.ies.
2   In the early 2000s the Tanaiste, Mary Harney, made reference to Ireland being closer to Boston than to Berlin. The Minister for Arts, Culture & Heritage, Sile De Valera, has suggested that the effect of EU legislation in the form of directives and regulations on Irish culture has been negative. Eamon O'Cuiv, junior Minister for Agriculture, revealed in the aftermath of the Treaty of Nice referendum that, despite campaigning for a 'Yes' vote, he had in fact voted 'No'. Charlie McCreevy, the Minister for Finance, and the Attorney-General, Michael McDowell, have both publicly questioned the future direction of the EU.
3   The TEU is frequently referred to as the Maastricht Treaty, after the town in the Netherlands where it was signed by EU leaders in 1992, and came into force in November 1993.
4   The Irish electorate, on a turnout of 57 per cent, ratified the TEU by a margin of 69.1 per cent to 30.9 per cent.
5   In the 1972 referendum on Irish accession to the EU, over four out of five Irish voters voted 'Yes', on a relatively high turnout of 70.3 per cent. In the early 1980s Ireland lagged somewhat behind the EC as a whole on the issue of whether membership was a good thing (European Commission 2002: 10). Support then rapidly rose. The 1987 referendum on ratification of the Single European Act was won by a lower margin on a lower turnout, but, nevertheless, 69.9 per cent in favour was a highly respectable outcome. The 1998 referendum on the Treaty of Amsterdam was the least contentious of all Irish referendums on EU matters and again approved ratification, by 61.7 per cent on a turnout of 56.3 per cent.

6   At the second Nice referendum in October 2002 some 62.89 per cent of the Irish electorate voted in favour of the treaty, against 37.11 per cent who said 'No'. Turnout was again disappointing, with just under 50 per cent using their vote.

Further reading

Anderson, S.S. and Eliassen, K.A. (2001) *Making Policy in Europe*, 2nd edn, London: Sage.

Cini, M. (ed.) (2003) *European Union Politics*, Oxford: Oxford University Press.

McGowan, L. and Murphy, M. (2003) 'Northern Ireland under Devolution: Facing the Challenge of Institutional Adaptation to EU Policy Formulation', *Regional and Federal Studies* (forthcoming).

Nugent, N. (2002) *The Government and Politics of the European Union*, 5th edn, London: Macmillan.

Peterson, J. and Bomberg, E. (1999) *Decision Making in the European Union*, Basingstoke: Macmillan.

Wallace, H. and Wallace, W. (eds) (2000) *Policy-making in the European Union*, 4th edn, Oxford: Oxford University Press.

12 Globalisation

Ireland in a global context

Paul Sweeney

Introduction

Globalisation is not new. What is new is that the trend of globalisation is accelerating; that it appears to be beyond the control of people and even of nation-states; that it is transferring power to corporations; and that, while there are many benefits, their distribution is uneven and thus it appears to be bringing new problems. 'Globalisation' is also a poorly understood term; it has different meanings and is 'blamed' for many ills in the modern world.

Globalisation is the process of internationalisation of business, of investment, of migration, of travel and of social relations. It is 'simply a story about the causes and consequences of an increase in mobility. For most of human history, neither goods nor capital nor most people nor many ideas moved very far from their place of origin', according to Weber (2001: 3). In the past few hundred years there has been an increase in mobility, but in the recent past it has greatly accelerated and in communications it is instant.

It is this rapid and apparently uncontrolled acceleration in mobility, this helter-skelter, which has caused a reaction, hostility to globalisation amongst many people. Some see globalisation as modernising and raising living standards, while others see it as converging and homogenising, with democratic governments and people being pushed into the background by market forces and the powerful, particularly corporations, gaining most. Globalisation is also associated with Americanisation because the influence of the US, as the dominant world power, is pervasive.

Globalisation can be defined as 'the process by which markets and production in different countries are becoming increasingly interdependent due to the dynamics of trade in goods and services and flows of capital and technology' (*European Economy* 1997: 45). Another definition of globalisation is that 'it is the result of the removal of rules, regulations, quotas and barriers to trade, which has resulted in the freeing up of movement of goods, services and, particularly, capital, between countries' (Sweeney 1999: 28). Globalisation has occurred because governments have decided to open up, or have been forced to do so by mobile capital. To this economic and financial definition must be added the social, the migration of peoples. This, in turn, includes travel, tourism and migrants seeking economic improvement and asylum. Migration, of course, is inexorably linked to the economic. The environment must also be considered when studying globalisation, because pollution, from Chernobyl, Sellafield, Alaskan oilfields or wherever, recognises no frontiers. Communications, particularly the media and the leisure industry, must also be analysed because both are increasingly globalised, increasingly controlled by large corporations, and in many ways define what and how people the world over think, act politically, spend their spare time and much of their increasing disposable income. Globalisation is not just about economics, trade, foreign direct investment (FDI) and financial flows, but includes migration, tourism, the environment, the media and the leisure industry. Globalisation is about the integration of the world's economies. The recession in the early 1990s hit the West, but Japan and Asia continued to grow; a short ten years later, the recession in 2001/2 affected all the world economies. Finally, and importantly, globalisation is about power.

Strange argues that it is impossible to study economics without examining the 'the role of power in economic life' (1994: 23). Whatever happens in a recession or boom is the result of action taken by those in authority, she holds – they set the rules of markets. While globalisation appears to be an independent force which develops automatically, it is, in fact, is a complex process, which is made up of many political choices. There are many alternative strategies which could be pursued in the economic social, political and cultural areas, though the key choices in the process are economic. Mary Robinson, former President of Ireland and UN High Commissioner on Human Rights said that 'globalisation is the privatisation of power. Governments are able to do less as a result'. She said that was why the UN was drawing up a 'Global Compact' with business to promote respect for human rights, labour standards and sustainable environmental policies (*Irish Independent*, 18 January 2002).

The growth in world trade (which has been at almost double the rate of economic growth for decades) and the acceleration of foreign direct investment, which is now more important than trade, have both accelerated the process of globalisation. So too has the fall in the costs of transport and communications, technological change in communications, the formation of the European Single Market, the fall of the Berlin Wall, the GATT (General Agreement on Tariffs and Trade) agreements under the World Trade Organisation (WTO), the huge rise in tourism, travel and the pent-up but controlled rise in economic migration. World trade grew by 7 per cent a year in the 1990s (though it and FDI stagnated in 2001). Revenues of foreign subsidiaries of multinational corporations (MNCs) had risen from $3 billion in 1990 to $14 billion by 1999 and were twice the level of all international exports. Thus FDI and international production by MNCs are more important than exports. The largest recipient of FDI is the US, the world's largest economy, at around 25 per cent, and it is also the largest investing country. Ireland is the top country in the world for FDI on a per capita basis.

Many developing countries which would have been protectionist in the past have opened up to freer trade in foreign investment in recent years. The sincere attempts at self-sufficiency in many developing countries after independence, which initially developed into varying forms of state socialism, regressed into cronyism and corruption in too many cases. While wary of free markets, many of these developing states have been abandoning protectionism in recent years. The more successful are not embracing 'free markets' with open arms, but 'use trade as part of a home-grown strategy that includes building sound political and legal institutions', according to Dani Rodrik of Harvard (*Fortune*, 26 November 2001).

Developing Weber's definition of globalisation as 'increased mobility', Held *et al.* state that 'in its simplest sense, globalisation refers to the widening, deepening and speeding up of global interconnectedness' (1999: 14). They hold that, while there is a wide variety of use of the term by different academics in different disciplines, the concept of globalisation embodies three main themes: extensity, intensity and velocity.

Extensity means that social, political and economic activities are now moving across frontiers, with events in one part of the world having significant effects on another. *Intensity* means the intensification of this interconnectedness, with widening social networks which may transcend established societies and states. *Velocity* is the way in which the growing extensity and intensity of global interconnection is reflected in an acceleration of global interactions and processes as transport and communication systems speed up the potential for the diffusion of ideas, goods, information, capital and people. Globalisation can be thought of as

> a process (or set of processes) which embodies a transformation in the spatial organisation of social relations and transactions – assessed in terms of their extensity, intensity, velocity and impact – generating transcontinental or interregional flows and networks of activity, interaction, and the exercise of power.
>
> (Held *et al.* 1999: 16)

Brief review of the evolution of globalisation approaches

Globalisation began in earnest in the mid-nineteenth century, with the railways, steamships and other technological innovations which led to increased mobility. Indeed, it has been argued that the type of globalisation which is taking place at the beginning of the twenty-first century is not as encompassing as that of over a century ago. The level of trade and foreign investment at the end of the nineteenth century and early twentieth was similar to today's, in proportion to the relative size of economies. At the beginning of the First World War the level of trade for the major powers – the UK, Germany, France, Japan and the US – was much the same as it is today, and the level of capital flows was also very high.

There are major differences between the globalisation process of a century ago and today's. First, capital flows were in more passive investment (indirect – through bonds and shares) a century ago and trade was in finished goods, whereas today there is far more FDI by companies in physical plant and subsidiaries. Second, in today's globalisation the migration of people is greatly constrained compared to that in the past. Migration is now greatly limited by state regulation and control. In the nineteenth and early twentieth century there was massive migration, particularly to the new worlds of North and South America, Africa, and Australia and New Zealand from Europe. In relative terms, the migration of people today is small compared to those times. In the three decades after the Second World War there was major migration from the peripheries of Europe (including Ireland) and the former colonies to urban centres in the core.

While the 'wide open plains' are no longer so under-populated, the industrialised world has closed its doors to economic migrants. A greater proportion of migration today is not economic but involuntary – refugees and asylum-seekers. Thus the nation-states of the rich countries have intervened in the international labour market by preventing the free movement of people. Ironically, nation-states have opened up to freer trade and to unregulated flows of capital while regulating the flows of people.

Another aspect of globalisation, of people's increased mobility – tourism – has grown phenomenally and may face forms of regulation in the future because of its potential impact on the environment. It is also ironic that the mobility of economic migrants is greatly regulated, while tourism mobility is encouraged by states. Furthermore, on the other side, some of the harshest critics of the globalisation of markets by corporations are the people who travel to distant and obscure places, bringing Western cultural mores and money with them – spreading the globalisation process in their own small way. Indeed, a long-distance flight of one economy passenger causes more greenhouse-gas production than one African produces in a year. Together with many other travellers, he/she adds up to mass tourism, which is one of the most rapidly growing aspects of the globalisation process. International tourism is growing at very high rates and tourism is penetrating all corners of the globe, impacting on cultures, economies and peoples.

There is a further contradiction in industrialised states' behaviour towards globalisation, which is that there is another area where governments of the industrialised countries intervene substantially in the marketplace, regulate trade, pay large subsidies out of taxes, impose high prices on their own citizens for food and endanger their environment with over-production. This is agriculture. The three industrialised trading blocks, US, Japan and Europe, all greatly protect their farmers with huge state subsidies, consumer subsidies, and bonuses on exports and restrictions on imports. This interventionist policy, which is enormously costly and regressive, damages the environment and is against fair and free trade, is not changed even when conservative pro-free-market parties come to power. 'Subsidies for farmers in rich countries are worth around $1 billion a day – more than six times as much as the rich countries' entire foreign aid budget' (*Economist*, 2 February 2002: 63).

Another important aspect of modern globalisation where borders do not matter, one which can only be dealt with by international co-operation between

market-setting states, is the environment. Environmental globalisation is a relatively new phenomenon, with ozone depletion, global warming, acid rain and
nuclear pollution (as well as AIDS) spreading across borders with impunity. At
the same time a new trade in toxic and nuclear waste has developed.

Technological change, driving much of the increase in mobility, has been
rapid in communications, which are now instant, with satellite and mobile
communications. A new and important political aspect of the globalisation
process is the growth of multinational media corporations which transcend
borders and governments and have political as well as commercial agendas.

While the process of globalisation is increasing, its impact is uneven. Some
countries have hardly opened up to its influences, while others are regressing, in
the sense of declining trade and falling FDI. Most FDI is between the rich countries. A few developing countries have increased their trade and these are the
ones that have gained most FDI. Twenty-four such countries, including China,
Argentina, Brazil, India and the Philippines, have grown their trade to national
income ratios since the early 1980s, according to a World Bank study quoted in
the *Economist* (2 February 2002). Growth averaged 5 per cent a year in the 1990s
(compared to rich countries, which grew by 2 per cent) and poverty rates
declined. But in poorer countries, such as Pakistan and most of Africa, trade
declined in relation to income per head, falling by 1 per cent a year in the 1990s,
when growth was stagnant and poverty rose. 'In short', according to the
Economist, 'globalisation is not, and never was, global. Much of the world, home
to one-third of its people and including large tracts of Africa and many Muslim
countries, has simply failed to participate' (2 February 2002). The *Economist*
(2001) book on globalisation, which is pro-free market and pro-globalisation,
makes the point that poor countries are not being 'raped' by globalisation and
foreign investment. In 2000 just 1 per cent of US FDI went to low-income countries, while 81 per cent went to high-income countries (*Economist* 2001: 13).
Ireland benefits disproportionately from US FDI and most of Ireland's FDI is
also to rich countries – the US, the UK and Europe.

Mainstream variants of globalisation in contemporary usage

The neo-classical, free-market schools hold that globalisation is modernising and
brings convergence between countries, whereas others place varying levels of
emphasis on the impact of institutions which have developed over time and
which alter the impact of globalisation in specific ways (Hay 2000). Weiss argues
that differing institutions and practices produce further divergences with globalisation – 'contrary to globalist predictions I propose that national differences are
likely to become more rather than less pronounced in a highly institutionalised
environment, thus exacerbating rather than diminishing current differences
between strong and weak states' (Weiss 1998: 188). Weiss is arguing for a qualitative improvement in institutions and state intervention, such as co-ordination

between, for example, the regulatory regime and the strategy of national competitiveness.

There are many theoretical perspectives on globalisation, ranging from proponents of totally free markets, at one extreme, to anti-globalisation protesters at the other, some of whom are anti-capitalist and others anti-change, anti-modern. In between are a wide range of views – emotionally hostile, passionately in favour but critical of aspects, etc.

Sklair (1999) categorises globalisation on the basis of four research clusters – first, the world systems approach; second, the global culture approach; third, the global society approach; and, fourth, the global capitalism approach – and he favours the last as the 'most productive'. Held *et al.* (1999) see it in terms of spatio-temporal dimensions, on the one hand, and of organisational dimensions on the other. Perhaps the best approach is the political. There are three broad schools, as in international relations, from the left/radical liberal in the middle to the realists on the right. Many anti-globalisation supporters are anti-capitalist, anti-big business – which, as has been seen, is a key driver of the process – and are on the left, while others on the left favour varying forms of regulation of globalisation. Many social democrats and socialists favour the process, but can be very critical of its present form with its lack of regulation. The liberals or free-marketeers favour the existing system of globalisation, but some schools support more intervention by states than others. On the right are many who see the process as modernising, enriching and spreading democratic values, while others on the right favour much less regulation and far freer markets. The realists, in general, are those who see the state as the main unit of international political economy and generally hold that state intervention distorts markets. The position broadly taken in this chapter is closer to those who favour greater regulation by the state in the process of globalisation.

Some neo-liberal economists, such as Jagdish Bhagwati (1993), see formations such as the European Union (EU) as an attack on free trade and a block on global integration. There is the contrary view of regional trading blocks, particularly the EU, which is that they force the imposition of the neo-liberal agenda on its people. Stephen Gill (1997) argues that the formation of the Union, which was social in its origin and objectives, has mutated into a charter of economic liberalisation and marketisation. It is clear that the EU competition rules and regulations have helped to eliminate many state companies, particularly as vehicles of social regional policy and universal service; the Stability Pact rules have curtailed governments' ability to deal with fiscal crises (though it may steer them from creating such crises in the first place); the monetary union has taken monetary policy away from the state – and these changes have led to what Gill (1997) calls 'disciplinary neo-liberalism'.

Other economists argue that the disadvantages of the Single Market have been outweighed (to date) by its benefits for Ireland (Bradley *et al.* 1992). It is clear that there are already competitive downward tax reductions between EU member states (led by Ireland on low taxes on corporations) on employer social charges and on labour regulation, and there will be further pressure for reductions in public spending. It is the policy of Forfas, the policy development agency of the Irish government, to continue this through the WTO 'by removing tax and regulatory barriers to investment flows through international agreements' (Forfas 2001: 33). There is an undoubted tension between the European Social Model and neo-liberal policies pursued by Brussels and some governments. This debate will continue.

On one side, there is a growing level of popular discontent with corporate power, which is not yet reflected by government action, but is illustrated by a number of highly popular business books, which have sold widely. The leading one is by Naomi Klein, whose *No Logo* (2001) is an internationally best-selling business book which became the bible of the anti-globalisation protesters in Seattle, Genoa, etc. Klein argues that the dominance of brands/logos has gone too far, and she focuses on the rise of corporations, the weakness of nation-states, the subservience of the product to the label, the use of sweatshops by many multinationals in the developing world, where 'cool' products are produced, on how local culture is subsumed by brands and even how companies are taking control of aspects of education. Similarly, George Monbiot, in the *Captive State* (2000), holds that Britain has been taken over by corporations. He argues that 'the struggle between people and corporations will be the defining battle of the twenty-first century. If corporations win, liberal democracy will come to an end' (Monbiot 2000: 7). Monbiot is particularly critical of the European Round Table of Industrialists, the association of the chief executives of the forty-six largest companies in Europe, which he believes exerts enormous influence on the European Commission and on governments and, in many ways, sets the EU's agenda.

On the other side, Micklethwait and Wooldridge celebrate globalisation because it brings not just 'economic efficiency' but also 'freedom' (2000: xxii). They argue that globalisation frees individuals and companies from control by governments and that 'free trade makes it easier for businesspeople to escape from interfering officials by moving their money and operations abroad' (Micklethwait and Wooldridge 2000: 337). They admit that, while it greatly lessens government influence, it transfers power to corporations, 'to the knuckle-head in the boardroom, or if you work in the *Académie Français*, by the illiterate in Hollywood'. Nevertheless, they believe that companies will not be able to control markets and that the 'forces of globalisation favour small companies' (Micklethwait and Wooldridge 2000: 338).

The position of states and markets in a globalising world

With globalisation, it appears initially that the nation-state can be largely ignored by foreign investors, MNCs and speculators. The integration of the world economy appears inevitable, with the convergence of economic factors like interest rates and the pressure to reduce taxes and therefore public spending. Unskilled jobs seem to be shifting from industrialised countries to newly industrialising ones, a trend that worries trade unions in the US and other developed countries. In the US, for example, trade unions that are strongly opposed to free trade even managed to persuade an avid conservative like George Bush to introduce protectionism against trade in steel in early 2002.

Hirst and Thompson state that that the world economy 'is dominated by uncontrollable global forces and has as its principal actors and major agents of change truly trans-national corporations, which owe allegiance to no nation state and locate wherever the global market advantage dictates' (1996: 287). But they also argue that there is much that states can and should do about MNCs, foreign investment and capital flows.

Today's world economy is still far from integrated in terms of prices of goods and services, labour, access to capital, interest rates and tax rates. Most importantly, governments still have a lot of power and, while it is a little less than before, particularly for small open economies like Ireland, it is still considerable. The Irish state, for example, may have less power over macroeconomic instruments than in the past, but it has substantial power over many other areas, especially microeconomic factors such as company law, taxation and labour regulations. Moreover, governments acting together can achieve much, as the fifteen member states of the EU are still learning. The introduction of the Euro in 1999, despite a shaky start, should strengthen the Eurozone and the EU. Whilst it is popular to state that the turnover of some companies exceeds that of many nation-states, the real comparison is between a company's value added and the gross domestic product (GDP) of a country, which is a measure of its value added. By this criterion, companies become a lot smaller – by about 70–80 per cent, and of course they do not have the power to raise taxes, make laws, or arrest people, etc. (*Financial Times*, 6 February 2001).

The competitive down-bidding for FDI by EU governments, using costly incentives, is a case of democratic countries weakening their own power instead of working together to set clear rules for corporate behaviour. Governments, particularly in the EU, will have to act together on broad policy issues for their peoples' welfare, while competing ferociously, if necessary, for FDI after new ground rules have been agreed.

While world trade and foreign investment by MNCs are growing rapidly, fears of globalisation and the power of MNCs are exaggerated. Nonetheless, it is important that governments do not let power slip easily to corporate boardrooms. The extraordinary influence of corporations on US politics was highlighted by the corrupt practices of Enron, the energy giant that backed George Bush and many politicians of both parties.

The fact that markets are shaped by man, companies and institutions was very clearly articulated by Kenneth Lay, the head of Enron, the world's seventh-largest company, which collapsed spectacularly in early 2002. Lay did not believe that markets were beyond human control or were 'objective'. He and Enron believed in pressurised lobbying to change and secure the marketplace for itself. Enron was the major financial backer of George Bush and of many US politicians. Kenneth Lay said, 'we are going to be the most important company in the world. We are going to change every market' (*Financial Times*, 9 February 2002).

Enron grew rapidly, greatly assisted by lobbying from a small pipeline company. As is now happening with some of the larger Irish companies, Enron placed many former government officials on its payroll to give it an insider's advantage, always with the objective of changing the market to suit the corporation. It was the major force behind the deregulation of US energy markets, which assisted its growth and was a key factor in the Californian blackouts in the late 1990s. It dominated Texas with its lawyers, Vinson and Elkins, its consultants, McKinseys, and its accountants, Arthur Andersen, who fiddled its books and tried to shred the evidence afterwards.

Enron and the other oil majors appeared to have directed energy policy in the US. The integration of the world economies is accelerating and the dominant economies are the major beneficiaries. The leading companies are the greatest direct investors, they have great influence and their boards are not democratically accountable. They are not supposed to be democratic entities, and, because their power is increasing, the issues of governance, accountability and social responsibility are of concern to all. They are theoretically accountable to their shareholders, who are largely other corporations or pension and corporate funds – but this means that they are not fully democratic, in the sense that they are not publicly accountable.

Held *et al.* hold that 'there are good reasons for doubting...claims that nation states are being eclipsed by contemporary patterns of globalisation. While regional and global interaction networks are strengthening, they have multiple and variable impacts across diverse locales' (1999: 441). They also argue that international human rights laws supersede those of states, and, while many governments have not signed up to the conventions, there has been a gradual shift away from the principle that state sovereignty is always above the rights of individuals. Held *et al.* are highly critical of the political fatalism of the 'hyper-globalisers', arguing that, although these advocates present much evidence of a significant politicisation of a growing array of issue areas, it has been accompanied by the growth of many new institutions and networks of political mobilisation and regulatory activity across borders. Because of this, they suggest that it is anachronistic to believe that politics can only be understood by reference to national structures and mechanisms (Held *et al.* 1999: 444–5).

Beck holds that nation-states must work together 'to limit or obstruct global firms from minimizing their tax obligations and maximizing state subsidies' (2000: 30). Arguing that 'with globalisation there is a growing need for binding international regulation for international conventions and institutions which cover cross-border transactions', Beck sees this as one of many responses to the process, which he terms as the response of 'the social democratic modernizers' (2000: 30). Another response is that of 'inclusive sovereignty', where the surrender of sovereignty rights is accompanied by a gain through transnational co-operation. Beck suggests several other approaches to reasserting the primacy of politics into the globalisation process, arguing that unless there is a more constructive approach to globalisation, the neo-liberals will have won – 'even against themselves. The social state [will be] in ruins and a type of anarchy or

"Brazilianisation" will have occurred' (2000: 160). In this scenario, Beck suggests that taxes will have long become 'a matter of voluntary contributions' (2000: 161).

John Gray, a former conservative turned radical critic of laissez-faire capitalism, believes that a truly global economy is being 'created by the spread of new technologies, not by the spread of free markets'. This spread of technologies has 'resulted in the emancipation of market forces from social and political control' and this will ultimately lead to servitude (Gray 1998: 208). The idea of a single, global market based on Anglo-American values has not been challenged. Gray argues that the 'global free market is not an iron law of historical development but a political project' and, echoing Joseph Schumpeter, states that global markets are 'inherently unstable, predicting that they will lead to the rise of fundamentalism, new varieties of nationalism and the breakdown of social cohesion' (1998: 210).

Case study: globalisation and Ireland

The impact of globalisation on Ireland has been profound and in many ways has brought great benefits to the majority of people in most, though not all, areas. Living standards have risen from around half the European average in the 1950s to close to it today, and the rise has been most rapid in the 'Celtic Tiger' years, between 1994 and 2000. Ireland is one of the most open economies in the world. In 2002 imports and exports exceeded GDP, at 176 per cent. This is not unusual, as small economies, by their size, have a high level of trade. Where Ireland is different from other small economies is in the level of its success in developing its economy through open trade. The Irish economy was a late-developing economy, in that when the rest of Europe was growing rapidly in the late 1940s and 1950s, Ireland's economy was stagnating (O'Malley 1989).

Since the 1950s, Irish public policy has been geared to openness, to trade and to FDI – objectives which have been consistently pursued by successive governments. Regrettably, they were also accompanied by large-scale outward migration. In proportion to its population, Ireland has had one of the largest emigrations for over two centuries. State agencies like the Industrial Development Authority (IDA) sought FDI and marketed Ireland as a country with a highly educated and flexible English-speaking workforce, with low taxes on companies (which has had to be partly paid for by high taxes on spending and incomes), access to the EU, good financial and professional services, and political stability. Ireland has pursued intervention in the global marketplace with its strong 'visible hand' of a coherent industrial policy through well-funded industrial development agencies, grants, tax breaks and broad assistance to investors. It is now extending the support of its agencies internationally to Irish firms that are investing abroad.

The first phase of opening up to foreign investment brought economic success in the 1960s, plus the high borrowing in the late 1970s that led to a severe debt problem and very low growth for most of the 1980s. However, the

1990s saw the most rapid and sustained growth levels of virtually any European country in the twentieth century. Key factors in this economic growth were: high employment growth – up by over 50 per cent in total jobs in just six years; rapidly falling unemployment and rising real incomes; and FDI. The FDI of the 1990s was of a different quality to that in the 1960s, when Irish companies were responsible for *assemblage* of products, rather than production (the so-called 'screwdriver' or assembly operations in a low-wage economy). The 1990s, by contrast, saw a higher-wage economy with well-paid jobs in some of the leading multinationals.

This did not occur by chance, by passively accepting the impact of global markets, but was the result of conscious and consistent policy by governments in driving industrialisation. The industrial promotion agencies, Forfas, the policy body, Enterprise Ireland and particularly the IDA Ireland, sought out companies in three sectors, which they identified, correctly, for their growth potential. These were computers and related areas, chemical and pharmaceuticals, and health-care. Government agencies were very successful in attracting the leading companies in these sectors to establish plants in Ireland, and this was under-pinned by other policies such as investment in education, fiscal reform, institutional reform and consensus through social partnership.

Comparatively speaking, Ireland is a very small economy, comprising just 1 per cent of the EU's GDP and disproportionately dependent on trade. It is the twenty-second-largest exporter in the world in absolute terms (excluding the micro-states like Singapore). For every $100 generated globally by exports in 2000, $1.30 accrued to Ireland (Forfas 2002). More importantly, Ireland is the highest per capita exporter in the world and is also now the largest recipient of FDI in the world on a per capita basis (Forfas 2002). Thus, for its size, Ireland is also a major player in generating FDI. Again, relative to its size, Ireland also has the largest emigration for over two centuries and its citizens are the most trav-elled. Ireland is therefore a country that has benefited from globalisation and also now contributes to the process. It is a truly globalised economy.

Whilst world trade has been growing at a much faster rate than the growth of the world's economies and FDI by multinationals has been growing even more rapidly than trade, Ireland has disproportionately benefited from FDI (on a per capita basis) and this was a key contributor to the 1990s' Celtic Tiger growth phase. In the era of globalisation, small open economies have little choice but to encourage FDI while attempting to build strong indigenous companies and stronger linkages between domestic and foreign companies. Ireland has been successful in both respects in recent times, but change is constant in maintaining these linkages, maintaining the attraction for FDI and retaining the larger indigenous headquarters operations.

To date, Ireland has been a recipient of a high proportion of US FDI. Leading US companies such as Apple, Intel, IBM, Microsoft, SmithKline Glaxo, etc. have plants here. In recent years, Ireland too has contributed to the process of globalisation through the takeover of firms in other countries. The leading Irish companies have been buying firms in many countries. There are around fifty Irish companies with subsidiaries of some size in other countries. In 2002 a smaller number of around fifteen are what might be termed 'Irish multinationals', but these would be small MNCs by international standards. Although the target countries are largely the UK and US, there are Irish subsidiaries in all continents.

In this context, Irish trade unions have tended not to be critical of globalisation, but have instead welcomed FDI since the early 1960s. This is in spite of the job losses in traditional industries and the fact that many, though not all, of the US investing companies have been anti-union. The unions believe that FDI brought in more and better-paying jobs than were displaced. This is in contrast to the autarky of unions in the US and elsewhere.

Addressing a Dublin business conference on the success of the Celtic Tiger and on migration on 1 December 2000, the *Financial Times* columnist Samuel Brittan argued that 'Ireland is better placed than most other EU countries to follow an open door policy in line with the words on the American Statue of Liberty':

> *Give me your tired, your poor,*
> *Your huddled masses yearning to breathe free,*
> *The wretched refuse of your teeming shore.*
> *Send these, the homeless, tempest-tossed to me,*
> *I lift my lamp beside the golden door!*

(quoted in Brittan 2000)

Ireland had one of the highest rates of emigration in the world for its size for over two centuries, yet its recent economic success has led to a rapid and complete reversal, with net immigration. This aspect of globalisation is bringing new challenges.

Some critics might see foreign investment by Irish firms as an indication of economic decline, but, on the contrary, it could easily be argued that it reflects the growing strength of Irish firms seeking to expand from the very small domestic market. If they are successful, the home economy gains from being the location of the higher value-added functions such as head office operations with higher salaries and research and development. Most Irish companies invest abroad to access new markets and acquire new technologies. They have, however, not invested abroad to reduce costs, as has been case with many US and UK firms, though they may move to lower-cost locations in the future. While there was justification in the argument against an over-dependence on foreign multinationals, the success has far outweighed the decline of traditional firms which were unable to adapt to foreign competition. The policy of openness has also attracted better-quality investment, higher-value jobs and the building of linkages with local firms, and many local firms have expanded abroad or been taken over by multinationals.

The best response to the dependence on foreign investment is to ensure that investing MNCs remain in Ireland, set down roots, build linkages with the local economy and wish to expand here as many of them are currently doing and that they behave as good corporate citizens.

(Sweeney 1999: 148)

It is believed by some that Ireland is becoming an outpost of the US and is too dependent on US FDI. However, according to Holger (2000), the level of Irish investment in the US almost equalled that of US companies in Ireland by 1999. He found that Irish FDI stocks in the US increased from $174 million in 1980 to $17,222 million in 1999 in real terms. This compares with an increase in US investment stocks in Ireland from $3,957 million to $18,998 million over the same period. He found that the number of jobs in Irish-owned subsidiaries in the US was 64,800 in 1998, compared to 100,000 jobs in Ireland in US firms. As this figure excluded jobs in Irish banks in the US, and as Allied Irish Bank (AIB) employed 5,658 in the US in 2000 and there were a number of additional takeovers in 1999 and 2000, the number of jobs in Irish-owned firms in the US clearly exceeded 70,000 by 2000. The key difference is that the US firms created most of the jobs in greenfield sites, whereas the US jobs of Irish firms were generally takeovers of existing firms and jobs.

In 2001 Irish firms invested 2.7 billion in acquisitions, domestically and abroad, down substantially from the 9 billion spent by them in 2000. In contrast, takeovers of Irish firms amounted to 4.3 billion in 2001 and 10 billion in 2000. The 2000 figures for the takeovers of Irish firms were distorted by the 4.5 billion takeover of the former state company subsidiary Eircell by Vodafone and British Telecom's 2.4 billion takeover of Esat.

Two state-owned companies, the Electricity Supply Board (ESB) and *Aer Rianta*, have operations in many foreign countries. *Aer Rianta* part owns and operates the airports at Birmingham, Dusseldorf and Hamburg, and the ESB has operations in over thirty-five countries. ESB was the leading bidder in a major takeover of eight Polish utilities, but was blocked by the government in 2001, because it did not want a state-owned company to expand further internationally on such a scale. Consistent with this policy, the largest indigenous Irish company, Eircom, was privatised and split, and the mobile part was sold to Vodafone and the fixed-line business to US venture capitalists led by Tony O'Reilly.

Cement Roadstone Haulage (CRH) and Irish globalisation

CRH is worth examining more closely as the leading Irish MNC at the beginning of the twenty-first century. It was amongst the largest investing Irish firms abroad, spending almost 1.3 billion, largely in the US and Europe in 2001 on over fifty acquisitions (CRH, *Annual Report 2001*; *Irish Times*, various dates). CRH is a building materials company and it is the largest Irish company ranked by turnover. It would be around the 600th largest company in the world by turnover in 2000. It was ranked 720th in market capitalisation in the top 1,000 global companies in the *Business Week* league in 2000. It was the 216th largest European company in 2001, also by market capitalisation (*Financial Times*), and fourth in the construction and building materials sector of the *Financial Times* league for shareholder return in the five years to 2000.

CRH's turnover was 10.4 billion, with profits of 803 million in 2001. In 2001 only 7.1 per cent of its turnover was in Ireland (though Ireland was disproportionately profitable – generating 16 per cent of profits). Thus it is a major multinational, headquartered in Ireland. The company has grown by taking over small and medium-size companies in the US, Europe and South America. Its turnover grew from 1.6 billion in 1995 to just over 10 billion in 2001. It retains the names of its takeovers and so trades under hundreds of different names. With the differing names and because it is not in consumer products, it has a low profile. It had around forty US subsidiaries with differing names in 2001. It has operations in eleven of the fifteen EU member states, in Poland, Estonia, Latvia, Ukraine, Switzerland, Israel, the US, Canada, Argentina and Chile. Its Americas division employed 26,000 in over 670 locations, and it leads the market in many products. In Europe it employs over 21,000 in 330 locations and is the fourth-largest building materials company in the continent.

CRH was founded by the merger of the private cement monopoly Cement Ltd and a materials company, Roadstone, in order to avoid a takeover by a foreign company. It grew on the domestic market from the 1960s as a monopoly which many would say enjoyed state protection. Thus, under the implicit protection of the state, it grew from an infant industry to a successful diversified multinational in similar products worldwide. Today it is managed and controlled from Ireland and its largest shareholders are Irish financial institutions.

Summary review of theoretical utility

We have seen that globalisation encompasses mobility in three main areas: trade, capital and people. It is about increased mobility in an era of technological change, so that markets and production all over the globe are becoming increasingly interdependent. The removal of rules, regulations, quotas and barriers to trade, the end of the Berlin Wall, the formation of the Single Market in Europe, the continuing fall in transport costs and instant communications are all accelerating the process and promoting mobility in three areas: trade, capital and people. Globalisation is not just about economics, about free trade and FDI, but includes the migration of peoples, mass tourism, the environment, media control and culture.

Globalisation and the mobility of investment are important because they create serious challenges to the democratic state. Globalisation is provoking a race to the bottom between democratic governments to reduce taxes, regulations and to increase subsidies and services to companies. Still, however, governments remain immensely powerful economically, and when they co-operate they can and do change the rules on corporate behaviour. The rules of the marketplace are made by people and can be changed by them and their representatives. At the moment, however, it appears that this is more clearly understood by large corporations' executives than by economists or even those whom they lobby, the politicians and senior government officials. While globalisation is sweeping through many rules and regulations, it is a process made by people and is amended by them. Events like 11 September, the collapse of the Argentinian economy in 2001/2 and wars can and do change the direction and the rules of the globalisation process. A complete understanding of the globalisation concept is therefore useful because it helps us to understand more fully the context and environment in which public policy is made.

Continuing globalisation is not inevitable. It is not an inexorable process. The First World War brought the process of globalisation to a halt and it was followed by a deep depression, a further series of wars and the Holocaust. Globalisation, trade, FDI and migration ceased for thirty-one years and the world's economies stagnated, with millions unemployed.

Still, the progress of globalisation is far more complex than a choice between such stagnation and the triumph of the untrammelled marketplace, the evisceration of the democratic state and the privatisation of power. The increase in the mobility in trade, in capital flows and, importantly, in migration, which are the components of globalisation, can occur in ways which enrich the greatest number of people, materially and in other ways. Modern globalisation does impose limits on national politics while simultaneously opening up wider choices. However, political institutions for global governance can be formed or evolve to civilise and democratise the process. The choice is not whether globalisation should be opposed, but how to civilise it.

The international mobilisation and popularisation of global issues has led to a shift in thinking by many in the key organisations in the globalisation process, such as the WTO, the World Bank, some MNCs and many governments. The *Financial Times* argued that the globalisation process got a shock with the 11 September attacks. It meant that the

> serious protestors who are concerned about the marginalisation of the poorest countries, about the ways of alleviating their intolerable debt burden and how to give them access to rich country markets, have been reinforced in their convictions. They would argue that global security, both economic and physical, can best be ensured by reducing poverty and investing more in development.
>
> (Editorial, *Financial Times*, 1 February 2002)

Its editorial concluded that 'those protestors deserve a hearing'.

Globalisation raises three questions for the nation-state. First, how can it benefit from globalisation and the growth of international trade, investment and capital flows? Second, how does it regulate it? Third, can governments exert more influence over the larger firms' corporate governance and social responsibility? In answer to the first question, Ireland's economic success, particularly in the 1990s, is perhaps the case study for understanding how globalisation can bring success to a late-developing economy (see Sweeney 1999), though the history, institutions and phase of development of each country are vitally important. The answer to the second question is that no country, especially a small country, can regulate the process of internationalisation of globalisation on its own, but regions or groups of countries, especially the EU, can. The growth of the power and influence of companies is beyond the influence of most nation-states, but by working together they can set rules and regulations for corporate governance of these companies. Some economists believe that companies must act in a responsible way if they are to be successful. Others believe that such rules interfere in the marketplace and are unnecessary.

In relation to the third question, the 'race to the bottom' – lowest taxes on profits, on share options, the fewest labour regulations, etc. – by governments in competition with each other to attract FDI is one where the losers may be democratic governments. Governments are weakening their own power by participating in such competition instead of working together to establish clear rules. There is the understandable temptation to get first-mover advantage by cutting taxes first, and Ireland has sought and achieved this in a number of areas. Governments, particularly in the EU, will have to act together on broad policy issues for their peoples' welfare, while competing for FDI after they have established clear ground rules on governance, taxes, the environment, labour law, etc.

Nonetheless, while economic power has shifted to the boards of MNCs, companies still have to obey the laws in each country in which they operate. Many spend a great deal lobbying Brussels, Washington and every capital city and leave little to market forces. Most MNCs still have most of their investments in their home country, but the MNCs headquartered in small countries like Ireland have more investment abroad than at home, and they are the exceptions in this regard.

The shift to free markets and globalisation is not guaranteed to be successful. The largest debt default ever was by Argentina in December 2001, on debts of $155 billion. Throughout the 1990s, those to the right on the globalisation debated promoted Argentina as an exemplar case – the leading light in pursuing free-market policies. It abolished its trade barriers, opened up its capital markets and privatised most of its state enterprises, including banks, airlines and ports, selling most of them to foreign multinationals. Yet it collapsed into economic and political chaos in early 2002.

It has been argued that the Irish economy has gained remarkably from globalisation, with a growth in employment of over 50 per cent in under ten years, with a sharp reduction in unemployment, in poverty and a rise in real incomes. There have, however, been losers, and the gap between the better off in society and those on low incomes and welfare has widened. There has also been a loss in traditional jobs. Moreover, as incomes rose, governments and public policy-makers have not attempted any serious redistribution of income or wealth. Monetary policy was allowed to shift to Bonn in return for low interest rates, and the pound was traded for the euro.

Taking a longer-term view, Irish public policy, which engaged in a costly trade war with Britain in the 1930s, was slow to open to free trade and foreign investment. The opening up in the 1960s brought prosperity and growth, and while based on low wages and the assembly or 'screwdriver operations' of foreign firms, it eventually led to the second phase of industrial development, with greater linkages, more research and development, the international financial services sector, etc. It also helped to open up Ireland culturally and socially. The 1990s Celtic Tiger phase was particularly successful and it brought many additional benefits, including incomes rising to close to the average EU level, better-quality multinational subsidiaries with better linkages to the domestic economy, and the expansion of a number of Irish companies into globalised multinationals.

Just as there has been a large flow of FDI into Ireland, with some of the world's leading corporations creating jobs here, so there has been a flow of investment from Ireland to other countries in Europe and particularly to the US. At the beginning of the twenty-first century the stock of Irish foreign investment in the US is almost as large as that of US investment in Ireland, and the number of jobs in Irish firms in the US, at around 70,000 in 2000, is not far off the number of US jobs in Ireland. This note only illustrates the internationalisation of Irish indigenous industry and the contribution of Ireland to the process of globalisation, but it also demonstrates that the process of globalisation cannot be seen as a one-way process.

The case study was of CRH, an indigenous Irish company which grew out of the Irish construction supply industry. It was the result of a merger of two major companies, Cement, a monopoly cement producer, and Roadstone, an aggregates company. The construction industry grew with large-scale public investment in roads, housing, hospitals and other areas over the years. The cement monopoly, which may have been protected by the state, allowed it to accumulate capital and eventually to invest outside the small domestic market and become one of the world's leading construction companies, with operations in many countries.

In conclusion, globalisation is not universal and the benefits, which are many, are unevenly spread, geographically and between peoples. Globalisation of markets and the internationalisation of capitalism are not even: the richer countries and larger corporations gain most from the process. The rich countries that are the most globalised are most open to trade and investment, and they benefit most. It is their companies which are the engines of globalisation, and these benefit most.

If there was a collapse in the process of globalisation, in the same way as it stopped in 1914 for thirty-one years, the impact on the world, its economies and its peoples would far outweigh its negative aspects, even if the stop was not accompanied by war. Indeed, without the artificial stimulus of war, with its increased public spending, its mobilisation and its creative destruction, such a breakdown in globalisation would lead to a prolonged and severe economic depression. Given the progress of globalisation to date, however, this time such a depression would not be confined to the West. It is therefore clear that the process of globalisation is one which is worth taming and civilising so that it may work for the benefit of more people.

Many in the anti-globalisation movement are aiming at the wrong target. Just as King Canute's orders were unable to stop the tide's return, so many are attempting to stop a process which, while not inexorable, cannot be rolled back, particularly as it does benefit more than harm. The real issue is what kind of globalisation is of most benefit to most people. Governments can and do interfere in markets and in global markets. Governments have interfered very strongly in the globalised labour market. They have, at the behest of their peoples, for good or bad reasons, greatly curbed international migration, one of the key elements of globalisation. Governments already intervene in international markets individually and collectively through WTO, the International Monetary Fund (IMF), the World Bank (all UN bodies) and the EU. Similarly, if motivated, they could intervene in international financial markets as they have in labour markets through curbing migration.

Further reading

Beck, U. (2000) *What Is Globalisation?*, Cambridge: Polity Press.

Hay, C. (2000) 'Globalisation, European Integration and the Contingent Convergence of European Social Models', *Review of International Studies* 26: 509–31.

Held, D., McGrew, A., Goldblatt, D. and Perraton, J. (1999) *Global Transformations: Politics, Economics and Culture*, Cambridge: Polity Press.

Hirst, P. and Thompson, G. (1999) *Globalisation in Question: The International Economy and the Possibilities of Governance*, Cambridge: Polity Press.

Sweeney, P. (1999) *The Celtic Tiger, Ireland's Continuing Economic Miracle*, Dublin: Oak Tree Press.

Weber, S. (ed.) (2001) *Globalisation and the European Political Economy*, New York: Columbia University Press.

Bibliography

Adler, E. and Haas, P. (1992) 'Conclusion: Epistemic Communities, World Order, and the Creation of a Coordination', *International Organization* 46: 367–90.

Adshead, M. (1996) 'Beyond Clientelism: Agricultural Networks in Ireland and the EU', *West European Politics* 19: 583–608.

Adshead, M. (2002) *Developing European Regions? Comparative Governance, Policy Networks and European Integration*, Aldershot: Ashgate.

Adshead, M. and Quinn, B. (1998) 'The Move from Government to Governance: Irish Development Policy's Paradigm Shift', *Policy and Politics* 26: 209–25.

All-Party Oireachtas Committee on the Constitution (2002) *Parliament: Seventh Progress Report*, Dublin: Stationery Office.

Allen, K. (2000) *The Celtic Tiger: The Myth of Social Partnership in Ireland*, Manchester: Manchester University Press.

Althusser, L. (1970) 'Ideology and the Ideological State Apparatuses', in L. Althusser (ed.) *Lenin and Philosophy*, London: New Left Books.

Anderson, C.W. (1978) 'The Logic of Public Problems: Evaluation in Comparative Policy Research', in D. Ashford (ed.) *Comparing Public Policies*, Beverly Hills, CA: Sage.

Anderson, P. (1974) *Lineages of the Absolutist State*, London: Verso.

Anderson, S.S. and Eliassen, K.A. (2001) *Making Policy in Europe*, 2nd edn, London: Sage.

Arensberg, C. and. Kimball, S.T. (1940) *Family and Community in Ireland*, Cambridge, MA: Harvard University Press.

Arrow, K.J. (1951) *Social Choice and Individual Values*, New York: John Wiley.

Aspinwall, M.D. and Schneider, G. (2000) 'Same Menu, Separate Table: The Institutionalist Turn in Political Science and the Study of European Integration', *European Journal of Political Research* 38: 1–36.

Baccaro, L. (2000) 'Negotiating the Italian Pension Reform with the Unions: Lessons for Corporatist Theory', unpublished paper, International Institute for Labour Studies, International Labour Office, Geneva.

Baccaro, L. (2001) 'The Construction of "Democratic Corporatism" in Italy', unpublished paper, International Institute for Labour Studies, International Labour Office, Geneva.

Bacchi, C. (1996) *The Politics of Affirmative Action*, London: Sage.

Bacon, P. (1998) *An Economic Assessment of Recent House Price Developments: Report Submitted to the Minister for Housing and Urban Renewal*, Dublin: Stationery Office.

Bacon, P. (1999) *The Housing Market: An Economic Review and Assessment: Report Submitted to the Minister for Housing and Urban Renewal*, Dublin: Stationery Office.

Bacon, P. (2000) *The Housing Market in Ireland: An Economic Evaluation of Trends and Prospects*, Dublin: Stationery Office.

Baker, T., Fitzgerald, J. and Honohan, I. (1996) *Economic Implications for Ireland of EMU*, Dublin: Economic and Social Research Institute.

Ball, A.R. and Peters, B.G. (2000) *Modern Politics and Government*, 6th edn, London: Macmillan.

Barrington, R. (1987) *Health, Medicine and Politics in Ireland 1900–1970*, Dublin: Institute of Public Administration.

Barrington, T.J. (1980) *The Irish Administrative System*, Dublin: Institute for Public Administration.

Barry, F. (ed.) (1999) *Understanding Ireland's Economic Growth*, London: Macmillan.

Barry, U. (1998) 'Women, Equality and Public Policy', in S. Healy and B. Reynolds (eds) *Social Policy in Ireland*, Dublin: Oak Tree Press.

Bax, M. (1976) *Harp Strings and Confessions: Machine-style Politics in the Irish Republic*, Assen: Van Gorcum.

Beck, U. (2000) *What Is Globalisation?*, Cambridge: Polity Press.

Bennett, C.J. (1991) 'Different Processes, One Result: The Convergence of Data Protection Policy in Europe and the United States', *Governance* 1: 162–83.

Benson, J.K. (1982) 'A Framework for Policy Analysis', in D. Rogers (ed.) Whitten and Associates, *Inter-organisation Coordination*, Ames, IO: Iowa State University Press.

Bentley, A. (1967) *The Process of Government*, Chicago: University of Chicago Press.

Bergson, A. (1938) 'A Reformulation of Certain Aspects of Welfare Economics', *Quarterly Journal of Economics* 52: 353–95.

Bew, P. and Patterson, H. (1982) *Sean Lemass and the Making of Modern Ireland*, Dublin: Gill and Macmillan.

Bhagwati, J. (1982) 'Directly Unproductive Profit Seeking Activities', *Journal of Political Economy* 90: 988–1,002.

Bhagwati, J. (1993) 'Regionalism and Multilateralism, An Overview', in J. de Melo and A. Panagariya (eds) *New Dimensions in Regional Integration*, Cambridge: Cambridge University Press.

Birch, A. (1993) *The Concepts and Theories of Modern Democracy*, London: Routledge.

Black, D. (1948) 'On the Rationale of Group Decision Making', *Journal of Political Economy* 56: 23–34.

Block, F. (1977) 'The Ruling Class Does Not Rule', *Socialist Revolution* 3: 6–28.

Block, F. (1980) 'Beyond Relative Autonomy: State Managers as Historical Subjects', in R. Miliband and J. Saville (eds) *Socialist Register*, London: Merlin Press.

Block, F. (1987) *Revising State Theory: Essays in Politics and Post Industrialism*, Philadelphia: Temple University Press.

Bomberg, E. (1994) 'Policy Networks on the Periphery: EU Environmental Policy and Scotland', *Regional Politics and Policy* 4: 45–61.

Börzel, T.A. (2001) *The Domestic Impact of Europe: Institutional Adaptation to Germany and Spain*, Cambridge: Cambridge University Press.

Bowler, S. and Farrell, D. (1993) 'Legislator Shirking and Voter Monitoring: Impacts of European Parliament Electoral Systems upon Legislator–Voter Relationships', *Journal of Common Market Studies* 31: 45–69.

Brachet-Marquez, V. (1992) 'Explaining Socio-political Change in Latin America', *Latin American Research Review* 3: 91–122.

Bradley, J. (2000) 'The Irish economy in comparative perspective', in B. Nolan, P.J. O'Connell and C.T. Whelan (eds) *Bust to Boom? The Irish Experience of Growth and Inequality*, Dublin: Institute of Public Administration.

Bradley, J., Fitzgerald, J. and Kearney, I. (1992) *The Role of the Structural Funds: Analysis of the Consequences for Ireland in the Context of 1992*, Dublin: Economic and Social Research Institute.

Brittan, Samuel (2000) *The Euro and the Future of the Irish Boom*, 1 December; available at http://www.samuelbrittan.co.uk (accessed 30 November 2002).

Brooke, S. (2001) *Social Housing for the Future: Can Housing Associations Meet the Challenge?*, Blue Paper No. 8. Dublin: Policy Institute.

Browne, N. (1986) *Against the Tide*, Dublin: Gill and Macmillan.

Brusco, V., Nazareno, M. and Stokes, S. (2001) 'Clientelism and Democracy: An Analysis of Ecological Data from Argentina', paper presented at Annual Meeting of the American Political Science Association, San Francisco, August–September.

Buchanan, J.M. (1980) 'Rent Seeking and Profit Seeking', in J.M. Buchanan, R.D. Tollison and G. Tullock (eds) *Towards a Theory of the Rent Seeking Society*, College Station, Texas: A&M Press.

Buchanan, J.M. (1984) 'Politics Without Romance', in J.M. Buchanan and R.D. Tollison (eds) *The Theory of Public Choice II*, Ann Arbor, MI: University of Michigan Press.

Budge, I. and Newton, K. (1997) *The Politics of the New Europe: Atlantic to Urals*, London: Longman.

Bulmer, S. (1994) 'The Governance of the European Union: A New Institutionalist Approach', *Journal of Public Policy* 13: 351–80.

Bulmer, S. and Burch, M. (2000) 'The Europeanisation of Central Government: The UK and Germany in Historical Institutionalist Perspective', in M. Aspinwall and G. Schneider (eds) *The Rules of Integration*, Manchester: Manchester University Press.

Burnham, J. (1972) *The Managerial Revolution*, Westport, CO: Greenwood Press.

Calmfors, L. and Driffill, J. (1988) 'Bargaining Structure, Corporatism and Macroeconomic Performance', *Economic Policy: A European Forum* 6: 13–61.

Calvert, P. and Calvert, S. (2001) *Politics and Society in the Third World*, 2nd edn, Harlow: Longman.

Cammack, P. (1989) 'Bringing the State Back In: A Polemic', *British Journal of Political Science* 19: 261–90.

Canadian Government (1990) *Beneath the Veneer*, Ottawa: Government Publications.

Carty, R.K. (1981) *Party and Parish Pump*, Ontario: Wilfrid Laurier University Press.

Cawson, A. (ed.) (1985) *Organised Interests and the State: Studies in Meso-Corporatism*, London: Sage.

CEC (1993) *Agreement on the Implementation of the Global Grant under Decision C (92) 2145 of September 1992*, Luxembourg: Office for Official Publications of the European Communities.

CEC (1998) *European Cooperation in Quality Assurance in Higher Education*, EC 561/98, Brussels: European Commission.

CEC (1999) *White Paper on Food Safety*, COM 1999/719, Brussels: European Commission.

Central Statistics Office (2002) *Quarterly National Household Survey: First Quarter 2002*, Dublin: Central Statistics Office.

Chambliss, W.J. (1964) 'A Sociological Analysis of the Law of Vagrancy', *Social Problems* 12: 67–77.

Cheng, C. (ed.) (1996) *Masculinities in Organisations*, London: Sage.

CHIU (Conference of Heads of Irish Universities) (1995) 'Proposals for Quality Improvement and Quality Assurance', unpublished report, Dublin: CHIU.

Chodorow, N. (1978) *The Reproduction of Mothering*, Berkeley, CA: University of California Press.

Chong, D. (1995) 'Rational Choice Theory's Mysterious Rivals', *Critical Review* 9: 37–57.

Chubb, B. (1963) 'Going about Persecuting Civil Servants: The Role of the Irish Parliamentary Representative', *Political Studies* 10: 272–86.

Chubb, B. (1982) *The Government and Politics of Ireland*, 2nd edn, London: Longman.

Chubb, B. (1992) *The Government and Politics of Ireland*, 3rd edn, London: Longman.

Cini, M. (ed.) (2003) *European Union Politics*, Oxford: Oxford University Press.

Clapham, C. (1982) 'Clientelism and the State', in C. Clapham (ed.) *Private Patronage and Public Power*, London: Frances Pinter.

Clare, A. (2000) *On Men: Masculinity in Crisis*, London: Chatto and Windus.

Coakley, J. (1999) 'The Foundations of Statehood', in J. Coakley and M. Gallagher (eds) *Politics in the Republic of Ireland*, 3rd edn, London: Routledge.

Cockburn, C. (1991) *In the Way of Women*, London: Macmillan.

Collins, N. (1987) *Local Government Managers at Work: The City and County Manager System of Local Government in the Republic of Ireland*, Dublin: Institute of Public Administration.

Collins, N. (1993) 'Still Recognisably Pluralist? State–Farmer Relations in Ireland', in R.J. Hill and M. Marsh (eds) *Modern Irish Democracy: Essays in Honour of Basil Chubb*, Dublin: Irish Academic Press.

Collins, N. and Cradden, T. (2001) *Irish Politics Today*, 4th edn, Manchester: Manchester University Press.

Collins, S. (2000) *The Power Game: Fianna Fail since Lemass*, Dublin: O'Brien Press.

Committee on the Price of Building Land (1973) *Report to the Minister for Local Government*, Dublin: Stationery Office.

Connell, R.W. (1994) 'The State, Gender and Sexual Politics, Theory and Appraisal', in H.L. Radtke and H.J. Stam (eds) *Power/Gender: Social Relations in Theory and Practice*, London: Sage.

Connell, R.W. ([1995a] 1987) *Gender and Power*, Oxford: Blackwell.

Connell, R.W. (1995b) *Masculinities*, Cambridge: Polity Press.

Connolly, E. and O'Halpin, E. (1999) 'The Government and the Governmental System', in J. Coakley and M. Gallagher (eds) *Politics in the Republic of Ireland*, 3rd edn, London: Routledge.

Connolly, L. (1996) 'The Women's Movement in Ireland 1970–1995: A Social Movement Analysis', *Irish Journal of Feminist Studies* 1: 43–77.

Connolly, L. (2001) *The Irish Women's Movement: From Revolution to Devolution*, London: Palgrave.

Conroy-Jackson, P. (1987) 'Women's Movement and Abortion: The Criminalization of Irish Women', in D. Dahlerup (ed.) *The New Women's Movement: Feminism and Political Power in Europe and the USA*, London: Sage.

Cowles, M., Green, J., Caporaso, A. and Risse T. (eds) (2001) *Transforming Europe: Europeanisation and Domestic Change*, Ithaca, NY: Cornell University Press.

Cox, P. (2001) 'Reflections on the No to Nice', address to the Institute of European Affairs, Dublin, November.

Cradden, T. (1993) *Trade Unionism, Socialism and Partition*, Belfast: December Publications.

Cradden, T. (1999) 'Social Partnership in Ireland: Against the Trend', in N. Collins (ed.) *Political Issues in Ireland Today*, Manchester: Manchester University Press.

CRE (Conference of Rectors in Europe) (2001) *Towards Accreditation Schemes for Higher Education in Europe: Final Project Report*, Geneva: CRE.

Crehan, J., Lyons, N. and Laver, M. (1987) 'The Effects of Self-Care Skills and Homelessness on the Independent Living Potential of Long-Stay Psychiatric Patients', Galway: University College Galway, Social Sciences Research Centre.

Cross, J.C. (1997) 'Breaking down Clientelism: The Formalization of Street Vending in Mexico City', English translation of 'Debilitando al clientelismo: la formalisación del ambulantaje en la Ciudad de Mexico', *Revista Mexicana de Sociologia* 59(4), 1997; available at http: //www.ss.net/archive/papers/1(1)cross.htm) (accessed 10 August 2002).

Crouch, C. and Dore, R. (eds) (1990) *Corporatism and Accountability: Organised Interests in British Public Life*, Oxford: Oxford University Press.

Crouch, C. and Pizzorno, A. (eds) (1978) *The Resurgence of Class Conflict in Western Europe Since 1968*, 2nd edn, London: Macmillan.

Cullen, P. (2002) *With a Little Help from my Friends: Planning Corruption in Ireland*, Dublin: Gill and Macmillan.

Dahl, R. (1956) *A Preface to Democratic Theory*, Chicago: Chicago University Press.

Dahl, R. (1958) 'A Critique of the Ruling Elite Model', *American Political Science Review* 52: 463–9.

Dahl, R. (1961) *Who Governs? Democracy and Power in an American City*, New Haven: Yale University Press.

Dahl, R. (1970) *After the Revolution? Authority in a Good Society*, New Haven: Yale University Press.

Dahl, R. (1971) *Polyarchy*, New Haven: Yale University Press.

Dahl, R. (1977) 'Governing the Giant Corporation', *Political Science Quarterly* 92: 1–19.

Dahl, R. (1982) *Dilemmas of Pluralist Democracy*, New Haven: Yale University Press.

Dahl, R. (1985) *A Preface to Economic Democracy*, Cambridge: Polity Press.

Daly, M. (1999) 'The State in Independent Ireland', in R. English and C. Townsend (eds) *The State: Historical and Political Dimensions*, London: Routledge.

De Blacam, M. (1992) *The Control of Private Rented Dwellings*, Dublin: Round Hall Press.

Department of Education (1992) *Education for a Changing World*, Green Paper on Education, Dublin: Stationery Office.

Department of Education (1995) *Charting our Education Future*, White Paper on Education, Dublin: Stationery Office.

Department of Finance (2001a) *Gender Equality for the Civil Service*, Dublin: Stationery Office.

Department of Finance (2001b) *Making Gender Equality Happen: Guidance on Affirmative Action in Gender Equality*, Dublin: Stationery Office.

Department of Justice, Equality and Law Reform (1999) *Equal Opportunities in the State Sponsored Sector*, Dublin: Stationery Office.

Department of Justice, Equality and Law Reform (2001) *National Plan for Women (2001–2005) Draft*, Dublin: Stationery Office.

Department of the Environment (1995) *Social Housing – The Way Ahead*, Dublin: Stationery Office.

Department of the Environment (1998) *Housing Statistics Bulletin, Quarterly and Annual Report*, Dublin: Department of the Environment.

Department of the Environment (1999) *Housing Statistics Bulletin, Quarterly and Annual Report*, Dublin: Department of the Environment.

Department of the Environment (2000) *Housing Statistics Bulletin, Quarterly and Annual Report*, Dublin: Department of the Environment.

Department of the Environment (2001) *Housing Statistics Bulletin, Quarterly and Annual Report*, Dublin: Department of the Environment.

Department of the Environment and Local Government (1991) *A Plan for Social Housing*, Dublin: Stationery Office.

Department of the Environment and Local Government (1998a) *Action on House Prices*, Dublin: Stationery Office.

Department of the Environment and Local Government (1998b) *Annual Housing Statistics Bulletin*, Dublin: Department of the Environment and Local Government.

Department of the Environment and Local Government (1999a) *Action on the Housing Market*, Dublin: Stationery Office.

Department of the Environment and Local Government (1999b) *Administration of Rent and Mortgage Interest Assistance: A Report of the Inter-Departmental Committee on Issues Relating to Possible Transfer Administration of Rent and Mortgage Interest Supplementation from Health Boards to Local Authorities*, Dublin: Stationery Office.

Department of the Environment and Local Government (1999c) *Annual Housing Statistics Bulletin*, Dublin: Department of the Environment and Local Government.

Department of the Environment and Local Government (2000a) *Annual Housing Statistics Bulletin*, Dublin: Department of the Environment and Local Government.

Department of the Environment and Local Government (2000b) *Homelessness – An Integrated Strategy*, Dublin: Stationery Office.

Department of the Environment and Local Government (2000c) *Report of the Commission on the Private Rented Sector*, Dublin: Stationery Office.

Department of the Environment and Local Government (2001) *Annual Housing Statistics Bulletin*, Dublin: Department of the Environment and Local Government.

Department of the Environment and Local Government, Department of Health and Children, Department of Education and Science (2002) *Homeless Preventative Strategy: A Strategy to Prevent Homelessness: Patients Leaving Hospital and Mental Health Care, Adult Prisoners and Young Offenders Leaving Custody and Young People Leaving Care*, Dublin: Stationery Office.

Department of the Taoiseach (2001) *Gender Equality Policy*, Dublin: Stationery Office.

DiMaggio, P.J. and Powell, W.W. (1991) 'Introduction', in W.W. Powell and P.J. DiMaggio (eds) *The New Institutionalism in Organisational Analysis*, Chicago: Chicago University Press.

Dinnerstein, D. (1977) *The Mermaid and the Minotaur: Sexual Arrangements and Human Malaise*, New York: Harper Colophon Books.

Doherty, R. (2000) 'Passivity versus Engagement? The Impact of an Emerging European Security Architecture on Irish Neutrality', unpublished thesis, University of Ulster.

Doling, J. (1997) *Comparative Housing Policy: Government and Housing in Advanced Industrialised Countries*, Basingstoke: Macmillan.

Dolowitz, D.P. (1996) 'The Origins of the Child Support Agency: Learning from the American Experience?', No. 17, Muirhead Paper series, University of Birmingham.

Dolowitz, D.P. and Marsh, D. (1996) 'Who Learns What from Whom? A Review of the Policy Transfer Literature', *Political Studies* 44: 343–57.

Domhoff, G.W. (1967) *Who Rules America?*, New York: Prentice-Hall.

Domhoff, G.W. (1970) *The Higher Circles: The Governing Class in America*, New York: Random House.

Dooge, J. and Keatinge, P. (eds) (2001) *What the Treaty of Nice Means*, Dublin: Institute of European Affairs.

Dooney, S. and O'Toole, J. (1998) *Irish Government Today*, 2nd edn, Dublin: Gill and Macmillan.

Dorr, D. (1992) *Option for the Poor: A Hundred Years of Vatican Social Teaching*, Dublin: Gill and Macmillan.

Dowding, K. (1994) 'Policy Networks: Don't Stretch a Good Idea Too Far', in P. Dunleavy and J. Stanyer (eds) *Contemporary Political Studies, 1994*, Belfast: Political Studies Association.

Dowding, K. (1995) 'Model or Metaphor: A Critical Review of the Policy Network Approach', *Political Studies* 43: 265–77.

Dowding, K. (2001) 'There Must Be an End to Confusion: Policy Networks, Intellectual Fatigue, and the Need for Political Science Methods Courses in British Universities', *Political Studies* 49: 89–105.

Downey, D. (1998) *New Realities in Irish Housing: A Study on Housing Affordability and the Economy*, Dublin: Threshold and the Consultancy and Research Unit for the Built Environment, Dublin Institute of Technology.

Downs, A. (1957) *An Economic Theory of Democracy*, Boston, MA: Harper and Row.

Doyle, A. (1999) 'Employment Equality since Accession to the European Union', in G. Kiely, A. O'Donnell, P. Kennedy and S. Quin (eds) *Irish Social Policy in Context*, Dublin: UCD Press.

Drudy, P.J. (2001) 'Towards Affordable Housing: The Case for a New Approach', in P.J. Drudy and A. MacLaran (eds) *Dublin: Economic and Social Trends*, Dublin: Centre for Urban and Regional Studies, Trinity College Dublin.

Drudy, P.J. and Punch, M. (2001) 'Housing and Inequality in Ireland', in S. Cantillon, C. Corrigan, P. Kirby and J. O'Flynn (eds) *Rich and Poor: Perspectives on Tackling Inequality in Ireland*, Dublin: Oaktree Press.

Drudy, P.J. and Punch, M. (2002) 'Housing Models and Inequality: Perspectives on Recent Irish Experience', *Housing Studies* 17: 657–72.

Dublin Simon Community with Focus Ireland and Dublin Corporation (2000) *Report on Street Count*, Dublin: Simon Community.

Duffy, D. (2002) 'A Descriptive Analysis of the Irish Housing Market', *Quarterly Economic Commentary*, summer: 40–55.

Dunleavy, P. and O'Leary, B. (1987) *Theories of the State*, London: Macmillan.

Dunlop, C. (2000) 'Epistemic Communities: A Reply to Toke', *Politics* 20: 137–44.

Dyson, K. (2002) *European States and the Euro*, Oxford: Oxford University Press.

Dyson, K. and Featherstone, K. (1999) *The Road to Maastricht: Negotiating Economic and Monetary Union*, Oxford: Open University Press.

EC (1994) *Bulletin on Women in Employment 1994*, Brussels: European Commission.

Economist (2001) *Globalisation: Making Sense of an Integrating World*, London: Profile Books.

Eising, R. and Kohler-Koch, B. (eds) (1999) *Transformation of Governance in the European Union*, London: Routledge.

Elliot, M. and Krivo, L.J. (1991) 'Structural Determinants of Homelessness in the United States', *Social Problems* 38: 113–31.

Engels, F. ([1887] 1942) *The Housing Question*, London: Lawrence and Wishart.

Erridge, A. and Connolly, M. (1990) 'Tripartite Industrial Training Systems: A Comparative Study', in C. Crouch and R. Dore (eds) *Corporatism and Accountability: Organised Interests in British Public Life*, Oxford: Oxford University Press.

European Commission (1995) 'The European Report on the European Pilot Project for the Evaluation of Quality in Higher Education', unpublished report, Brussels: European Commission.

European Commission (2001) *Eurobarometer Report 56*, Brussels: European Commission; available at http://www.europa.eu.int/comm/dg10/epo (accessed. 25 March 2002).

European Commission (2002) *Eurobarometer Report 57*, Brussels: European Commission.

European Commission DG X (1992) *Voters and Interest Groups: Representation at the European Level*, Brussels: Final Report to European Commission DG X.

European Economy (1997) 45, European Commission: Brussels.

European Ministers of Education (1998) *Joint Declaration on Harmonization of the Architecture of the European Higher Education System*, Sorbonne, 25 May.

European Ministers of Education (1999) *Joint Declaration: The European Higher Education Area*, Bologna, 19 June.

European Ministers of Education (2001) *Communique: Towards The European Higher Education Area*, Prague, 19 May.

Evans, P.B., Rieschemeyer, D. and Skocpol, T. (eds) (1985) *Bringing the State Back In*, Cambridge: Cambridge University Press.

Fahey, T. (ed.) (1999a) *Social Housing in Ireland: A Study of Success, Failure and Lessons Learned*, Dublin: Oak Tress Press in association with the Katharine Howard Foundation and the Combat Poverty Agency.

Fahey, T. (1999b) 'Social Housing in Ireland: The Need for an Expanded Role?', *Irish Banking Review*, autumn: 25–38.

Fahey, T. (2002) 'The Family Economy in the Development of Welfare Regimes: A Case Study', *European Sociological Review* 18: 51–64.

Fahey, T. and Watson, D. (1995) *An Analysis of Social Housing Need*, General Research Series, Paper No. 168, Dublin: Economic and Social Research Institute.

Fajertag J. and Pochet P. (eds) (2000) *Social Pacts in Europe – New Dynamics*, Brussels: European Trade Union Institute.

Farnham, D. and Horton, S. (1993) *Managing the New Public Services*, London: Macmillan.

Farrell, B. (1983) 'Ireland: from Friends and Neighbours to Clients and Partisans: Some Dimensions of Parliamentary Representation under PR STV', in V. Bogdanor (ed.) *Coalition Government in Western Europe*, London: Heinemann.

Featherstone, K. and Kazamias, G. (2001) *Europeanisation and the Southern Periphery*, London: Frank Cass.

Ferejohn, J. (1991) 'Rationality and Interpretation: Parliamentary Elections in Early Stuart England', in K. Monroe (ed.) *The Economic Approach to Politics*, New York: HarperCollins.

Finer, H. (1932) *The Theory and Practice of Modern Government*, London: Macmillan.

Finer, H. (1954) *The Theory and Practice of Modern Government* (abridged) London: Methuen.

Finlay, F. (1998) *Snakes and Ladders*, Dublin: New Island Books.

Fiorina, M.P. (1981) *Retrospective Voting in American National Elections*, New Haven: Yale University Press.

Fitzgerald, E. (1990) 'Housing at a Turning Point', in J. Blackwell, B. Harvey, M. Higgins and J. Walsh (eds) *Housing: Moving into Crisis?*, Dublin: National Campaign for the Homeless/Combat Poverty Agency.

Fitzgerald, Garret (1991) *All in a Life*, Dublin: Gill and Macmillan.

Fitzgerald, J. (2001) 'Managing an Economy under EMU: The Case of Ireland', *World Economy* 24: 1,353–71.

Fitzgerald, R. and Girvin, B. (2000) 'Political Culture, Growth and the Conditions for Success in the Irish Economy', in B. Nolan, P.J. O'Connell and C.T. Whelan (eds) *Bust to Boom? The Irish Experience of Growth and Inequality*, Dublin: Institute of Public Administration.

Fitzmaurice, J. (1988) 'An Analysis of the EC's Cooperation Procedure', *Journal of Common Market Studies* 16: 389–400.

Fitzpatrick, S. (1998) 'Homelessness in the European Union', in M. Kleinman, W. Matznetter and M. Stephens (eds) *European Integration and Housing Policy*, London: Routledge.

Flood, F. (2002) *The Second Interim Report of the Tribunal of Inquiry into Certain Planning Matters and Payments*, Dublin: Stationery Office.

Ford, G. and Lake, G. (1991) 'Evolution of European Science and Technology Policy', *Science and Public Policy* 18: 38–50.

Forfas (2001) *Statement on Outward Direct Investment*, Dublin: Forfas (October).

Forfas (2002) *International Trade and Investment Report 2001*, Dublin: Forfas (January).

Foster-Carter, A. (1985) *The Sociology of Development*, Ormskirk: Causeway Press.

Fourth Report of the Fourth Joint Oireachtas Committee on Women's Rights (1996) *The Impact of European Equality Legislation on Women's Affairs in Dublin*, Dublin: Stationery Office.

Franzway, S., Court, D. and Connell, R.W. (1989) *Staking a Claim: Feminism, Bureaucracy and the State*, London: Allen and Unwin.

Fraser, M. (1996) *John Bull's Other Homes: State Housing and British Policy in Ireland, 1883–1922*, Liverpool: Liverpool University Press.

Frey, B.S. and Schneider, F. (1978) 'A Politico-Economic Model of the United Kingdom', *Economic Journal* 88: 243–53. Friedan, B. (1963) *The Feminine Mystique*, London: Gollantz.

Friedan, B. (1981) *The Second Stage*, New York: Summit Books.

Friedman, J. (1995) 'Economic Approaches to Politics', *Critical Review* 9: 1–24.

Gallagher, M. and Komito, L. (1992) 'Dáil Deputies and Their Constituency Work', in J. Coakley, and M. Gallagher (eds) *Politics in the Republic of Ireland*, Galway: PSAI Press.

Gallagher, M. and Komito, L. (1999) 'The Constituency Role of TDs', in J. Coakley and M. Gallagher (eds) *Politics in the Republic of Ireland*, London: Routledge.

Gallagher, M. and Marsh, M. (2002) *Days of Blue Loyalty: The Politics and Membership of the Fine Gael Party*, Dublin, PSAI Press.

Gallagher, M., Laver, M. and Mair, P. (2001) *Representative Government in Modern Europe: Institutions, Parties, and Governments*, 3rd edn, New York: McGraw-Hill.

Galligan, Y. (1998) *Women and Politics in Contemporary Ireland: From the Margins to the Mainstream*, London: Pinter.

Galligan, Y. (1999) 'Candidate Selection', in J. Coakley and M. Gallagher (eds) *Politics in the Republic of Ireland*, 3rd edn, London: Routledge.

Gamble, A., Marsh, D. and T. Tant (eds) (1999) *Marxism and Social Science*, Basingstoke: Macmillan.

Gardiner, F. (ed.) (1997) *Sex Equality Policy in Western Europe*, London: Routledge.

Garvie, S. (2001) 'Lessons to be Learned? – An Irish Perspective', paper presented at the Sixth Quality in Higher Education Seminar on 'The End of Quality?', Birmingham 25–26 May.

Garvin, T. (1981) *The Evolution of Irish Nationalist Politics*, Dublin: Gill and Macmillan.

George, S. (2001) 'The Europeanisation of UK Politics and Policy-Making: The Effect of European Integration on the UK', Queen's Papers on Europeanisation, No.8, Institute of European Studies, Queen's University Belfast.

George, S. and Bache, I. (2001) *Politics in the European Union*, Oxford: Oxford University Press.

Geyer, R. (1996) 'EU Social Policy in the 1990s: Does Maastricht Matter?', *Journal of European Integration* 20: 5–33.

Gill, S. (1997) *Globalisation, Democratisation and Multilateralism*, London: Macmillan.

Girvin, B. (1986) 'Social Change and Moral Politics: The Irish Constitutional Referendum 1983', *Political Studies* 34: 61–81.

Girvin, B. (1987) 'The Divorce Referendum in the Republic, June 1986', *Irish Political Studies* 2: 93–9.

Girvin, B. (1993) 'The Referendums on Abortion 1992', *Irish Political Studies* 8: 118–24.

Girvin, B. (1996) 'The Irish Divorce Referendum, November 1995', *Irish Political Studies* 11: 74–81.

Goetschy, J. (2000) 'The European Union and National Social Pacts: Employment and Social Protection Put to the Test', in J. Fajertag and P. Pochet (eds) *Social Pacts in Europe – New Dynamics*, Brussels: European Trade Union Institute.

Goetx, K.H. and Hix, S. (eds) (2001) *Europeanised Politics: European Integration and National Political Systems*, London: Frank Cass.

Goldthorpe, J.H. (ed.) (1984) *Order and Conflict in Contemporary Capitalism: Studies in the Political Economy of West European Nations*, Oxford: Clarendon Press.

Good, A. (2001) 'Femocrats Work with Feminists and the EU against Gender Bias in Ireland', in A. Mazur (ed.) *State Feminism, Women's Movements, and Job Training: Making Democracies Work in the Global Economy*, London: Routledge.

Gorges, M.J. (2001) 'New Institutionalists' Explanations for Institutional Change: A Note of Caution', *Politics* 21: 137–45.

Government of Ireland (1971) *White Paper: Local Government Reorganisation*, Dublin: Stationery Office.

Government of Ireland (1973) *Local Government Discussion Document*, Dublin: Stationery Office.

Government of Ireland (1985) *Local Government Reform*, Dublin: Stationery Office.

Government of Ireland (1991) *Local Government Reorganisation and Reform*, Dublin: Stationery Office.

Government of Ireland (1993) *National Development Plan 1994–1999*, Dublin: Stationery Office.

Government of Ireland (1994) *Government of Renewal – 1994 Programme for Government*, Dublin: Stationery Office.

Government of Ireland (1996) *Better Local Government: A Programme for Change*, Dublin: Stationery Office.

Government of Ireland (1997) *An Action Programme for the New Millennium*, Dublin: Stationery Office.

Government of Ireland (1998) *Belfast Agreement*, Dublin: Stationery Office.

Government of Ireland (2002) *Homelessness Prevention Strategy of Ireland*, Dublin: Stationery Office.

Gramsci, A. (1971) *Selections from Prison Notebooks*, London: Lawrence and Wishart.

Gramsci, A. (1977) *Selections from Political Writings (1910–1920)*, London: Lawrence and Wishart.

Grant, W.P., Paterson, W. and Whitson, C. (1988) *Government and the Chemical Industry*, Oxford: Clarendon.

Gray, J. (1998) *False Dawn*, London: Granta Books.

Green, D.P. and Shapiro, I. (1994) *Pathologies of Rational Choice Theory: A Critique of Applications in Political Science*, New Haven: Yale University Press.

Greenwood, J. and Aspinwall, M. (eds) (1998) *Collective Action in the European Union: Interests and the New Politics of Associability*, London: Routledge.

Guerin, D. (1999) *Housing Income Support in the Private Rented Sector: A Survey of Recipients of SWA Rent Supplement*, Dublin: Combat Poverty Agency.

Guttsman, W. (1963) *The British Political Elite*, London: MacGibbon and Kee.

Haas, E. (1989) 'Do Regimes Matter? Epistemic Communities and Mediterranean Pollution Control', *International Organisation* 143: 233–43.

Haas, E. (1990) *When Knowledge is Power: Three Models of Change in International Organizations*, Berkeley, CA: University of California Press.

Haas, P.M. (1992) 'Epistemic Communities and International Policy Co-ordination: Introduction', *International Organisations* 46: 1–35.

Hakim, C. (1995) 'Five Feminist Myths about Women's Employment', *British Journal of Sociology* 46: 429–57.

Halford, S. (1992) 'Feminist Change in a Patriarchal Organisation', in M. Savage and A. Witz (eds) *Gender and Bureaucracy*, Oxford: Blackwell.

Hall, P.A and Taylor, C.R. (1996) 'Political Science and the Three New Institutionalisms', *Political Studies* 44: 936–57.

Halpenny, A.M., Keogh, A.F. and Gilligan, R. (2002) *A Place for the Children? Children in Families Living in Emergency Accommodation: The Perspectives of Children, Parents and Professionals*, Dublin: Children's Research Centre/Homeless Agency.

Halpenny, A.M., Greene, S., Hogan, D., Smith, M. and McGee, H. (2001) *Children of Homeless Mothers: The Daily Life Experience and Well-being of Children in Homeless Families*, Dublin: Children's Research Centre/Royal College of Surgeons in Ireland.

Hamilton, C.V. (1979) 'The Patron–Recipient Relationship and Minority Politics in New York City', *Political Science Quarterly* 94: 211–27.

Hanf, K. and Scharpf, F.W. (eds) (1978) *Inter-organisational Policy-making*, London: Sage.

Hansard Society (1990) *Report of the Commission on Women at the Top*, London: HMSO.

Hardiman, N. (1988) *Pay, Politics and Economic Performance in Ireland 1970–1987*, Oxford: Clarendon Press.

Hardiman, N. (2000) 'Social Partnership, Wage Bargaining and Growth', in B. Nolan, P.J. O'Connell and C.T. Whelan (eds) *Bust to Boom? The Irish Experience of Growth and Inequality*, Dublin: Institute of Public Administration.

Harmsen, R. (1999) 'The Europeanisation of National Administrations: A Comparative Study of France and the Netherlands', *Governance* 12: 81–113.

Harmsen, R. and Wilson M. (2000) 'Introduction: Approaches to Europeanisation', in R. Harmsen and M. Wilson (eds) *Europeanisation: Institutions, Identities and Citizenship*, Amsterdam: Rodopi.

Harrison, D. (1988) *The Sociology of Modernization and Development*, London: Routledge.

Hartmann, H. ([1981] 1994) 'The Unhappy Marriage of Marxism and Feminism', in J. Kourany, J.P Sterba and R. Tong (eds) *Feminist Philosophies: Problems, Theories and Applications*, London: Harvester Wheatsheaf.

Harvey, B. (1995) 'The Use of Legislation to Address a Social Problem: The Example of the Housing Act 1988', *Administration* 43: 76–85.

Haug, G. and Tauch, C. (2001) 'Towards a Coherent European Higher Education Space: From Bologna to Prague', paper presented at the Convention of European Higher Education Institutions, Salamanca 29–30 March.

Hay, C. (1995) 'Structure and Agency', in G. Stoker and D. Marsh (eds) *Theory and Methods in Political Science*, London: Macmillan.

Hay, C. (1999) 'Marxism and the State', in A. Gamble, D. Marsh and T. Tant (eds) *Marxism and Social Science*, Basingstoke: Macmillan.

Hay, C. (2000) 'Globalisation, European Integration and the Contingent Convergence of European Social Models', *Review of International Studies* 26: 509–31.

Hazelkorn, E. (1986) 'Class, Clientelism and the Political Process in the Republic of Ireland', in P. Clancy, S. Drudy, K. Lynch and L. Dowd (eds) *Ireland: A Sociological Profile*, Dublin: Institute of Public Administration.

HEA (1994) 'Quality and Equity and their Correlation in Higher Education', unpublished report, Dublin.

Healy, S. and Reynolds, B. (1999) *Social Partnership in a New Century*, Dublin: CORI Justice Commission.

Heclo, H. (1978) 'Issue Networks and the Executive Establishment', in A. King (ed.) *The New American Political System*, Washington, DC: American Enterprise Inc.

Heclo, H. and Wildavsky, A. (1974) *The Private Government of Public Money*, London: Macmillan.

Held, D., McGrew, A., Goldblatt, D. and Perraton, J. (1999) *Global Transformations: Politics, Economics and Culture*, Cambridge: Polity Press.

Hemingway, J. (1978) *Conflict and Democracy: Studies in Union Government*, Oxford: Clarendon Press.

Heritier, A. (1993) 'Policy Netzwerkanalyse als Untersuchunginstrument im Europaischen Kontext: Folgerungen aus einer empirischen Studie regulativer Politik', in A. Heritier (ed.) *Policy-Analyse, Kritik und Neuorientierung*, Opladen: Westdeutscher Verlag.

Hesketh, T. (1990) *The Second Partitioning of Ireland: The Abortion Referendum of 1983*, Dublin: Bandsman Books.

Heywood, A. (1997) *Politics*, London: Macmillan.

Higgins, M. (2001) *Shaping the Future: An Action Plan on Homelessness in Dublin, 2001–2003*, Dublin: Homeless Agency.

Higgins, M.D. (1982) 'The Limits of Clientelism: Towards an Assessment of Irish Politics', in C. Clapham (ed.) *Private Patronage and Public Power: Political Clientelism in the Modern State*, London: Frances Pinter.

Hill, M. (1997) *The Policy Process in the Modern State*, 3rd edn, London: Prentice-Hall.

Hirdman, Y. (1998) 'State Policy and Gender Contracts: The Swedish Experience', in E. Drew, R. Emerek and E. Mahon (eds) *Women, Work and Family in Europe*, London: Routledge.

Hirst, P. (1993) 'Associational Democracy', in D. Held (ed.) *Prospects for Democracy*, Cambridge: Polity Press.

Hirst, P. and Thompson, G. (1996) *Globalisation in Question: The International Economy and the Possibilities of Governance*, 1st edn, Cambridge: Polity.

Hirst, P. and Thompson, G. (1999) *Globalisation in Question: The International Economy and the Possibilities of Governance*, 2nd edn, Cambridge: Polity Press.

Hix, S. (1999) *The Political System of the European Union*, Basingstoke: Macmillan.

Hobbes, T. (1968) *The Leviathan*, London: Penguin Books.

Hodson, D. and Maher, I. (2001) 'The Open Method as a New Mode of Governance: The Case of Soft Economic Policy Co-ordination', *Journal of Common Market Studies* 39: 719–46.

Holger, G. (2000) 'Irish Direct Investment in the US: Evidence and Further Issues', *Journal of the Statistical and Social Inquiry Society of Ireland* 3: 33–64.

Holmes, M. (1999) 'Organisational Preparation and Political Marketing', in J. Coakley and M. Gallagher (eds) *Politics in the Republic of Ireland*, 3rd edn, London: Routledge.

Hoogvelt, A. and Margaretha, M. (1978) *The Sociology of Developing Societies*, 2nd edn, London: Macmillan.

Hooke and McDonald (2001) *The Apartment Market in Ireland*, Dublin: Hooke and McDonald.

Horgan, J. (2000) *Passionate Outsider*, Dublin: Gill and Macmillan.

Hotelling, H. (1929) 'Stability in Competition', *Economic Journal* 39: 41–57.

Houghton, F.T. and Hickey, C. (2000) *Focussing on B and Bs: The Unacceptable Growth of Emergency B and B Placement in Dublin*, Dublin: Focus Ireland.

Howlett, M. and Ramesh, M. (1995) *Studying Public Policy: Policy Cycles and Policy Subsystems*, Oxford: Oxford University Press.

Hug, C. (1999) *The Politics of Sexual Morality in Ireland*, London: Macmillan.

Humphreys, P.C., Drew, E. and Murphy, C. (1999) *Gender Equality in the Irish Civil Service*, Dublin: Institute of Public Administration.

Hussey, G. (1993) *Ireland Today: The Anatomy of a Changing State*, Dublin: Townhouse Viking.

ICTU (Irish Congress of Trade Unions) (1993) *New Forms of Work Organisation: Options for Unions*, Dublin: Irish Congress of Trade Unions.

ICTU (Irish Congress of Trade Unions) (1998) *What People Think of Trade Unions: Results of a National Survey Conducted by Research and Evaluation Services for the Irish Congress of Trade Unions*, Dublin: Irish Congress of Trade Unions.

ICTU (Irish Congress of Trade Unions) (2001) *Unions and Work: Highlights of a Survey of Attitudes Conducted by Research and Evaluation Services for the Irish Congress of Trade Unions*, Dublin: Irish Congress of Trade Unions.

Immergut, E.M. (1992) 'The Rules of the Game: The Logic of Health Policy-making in France, Switzerland and Sweden', in S. Steinmo, K. Thelen and F. Longstreth (eds) *Structuring Politics: Historical Institutionalism in Comparative Analysis*, Cambridge: Cambridge University Press.

Immergut, E.M. (1998) 'The Theoretical Core of the New Institutionalism', *Politics and Society* 26: 5–34.

IMS (Irish Marketing Surveys) (1997) *Irish Independent/IMS Poll: Election 1997 Poll No. 1*, Dublin: Irish Marketing Surveys.

IPA (Institute for Public Administration) (1997) *Annual Directory*, Dublin: IPA.

Irigaray, I. (1993) *Je, Tu, Nous, Towards a Culture of Difference*, trans. A. Martin, London: Routledge.

Jencks, C. (1994) *The Homeless*, Cambridge, MA: Harvard University Press.

Jepperson, R.L. (1991) 'Institutions, Institutional Effects and Institutionalism', in W.W. Powell and P.J. DiMaggio (eds) (1991) *The New Institutionalism in Organisational Analysis*, Chicago: Chicago University Press.

Jessop, B. (1977) 'Recent Theories of the Capitalist State', *Cambridge Journal of Economics* 1: 353–72.

Jessop, B. (1990a) *State Theory: Putting Capitalist States in their Place*, Cambridge: Polity Press.

Jessop, B. (1990b) 'Regulation Theories in Retrospect and Prospect', *Economy and Society* 19: 153–216.

Jessop, B. (1992) 'Towards the Schumpeterian Workfare State', Lancaster Regionalism Group Working Paper.

Jessop, B. (2001) 'Bringing the State Back In (Yet Again): Reviews, Revisions, Rejections, and Redirections', *International Review of Sociology* 11: 149–73.

Jessop, B. (2002) *The Future of the Capitalist State*, London: Blackwell.

Johansen, L. (1976) *The Theory of Public Goods: Misplaced Emphasis*, Oslo: Institute of Economics, University of Oslo.

Jones, J. (2001) *In Your Opinion: Political and Social Trends in Ireland through the Eyes of the Electorate*, Dublin: Town House.

Jordan, A.G. (1990a) 'The Pluralism of Pluralism: An Anti Theory', *Political Studies* 38: 286–301.

Jordan, A.G. (1990b) 'Sub-government, Policy Communities and Networks: Refilling the Old Bottles', *Journal of Theoretical Politics* 2: 319–18.

Jordan, A.G. and Richardson, J.J. (1987) *Government and Pressure Groups in Britain*, Oxford: Clarendon Press.

Jordan, A.G. and Schubert, K. (1992) 'A Preliminary Ordering of Policy Network Labels', *European Journal of Political Research* 21: 7–27.

Kadushin, C. (1974) *The American Intellectual Elite*, Boston, MA: Little Brown.

Kassim, H. (2000) 'Conclusion', in H. Kassim, B.G. Peters and V. Wright (eds) *The National Co-ordination of EU Policy*, Oxford: Oxford University Press.

Kato, J. (1996) 'Review Article: Institutions and Rationality in Politics – Three Varieties of Neo-Institutionalists', *British Journal of Political Science* 27: 553–82.

Katzenstein, P.J. (1985) *Small States in World Markets*, Ithaca, NY: Cornell University Press.

Kavanagh, D. (1991) 'Why Political Science Needs History', *Political Studies* 39: 479–95.

Keane, J.B. (1967) *Letters of a Successful T.D.*, Cork: Mercier Press.

Keane, J.B. (1978) *Letters of an Irish Minister of State*, Cork: Mercier Press.

Kearns, K.C. (1984) 'Homelessness in Dublin. An Irish Urban Disorder', *American Journal of Economics and Sociology* 43: 217–33.

Kelly, D. (1999) 'The Strategic-Relational View of the State', *Politics* 19: 109–15.

Kemeny, J. (1981) *The Myth of Home Ownership: Public Versus Private Choices in Housing Tenure*, London: Routledge.

Kemeny, J. (1992) *Housing and Social Theory*, London: Routledge.

Kemeny, J. (1995) *From Public Housing to the Social Market. Rental Policy Strategies in Comparative Perspective*, London: Routledge.

Kemp, P.A., Lynch, E., and McKay, D. (2001) *Structural Trends and Homelessness: A Quantitative Analysis*, Homelessness Task Force Research Series, Edinburgh: Scottish Executive Central Research Unit.

Kenis, P. and Schneider, V. (1991) 'Policy Networks and Policy Analysis: Scrutinizing a New Analytical Toolbox', in B. Martin and R. Mayntz (eds) *Policy Network: Empirical Evidence and Theoretical Considerations*, Frankfurt am Main: Campus Verlag.

Kenna, P. (2000) 'Assessing Policy Approaches to Homelessness', *Poverty Today* (48), Dublin: Combat Poverty.

Kennedy, P. (1999) 'Women and Social Policy', in G. Kiely, A. O'Donnell, P. Kennedy and S. Quin (eds) *Irish Social Policy in Context*, Dublin: UCD Press.

Kennelly, B. and Ward, E. (1993) 'The Abortion Referendums', in M. Gallagher and M. Laver (eds) *How Ireland Voted 1992*, Dublin: Folens and PSAI Press.

Kenny, Justice (1973) *Report of the Committee on the Price of Building Land*, Dublin: Stationery Office.

Kenny, M. (1999) 'Marxism and Regulation Theory', in A. Gamble, D. Marsh, and T. Tant (eds) *Marxism and Social Science*, Basingstoke: Macmillan.

Keohane, R.O. and Hoffman, S. (1990) 'Community Politics and Institutional Change', in W. Wallace (ed.) *The Dynamics of European Integration*, London: Pinter.

Keohane, R. and Nye, J. (1977) *Power and Interdependence*, Boston, MA: Little Brown.

Kickert, W.J., Klijn, E. and Koppenjan, J. (1997) *Managing Complex Networks*, London: Sage.

Kimber, R. and Richardson, J.J. (eds) (1974) *Pressure Groups in Britain*, London: Dent and Co.

Kirby, P. (2002) *The Celtic Tiger in Distress: Growth with Inequality in Ireland*, London: Palgrave.

Klein, N. (2001) *No Logo*, London: Flamingo.

Klijn, E. (1997) 'Policy Networks: An Overview', in W.J. Kickert, E. Klijn and J. Koppenjan (eds) *Managing Complex Networks*, London: Sage.

Knapp, A. and Wright, V. (2001) *The Government and Politics of France*, 4th edn, London: Routledge.

Koeble, T.A. (1995) 'The New Institutionalism in Political Science and Sociology', in *Comparative Politics* 27: 231–43.

Kohler-Koch, B. (1996) 'Catching Up with Change. The Transformation of Governance in the European Union', *Journal of European Public Policy* 3: 359–80.

Kohler-Koch, B. (1997) 'Organized Interests in European Integration. The Evolution of a New Type of Governance', in H. Wallace and A. Young (eds) *Participation and Policy Making in the European Union*, Oxford: Oxford University Press.

Kohler-Koch, B. (1999) 'The Evolution and Transformation of European Governance', in Eising, R. and Kohler-Koch, B. (eds) *Transformation of Governance in the European Union*, London: Routledge.

Komito, L. (1985) 'Politics and Clientelism in Urban Ireland: Information, Reputation, and Brokerage'; available at http: //www.ucd.ie/lis/staff/komito/ (accessed 10 August 2002).

Kourany, J., Sterba, J.P. and Tong, R. (eds) (1993) *Feminist Philosophies: Problems, Theories and Applications*, London: Harvester Wheatsheaf.

Krasner, S.D. (ed.) (1983) *International Regimes*, Ithaca, NY: Cornell University Press.

Ladrech, R. (1994) 'Europeanisation of Domestic Politics and Institutions: The Case of France', *Journal of Common Market Studies* 32: 69–88.

Laffan, B. (1989) 'While You're Over There in Brussels, Get Us a Grant: The Management of the Structural Funds in Ireland', *Irish Political Studies* 4: 43–57.

Laffan, B. (2001) 'Organising for a Changing Europe: Irish Central Government and the European Union', Blue Paper 7, Dublin: Policy Institute, Trinity College Dublin.

Lasswell, H.D. (1936) *Politics: Who Gets What, When and How?*, New York: McGraw-Hill.

Laumann, E. (1976) *Networks of Collective Action: A Perspective on Community Influence Systems*, New York: Academic.

Laumann, E. and Pappi, F. (1973) 'New Directions in the Study of Community Elites', *American Sociological Review* 38: 212–29.

Laumann, E., Marsden, P.V. and Galaskiewicz, J. (1977) 'Community–Elite Influence Structures: Extension of a Network Approach', *American Journal of Sociology* 83: 594–631.

Laver, M. and Schofield, N. (1990) *Multiparty Government*, Oxford: Oxford University Press.

Laver, M. and Shepsle, K. (1990) 'Coalitions and Cabinet Government', *American Political Science Review* 84: 843–90.

Laver, M. and Shepsle, K. (1996) *Making and Breaking Governments: Cabinets and Legislatures in Parliamentary Democracies*, Cambridge: Cambridge University Press.

Lee, J.J. (1989) *Ireland 1912–1985: Politics and Society*, Cambridge: Cambridge University Press.

Lenin, V.I. ([1918] 1943) *State and Revolution*, New York: International Publishers.

Lenschow, A. (1999) 'Transformation in European Environmental Governance', in R. Eising and B. Kohler-Koch (eds) *Transformation of Governance in the European Union*, London: Routledge.

Levine, A. (1987) *The End of the State*, London: Verso Books.

Levinson, D., Aamador, A.C. and Pari, J.L. (1992) *A Question of Equity: Women and the Glass Ceiling in the Federal Government*, Washington: US Merit Systems Board.

Lewis, S. and Lewis, J. (1996) *The Work–Family Challenge: Rethinking Employment*, London: Sage.

Lijphart, A. (1968) *The Politics of Accommodation, Pluralism and Democracy in the Netherlands*, Berkeley and Los Angeles: University of California Press.

Lindblom, C. (1977) *Politics and Markets*, New York: Basic Books.

Lindblom, C. (1980) *The Policymaking Process*, New Jersey: Prentice-Hall.

Lindblom, C. (1982) 'The Market as Prison', *The Journal of Politics* 44: 324–36.

Lohmann, S. (1995) 'The Poverty of Green and Shapiro', *Critical Review* 9: 127–54.

Lovenduski, J. (1997) 'Sex Equality and the Rules of the Game', in F. Gardiner (ed.) *Sex Equality Policy in Western Europe*, London: Routledge.

Lowi, T. (1969) *The End of Liberalism*, New York: Norton.

Lowi, T.A. (1972) 'Four Systems of Policy, Politics and Choice', *Public Administration Review* 32: 298–310.

Lowndes, V. (1996) 'Varieties of New Institutionalism: A Critical Appraisal', *Public Administration* 74: 181–97.

Lynch, K. (1989) 'Solidarity Labour: Its Nature and Marginalisation', *Sociological Review* 37: 1–14.

Lynch, K. and McLaughlin, E. (1995) 'Caring Labour and Love Labour', in P. Clancy, S. Drudy, K. Lynch and L. O'Dowd (eds) *Irish Society: Sociological Perspectives*, Dublin: Institute of Public Administration.

Lyons, F.S.L. (1973) *Ireland since the Famine*, London: Fontana Press.

McCann, D. (1993) 'Business Power and Collective Action: The State and the Confederation of Irish Industry 1970–1990', *Irish Political Studies* 8: 37–53.

McCarthy, C. (1977) *Trade Unions in Ireland 1894–1960*, Dublin: Institute of Public Administration.

McCarthy, W.E.J., O'Brien, J. and O'Dowd, V.G. (1975) *Wage Inflation and Wage Leadership*, Dublin: Economic and Social Research Institute.

McCashin, A. (2000) The Private Rented Sector in the 21st Century: Policy Choices, Dublin: Threshold and St Pancras Housing Association.

McConnell, G. (1996) *Private Power and American Democracy*, New York: Knopf.

McCormick, J. (2002) *Understanding the European Union*, 2nd edn, Basingstoke: Macmillan.

McFarland, A. (1987) 'Interest Groups and Theories of Power in America', *British Journal of Political Science* 17: 129–47.

McGowan, L. and Murphy, M. (2003) 'Northern Ireland under Devolution: Facing the Challenge of Institutional Adaptation to EU Policy Formulation', *Regional and Federal Studies* (forthcoming).

Machiavelli, N. (1961) *The Prince*, London: Penguin Books.

MacKinnon, C. (1982) 'Feminism, Marxism, Method, and the State: An Agenda for Theory', *Signs* 8: 515–44.

McNamara, T. (1995) 'Strategic Management in the Irish Civil Service', *Administration* 43: 4–152.

Mac Neela, P. (1999) Homelessness in Galway: A Report on Homelessness and People Sleeping Rough in Galway City, Galway: Simon.

McSharry, R. and White, P. (1999) *The Making of the Celtic Tiger: The Inside Story of Ireland's Boom Economy*, Cork: Mercier Press.

Mahon, E. (1991) *Motherhood, Work and Equal Opportunity: First Report of the Third Joint Oireachtas Committee on Women's Rights*, Dublin: Stationery Office.

Mahon, E. (1995) 'From Democracy to Femocracy: The Women's Movement in the Republic of Ireland', in P. Clancy, S. Drudy, K. Lynch and L. O'Dowd (eds) *Irish Society: Sociological Perspectives*, Dublin: Institute of Public Administration.

Mahon, E. (1998) 'Class, Mothers and Equal Opportunities to Work', in E. Drew, R Emerek and E Mahon (eds) *Women, Work and the Family in Europe*, London: Routledge.

Maier, C.S. (1984) 'Preconditions for Corporatism', in J.H. Goldthorpe (ed.) *Order and Conflict in Contemporary Capitalism: Studies in the Political Economy of West European Nations*, Oxford: Clarendon Press.

Mair, P. (1999) 'Parties and Voters', in J. Coakley and M. Gallagher (eds) *Politics in the Republic of Ireland*, 3rd edn, London: Routledge.

Majone, G. (1991) 'Cross National Sources of Regulatory Policy Making in Europe and the United States', *Journal of Public Policy* 11: 79–106.

Majone, G. (1996) *Regulating Europe*, London: Routledge.

Majone, G. (2000) 'The Credibility Crisis of Community Regulation', *Journal of Common Market Studies* 38: 271–300.

Mann, M. (1970) 'The Social Cohesion of Liberal Democracy', *American Sociological Review* 35: 423–39.

Mann, M. (1988) *States, War and Capitalism*, New York: Basil Blackwell.

Manning, M. (1999) *James Dillon: A Biography*, Dublin: Wolfhound Press.

March, J.G. and Olsen, J.P. (1984) 'The New Institutionalism: Organisational Factors in Political Life', *American Political Science Review* 78: 734–49.

March, J.G. and Olsen, J.P. (1989) *Rediscovering Institutions: The Organisational Basis of Politics*, New York: Free Press.

March, J.G. and Olsen, J.P. (1997) 'Institutional Perspectives on Political Institutions', in M. Hill (ed.) *Theories of the Policy Process: A Reader*, 2nd edn, London: Harvester Wheatsheaf.

March, J.G. and Simon, H.A. (1958) *Organisations*, New York: John Wiley.

Marcuse, P. (1988) 'Neutralising Homelessness', *Socialist Review* 1: 69–96.

Marcuse, P. (1996) 'Space and Race in the Post-Fordist City: The Outcast Ghetto and Advanced Homelessness in the United States Today', in E. Mingione (ed.) *Urban Poverty and the Underclass*, Oxford: Blackwell.

Marks, G., Nielsen, F., Ray, L. and Salk, J. (1996a) 'Competencies, Cracks and Conflicts: Regional Mobilization in the European Union', in G. Marks, F.W. Scharpf, P.C. Schmitter and W. Streeck (eds) *Governance in the European Union*, London: Sage.

Marks, G., Nielsen, F., Ray, L., Salk, J., Marks, G., Hooghe, L. and Blank, K. (1996b) 'European Integration from the 1980s: State-centric versus Multi-level Governance', *Journal of Common Market Studies* 34: 341–76.

Marsh, D. (1983) 'Interest Group Activity and Structural Power: Lindblom's Politics and Markets', *Western European Politics* 6: 3–13.

Marsh, D. (ed.) (1998) *Comparing Policy Networks*, Milton Keynes: Open University Press.

Marsh, D. (2002) 'Marxism', in D. Marsh and G. Stoker (eds) *Theory and Methods in Political Science*, 2nd edn, Basingstoke: Macmillan.

Marsh, D. and Rhodes, R.A.W. (eds) (1992) *Policy Networks in British Government*, Oxford: Clarendon Press.

Marsh, D. and Smith, M. (2000) 'Understanding Policy Networks: Towards a Dialectical Approach', *Political Studies* 48: 4–21.

Marsh, M. and Sinnott, R. (1999) 'The Behaviour of the Irish Voter', in M. Marsh and P. Mitchell (eds) *How Ireland voted 1997*, Boulder, CO: Westview Press.

Martin, B. and Mayntz, R. (eds) (1991) *Policy Network: Empirical Evidence and Theoretical Considerations*, Frankfurt am Main: Campus Verlag.

Martin, M. (2003) *The Freedom to Choose: The Formation of the Irish Party Political Parties 1918–1932*, Cork: Collins Press (forthcoming).

Marx, K. and Engels, F. ([1848] 1967) *The Communist Manifesto*, Harmondsworth: Penguin.

May, K.O. (1952) 'A Set of Independent, Necessary and Sufficient Conditions for Simple Majority Rule', *Econometrica* 15: 680–4.

Mayntz, R. (1994) 'Modernization and the logic of interorganizational networks', MIPGF Working Paper No. 4, Koln: Max-Planck-Institut fur Gesellschaftsforschung.

Mazey, S. and Richardson, J. (1996) 'The Logic of Organisation: Interest Groups', in J. Richardson (ed.) *European Union: Power and Policy-Making*, London: Routledge.

Mazur, A.G (ed.) (2001) *State Feminism, Women's Movements, and Job Training: Making Democracies Work in the Global Economy*, London: Routledge.

Meltzer, A.H. and Richards, S.F. (1981) 'A Rational Theory of the Size of Government', *Journal of Political Economy* 89: 914–27.

Memery, C. (2000) 'The Housing System and the Celtic Tiger: The State Response to a Housing Crisis of Affordability and Access', *European Journal of Housing Policy* 1: 79–104.

Memery, C. and Kerrins, L. (2000) 'Investors in the Private Rented Residential Sector', Threshold Findings, Dublin: Threshold.

Mény, Y. and Knapp, A. (1998) *Government and Politics in Western Europe*, 3rd edn, Oxford: Oxford University Press.

Michels, R. ([1911] 1962) *Political Parties*, New York: Free Press.

Micklethwait, J. and Wooldridge, A. (2000) *A Future Perfect: The Challenge and Hidden Promise of Globalisation*, Heinemann: London.

Miliband, R. (1969) *The State in Capitalist Society: An Analysis of the Western System of Power*, London: Weidenfeld and Nicolson.

Miliband, R. (1970) 'The Capitalist State: Reply to Poulantzas', *New Left Review* 59: 53–60.

Miliband, R. (1973) 'Poulantzas and the Capitalist State', *New Left Review* 82: 83–92.

Miliband, R. (1977) *Marxism and Politics*, Oxford: Oxford University Press.

Miller, N.R. (1987) 'Voting', in J. Eatwell, M. Millgate and P. Newman (eds) *The New Palgrave: A Dictionary of Economics*, London: Macmillan Press.

Mills, C.W. (1956) *The Power Elite*, New York: Oxford University Press.

Monbiot, G. (2000) *Captive State? The Corporate Takeover of Britain*, London: Macmillan.

Monroe, K.R. (1991) 'The Theory of Rational Action: What Is It? How Useful Is It for Political Science', in W. Crotty (ed.) *Political Science: Looking to the Future*, Evanston, IL: Northwestern University Press.

Moore, J. (1994) *B and B in Focus: The Use of Bed and Breakfast Accommodation for Homeless Adults in Dublin*, Dublin: Focus Point.

Moravscik, A. (1998) *The Choice for Europe*, London: UCL Press.

Mosca, G. ([1896] 1939) *The Ruling Class*, New York: McGraw-Hill.

MRBI (1992) *Mna na hEireann Inniu: An MRBI Perspective on Women in Irish Society To-Day*, Dublin: Market Research Bureau of Ireland.

Mueller, D.C. (1989) *Public Choice II*, Cambridge: Cambridge University Press.

Mule, R. (1999) 'New Institutionalism: Distilling Some "Hard Core" Propositions in the Works of Williamson and March and Olsen', *Politics* 19: 145–51.

Murphy, G. (1999) 'The Role of Interest Groups in the Policy Process', in J. Coakley and M. Gallagher (eds) *Politics in the Republic of Ireland*, 3rd edn, London: Routledge.

Murphy, L. (1994) 'The Downside of Home Ownership: Housing Change and Mortgage Arrears in the Republic of Ireland', *Housing Studies* 9: 183–98.

Murphy, L. (1995) 'Mortgage Finance and Housing Provision in Ireland 1970–90', *Urban Studies* 32: 135–54.

Nadel, M. (1975) 'The Hidden Dimension of Public Policy: Private Government and the Policy', *Journal of Politics* 37: 2–34.

National Development Plan (2001) *Gender Equality in Training*, Dublin: Department of Justice, Equality and Law Reform.

National Economic and Social Council (1988) *A Review of Housing Policy*, Dublin: National Economic and Social Council.

National Economic and Social Forum (2000) *Social and Affordable Housing and Accommodation: Building the Future*, Forum Report No. 18, Dublin: NESF.

Neale, J. (1997) 'Homelessness and Theory Reconsidered', *Housing Studies* 12: 47–61.

Neunreither, K.H. and Wiener, A. (2000a) *European Integration after Amsterdam: Institutional Dynamics and Prospects for Democracy*, Oxford: Oxford University Press.

Neunreither, K.H. and Wiener, A. (2000b) 'Amsterdam and Beyond', in K.H. Neunreither and A. Wiener (eds) *European Integration after Amsterdam*, Oxford: Oxford University Press.

Nicoll, W. (1984) 'The Luxembourg Compromise', *Journal of Common Market Studies* 23: 35–43.

Niskanen, W.A. (1971) *Bureaucracy and Representative Government*, Chicago: Aldine Atherton.

Nordhaus, W.D. (1975) 'The Political Business Cycle', *Review of Economic Studies* 42: 169–90.

North, D.C. and Weingast, B.W. (1989) 'The Evolution of Institutions Governing Public Choice in 17th Century England', *Journal of Economic History* 49: 803–32.

Nugent, N. (2002) *The Government and Politics of the European Union*, 5th edn, London: Macmillan.

O'Brien, L. and Dillon, B. (1982) *Private Rented. The Forgotten Sector of Irish Housing*, Dublin: Threshold.

O'Brien, M. and Penna, S. (1998) *Theorising Welfare: Enlightenment and Modern Society*, London: Sage.

O'Carroll, J.P. (1987) 'Strokes, Cute Hoors and Sneaking Regarders: The Influence of Local Culture on Irish Political Style', *Irish Political Studies* 2: 77–92.

O'Cinneide, S. (1998) 'Democracy and the Constitution', *Administration* 46: 41–58.

O'Connor, P. (1996) 'Organisational Culture as a Barrier to Women's Promotion', *Economic and Social Review* 27: 187–216.

O'Connor, P. (1998) *Emerging Voices: Women in Contemporary Irish Society*, Dublin: Institute of Public Administration.

O'Connor, P. (2000a) 'Ireland: A Man's World?', *Economic and Social Review* 31: 81–102.

O'Connor, P. (2000b) 'Structure, Culture and Passivity: A Case Study of Women in a Semi-state Organisation', *Public Administration and Development* 20: 265–75.

O'Connor, P. (2002) 'A Bird's Eye View…Resistance in Academia', *Irish Journal of Sociology* 10: 86–104.

O'Donnell, I. and O'Sullivan, E. (2001) *Crime Control in Ireland: The Politics of Intolerance*, Cork: Cork University Press.

O'Donnell, R. (ed.) (2000) *Europe: The Irish Experience*, Dublin: Institute of European Affairs.

O'Donnell, R. and O'Riordan, C. (2000) 'Social Partnership in Ireland's Economic Trans-formation', in J. Fajertag and P. Pochet (eds) *Social Pacts in Europe – New Dynamics*, Brussels: European Trade Union Institute.

O'Donnell, R. and Thomas, D. (1998) 'Partnership and Policy-Making', in S. Healy and B. Reynolds (eds) *Social Policy in Ireland: Principles, Practice and Problems*, Dublin: Oak Tree Press.

O'Flaherty, B. (1996) *Making Room: The Economics of Homelessness*, Cambridge, MA: Harvard University Press.

O'Halpin, E. and Connolly, E. (1998) 'Parliaments and Pressure Groups: The Irish Experi-ence of Change', in P. Norton (ed.) *Parliaments and Pressure Groups in Western Europe*, London: Frank Cass.

O'Hearn, D. (1998) *Inside the Celtic Tiger: The Irish Economy and the Asian Model*, London: Pluto Press.

O'Leary, C. and Hesketh, T. (1988) 'The Irish Abortion and Divorce Referendum Campaigns', *Irish Political Studies* 3: 43–62.

O'Leary, D. (2000) *Vocationalism and Social Catholicism in Twentieth Century Ireland*, Dublin: Irish Academic Press.

O'Mahony, J. (2001) 'Not So Nice: The Treaty of Nice, the International Criminal Court, the Abolition of the Death Penalty – The 2001 Referendum Experience', *Irish Political Studies*, 16: 201–13.

O'Malley, E. (1989) *Industry and Economic Development: The Challenge for the Latecomer*, Dublin: Gill and Macmillan.

O'Reilly, E. (1992) *Masterminds of the Right*, Dublin: Attic Press.

O'Riain, S. and O'Connell, P.J. (2000) 'The Role of the State in Growth and Welfare', in B. Nolan, P.J. O'Connell and C.T. Whelan (eds) *Bust to Boom? The Irish Experience of Growth and Inequality*, Dublin: Institute of Public Administration.

O'Sullivan, E. (1996) *Homelessness and Social Policy in the Republic of Ireland*, Department of Social Studies Occasional Paper No. 5, Dublin: Trinity College Dublin.

O'Sullivan, E. (1998) 'The Other Housing Crisis', paper presented at the 13th Annual Conference of the Foundation for Fiscal Studies, Dublin, October.

O'Sullivan, E. (2001) *Access to Housing in the Republic of Ireland*, Brussels: European Observatory on Homelessness.

O'Sullivan, E. (2002) *Homelessness in the Republic of Ireland: A Descriptive Analysis, 1988–2001*, Brussels: European Observatory on Homelessness.

O'Sullivan, E. and Higgins, M. (2001) 'Women, the Welfare State and Homelessness in the Republic of Ireland', in B. Edgar, J. Doherty, and A. Mina-Couell (eds) *Women and Homelessness in Europe*, Bristol: Policy Press.

O'Sullivan, M.C. (1999) 'The Social and Political Characteristics of the Twenty-eighth Dáil', in M. Marsh and P. Mitchell (eds) *How Ireland Voted 1997*, Boulder, CO: Westview Press.

O'Toole, F. (1995) *Meanwhile Back at the Ranch*, London: Vintage.

OECD (1996) *Ireland: Local Partnerships and Social Innovation*, Paris: OECD.

Offe, C. (1975) 'The Theory of the Capitalist State and the Problem of Policy Formation', in L.N. Lindberg (ed.) *Stress and Contradiction in Modern Capitalism*, Lexington: D.H. Heath.

Oldersma, J., Portegijs, W. and Janzen-Marquard, M. (1999) 'The Iron Ring in Dutch Politics Revisited', *Public Administration* 77: 335–60.

Olsen, J.P. (2002) 'The Many Faces of Europeanisation', ARENA (Advanced Research on the Europeanisation of the Nation-State) Working Papers, WP01/2, Oslo: University of Oslo; available at http://www.arena.uio.no/research%20focus/aboutARENA.html (accessed 4 November 2002).

Olsen, M. and Marger, M. (1993) *Power in Modern Societies*, Oxford: Westview Press.

Olson, M. (1965a) *The Logic of Collective Action: Public Goods and the Theory of Groups*, Cambridge, MA: Harvard University Press.

Olson, M. (1965b) *The Rise and Decline of Nations: Economic Growth, Economic Rigidities and Stagflation*, New Haven: Yale University Press.

Olson, M. (1985) *The Rise and Decline of Nations: Economic Growth, Economic Rigidities and Stagflation*, New Haven, CT: Yale University Press.

Panitch, L. (1980) 'Recent Theorisations of Corporatism: Reflections on a Growth Industry', *British Journal of Sociology* 31: 159–85.

Pareto, V. (1935) *The Mind and Society*, London: Cape.

Pareto, V. (1966) *Sociological Writings*, London: Pall Mall.

Parsons, W. (1995) *Public Policy: An Introduction to the Theory and Practice of Policy Analysis*, Cheltenham: Edward Elgar.

Peltzman, S. (1980) 'The Growth of Government', *Journal of Law and Economics* 23: 209–88.

Perrott, R. (1968) *The Aristocrats*, London: Weidenfeld and Nicolson.

Peters, B.G. and Pierre, J. (1986) 'Governing Without Government: Rethinking Public Administration', *Journal of Public Administration and Theory* 8: 223–42.

Peterson, J. and Bomberg, E. (1999) *Decision Making in the European Union*, Basingstoke: Macmillan.

Peterson, J. and Bomberg, E. (2000) 'Policy Transfer and Europeanisation: Passing the Heineken Test', Queen's Papers on Europeanisation, No.2, Institute of European Studies, Queens University Belfast.

Peterson, J. and Shackleton, M. (2002) *The Institutions of the European Union*, Oxford: Oxford University Press.

Phillips, A.W. (1954) 'Stabilisation Policy in a Closed Economy', *Economic Journal* 64: 290–322.

Pierre, J. and Peters, B.G. (2000) *Governance, Politics and the State*, London: Macmillan.

Pierson, C. (1996) *The Modern State*, London: Routledge.

Pierson, C. (1998) *Beyond the Welfare State: The New Political Economy of Welfare*, 2nd edn, Cambridge: Polity Press.

Pierson, C. (1999) 'Marxism and the Welfare State', in A. Gamble, D. Marsh and T. Tant (eds) *Marxism and Social Science*, Basingstoke: Macmillan.

Pinder, J. (2001) *The European Union: A Very Short Introduction*, Oxford: Oxford University Press.

Plato (1951) *The Republic*, trans. W. Hamilton, London: Penguin Books.

Pochet, P. and Fajertag, J. (2000) 'A New Era for Social Pacts in Europe', in J. Fajertag and P. Pochet (eds) *Social Pacts in Europe – New Dynamics*, Brussels: European Trade Union Institute.

Pollack, M. (2000) 'The End of Creeping Competence? Policy Making since Maastricht', *Journal of Common Market Studies* 38: 519–38.

Polsby, N. (1963) *Community Power and Democratic Theory*, New Haven: Yale University Press.

Polsby, N. (1984) *Political Innovation in America*, New Haven: Yale University Press.

Poulantzas, N. (1969) 'The Problems of the Capitalist State', *New Left Review* 58: 67–78.

Poulantzas, N. (1974) *Political Power and Social Classes*, London: New Left Books.

Poulantzas, N. (1975) *Classes in Contemporary Capitalism*, London: New Left Books.

Poulantzas, N. (1976) 'The Capitalist State: A Reply to Miliband and Laclau', *New Left Review* 95: 63–83.

Poulantzas, N. (1978) *State, Power, Socialism*, London: New Left Books.

Powell, W.W. and DiMaggio, P.J. (eds) (1991) *The New Institutionalism in Organisational Analysis*, Chicago: Chicago University Press.

Quigley, J.M. and Raphael, S. (2001) 'The Economics of Homelessness: The Evidence from North America', *European Journal of Housing Policy* 1: 323–36.

Radaelli, C. (1995) 'The Role of Knowledge in the Policy Process', *Journal of European Public Policy* 2: 159–83.

Radaelli, C. (1999) 'The Public Policy of the European Union: Whither Politics of Expertise?', *Journal of European Public Policy* 6: 757–74.

Radaelli, C. (2000) 'Policy Transfer in the European Union: Institutional Isomorphism as a Source of Legitimacy', *Governance* 13: 25–43.

Redmond, D. (2001) 'Social Housing in Ireland: Under New Management?', *European Journal of Housing Policy* 1: 291–306.

Regini, M. (1996) 'Still Engaging in Corporatism?', paper presented at International Conference on Socio-Economics, Geneva, July.

Rhodes, M. (1998) 'Globalization, Labour Markets and Welfare States: A Future of "Competitive Corporatism"?', in M. Rhodes and Y. Meny (eds) *The Future of European Welfare: A New Social Contract?*, London: Sage.

Rhodes, M., Heyward P. and Wright, V. (1997) *Developments in Western European Politics*, Basingstoke: Macmillan.

Rhodes, R.A.W. (1981a) *Control and Power in Central–Local Relations*, Aldershot: Gower.

Rhodes, R.A.W. (1981b) 'The Changing Pattern of Local Government in England: Reform or Reorganisation?', in A.B. Gunlicks (ed.) *Local Government Reform and Reorganisation: an International Perspective*, London: Kennikat Press.

Rhodes, R.A.W. (1986) *The National World of Local Government*, London: Allen and Unwin.

Rhodes, R.A.W. (1988) *Beyond Westminster and Whitehall*, London: Unwin Hyman.

Rhodes, R.A.W. (1994) 'The Hollowing Out of the State', *Political Quarterly* 65: 138–51.

Rhodes, R.A.W (1996a) 'The New Governance: Governing without Government', *Political Studies* XLIV: 652–67.

Rhodes, R.A.W (1996b) 'The Institutional Approach', in D. Marsh and G. Stoker (eds) *Theory and Methods in Political Science*, Basingstoke: Macmillan.

Rhodes, R.A.W (1997) *Understanding Governance: Policy Networks, Governance, Reflexivity and Accountability*, Buckingham: Open University Press.

Rhodes, R.A.W. and Marsh, D. (1992) 'New Directions in the Study of Policy Networks', *European Journal of Political Research* 21: 181–205.

Richardson, J.J. (ed.) (1993) *Pressure Groups*, Oxford: Oxford University Press.

Richardson, J.J. (2001) *Power and Policy Making in the European Union*, 2nd edn, London: Routledge.

Richardson, J.J. and Jordan, G. (1979) *Governing under Pressure: The Policy Process in a Post-parliamentary Democracy*, Oxford: Martin Robertson.

Richardson, J.J. and Jordan, G. (1982) *Policy Styles in Western Europe*, London: George Allen and Unwin.

Risse, T., Cowles, M. and Caporaso, J. (2000) 'Introduction', in M. Cowles, M. Green, J. Caporaso and T. Risse (eds) *Transforming Europe: Europeanisation and Domestic Change*, Ithaca, NY: Cornell University Press.

Risse-Kappen, T. (1996) 'Exploring the Nature of the Beast: International Relations Theory and Comparative Policy Analysis Meet the European Union', *Journal of Common Market Studies* 34: 53–80.

Roche, W.K. (1997) 'Pay Determination, the State and the Politics of Industrial Relations', in T.V. Murphy and W.K. Roche (eds) *Irish Industrial Relations in Practice*, 2nd edn, Dublin: Oak Tree Press.

Roche, W.K. and Geary, J. (2000) ' "Collaborative Production" and the Irish Boom: Work Organization, Partnership and Direct Investment in Irish Workplaces', *Economic and Social Review* 31: 1–36.

Rose, R. (1991) 'What is Lesson Drawing?', *Journal of Public Policy* 11: 3–30.

Rose, R. (1993) *Lesson Drawing in Public Policy: A Guide to Learning Across Time and Space*, New Jersey: Chatham House.

Rostow, W.W. (1971) 'The Stages of Economic Growth: A Non-Communist Manifesto', in A. Foster-Carter, *The Sociology of Development*, Ormskirk: Causeway Books.

Sacks, P.M. (1976) *The Donegal Mafia: An Irish political machine*, New Haven: Yale University Press.

Sampson, A. (1962) *The Anatomy of Britain*, London: Hodder and Stoughton.

Sampson, A. (1965) *The Anatomy of Britain Today*, London: Hodder and Stoughton.

Sampson, A. (1971) *The New Anatomy of Britain*, London: Hodder and Stoughton.

Sampson, A. (1982) *The Changing Anatomy of Britain*, London: Hodder and Stoughton.

Saunders, D. (1995) 'Behavioural Analysis', in D. Marsh and G. Stoker (eds) *Theory and Methods in Political Science*, London: Macmillan.

Saunders, P. (1990) *A Nation of Home Owners*, London: Unwin Hyman.

Schmidt, D.E. (1973) *The Irony of Irish Democracy: The Impact of Political Culture on Administrative and Democratic Political Development in Ireland*, London: Lexington Books.

Schmitter, P.C. (1974) 'Still the Century of Corporatism', *Review of Politics* 36: 85–131.

Schmitter, P.C. (1979) 'Still the Century of Corporatism', in P.C. Schmitter and G. Lehmbruch (eds) *Trends Towards Corporatist Intermediation*, London and Beverly Hills, CA: Sage.

Schmitter, P.C. and Lehmbruch, G. (eds) (1979) *Trends Towards Corporatist Intermediation*, London and Beverly Hills, CA: Sage.

Scott, D. (1994) *Ireland's Contribution to the European Union*, Occasional Paper No. 4, Dublin: Institute of European Affairs.

Scott, J. (1991) *Who Rules Britain?*, Cambridge: Polity Press.

Scott, J.C. (1977) 'Political Clientelism: A Bibliographic Essay', in Steffen W. Schmidt, J.C. Scott, C. Lande and L. Guasti (eds) *Friends, Followers, and Factions*, Berkeley, CA: University of California Press.

Scott, R. and Meyer, J.W. (1983) *Organizational Environments*, Beverly Hills, CA: Sage.

Searing, D. (1985) 'The Role of the Good Constituency Member and the Practice of Representation in Great Britain', *Journal of Politics* 47: 348–81.

Searing, D. (1991) 'Role, Rules and Rationality in the New Institutionalism', *American Political Science Review* 85: 1,239–60.

Selznick, D. (1949) *TVA and the Grass Roots*, Berkeley, CA: University of California Press.

Sen, A.K. (1977) 'Rational Fools: A Critique of the Behavioural Assumptions of Economic Theory', *Philosophy and Public Affairs* 6: 317–44.

Sen, A.K. (2001) 'The Discipline of Cost–Benefit Analysis', *Journal of Legal Studies* 29: 931–52.

Simon Community (1992) *Still Waiting for the Future*, Submission for the Simon Community to the Minister and Department of Health.

Sinclair, A. (1968) *The Last of the Best*, London: Weidenfeld and Nicolson.

Sinnott, R. (1995) *Irish Voters Decide. Voting Behaviour in Elections and Referendums since 1918*, Manchester: Manchester University Press.

Sinnott, R. (1999) 'Party Competition and the Changing Party System', in J. Coakley and M. Gallagher (eds) *Politics in the Republic of Ireland*, 3rd edn, London: Routledge.

Sklair, L. (1999) 'Competing Conceptions of Globalisation', *Journal of World Systems Research* 2: 143–62.

Skocpol, T. (1979) *States and Social Revolutions*, Cambridge: Cambridge University Press.

Skocpol, T. (1985) 'Bringing the State Back In: Strategies of Analysis in Current Research', in P.B. Evans, D. Rieschemeyer and T. Skocpol (eds) *Bringing the State Back In*, Cambridge: Cambridge University Press.

Smith, M.J. (1990) 'Pluralism, Reformed Pluralism and Neopluralism: The Role of Pressure Groups in Policy-Making', *Political Studies* 38: 302–22.

Smith, M.J. (2000) *Rethinking State Theory*, London: Routledge.

Smyth, A. (1992) *The Abortion Papers: Ireland*, Dublin: Attic Press.

Smyth, A. (1993) 'The Women's Movement in the Republic of Ireland', in A. Smyth (ed.) *Irish Women's Studies Reader*, Dublin: Attic Press.

Soetendorp, H and Hanf, K. (eds) (1998) *Adapting to European Integration: Small States in the EU*, Harlow: Longman.

Soysal, Y. (1994) *Limits of Citizenship: Migrants and Postnational Membership in Europe*, Chicago: University of Chicago Press.

Steinmo, S., Thelen, K. and Longstreth, F. (eds) *Structuring Politics: Historical Institutionalism in Comparative Analysis*, Cambridge: Cambridge University Press.

Strange, S. (1994) *States and Markets*, Pinter: London.

Studlar, D.T. and McAllister, I. (1996) 'Constituency Activity and Representational Roles among Australian Legislators', *Journal of Politics* 58: 69–70.

Sweeney, P. (1990) *The Politics of Public Enterprise and Privatisation*, Dublin: Tomar.

Sweeney, P. (1999) *The Celtic Tiger, Ireland's Continuing Economic Miracle*, Dublin: Oak Tree Press.

Taylor, G. (1995) 'Marxism', in D. Marsh and G. Stoker (eds) *Theory and Methods in Political Science*, Basingstoke: Macmillan.

Taylor, G. (2001) *Conserving the Emerald Tiger: The Politics of Environmental Regulation*, Galway: Arlen House Press.

Taylor, G. and Millar, M. (2002a) 'The Appliance of Science: The Politics of European Food Regulation and Reform', *Public Policy and Administration* 17: 125–46.

Taylor, G. and Millar, M. (2002b) ' "The Buffalo Can Still Be Heard Running": The Politics of Food Regulation and Reform in Ireland', SSRC Working Paper No.7, Galway: NUI.

Teague, P. and Donaghey, J. (2003) 'European Economic Government and the Corporatist Quid Pro Quo', *Industrial Relations Journal* 34 (forthcoming).

Teasdale, A.L. (1993) 'The Life and Death of the Luxembourg Compromise', *Journal of Common Market Studies* 31: 567–79.

Thelen, K. and Steinmo, S. (1992) 'Historical Institutionalism in Comparative Politics', in S. Steinmo, K. Thelen and F. Longstreth (eds) *Structuring Politics: Historical Institutionalism in Comparative Analysis*, Cambridge: Cambridge University Press.

Therborn, G. (1995) *European Modernity and Beyond: The Trajectory of European Societies 1945–2000*, London: Sage.

Thorns, D.C. (1991) 'The Production of Homelessness: From Individual Failure to System Inadequacies', *Housing Studies* 4: 253–66.

Thune, C. (1998) *Evaluation of European Higher Education: A Status Report*, Copenhagen: Centre for Quality Assurance and Evaluation of Higher Education.

Toinet, M. and Glenn, I. (1982) 'Clientelism and Corruption in the "Open" Society: The Case of the United. States', in Christopher Clapham (ed.) *Private Patronage and Public Power: Political Clientelism in the Modern State*, London: Frances Pinter.

Toke, D. (1999) 'Epistemic Communities and Environmental Groups', *Politics* 19: 97–102.

Tong, R.P. (1998) *Feminist Thought*, Oxford: Westview Press.

Tonra, B. (1991) *The Europeanisation of National Foreign Policy: Dutch, Danish and Irish Foreign Policy*, Aldershot: Ashgate.

Tony, S. (1992) *Social Change, Development and Dependency*, Oxford: Blackwell.

Traxler, F. (2000) 'National Pacts and Wage Regulation in Europe: A Comparative Analysis', in J. Fajertag and P. Pochet (eds) *Social Pacts in Europe – New Dynamics*, Brussels: European Trade Union Institute.

Traxler, F., Blaschke, S. and Kittel, B. (2001) *National Labour Relations in Internationalized Markets: A Comparative Study of Institutions, Change and Performance*, Oxford: Oxford University Press.

Truman, D. (1951) *The Governmental Process: Political Interests and Public Opinion*, New York: Knopf Press.

Tullock, G. (1967) 'The Welfare Costs of Tariffs, Monopolies and Theft', *Western Economic Journal* 5: 224–32.

Tullock, G. (1976) *The Vote Motive*, London: Institute for Economic Affairs.

Tullock, G. (1988) *Wealth, Poverty and Politics*, Oxford: Basil Blackwell.

UNCTAD (2001) *World Investment Report 2001*, New York and Geneva.

United Nations Report (2000) *Human Development Report*, New York: UNP.

Van Waarden, F. (1992) 'Dimensions and Types of Policy Networks', *European Journal of Political Research* 21: 29–52.

Verdun, A. (1999) 'The Role of the Delors Committee in the Creation of EMU: An Epistemic Community?', *Journal of European Public Policy* 6: 308–28.

Visser, J. and Hemerijck, A. (1997) *A Dutch Miracle': Job Growth, Welfare Reform and Corporatism in the Netherlands*, Amsterdam: Amsterdam University Press.

Vlachos-Dengler, K. (2000) 'Greek Civil Society and the Impact of Globalisation', paper presented at 'Greece's New Geopolitical Role' conference, Athens, November–December.

von Prondzynski, F. (1992) 'Ireland: Between Centralism and the Market', in R. Hyman and A. Ferner (eds) *Industrial Relations in the New Europe*, Oxford: Blackwell.

Walby, S. (1990) *Theorizing Patriarchy*, Oxford: Blackwell.

Walker, J. (1969) 'The Diffusion of Innovations among the American states', *American Political Science Review* 33: 880–99.

Wallace, H. and Wallace, W. (eds) (2000) *Policy-making in the European Union*, 4th edn, Oxford: Oxford University Press.

Walsh, J. (1995) 'Local Development Theory and Practice: Recent Experience in Ireland', paper presented at International seminar on marginal regions, St Patrick's College, Maynooth, July.

Walshe, J. (1999) *A New Partnership in Education: From Consultation to Legislation in the Nineties*, Dublin: Institute of Public Administration.

Walt, G. (1994) *Health Policy: An Introduction to Process and Power*, London: Zed Books.

Walter, N. (1998) *The New Feminism*, London: Little Brown.

Walton, R.E. and McKersie, R.B. (1965) *A Behavioural Theory of Labour Negotiations*, New York: McGraw-Hill.

Weber, S. (ed.) (2001) *Globalisation and the European Political Economy*, New York: Columbia University Press.

Weiss, L. (1998) *The Myth of the Powerless State: Governing the Economy in a Global Era*, Cambridge: Polity Press.

Whitehead, S. and Moodley, R. (eds) (1999) *Transforming Managers: Gendering Change in the Public Sector*, London: UCL Press.

Whyte, J.H. (1980) *Church and State in Modern Ireland 1923–1979*, 2nd edn, Dublin: Gill and Macmillan.

Wilkes, S. and Wright, M. (eds) (1987) *Comparing Government–Industry Relations: Western Europe, the United States, and Japan*, Oxford: Clarendon Press.

Williams, J. and O'Connor, M. (1999) *Counted In: The Report of the 1999 Assessment of Homelessness in Dublin, Kildare and Wicklow*, Dublin: Economic and Social Reseach Institute/Homeless Initiative.

Williamson, O. (1985) *Markets and Hierarchies*, New York: Free Press.

Williamson, P. (1985) *Varieties of Corporatism*, Cambridge: Cambridge University Press.

Wilson, G.K. (1991) *Interest Groups*, Oxford: Basil Blackwell.

Winchester, S. (1981) *Their Noble Lordships*, London: Faber and Faber.

Wistow, G. (1992) 'The Health Service Policy Community, Professionals Pre-eminent or under Challenge', in D. Marsh and R.A.W. Rhodes (eds) *Policy Networks in British Government*, Oxford: Clarendon Press.

Witz, A. and Savage, M. (1992) 'Theoretical Introduction', in M Savage and A. Witz (eds) *Gender and Bureaucracy*, Oxford: Blackwell.

Wood, D.M. and Young, G. (1997) 'Comparing Constituency Activity by Junior Legislators in Great Britain and Ireland', *Legislative Studies Quarterly* 22: 217–32.

World Bank (2000) *The Quality of Growth*, Oxford: Oxford University Press.

World Bank (2002) *World Development Report 2002: Building Institutions for Markets*, Oxford: Oxford University Press.

Zeigler, J.N. (2001) 'Corporate Governance in Germany', in S. Weber (ed.) *Globalisation and the European Political Economy*, New York: Columbia University Press.

Newspapers

Business and Finance, September 1996, 'Talking to the Grassroots'.

Economist, 2 February 2002, Supplement Globalisation.

Financial Times, 6 February 2001, 'Countries Still Rule the World', M. Wolf.

Financial Times, 29 June 2001, 'European Performance League'.

Financial Times, 1 February 2002, Editorial 'Global Warnings'.

Financial Times, 1 February 2002, 'How Enron Money Won the Right Friends', S. McNulty.

Financial Times, 9 February 2002, 'How Enron Money Won the Right Friends', S. McNulty.

Financial Times, 10 May 2002, 'FT 500 The World's Largest Companies'.

Fortune, 26 November 2001, 'Globalisation', J. Useem.

Industrial Relations News (1999) no. 9.

Industrial Relations News (1999) no.18.

Industrial Relations News (1999) no. 24.

Industrial Relations News (1999) no. 42.

Industrial Relations News (2000) no. 47.

Industrial Relations News (2002) no. 6.

Irish Independent, 18 January 2002, 'New Thinking Needed to Address Globalisation', B. Keenan.

Irish Times, 27 November 1995, 'Government Owes Yes Victory to Voluntary Groups', C. Coulter.

Irish Times, 29 November 1995, 'Groups Opposed to Divorce Expected to Confirm Legal Challenge to Poll', M. Brennock.

Irish Times, 31 July 1996, 'Bill Given General Welcome', J. Connolly.

Irish Times, 1 November 1996, 'Universities Bill a Muzzle on Intellectual Independence', M. Martin.

Irish Times, 11 December 1996, 'FF Tables Amendments to "Flawed" Universities Bill', J. Connolly.

Irish Times, 23 May 1997, 'Putting Food Safety on the Political Menu', K. O'Sullivan.

Irish Times, 3 June 1997, 'Labour Has to Rethink Why it Wants to Be in Politics', F. O'Toole.

Irish Times, 16 January 2001, 'CRH Spent £1.5bn in 2000 on Development Investments', C. Brennan.

Irish Times, 28 February 2001, 'Irish Firms Involved in Takeovers, Acquisitions Worth 7.6bn', B. McGrath.

Irish Times, 13 March 2001, 'CRH Plans 750m Bond Issue', B. McGrath.

Irish Times, 2 June 2001, 'Yes Side Still Leads but the Gap is Still Narrowing', R. Sinnott.

Irish Times, 2 March 2002, 'How It Started 21 Years Ago and Why I Intend to Vote No', G. Fitzgerald.

Irish Times, 8 March 2002, 'Six Years of Work Go Up in Smoke for Ahern', D. Coughlin.

Irish Times, 13 April 2002, 'Yet Again, Irish Politics is Rocked by Repercussions of Sex Abuse Case', F. O'Toole.

Irish Times, 20 April 2002, 'Why Helping Voters Can Be a Noble or a Grubby Business', G. Fitzgerald.

Irish Times, 11 July 2002, 'CRH Spends 630m Expanding Firm', C. Lally.

Sunday Business Post, 14 April 2002, Editorial.

INDEX